ENGLISH AND ITALIAN LITERATURE
FROM DANTE TO SHAKESPEARE

Longman Medieval and Renaissance Library

General Editors:
Charlotte Brewer, Hertford College, Oxford
N.H. Keeble, University of Stirling

Published Titles:

Piers Plowman: An Introduction to the B-Text
James Simpson

Shakespeare's Mouldy Tales: Recurrent Plot Motifs in Shakespearian Drama
Leah Scragg

English Medieval Mystics: Games of Faith
Marion Glasscoe

The Fabliau in English
John Hines

The Classical Legacy in Renaissance Poetry
Robin Sowerby

Regaining Paradise Lost
Thomas Corns

Speaking Pictures: English Emblem Books and Renaissance Culture
Michael Bath

Robin Kirkpatrick

ENGLISH AND ITALIAN LITERATURE FROM DANTE TO SHAKESPEARE

A Study of Source, Analogue and Divergence

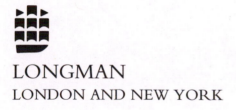

LONGMAN

LONDON AND NEW YORK

Longman Group Limited,
Longman House, Burnt Mill,
Harlow, Essex CM20 2JE, England
and Associated Companies throughout the world.

Published in the United States of America
by Longman Publishing, New York
© Longman Group Limited 1995

First Published 1995

ISBN 0 582 065593 CSD
ISBN 0 582 065585 PPR

British Library Cataloging-in-Publication Data
A catalogue record for this book is available from the British Library

Library of Congress Cataloguing-in-Publication Data
Kirkpatrick, Robin, 1943–
    English and Italian literature from Dante to Shakespeare : a study
of source, analogue, and divergence / Robin Kirkpatrick.
        p.   cm. — (Longman medieval and Renaissance library)
    Includes bibliographical references and index.
    ISBN 0-582-06559-3. — ISBN 0-582-06558-5 (pbk.)
    1. Literature, Comparative–Italian and English.   2. Literature,
Comparative—English and Italian.   3. Italian literature—To 1400
History and criticism.   4. Italian literature—15th century-
History and criticism.   5. Italian literature—16th century-
History and criticism.   6. English literature—Italian influences.
I. Title.   II. Series.
PQ4050.E5K57   1995
820.9—dc20   94-21998
                                                              CIP

Set by 8 in 10/12pt Bembo
Produced by Longman Singapore Publishers (Pte) Ltd.
Printed in Singapore

Contents

Preface

In 1979, Seamus Heaney included among the poems collected in *Field Work* a translation of Dante's *Inferno,* Canto XXXIII. Six hundred years earlier, in the Monk's Tale, Chaucer had offered his own version of the same canto.

From Chaucer to Heaney, there runs an uninterrupted history of similar affiliations between English and Italian literature. The present volume will concentrate upon the first two centuries of that history. Yet the tradition continues; and this book would hardly have been written if it did not. The names which figure in the following pages – Chaucer, Wyatt, Spenser, Sidney and Shakespeare – could well have been matched by others – Milton, Byron, Keats, Tennyson, Joyce and Eliot – deserving at least equal attention. Indeed, there is reason to look as much to the future as to the past. Almost all the following chapters began as lectures or seminars in the English Faculty at Cambridge; and my principal debt is to the many members of that audience who revealed to me the areas in which close attention to the Italian text might continue to illuminate the English analogue.

None of this means that the English reader has been or should be uncritical in approaching Italian literature. It is true that for the greater part of the period I shall be considering, Italian culture provides, on the literary as on other fronts, the more progressive example; and it would be impossible to account for the developments that occurred in English literature during this period, without acknowledging the stimulus and example of the Italian. Yet by the end of the sixteenth century, Italian culture was in decline, or at least was perceived as being so by the English, who in this same period were increasingly conscious of their own intellectual and political success. Ascham famously declares that 'an Englishman italianate is the devil incarnate', while Nashe in *Have with you to Saffron Walden* (1596) derides Gabriel Harvey for his attempt to speak English with an Italian accent. More productively, Spenser at the end of the period sets himself to outdo Ariosto while already at the beginning of the period Chaucer has directed a keenly analytical eye upon the writings of the three founders of the Italian literary tradition, Dante, Petrarch and Boccaccio. (I shall devote an especially long chapter to Chaucer not least because his treatment of these three writers amounts even now to an excellent reading of their work.)

Such considerations have consequences for the modern critic. In the first place, it cannot be appropriate to speak only of the influence which Italian writers exerted over their English counterparts. There are already a number of valuable studies – often produced in the early years of the century – which offer comprehensive accounts in terms of influence, for instance Symond's *Shakespeare's Predecessors in the English Drama* (London 1889) and Einstein's *The Italian Renaissance in England* (New York 1902). Yet it is no less valuable to look at the differences which arise between the two literary traditions than at the similarities. This approach will imply no disparagement of Italian literature. On the contrary, in asking how English writers transformed the Italian original, one is bound to observe how seriously they themselves took that original and how closely they engaged in critical or technical debate with its detail. Often, the important question is not what the source might have been for this or that work, but rather why an identifiable Italian text should have attracted the English writer in the first place; and, often, to answer this question, one will need to investigate the Italian text not as a passive source but as a primary work to be viewed on a level with its English equivalent.

The attractions, stimuli and – occasionally – the repulsions which emerge on such a view are various in kind. Some may be said to be purely literary. The work of Italian writers did much to heighten both the technical and theoretical awareness of English readers, as will be evident from the discussion of the genres – lyric, epic, comic and prose-narrative – in Chapters 3 to 6. Likewise, in Chapter 7 I shall look at how the literary theory which developed in sixteenth-century Italy produced a notion of mixed genres which was particularly influential, as the same chapter will show, in stimulating an appetite for experiment among English dramatists from Marston to Webster, including Shakespeare himself.

But literary (and also, frequently, linguistic) considerations of this sort cannot be seen in isolation from their historical and cultural context. Throughout the period there is an especially close connection to be drawn between text and context. The influence of Italy extends far beyond the realm of literature to include, on the one hand, whole areas of visual style, etiquette or even cookery and, on the other, political theory and theological attitudes.

For that reason, I shall attempt to outline in the introductory chapter the historical developments in Italy over the early years of the modern period in a way which invites (even if there is no space to pursue them) comparisons with developments in England over the same period; likewise, in Chapter 2 I shall consider the social and intellectual developments that characterised the relationship between the two countries in the early Renaissance. It will, however, be important at all points to examine not only the facts of Italian history but also the myth of Italy as it seized and coloured the English imagination of English intellectuals. The myth is a potent one, exciting – even now, as it did in earlier times – impressions of both brilliance and decadence. Italy as, historically, it was, may have been transformed or deformed by the English myth; its importance is no less great on that account.

The many-sided nature of the literary relationship which is now to be examined has been brought home to me by friends and colleagues in many different disciplines. My thanks first and last are due to David Wallace, in recognition of a recurrent debt – sometimes reluctantly paid – to his understanding of the historical connections between England and Italy and for his extremely helpful reading of early versions of the book. In the literary sphere, the writings of Piero Boitani are a model of what cordial but critical relationship between England and Italy can produce, while the unfailing interest of all my colleagues in both the English and Italian Departments at Cambridge has sustained the work when its purpose dwindled. I am particularly grateful to Virginia Cox for reading Chapter 2 and to Matthew Reynolds of Trinity College for his comments on the final Chapter. I also wish to record my thanks to Dr Gillian Rogers and the staff of the English Faculty Library in Cambridge, where a generous stock of Italian texts and a welcoming atmosphere should make the continuing study of this subject as enjoyable for others as it has been for me. The failings of this book remain my own – and they are the more serious in that they are to be judged against a standard of ancient as well as modern enthusiasm for its subject. I remain confident that whatever the deficiencies of the present treatment, the subject itself will survive and prosper.

Acknowledgements

The illustration on page 199 from Book Two of Sebastiano Serlio's *De Architectura* is reproduced by kind permission of the Syndics of Cambridge University Library.

To

David Wallace

and

R. V. Weight

Introduction

In the two centuries between 1400 and 1600, England became a nation-state. By the end of the period, the Italian peninsula, too, was as near to being governed by a central authority as it would be until the Unification of Italy in the nineteenth century. In England, as in Spain and France, nationhood was the foundation for expansion and subsequently for imperial adventure. In Italy, however, the unification that occurred in the sixteenth century, was itself the result of foreign domination. During the last decade of the fifteenth century and the first three of the sixteenth, French and Spanish armies entered Italy, to compete over long-standing territorial and dynastic claims. Effectively, with these invasions there came to an end the system of independent city-states which had developed in Italy over the previous three or four hundred years.

This chapter is concerned largely with the history of the Italian city-state. Throughout the early years of the modern period, Italy represented the avant-garde of Europe not only in respect of art and literature but also in respect of political thinking and commercial expertise. Ironically enough, through their influence in these two fields, the Italian city-states contributed directly to the development of those nations which eventually would outdo or else destroy them. The early success of Italy depended upon the diversity of its political structure which often, though not always, was republican in character; the later success of England depended upon increasingly centralised and increasingly monarchical institutions. But Italian theorists could still reflect upon the issues which other states were later to put into practice.

Two illustrations, drawn from the visual arts, will serve to establish in outline how, politically, the two countries stood, in England at the time of Chaucer and in Italy at the time of Dante, Petrarch and Boccaccio. These examples will also suggest how deeply, throughout the period we are examining, questions of an ideological character are registered in the images, structures and practices of art.

The first of these examples, chronologically, is the *The Allegory of Good Government*, a fresco painted by Ambrogio Lorenzetti between 1337 and 1340 on the walls of the great council chamber in the Palazzo Pubblico at Siena. On one wall of the chamber, Lorenzetti paints an allegory which represents and celebrates the state of 'good government' in his city;[1] on other walls this huge fresco is matched by depictions of 'bad government' and by representations of urban activities or of life in the countryside around Siena. The second example is the Wilton Diptych now in the National Gallery, London. This was painted around 1395 by an unknown artist, or more probably by several artists employed in the court workshop. It is a small luxury object, costly in design and workmanship, and was probably made at royal command. The front of the diptych shows King Richard II of England, being presented by St Edward the Confessor, St Edmund and John the Baptist to the Christ Child, who appears on the right-hand panel in the arms of the Virgin Mary accompanied by eleven angels. The reverse of the Diptych carries Richard's own armorial bearings and the white hart, which was the King's personal badge or cognizance.

Consider first the English example.[1a] In every respect, the painting seeks to emphasise the dignity of the king and the sanctity of his office. Notably, Richard is depicted as a young man dressed as he would have been – twenty years before the Diptych was itself produced – at the age of eleven, in the coronation robes of 1377. This portrayal has been taken to reveal a narcissistic strand in Richard's personality, or else, more sympathetically, as evidence of an obsession with the triumphal culmination of his adolescent years; and such a view is consistent with the tragic account of Richard's career which is familiar from Shakespeare's treatment of the subject. Yet it would not adequately represent the artistic character or political significance of the Diptych.

It was in Richard's reign that notions of royal absolutism and claims

---

1. It has not been possible to reproduce these famous images in the present volume. The cover, however, shows a small detail of Lorenzetti's mural which suggests Lorenzetti's prevailing interest in both the mercantile life and the ideals which underlay the success of civic culture in thirteenth- and fourteenth-century Italy.

1a. See, for the Wilton Diptych, Dillan Gordon, *Making and Meaning: The Wilton Diptych* (London National Gallery 1993).   General bibliography here includes Gervase Mathew *The Court of Richard the Second* (London, 1968); K.B. McFarlane, *Lancastrian Kings and Lollard Knights* (Oxford, 1972); John A. F. Thompson, *The Transformation of Medieval England: 1370–1529* (London, 1983).   Maurice Keen, *England in the Later Middle Ages* (London, 1973); Mary McKisack, *The Fourteenth Century: 1307–1399* (Oxford, 1959; repr. 1991).

for the divine origins of royal authority began to appear as a part of monarchical policy. Since the Conquest, the position of the English King had been balanced by, and had often been subject to, the powers of his barons such as John of Gaunt, who, though a supporter of the King, could lay claim on his own account to the Throne of Castile. Yet developments were taking place in Europe at large as well as in England which pointed away from the ancient tendencies of feudal devolution, and encouraged instead a concentration of power in the hands of established dynasties. For instance, in France the successors of St Louis had been quick to assert that their rule was divinely sanctioned. In point of theory, too, absolutism was much discussed in the Late Middle Ages. Thinkers such as Giles of Rome and Marsilius of Padua had developed a conception of power as the expression of divine will and as the remedy – right or wrong – for human sinfulness. Dante, as we shall see, had his own version of this doctrine, while in England Wycliff had already spoken of the rights and responsibilities of secular authority. The Wars of the Roses were to be dynastic wars.

The Wilton Diptych may well have had a small part to play in a programme of propaganda which included, for instance, a through revision of Richard's Coronation Oath which emphasised the secular and dynastic authority of the Monarch. The fragility of the monarch's position (particularly as an hereditary minor) had been demonstrated as recently as the deposition of Edward II; and this was increased, externally, by the outbreak of the wars which would eventually lead to the loss of all British territory in France and, internally, by the aftermath of the Black Death which had struck in 1348. A poll-tax to pay for foreign ventures, along with economic shifts which, through a diminishing supply of labour, had tended to strengthen the hand of the labouring classes, combined to produce the Peasants' Revolt of 1381. Richard inherited the throne with apparent ease, buoyed up by the prestige of both his grandfather Edward III, whom he succeeded, and his dead father, the Black Prince; and he had already shown himself in the Peasants' Revolt to be a principle of unity against the barons. But opportunities were taken at the coronation and elsewhere to assert his Imperium and his absolute claims based on dynastic grounds.

It is the imagery of Imperium which the Diptych tends to stress. Just as Richard at his Coronation had sworn, unusually, to abide by the laws established in Edward the Confessor's reign and was subsequently buried in St Edward's chapel, so here he is presented to Christ by St Edmund the Martyr and by Edward, suggesting that the claims of his dynasty originated long before the Conquest and conspicuously reflected divine favour. Likewise – woven among the white does on Richard's corona-tion cape – there is the Imperial Eagle, an assertion of his right to rule in his own domain, as the chosen vessel of divine power, independent of the dictates of Pope or Holy Roman Emperor.[2] One hundred and fifty years after the failure Richard's absolutist enterprise, the notion of Imperium was again to become important. In the preamble to Henry VIII's *Act in Restraint of Appeals* (1533) one reads:

> Where by divers sundry old authentic histories and chronicles, it is manifestly declared and expressed that this Realm of England is an Empire.

Absolutism, to succeed, would need to be founded on the bureaucratic skills and economic expertise of the early Tudors. But Richard's reign had by then already brought painfully to light the institutional issues which English politics were bound to wrestle with.

There is little need here to speak of the cultural achievements which accompanied the political machinations of Richard's court; the Riccardian poetry of Chaucer along with Gower and others is proof enough of these.[3] But the Diptych does suggest a taste which was reflected in everything from cookery to palace-building from chivalry to styles of dress. And in style the painter of the Diptych may have owed something to the grace and delicate realism of the Sienese schools.

Yet if now one begins to turn to Lorenzetti's *Good Government*, dif-ferences at once emerge not only in regard to taste and style, but also – and most markedly – in respect of the political issues which are reflect-ed, however obliquely, in the Wilton Diptych.

Where the Diptych is a personal and private object, Lorenzetti's *Good Government* is monumental, and unambiguously public in character. Though there is a good deal of delicacy in the treatment of fabric, the terrestrial solidity of Giotto has its counterpart in Lorenzetti's work. In particular, the composition of *Good Government* is dominated by emphatic horizontal lines, which – as in Giotto's Arena Chapel frescoes of 1306 – associate the painting with the architectural features of the chamber in which they are painted. By contrast, in the Wilton Diptych the dominant compositional note is vertical, with expanses of gold over Richard's head and, in the left-hand panel, the airy upward orientation of angels' wings and fluttering penants. Here, the vertical, too, establishes the axis of divine sanction which Richard wishes to affirm. But Lorenzetti has clearly other ends in view. For while religious images are

2. Later in his reign Richard was to claim unsuccessfully the Holy Roman Empire.
3. See John Burrow, *Riccardian Poetry* (London, 1971).

of course to be found in his painting, the angelic representatives of Faith, Hope and Charity do not elevate the design but form, rather, a flat triangle which emphasises the horizontal length of the composition. Attention is focussed upon a grandiose figure, with Orb and Sceptre, who represents the Commune of Siena, commanding with its gaze the horizontal plane in which the onlooker stands.[4]

In theme and in composition, Lorenzetti's fresco is profoundly secular. In the allegory, the figures seated along the damask bench beside the Commune all represent virtues which are appropriate to the proper government of a city. Similarly – though largely in realistic rather than allegorical terms – the side walls carry a precisely observed depiction of city life and of the relationship between this and the surrounding countryside. Realism in the chivalric calligraphy of the Wilton Diptych is confined to moments of miniaturistic detail. In *Good Government*, however, Lorenzetti depicts to an unprecedented degree a coherent and comprehensible pictorial space in which the relationships underlying urban life can be fully represented; and while space is not, in any formal sense, perspectively organised, there is no mistaking the pleasure which Lorenzetti takes in representing roofs and walls and their decorative crenellations, or indeed the merchants who trade beneath them.

Good Government is a celebration of life in a successful Italian commune. It is an analysis, in both ideological and practical terms, of the activities which characterised such a commune. Painting itself was one of these activities; and while, perhaps, no painter is actually depicted in Lorenzetti's cityscape, it is remarkable that the one historical name recorded in the fresco is that of its creator, Ambrogio Lorenzetti. Where the Wilton Diptych, in celebrating the sovereign, imposes anonymity upon the artist or artists who created it, Lorenzetti is evidently free and confident enough to emblazon his own claims to attention beneath the fresco. The artist here is an intellectual with a full right to participate in the political life of his city and even to use his painting as an allegorical admonition to those councillors who would gather beneath it.[5]

Facing the allegory of *Good Government* in Lorenzetti's fresco is the allegory of *Bad Government* which is depicted in terms of demonic tyranny. This image admits the negative view, which is held at bay in the Wilton Diptych, and serves to throw into relief the high aspirations

---

4. See Frederick Hartt, *A History of Italian Renaissance Art* (London, 1970), pp. 119–20.
5. On Lorenzetti, see Quentin Skinner, 'Ambrogio Lorenzetti: The Artist as Political Philosopher', *Proceedings of British Academy*, 72 (1987). For Siena in this period see William M. Bowsky, *A Medieval Commune: Siena under the Nine (1287–1355)*, (Berkeley 1981).

of the facing panel. One notes in particular, the importance given to the elegant and relaxed figure at the geometric centre of *Good Government*. This figure represents Peace as a 'victorious force, her repose the outcome of a battle won against her darker enemies which include tyranny, war and internal civic dissension'.[6] And it appears – if proof were needed that Lorenzetti was a qualified political thinker – that such a conception of Peace draws upon a tradition of thought which had developed in the communes of Italy in the hundred years before Lorenzetti designed *Good Government*. Rome – and particularly Cicero's work – had been the inspiration of this tradition. Some might argue that Lorenzetti had been influenced by Aquinas and Aristotle. But Skinner convincingly suggests that, as in the pre-humanist political philosophy of Brunetto Latini,[7] so in Lorenzetti political activity is represented figuratively in terms of the crafts and trades of the city: justice is seen as a means of ensuring fair exchange between drapers and metal workers, while peace is an active power, levelling with plane in hand. One may add, finally, that the figure of Peace, though elegantly medieval in line, is itself modelled upon a Roman sarcophagus figure, still to be seen in Siena. Where Richard appeals to the traditions of pre-conquest Britain, Lorenzetti appeals to Rome.

It would be easy to suppose that the Italian work is the more forward-looking of the two examples; and certainly Lorenzetti's interest in the secular world reflects a development which, beginning in pre-humanists such as Brunetto Latini and Dante, can be traced throughout Europe as humanism-proper makes its advance. Yet the absolutist policies of Richard's reign are also an indication of what the future will be. Even in Richard's time, when Italians would have identified themselves as citizens of Siena, Florence or Venice, a potent sense of nationhood may already have been developing in England. In that perspective, the city republics of Italy proved incapable of maintaining the peace, order and justice which Lorenzetti held before Siena as an ideal. It is to the history of that ideal which, in its failure as well as in its realisation, would continue to inspire Italian artists, that we must now turn.

6. Cf. Skinner op.cit.
7. Brunetto Latini (*c.* 1230–1294) will appear frequently in the following pages. Though notoriously condemned to Hell by Dante, he was an intellectual of the highest order – being responsible for a translation of Cicero and for an encyclopaedic study, the *Trésor* – as well as acting as a chief secretary to the Florentine Civil service in the last quarter of the thirteenth century. See below pp. 12 and 88.

THE EARLY DEVELOPMENT OF THE ITALIAN CITY-STATE

Among the most surprising features of Italian civic culture to the English eye are the early date at which this culture established itself and the great diversity of forms which it assumed from one city to another.[8] By the time Chaucer visited Italy at the end of the fourteenth century, almost all the major cities of modern Italy, such as Venice, Milan and Florence (excepting the special cases of Rome and Turin) had been active, politically and economically, for periods ranging from 200 to 500 years; some – such as Amalfi and Pisa – had already passed their zenith and were perceptibly in decline. As to the modes of government adopted in these cities, a political map drawn in the fourteenth century would have revealed an exceptionally wide variety of constitutional colours, ranging from communes and republics, to merchant oligarchies, dynastic despotisms, theocracies, empires, feudal fiefdoms and foreign enclaves; and every part of the peninsula would have been seeking in its own way to maintain an independent existence, often by battle, sometimes by negotiation and occasionally by ideological debate.

One tends now to suppose that cities are the product of geography or the commercial opportunities offered by geographical circumstance. This largely holds true of the early Italian city. A long seaboard – projecting deep into the Mediterranean – produced, well before the year 1000, cities such as Bari, Amalfi and Pisa which served as entrepôts between the Near-East or the Arab world and the Italian hinterland and contributed directly to European culture by introducing scientific, mathematical and philosphical learning from the advanced Islamic civilisations.

Yet neither trade nor geography alone can explain the characteristics of Italian civic consciousness. There are considerations unique to Italy, many of which derive from the fact that Italy had once been the centre of the Roman Empire and was subsequently affected in a particular way by its decline. Not only could many Italian cities trace their origins to Roman triumphs, they could also recognise the consequences of a history which saw, first, the transference of Empire to Byzantium, and then –

8. A general bibliography here includes G. Procacci, *The History of the Italian People,* trans. Anthony Paul (London, 1970); J.K. Hyde, *Society and Politics in Medieval Italy* (London, 1973): J. Larner, *Italy in the Age of Dante and Petrarch* (London, 1980) and also his *Culture and Society in Italy 1290–1420* (London, 1971); G.A. Brucker, *Florentine Politics and Society, 1343–1378* (Princeton, 1962); Marvin B. Becker, *Florence in Transition,* (Baltimore, 1968). Brian Pullan, *A History of Early Renaissance Italy* (London, 1973); Chris Wickham *Early Medieval Italy: Culture Power and Local Society* (London, 1981).

after centuries of migratory invasions which greatly altered the ethnic character of the peninsula – the establishment of a feudal and Germanic successor with pretensions to the ancient Roman title and large claims upon Italian territory. It is an indication of what this might mean that, by the year 1000, there were at least two cities, Ravenna and Pavia, which could have claimed capital status (although by then no more important than they are now) as plausibly as Rome itself. Ravenna, until the eighth century was the admininistrative outpost of the Byzantine Empire, while Pavia – after the fall of the Byzantine Empire in Italy – had served the Lombards and Franks as the capital of their Italic kingdom. On the other hand, Venice, which eventually would provide a model for modern Imperial expansionism, owed its original existence to the migratory invasions of the Dark Ages.[9] There had been no Roman city of Venice. The lagoon began to be populated by inhabitants of the western mainland fleeing from Attila the Hun; and, turning east, the Venetian economy benefited greatly from the decline of nearby Ravenna; a trade was established with the Orient in salt, slaves and luxury goods which also produced – when conjoined with the complex ethnic origins of the city – a constitutional system with strong oriental colourations.

Inland cities tended to make their mark somewhat later than seaboard cities. In these cases, as the climate for commerce developed, trade was accompanied by advances in manufacturing industry. Milan, for example, promoted, among many other industrial activities, an expertise in metallurgy which eventually was to make it an international supplier of armaments, while Florence gained pre-eminence in the processing of wool and textiles. Notably, as the period progressed, merchants were to become bankers, as first the Sienese and later the Florentines put to use the capital they had accumulated in commerce and industry. By the beginning of the thirteenth century, Italian bankers were strong enough to fund – and indeed to bear the losses incurred by – English Kings. Few factors are more important in the development of Renaissance culture than the growth of Italian capitalism. The first fruits of Italian urban culture were often technological in character, involving, for example, production–line methods and state control in The Venetian Arsenal and elsewhere trading practices which involved insurance, currency speculation and double–entry book-keeping.

Yet development of the Italian city depended upon political as well as economic factors. Generally speaking, the inland cities were only free to

9. J.R. Hale (ed.), *Renaissance Venice* (London, 1973); D.S. Chambers, *The Imperial Age of Venice 1380–1580* (London, 1970).

advance when, as tended to happen around the year 1000, the strength-
ening of urban economies coincided with a weakening of the feudal ties
which had bound the cities territorially to the Germanic Empire. At this
critical point, civic independence came to be a real possibility, and was
often expressed through the displacement of civic authority from the
hands of a feudal count to those of a bishop. Milan in particular was an
ancient archbishopric and benefited during the eleventh century from a
sequence of politically ambitious and effective bishops. Soon, however,
the merchant classes were to take independence a step further. And this
process was promoted by a radical readjustment – with no counterpart
in England – of the relations between town and country. In many
regions, members of the erstwhile feudal nobility threw in their lot with
the new economic order. Alliegance to family usually remained
undimmed and was expressed architecturally in fortress-like clan towers
such as can still be seen in San Gimigniano. But the resources these families could muster were firmly wedded to the mercantile and banking
economy; and the countryside, though freer now from feudal overlord-
ship, was quickly re-subjected to the sovereignty of the towns by decree
and by armed aggression.

In this perspective, the cities began to introduce new constitutional
forms and governmental procedures intended to reflect the demands of
new economic and social interests. But these internal developments were
made more urgent – to the point at which they became a matter of conscious policy – by international developments during the thirteenth
century in relations between the Holy Roman Empire and the Church.

The history of opposition between Church and Empire which
stretches back to the time of Charlemagne entered a new phase, when
the Swabian Emperor Frederick II (1215–1250), who had inherited
Sicily through his mother, transferred the seat of Empire from its remote
Germanic base to southern Italy.[10] For a period of sixty or so years the
Imperial claims over Italy which had hitherto been in decline were
resuscitated with sufficient vigour to make the city-states defensively
aware of their developing freedoms. This awareness could only have
been sharpened by the policy and character of Frederick II himself.
Known in his own times both as anti-Christ and as *stupor mundi*,
Frederick was determined from the first to create a form of neo-feudalism in which all secular authority would be seen to lie in the hands of

---

10. On Frederick II, see Thomas Curtis Van Cleeve, *The Emperor Frederick II of
    Hohenstaufen* (Oxford, 1972) and – for a less adulatory view – D. Abulafia, *Frederick II:
    A Medieval Emperor* (London, 1990).

the Emperor. His policies were accompanied by theories – expressed most fully in the *Liber Augustalis* – which drew upon Roman conceptions of Law and Empire to assert that the Emperor should be regarded as the very embodiment of justice in the temporal world: *lex animata in terra*. This claim can be regarded as a major contribution to theories of law and justice which by the fourteenth century would produce in Italy a highly influential school of jurisprudence. However, in practical terms, Frederick's programme stood in direct opposition not only to the local power of the city-states but also to the authority of the Church. For implicit in Frederick's position was a demand that the Empire should be seen as the agent of God, directly commissioned to act as the vessel of Divine Justice in the temporal world and consequently needing no sanction from the Church. At any time – as subsequently in the Reformation – the Church would have violently resisted doctrines of this sort. But in the thirteenth century resistance was the greater because the Church itself had begun to pursue a policy of temporal expansion. Under Pope Innocent III (1160–1216) the political organisation of the Church was improved – to a point at which, in terms of governmental technique, its bureaucracy may now be regarded as the forerunner of state bureaucracies throughout the modern world.[11]

Initially, these developments tended to encourage an alliance between Church and city. The city could certainly find in the Church a bulwark against the feudal claims of Empire, offering, in return, the funds and services created by its capitalist ventures. Simultaneously, Church and city-state faced another common enemy in the form of various heretical and evangelical movements which, against both ecclesiatical and bourgeois interests, preached poverty and even, in some cases, the common possession of material goods.

The deleterious consequences of this agitated period are evident in the partisan strife which now arose both between and within Italian cities. The names Guelf and Ghibelline point to a constantly changing pattern of alliegances in which the original associations – of 'Ghibelline' with the Imperial power and 'Guelf' with the Church and the republic – were often lost or transformed into battle-cries adopted by rival families or warring economic interest groups. At the same time, the agitation of the period combined with the great interest which both Church and Empire showed in the technology of government to stimulate still further the tendency to constitutional experimentation within a city such as

---

11. See Randall Collins's discussion of Weber's analysis in *Weberian Sociological Theory* (Cambridge, 1986), p. 49.

Florence. In many cases, of course, new constitutions proved to be a blatant expression of partisan sympathy. For instance, the Florentine Ordinamenti di Giustizia included measures which limited the rights of defeated or declining factions; and it would certainly be anachronistic to expect that the cities would have been democratic in nature. But by the mid-fourteenth century, Florence was probably the most politically inclusive regime in Europe; and the concept of self-regulation had been established well before this period. On the level of government, this was expressed through the devising of checks and balances which in Florence ensured a three-monthly rotation of senior officials. But the city seems also to have been built on a tissue of small self-governing bodies – guilds, confraternities, universities and even poetic coteries – all with the rule-books and rituals needed to establish a consensual order. The fact that by the fourteenth century some city-states, such as Milan, had developed along despotic rather than republican lines only enhanced the pride which others, such as Florence, took in their own republican institutions.

As early as 1265, one finds in Florence inscribed over the gate to the palace of the military governor the words:

> Florence possesses both sea and land and indeed the whole globe. All Tuscany rejoices in her rule; and she sits as secure as Rome in her rule, triumphant for all time to come, demanding that all accept her judgement under the certain rule of law.

This assertion, which would be unthinkable in Norwich, York or even London at the same time, arrogates to the Guelf commune of Florence the prestige and responsibilities of Empire. Forty years earlier, the Emperor Frederick had turned to Rome not only for a philosophy of law but also for images and icons which might serve as propaganda in coins, statuary and architecture. Now, the city-states were following suit. Likewise, where Frederick's court had shown a highly developed interest in science and literature, so in the cities, secular studies began to develop – focussed upon law, rhetoric and mathematics – while universities were set up in Bologna, Padua and Florence with aims quite different from those of the great international foundations in Paris and Oxford where theology and speculative philosophy had been, and continued to be, supremely important. The cities increasingly discovered the practical importance of learning, and came to place a value upon classical study as a central facet of the secular life. The example which Brunetto Latini had set when, as head of the Guelf civil service in Florence, he had translated Cicero's *Rhetoric* was, as we have seen, alive at least a hundred years later in the mind of Lorenzetti.

CULTURE AND POLITICS IN FOURTEENTH-CENTURY FLORENCE

When Robert Browning's 'Italian person of quality' – marooned in a country villa – exclaims: 'Oh, a day in the city-square, there is no such pleasure in the life',[12] he identifies a fundamental characteristic of Italian political thinking, in which the city is understood to be the product of human intelligence and the proper sphere for human activity. Imagery drawn from nature – which might suggest, as in the Wilton Diptych, an organic harmony between the divine order and the divine rights of government – is less common than imagery which, as in Lorenzetti, suggests the dominance of the turreted city over its *contado* or represents urban life in the form of a sophisticated or courtly lady.[13] This is not, of course, to say that Italians lacked any conception of an absolutist order, rooted in the order of the created world. Thus, against the background of Frederick II's Imperial policy, Dante in *De Monarchia* develops a theory which sees the Emperor as a figure independent of the Pope elected by God alone – as was the Roman Empire – for the purpose of bringing justice into the world. In the Reformation this theory was to be cited in a distorted, if approving, form by Protestant propagandists.[14] Yet in Dante's case the theory represents a desire to redeem the city itself from the vicious partisan strife which had been aroused by years of economic and constitutional contention; and the ideal world which he pictures in Dante; *Paradiso,* Canto XV, is one in which the 'roots' of any true Florentine are distinctly placed in the defined spaces of a town. Though it is his exile which drives the poet to these theoretical straits, Dante never wholly loses touch with the humanist thought which led him to follow in the tracks of Brunetto Latini. Indeed, in the first line of the *Inferno*, where Dante wishes to invoke the confusion and barbarity of sin, he draws directly on Brunetto's *Tesoretto* in speaking, significantly, of a dark wood.

The phase in the history of the Italian city which runs from 1265 to

12. From 'Up at a Villa – Down in the City', in *Men and Women* (1855).
13. For the English countryside as a source of new political thought, see David Wallace, *Chaucerian Polity* (Stanford, forthcoming). For the myth of Florence, see Donald Weinstein, 'The Myth of Florence', in Nicolai Rubinstein (ed.), *Florentine Studies* (London, 1968) pp. 15–44.
14. John Bale (1495–1563) cites *De Monarchia* to show that Imperium does not depend upon the Church; Bishop John Jewel (1522–71) approves Dante's allusion to the Church as the 'whore of Babylon'. See Paget Toynbee, *Dante in English Literature: From Chaucer to Cary* (London, 1909) pp. 37 and 52.

around 1365 could well be described as one of proto-humanism; and Dante is both the finest product and the most trenchant critic of that phase. But by the time Chaucer visited Italy towards the end of the 1370s much had developed both socially and intellectually to translate the proto-humanism legacy of the Duecento into the foundation of its Renaissance equivalent. For one thing there had been the Black Death of 1348. This event – more disastrous in its effects than any in history – had reduced the population of Florence by between a quarter and a third. And its repercussions were manifold in Italy as well as in England. Yet in a certain sense it contributed directly to civic consciousness in revealing what it was that made a city function, and in many other respects modified the sensibility of the period, as becomes apparent in the response of Petrarch and Boccaccio.

In Petrarch's case, the Black Death seems to have confirmed a tendency to an otherworldliness which sought to avoid the moral temptations and mutability of the town, and which often expressed itself in a desire for the peace and quiet of an idyllic and idealised natural setting. Petrarch spent much of his life in Avignon, which in 1309 became the seat of a papal court, which returned to Rome only in 1377. And when the poet visited Italy, he came with an international reputation for scholarship, eloquence and philosophy which won him favour as much with Milanese despots and Venetian oligarchs as it did with his Florentine circle of admirers. Petrarch always spoke of himself as a Florentine. Yet his interest was not directly in the affairs of the Florentine republic. Indeed, there is a case for saying that he deliberately cultivated a certain detachment in regard to the practicalities of political life. He could be enthusiastic when in 1347 attempts were made by Cola di Rienzo to re-establish a Republic in Rome. But the enthusiasm was visionary in character, as was his concern to see Italy restored to its ancient glory. To some degree, of course, Petrarch's dealings with, say, the Visconti of Milan must have involved him in the practical affairs of a state which was often seen as the natural enemy of Florence. But he himself was largely silent about this, preferring – in common with later humanists – to preserve the appearance at least of scholarly detachment.

Boccaccio, on the other hand, came to know Florence in circumstances which if, initially tragic, seem to have inspired in him a deep understanding of the city and a deep devotion to the Florentine republic. In his early years he, like Petrarch, had inhabited a far more international world than Dante, spending his early years as a banker in the city of Naples. The exiled Dante had sought constantly to return to

Florence. But the careers of both Petrarch and Boccaccio indicate that, where commercial and diplomatic activity had established routes between Florence and the rest of Europe, intellectuals and their works were ready to follow. Throughout the Middle Ages the Church had produced its own form of international culture. By the time of Petrarch and Boccaccio, the secular culture of the Italian cities was itself about to develop a similarly extensive hegemony.

Trade took Boccaccio to Angevin Naples. But he found there a monarchical court,[15] and a culture which not only drew on all the resources of France but was also enlivened by influences from all over the Mediterranean basin. To Boccaccio this early experience was to provide the environment for his own early writings. At the same time, it impressed upon him the myth of an ideal world of cultured *otium* and aristocratic escape which would continue to influence him, especially in creating the garden setting of the *Decameron*. But in 1340 Boccaccio was called back to Florence, as the surviving head of a plague-stricken family; and the *Decameron* is the first extended indication of the concern which Boccaccio would henceforth display for the culture of the city.

In some respects Boccaccio may from this point be seen as the literary equivalent of Ambrogio Lorenzetti. The majority of his stories are plotted within a townscape rather than a landscape; and the protagonists of these stories are as likely to be cooks, notaries and fresco painters as aristocrats or legendary heroes. Equally, as in Lorenzetti, so in Boccaccio, the detail of the representation is accompanied by a profound attention to the principles or practical energies which sustain the life of a city. In the opening description of the plague, Boccaccio contemplates the destruction of many apparently immutable aspects of the old civic order. Yet far from submitting to this destruction, he proceeds to lay bare the appetites and stratagems which were to ensure within a few decades that Florentine culture would renew itself. It is as if, in viewing the collapse of the old order, Boccaccio had realised that the city was no given or absolute fact but rather the product of human hands and minds. And in the *Decameron* at large he vigorously pursues this understanding.

In the first place, composing what has suggestively been described as a mercantile epic,[16] Boccaccio depicts the often amoral pragmatism which ensures survival or success in the secular world: a merchant Landolfo in Day Two story four finds that there is a glut on the market of the goods

15. See below, p. 62
16. V. Branca, *Boccaccio medievale*, 3rd edn. (Florence 1970). A version is published in
    English as *Boccaccio: The Man and his Works* (New York, 1974).

in which he deals; to remedy that economic disaster he turns his entre-
preneurial skills to piracy, and for a time is successful, until shipwreck
lays him low again; even then, his primitive tenacity, in clinging to a
piece of flotsam, proves to be his salvation: the flotsam is a chest, bearing enough treasure to set him up for life.

The same tenacity is expressed more subtly in the group of young
Florentines, the *brigata*, who are the tellers of Boccaccio's tales. Faced
with the certainty of death if they remain in Florence, the brigata reject
all heroic posturings, and argue indeed that to remain would amount to
a blasphemous presumption of immortality. Once they arrive at their
country villa, however, the brigata immediately begin to establish a
new order, and one which, far from following the ruined conventions
of the old, sets up a system of regulation specifically designed to admit
the natural demands of human nature – be it a demand for recreation,
for story-telling or even for hair-washing.[17] The stories they tell recall
for the most part the life of Florence before the plague; it is as if these
were their household gods, immune to material disaster. But the order
which the brigata institute as a frame for their tales is inherently flexible: there are kings and queens here who rule over conduct for nine of
the days of story-telling; but the rulers are established by rote, and at
least one of their number demands – and is granted – the right to dis-
rupt, if he so desires, the settled order of proceeding. Order here lies in
the human hand. Boccaccio himself was subsequently prepared to write
(as in the *De Casibus*) vigorously in defence of republican as against
despotic forms of government and, like the *brigata*, he carried with him,
in spite of his experiences in Naples, a constant sense of the value of
the city culture.

CRISIS AND TRANSITION IN THE FOURTEENTH-CENTURY CITY

By 1400, the signs that, later, were taken to betoken the Renaissance
were clearly visible in many cities of Italy, though especially in Florence.
It is true that, for reasons considered in Chapter 2, vernacular literature
would not pursue the example set by Petrarch and Boccaccio for a good
century and a half. But in visual form the cities were already expressing
that capacity for construction and reconstruction that Boccaccio had

17. See Prologue to the Third Day. G. McWilliam's introduction to his translation
(London, 1972) is an excellent guide.

identified in the *Decameron*, and were consciously pursuing the principles of aesthetic grace and beauty which Petrarch had developed in his scholarly and poetic meditations. Wealth, however, was necessarily the engine of this development as in the patronage of the *Arte della Lana* which commissioned the work of Orcagna in Orsanmichele; and art was increasingly at the service of civic purposes as in the building of Brunelleschi's dome for the Cathedral, which could claim to be the most original piece of engineering since classical times.[18]

This is not to say, however, that tensions in the city, emanating often from before the Black Death, did not persist.[19] There were continual wars, and even when the partisan strife of the Guelfs and Ghibellines had diminished, wars needed to be fought to defend the independence of Florence or to expand its dominion over others. Equally, problems arose with the overextension of the economic base. But these tensions, like the Black Death itself, seem to have produced both a developing consciousness of the city and a new strategy to deal with the future, which included, by 1400, strategies for dealing with its own internal tensions. For instance, economic order was strained, particularly in 1339 when the English King Edward III, deeply involved in the opening phases of the Hundred Years War, reneged on his debts to the greatest Florentine bank, the Bardi.

Two particular episodes illustrate these developments, the first which involved the importation of a tyrant in the years 1342–3, the second that of the Ciompi involving the rebellion of the lesser guilds in 1378. At the same time, the response of the Bardi was, first, to attempt unsuccessfully to defend their position in Florence itself by a *coup d'état* and then – in association with other well-established families – to invite a foreign despot into the city as head of its administration. This tactic had been tried before in 1325 and the choice now fell on Walter of Brienne, who had been associated with the earlier attempt. Yet the ploy did not win the magnates the advantages they had hoped for. Walter himself proceeded to submit the affairs of the higher echelons to scrutiny, and even to grant privileges to certain of the minor guilds. Conspiracies against Walter proliferated and in 1343 he was driven out, apparently with universal approval.

Significantly, the cry which was to oust Walter was: 'Long live the people and the commune of Florence; long live liberty.' And it is plain

---

18. See R.C. Trexler, *Public Life in Renaissance Florence* (New York and London, 1980).
19. See especially, Hans Baron, *The Crisis of the Early Italian Renaissance* (Princeton, 1966) and Peter Burke, *Culture and Society in Renaissance Italy, 1420–1540* (London, 1972).

that in some respects the threat to civic liberties which the so-called Duke of Athens had seemingly posed helped to call into consciousness the Florentine commitment to a republican ideology. So Boccaccio writes indignantly against the imposition of a despotism, in accents which anticipate those of political humanism in the later Renaissance. Yet it could just as well be said that in this episode the higher guilds were here already beginning to manipulate the republican sentiments of the populace in an attempt to remedy the danger which their own mis-judgements had precipitated. In a similar way, any suggestion that the republic was democratic, or even high-principled, can at least be called into question by the events surrounding the rebellion in 1378 of the Ciompi, cloth workers who had lost their jobs through a decline in demand. As with the Peasants Revolt of 1381 in England, labour short-ages brought about by the Black Death may eventually have worked to the advantage of the lower social orders; and in 1378, as in 1343, liber-tarian slogans were heard in the streets, this time voiced directly by the people. Yet what seems most to have offended and terrified the ruling groups in Florence were certain – apparently modest – demands for guild status. This time, the higher guilds relied upon their own powers to resist the claims for reform.

Crisis, then, may have helped to stimulate republican theory in a city such as Florence. But it also led the established orders to strengthen their hand, sometimes by constitutional accommodation, sometimes by the manipulation both of the constitution and ideological principle. In fact, throughout Italy at this time, there was a closing of ranks among those classes who had profited by now for centuries from the established con-stitutional order.[20] And a reason for this lay in the need which ever-more successful cities conceived either for territorial expansion or for defence against expansion of this sort on the part of neighbouring states. In consequence, the social order became increasingly hierarchical; the old cities of Italy began to take on the characteristics of a court.

The influence exerted, even by the minor courts of the early six-teenth century, can be exemplified by the arrival in England of Castiglione to receive the Order of the Garter from Henry VII on behalf of the Duke of Urbino. But the subtext of such developments can be read in the history of the Medici who operated more from a 'cir-cle' than a court.

20. See Denys Hay and John Law (eds.), *Italy in the Age of the Renaissance, 1380–1530* (London, 1989).

Though eventually the Medici themselves were to become Dukes of Tuscany, they were never in their greatest days formally rulers of Florence. Having arrived in the early thirteenth century from the hilly Mugello, the Medici discreetly avoided the impression that they were building a dynastic court. Using methods which have been compared to those of the Mafia,[21] they slowly infiltrated the democratic system. They benefited from a large family network, built through advantageous marriage alliances, and eventually they developed a certain skill in the management of Republican voting procedures. But their greatest influence, both within Florence and without, derived from their success on the international banking scene where the Medici reputation was strong enough to secure the Pope himself as a client. The value of this international banking organisation – with its network of agents and its command of information was – needless to say, invaluable to Florence at large.

When Cosimo died in 1464, the title that was accorded to him was characteristically discreet and constitutionally neutral: *Pater Patriae*, Father of his Country. Cosimo had made no attempt, formally, to become anything more. Yet when foreign dignitaries came to Florence they were more often housed in the Medici rather than public palaces; Cosimo, in his time played host to no less than two Emperors. In this perspective, patronage of the arts became a diplomatic necessity and an expression of Medici wealth, as well as being a further instrument of policy and influence in Florence itself. Cosimo, while not actively a humanist, had a particular concern for architectural ventures and for book-collecting, where his interest in rare Greek manuscripts was to bear scholarly fruit after his death. Cosimo's activities were developed still further by Lorenzo the Magnificent who did practise as a humanist and poet; and the results are not only to be witnessed in the visual arts of the period but also, as will be seen in the second chapter, in the philosophical, educational and literary achievements of figures such as Ficino, Pico della Mirandola and Poliziano.

It should be emphasised that while the courtly circle of the Medici was establishing itself, political theorists never lost sight of the republican principles which they saw embodied in the history of their own city. It is a characteristic of humanist theorists, as we shall see, to distinguish themselves from their medieval counterparts by the interest they took in the Republican rather than the Imperial phase of Roman history.[22] This

21. J.R. Hale, *Florence and the Medici. The Pattern of Control* (London, 1977); D.V. Kent, *The Rise of the Medici Faction in Florence* (Oxford, 1977).
22. See below, p. 87.

interest, along with a lively sense of how Florence had stood out in the recent past against modern tyranny, led to a theoretical defence of liberty under civic rule which was voiced with particular eloquence in the first half of the fifteenth century by the Chancellor of Florence Leonardo Bruni (1370–1444). So reflecting on the role played by Giano della Bella in the internal disturbances which came to a head in Florence in 1295, Bruni records Giano's sentiments in these words:

> A good citizen, I think, ignores his own comfort when his country needs his advice; and he does not cut down his public statements to suit his private convenience. Therefore I shall speak my mind freely. It seems to me that the liberty of the people consists in two things: the laws and the judges. When the power of these two things prevails in the city over the power of any individual citizen, then liberty is preserved. But when some people scorn the laws and the judges with impunity, then it is fair to say that liberty is gone.
>
> (*History of Florence*, IV)[23]

Here Bruni draws on the mythic past of Florence; and if the myth is out of keeping with observable realities, that is simply a sign of its potency. These high principles were widespread enough to provide the terminological, if not the pragmatic, basis for alliances between city-states, as for instance in 1536 between Florence, Genoa and Venice against Milan, though when pragmatism dictated, the Medici's were quite capable of negotiating with the overtly despotic Milan.

But in the last decade of the Quattrocento, with the death of Lorenzo, the presuppositions which had governed both the practical politics and also the political theory of the foregoing half-century were violently called into question. In 1494 the Milanese broke ranks and invited French armies into Italy in pursuit of ancient territorial claims to Naples; this led the Spanish as the repository of the Empire to enter Italy also. For the next thirty years Italy and its city-state system was gradually dismantled in the face of the warring claims of the great international states.

Within Florence itself, the disappearance of Lorenzo led to an expression of pent-up resentment which found a focus in the figure of Savanarola. Preaching religious reform, Savanarola also sought to re-establish a city which was true to its ancient republican principles; and though his prophetic eloquence deeply impressed a number of major

23. For this and other extracts from Bruni's *History* (as well as pieces by Alberti and Savarola), see Renée Neu Watkins, *Humanism and Liberty: Writings on Freedom From Fifteenth-Century Florence* (Columbia, 1978).

humanists such as Pico della Mirandola and even Michelangelo, there was a great deal in his programme which stood in opposition to the style and political practices of the fourteenth-century Renaissance and harked back to the late Middle Ages. It is a sign that the principles of this age could not withstand the pressures of modern politics that, however deep the appeal of Savanarola's message, he too should be forced from power by the Medici, returning with international support.

There can be no doubt of the seriousness of the invasions which Italy and its culture suffered at this time. For thirty years or more, Italy was prey to artillery wars which culminated in the traumatic sack of Rome in 1527 where for three days the Swiss troops were to rampage throughout the city. These disasters were to resonate in the imagination of artists and poets in the sixteenth century, including even Ben Jonson who alludes to these events in *The Case is Alter'd*. Thus the contemporary historian Francesco Guicciardini was to write in the opening pages of his *History of Italy*:

> The misfortunes of Italy (to take account of what its condition was like then as well as the causes of so many troubles) tended to stir up men's minds with all the more displeasure and dread inasmuch as things in general were at that time most favourable and felicitous. It is obvious that ever since the Roman Empire, more than a thousand years ago . . . Italy had never enjoyed such prosperity or known so favourable a situation as that in which it found itself so securely at rest in the year of our Christian salvation 1490.

Yet the invasions, says Guicciardini, came to teach what Fortune could do when,

> summoned by our own princes, French troops began to stir up very great dissensions here . . . and Italy suffered for many years all those calamities with which miserable mortals are usually afflicted.[24]

It should not be supposed that the Italy of the sixteenth century was entirely destroyed, even though the city-states of the early Renaissance and the courts which succeeded them were to fall slowly into political decadence.[25] Rome itself now became for the first time important as a political and cultural centre of Italy (though Venice continued to maintain its separate history). Under the Popes – often now of Spanish extraction – the city which had, for most of the early Renaissance, been little more than a market town began to be transformed architecturally while, admin-

---

24. Guicciardini, *History of Italy*, Book I.
25. Eric Cochrane in Julius Kirshner (ed.), *Italy 1530–1630* (London, 1988).

istratively, its position was greatly enhanced. Certainly, with the Counter-Reformation and its response to Protestantism, the influence of Rome as a religious centre became ever stronger as a watchword to enemy as to friend. It should be recognised that the Counter-Reformation marked a profound desire, on the part of Catholics themselves, to reform the Church; and in Italy since at least Savanarola's time there was a marked movement towards reform which produced figures such as Bernardo d'Ochino who were influential even in a Protestant ambit. But the desire for orthodoxy and for a centralised authority represented a major response to the disintegration of an old order.

For all that, an age now began in which stimulus was to be found as much in questioning or in redirecting the ancient energies of the city; and of all the writers who appear in this period none displays its tensions and cross-currents more fully than Machiavelli in his political reflections on the failure of the Florentine city-state.

Machiavelli's name will appear frequently in the following chapters, as philosopher and humanist, as playwright and as the mythic Machia*villain* of the Elizabethan stage.[26] Here one need only record that the *realpolitik* for which Machiavelli has become notorious was developed paradoxically enough as a way of defending the civic values which had developed in Italy over the preceding four centuries. Machiavelli had himself been in France as a diplomat; and he seems to have understood very clearly that the political future of Europe lay with large centralised nation-states. He certainly realised that in such a state the realm of politics and power (increasingly allied to devastating military technology) would come to be governed by considerations quite different from those which governed the ethical life of the individual. In the small city, as in the Greek *polis*, it had been possible to believe, at least, that the rules of political conduct might be identical to those of personal conduct; and up to a point this may have been true, insofar as policy would be formed and executed through agencies of personal acquaintance. But with the invasions, this myth was no longer tenable. Machiavelli does not hesitate to criticise the lack of realism which in an international perspective his contemporaries displayed with their increasingly provincial policies. *The Prince* is an attempt to awaken the rulers of Italy – or of Florence – to the true nature of their political case. Yet the end to which Machiavellian means were directed remains one which would only have been possible within the context of Italian

26. See below, pp. 99–105 and 207–11.

Republican history. Liberty and glory, however redefined, are still his aim; and when Machiavelli looks back, in his own *History of Florence*, to the traumatic episode of Walter de Brienne's tyranny he can speak of a reign of terror – which might in other circumstances have attracted his admiration. He notes how Florentine citizens may for a time have been prepared to live 'seeing the majesty of their state in ruins, their laws annulled all upright ways of living corrupted and all civic decency extinguished' (*The Prince*, Chapter XXXVI, p. 197) and yet still, in the end, be prepared to take the cause of liberty into their own hands, 'whether noble or plebian' (ibid., 201).

CONCLUSION

The chapters that follow will at many points be concerned with response of English intellectuals to the Italian experience of civic life. There will be instances of excitement; there will be instances of resistance and redirection. But it needs to be noted here that, whatever the literary texts may reveal, there is a parallel history of diplomatic and commercial relationships between the two countries. It would require another – and different – volume to chart this progress. Yet one cannot ignore the early wave of commercial negotiations which may have sped Chaucer on his way to Italy and even have acquainted him with Italian merchants who were resident in England.[27] Nor can one ignore the contribution which the Lancastrians made to the development of Anglo-Italian history. Henry IV, while still in exile as Bolingbroke, was celebrated in Italian courts, and may have even have contemplated a marriage alliance with the Visconti. As for his sons, Henry V had begun to recognise the political implications of the new learning which by 1400 was well established in Italian cities;[28] Duke Humphrey in particular deserves close attention as patron to the University of Oxford in endowing the Bodleian Library with its first collection of humanist texts.[29] Then again, the first Tudors can be seen to have turned to Italy, and in particular to Polydore Virgil when they needed historians to bolster their new princedom;[30] and even if they were not wholly satisfied

27. See Wendy Childs, 'Anglo-Italian Contacts in the Fourteenth Century', in Piero Boitani (ed.), *Chaucer and the Italian Trecento* (Cambridge, 1983).
28. Mcfarlane, *op. cit.*
29. See below, pp. 91–2.
30. Denys Hay, *Polydore Virgil* (Oxford, 1952).

with the results, there was nevertheless a vigorous traffic between the two countries, in courtiers, churchmen and scholars by this time. By the end of the century, the traffic had come to include men like Bernardo d'Ochino, Florio and Giordano Bruno who were fleeing from persecution in their native land yet were prepared to teach the fundamentals of the language and thought which Italy had itself produced.[31]

It was men such as these, and in particular Florio, who realised that the language of Italy could usefully be taught to a nation which until that point seems to have trusted in its innate interest and adaptability to acquire a working knowledge of the tongue. And it is a sign of the competence that could be expected of contemporaries of Shakespeare that the printer John Woolfe – having trained in Florence – should set up his press in England and produce Italian language editions of texts such as Machiavelli's *Discorsi*, published in London in 1584. At the same time, there were always travellers who began the long-standing tradition of Italian journeys; and it is in one of them that the same curiosity, preciseness of observation and critical spirit is found which will animate the poets and dramatists who will be considered in the following pages. It was the puritan William Thomas – author of an Italian grammar in English – who, observing the procession of Pope Paul III on Christmas day 1547, wrote home:[32]

> O what a world it is to see the pride and abomination that the churchmen there maintain. What is a king? What is an emperor in his majesty? Anything like to the Roman bishop? No, surely nor would I wish them to be so.

Yet this same William Thomas maintains that the historical method which he pursued in his account of Italy is itself derived from an Italian, Machiavelli: 'a notable and learned man . . . I determined to take him for mine only author.'

---

31. On these matters see especially. Lewis Einstein, *The Italian Renaissance in England* (New York, 1902). Also on Florio as a teacher of the Italian language, see Frances A. Yates, *John Florio* (London, 1934).
32. William Thomas, *History of Italy 1550,* quoted in Einstein, op.cit., pp. 151–2 and 99–100.

Chapter 1

Chaucer and the Italians

INTRODUCTION

No English poet makes fuller or more critical use of Italian sources than Chaucer. It is probable that he alone, among his literary contemporaries, had travelled to Italy, where he would have met Italian intellectuals and would have been able to consult – in circulation – the manuscripts of major authors, possibly carrying copies back with him to England. Other poets of the period, as, for instance, Gower, may occasionally make reference to Italian texts;[1] and analogies are always likely to occur where English and Italian authors have drawn upon the same French or classical sources. Yet there is nothing in the fifteenth century to compare with Chaucer's revision of Boccaccio's *Filostrato* – which is so detailed as to have been inconceivable without a manuscript to hand – or the critical use to which, as we will be seen, Chaucer puts Dante's *Commedia* in *The House of Fame*.

A hundred and fifty years after Chaucer, printing and the development of libraries provided relatively easy access to Italian culture and also made it plausible that, when an English author such as Spenser alluded to or attempted to surpass an Italian original, the reader might recognise his artistic or intellectual intentions. These were advantages which Chaucer himself did not enjoy. Yet even in comparison with later writers, Chaucer's use of Italian is exceptionally intense and deliberate. The Italian authors to whom he paid attention – in particular Dante, Petrarch and Boccaccio – were all, in their differing ways, concerned to demonstrate the literary potentialities of their own vernacular tongue, revisiting but also revising the precedents they discovered in

---

1. Cf. *Confessio Amantis*: II 3095 ff. with *Inf.*, XIII. 64–66; and V 1419 ff. and *Inf.*, V. 58. I am grateful to James Simpson for these suggestions.

Latin, French and Occitan. Chaucer gave close attention both to the formal features of such experimentation and to the larger aspirations which inspired them. It was from the Italians that Chaucer learned what a modern vernacular was capable of achieving; and it is to the Italians, it seems, that he resorts at points, most conspicuously in *The House of Fame* and in *Troilus and Crisyede*, when he seeks stimulus on a technical or philosophical front.

This is not to say that Chaucer ever produces a slavish imitation of the original text. On the contrary, his understanding of the divergences which appear even between the major poets of the Italian tradition would have sanctioned the divergences which he himself seems knowingly to have pursued. It should also be emphasised that French traditions as well as the narrative and linguistic traditions of England itself remain vital components in Chaucer's art.[2] indeed, in terms simply of number and quantity, Chaucer's references to French and English source material far outweigh his reference to Dante, Petrarch or Boccaccio. In regard, however, to impetus, it was Italy, it appears, which led Chaucer to reflect – sometimes with evident irony – upon his own art and indeed upon the art of his Italian exemplars: as a literary 'maker' he measured himself against three of the most conscious craftsman of his era; as a thinker, he was no less able to establish a position of his own by inspecting the (often competing) models which Italian theorists established in their speculative writings.[3] Of course, Chaucer himself was not a theorist to anything like the same degree as Dante, Petrarch and Boccaccio: all that can be attributed to him in regard to theory must be deduced from the themes he addresses or from his poetic practice, and on this evidence he may indeed be thought to display a certain resistance to the theoretical projects of his Italian contemporaries. But the Italian works which Chaucer chose to read and imitate

---

2. For the English tradition see P. Boitani, *English Medieval Narrative in the 13th and 14th Centuries* (Cambridge,1982); for the French tradition, see Charles Muscatine, *Chaucer and the French Tradition* (Berkeley, 1956); for biography see D. Pearsall, *The Life of Geoffrey Chaucer: A Critical Biography* (Oxford, 1992).

3. It is no anachronism to attribute theoretical power to the Italians. Before he wrote the *Commedia*, Dante had written his philosophical prose work the *Convivio* and his study of language and poetics, *De Vulgari Eloquentia* while, during the writing of the *Commedia*, he also composed, in Latin, his treatise on world government, *De Monarchia*. Petrarch wrote in Latin many tracts such as *Contra Medicos* and *De Otio Religioso* and many letters – gathered in *Rerum Familiarum Libri* and *Rerum Senilium Libri* – which addressed the moral and intellectual controversies of his day. Boccaccio is responsible for a discussion of myth and literature, the *De Genealogia Deorum*, which was to continue to influence theoreticians as late as Sir Philip Sidney.

display, when taken together, an unparalleled range of philosophical, political and ethical issues – from the nature of our relations with God, to the formation of human societies, to a critique of the human constitution in regard to the intellect and the emotions; and these considerations are all very closely linked in the minds of the Italians to questions of expression, linguistic form and intellectual method. If, then, one proceeds first to consider how this debate was conducted in Italy, one will then be able to return to Chaucer's work himself and examine what he himself might have made of the intellectual ferment which he would have encountered in the Italy he visited in the 1370s and to investigate the literary forms which he subsequently developed to define his own position.

DANTE, PETRARCH AND BOCCACCIO

In his treatise *On His Own Ignorance and That of Many Others* (*c.* 1368), which represents one of his comprehensive accounts of ethics and culture, Petrarch declares: 'I do not adore Aristotle.' This disavowal of intellectual idolatry leads, as will appear in Chapter 2, to a position which anticipates many features of Renaissance humanism. But the treatise also identifies (in order to attack) the principles of philosophical procedure which, in the hands of scholastic philosophers such as Aquinas, had revolutionised religious thinking in the Late Middle Ages. Particularly during the thirteenth century, the rediscovery of Aristotle's work generated a profound confidence in reason and in the power of logic; philosophers now thought themselves able to analyse systematically the whole network of relations in the natural as well as the supernatural world which were thought to exist between God as Creator and the human creature. These same principles, only fifty years before Petrarch launched his attacked, had been for Dante a primary source of inspiration. That human beings should possess Aristotelian reason at all, is, he declares, itself 'a miracle';[4] and from his earliest philosophical investigations of natural phenomena until the highest reaches of religious experience in the *Commedia,* he expresses and gives meaning to the notion that the rational mind itself is capable of love: God, on this view, intended the cosmos to be known by the human mind; and human beings were capable of discovering their own human

---

4. *Convivio,* III. 7.

nature as well as God himself through a rational understanding of their own relation to the wisdom of God's created scheme. Thus, even in the *Paradiso*, Dante's statement of faith in the Christian God is expressed through a vocabulary which shows an equal faith in the Aristotelian vocabulary of physical motion:[5]

> Io credo in uno Dio
> solo ed eterno. che tutto il ciel move,
> non moto, con amore e disio.
>
> (*Par.*, XXIV. 130–2)

(I believe in one God, single and eternal, who unmoving moves the whole universe, with love and desire.)

From assertions such as this – many with an even higher incidence of technical terminology and argumentation – there derives the familiar understanding of the *Commedia* as a celebration of universal order. Much can be said in favour of this view;[6] and there is reason to suppose that Chaucer understood its implications.[7] Yet it needs to be emphasised that there are many aspects of Dante's poem which cannot be explained simply as a reflection of some medieval world picture. Its imaginative impact is by no means as systematic as modern critics have sometimes suggested;[8] and to read the poem as closely as Chaucer seems to have read it would have generated many suggestions which could not be explained by a purely Aristotelian interpretation.

In the first place, the *Commedia* is as much an account of disorder as it is of order. In the *Inferno* (though not exclusively there) Dante anatomises the psychological and social pressures which lead human beings to

5. On Dante's Aristotelianism see P. Boyde, *Dante Philomythes and Philosopher* (Cambridge, 1981) and *Perception and Passion in Dante's Comedy* (Cambridge, 1993). Also K. Foster, 'The Mind in Love' in John Freccero (ed.), *Dante: A Collection of Critical Essays* (Englewood Cliffs, 1965).

6. Support for this view on a political level emerges when one considers the emphasis which Dante came to place on the historical importance of the Roman Empire and on the universal order which would arise in the temporal human world under the authority of the Just Emperor. God in his view had commissioned the Empire to establish peace – and therefore happiness – in the temporal world. See below, p. 88.

7. This view is proposed especially by Piero Boitani in his 'What Dante meant to Chaucer', in *Chaucer and the Italian Trecento* (Cambridge, 1983), pp. 115–39. I shall return to this very important contention below at pp. 000 and 000.

8. See, for instance, C.S. Lewis who speaks of the *Commedia* as if it were created by the scholastic system independent of the author's control in *Studies in Medieval and Renaissance Literature* (Cambridge, 1966), p. 158. T.S. Eliot in *Dante* (London, Faber 1929) also stresses the extent to which Dante benefits from the established structures of scholastic thought.

destroy the harmonious universe which God had created them to enjoy. Sins for Dante are acts of treachery, betraying not only God but also the human self, insofar as the sinner misdirects – through a perversion of rational love – the potentialities of his or her own nature and temperament. In response to this disorder, Dante is not content simply to reaffirm the details of divine law (though he does not fail to do this). Rather, he takes upon himself the responsibilities (and pains) of a judge. The encounters depicted throughout the *Inferno* are invariably encounters in which particular judgements of cultural and political failure as well as spiritual failure are recorded, and in which the poet attempts to reaffirm for the benefit of the reader the powers of discrimination or rational courage which – as the actions of the damned display – can all too easily be obscured in the human mind. Dante's Aristotelian desire for order and clarity is accompanied by an equally strong desire to penetrate to the heart of darkness.

Two other complications follow, largely generated by Dante's imaginative conception of the other world and by his conduct of the narrative. First, there is the fact that the Aristotelian Dante chooses as his guide in Hell and Purgatory not Aristotle but rather the Roman poet Virgil; secondly, that on Dante's own account the central figure in his poem and in the journey it represents is the figure of his courtly lady, Beatrice.

In one sense, the choice of Virgil powerfully re-emphasises Dante's Aristotelianism: in Aristotle's view, there is nothing in the mind which is not first in the senses; and Dante in assimilating his own journey to the journey which Virgil's Aeneas makes to Rome out of the ruins of Troy represents his own acquisition of knowledge and orderly understanding as a progressive and dynamic encounter with the facts, personages and even the physical textures of the external world. Nothing is more palpable – in regard to sight, touch, hearing and smell – than the supposedly spiritual world of Dante's after-life. But, strikingly, this assimilation leads Dante away from formal logic (of which he shows himself capable in the *Convivio* and the *Monarchia*) into a realm which asserts the value of narrative form itself as a vehicle of intellectual inquiry: Virgil is no philosopher. Yet throughout the *Commedia* he is seen as a teller of truths; and there can be little doubt that it was a reading of Virgil's *Aeneid* which encouraged Dante (who, before the *Commedia*, had written no narrative poetry at all) to attempt a reconciliation of literary and philosophical aspirations. At the same time, the figure of Virgil in the *Commedia* is profoundly problematical. He may have given Dante the confidence to write narrative verse, and this (combined with the example of Ovid, Statius and Lucan) may have impelled him into the many revolutionary developments of form and fiction which are demonstrated in the *Commedia*. Yet Virgil is a pagan; and running through Dante's representation of him in the *Commedia* is a profound concern over the limits as well as the virtues which characterise the literary, discursive and ethical codes of the pagan world. Questions of the sort had been raised throughout the later Middle Ages and increase in intensity, through Petrarch, Boccaccio and Chaucer, as one approaches the Renaissance. But nowhere is the problem expressed in more acutely personal terms than when Dante writes of Virgil as one who carries a light for the benefit of others but not of himself (*Purg.*, XXII. 67–8).

If, in representing Virgil, Dante comes to terms with the possibilities and limitations of classical narrative and culture, so too in his treatment of Beatrice, he similarly re-engages with the codes of love which, from the troubadours onwards, had been central to the development of the vernacular lyric. As it is commonly understood, Dante's contribution to this development was to see the courtly lady not in social or even sexual terms but as a saint or mediator between himself and God. This interpretation cannot wholly be discounted; certainly it was a view which made a considerable impact on Petrarch. Yet to say only this would be to misapprehend very seriously Dante's understanding of Beatrice and to invite (particularly in the context of recent criticism) a dangerously distorted view of his moral and literary position.[9] From the *Vita nuova* – which is Dante's earliest account of Beatrice – to the final cantos of the *Paradiso*, Beatrice is seen not as an ideal but as an incarnation. In and through Beatrice, Dante envisages the possibility that human beings, as created by God, are intrinsically good and that such goodness, which God himself loves, is also the proper object of human love. It is in this sense that Beatrice reveals to Dante the truth of the Christian God, as a loving Creator. In this sense, too, it would be wrong to treat Beatrice allegorically, since her meaning lies not in some general conceptual truth which she serves to represent but in the undefinable reality of

9. For opposing views of Beatrice – particularly in the perspective of modern feminist thinking – see Joy Hambuechen Potter, 'Beatrice Dead or Alive: Love in the *Vita nuova*', and R. Kirkpatrick, 'Dante's Beatrice and the Politics of Singularity', both in David Wallace (ed.), *Texas Studies in Literature and Language,* (Vol. 32, No. 1, Spring 1990). Here and throughout this volume I shall contend that an understanding of Beatrice as the source of Dante's confidence in the value of human persons is central to an understanding of his poetry and thought. See especially below, pp. 300–1.

human goodness which she communicates to Dante. Of course, there is a sufficient amount of allegorising and idealising language in Dante's treatment of Beatrice to have misled even his immediate contemporaries. But in large part Dante's concern in the *Vita nuova* is to abandon the temptingly masterful interpretations of allegory. From the middle of the *Vita nuova* Beatrice is independent of interpretative generalisation. She moves freely around Florence as a particular human being, and is indeed capable of laughing at a lover who is still much encumbered by the codes and conventions of love literature.[10] In this respect the Beatrice of the *Vita nuova* is recognisably the forerunner of the Beatrice who speaks with irrepressibly disruptive power in the Earthly Paradise and the *Paradiso*. At all points, there is something singular and surprising about Beatrice which interrupts the predictable flow of narrative or of controlling logic. She often appears as a lyric epiphany, disturbing yet fulfilling the progress of the narrative. But she is also intimate – a *soave voce* – and in that regard she can rightly be seen as a voice which stimulates the poet to write in the vernacular (rather than in Latin) since in Dante's definition, the vernacular is specifically able to touch the heart and penetrate to the roots of the self.[11]

In contemplating Beatrice, Dante is always surprised by what she reveals about the excellence of human nature; and in that regard, his understanding of Beatrice is not ultimately incompatible with his understanding of Aristotle. The unifying principle of Dante's poetry demands that, even while writing of the other world, he should be utterly convinced of the value of this world. Aristotle may have given him the means to explore that world from a scientific – and also from a political – point of view, developing a language which is technically precise and descriptively trenchant in its evocation of natural or historical phenomena. It is, however, from Beatrice that Dante, on his own account, derives the confidence which allows him to value – indeed to love – the things and persons of the secular world,[12] and to recognise (in what must seem a plausibly Chaucerian vein) that God can be loved in and through the things of this world.

There is, then, certainly a synthesis and a high degree of order in Dante's thinking. But it is a synthesis, which depends as much upon a confident sense of the value of human beings, human culture and human

10. See especially her laughter at Dante's swooning adoration in *Vita nuova*, XIV.
11. See Dante's definition of the vernacular as the language we learn to speak at the breast, in *De Vulgari Eloquentia*, I. i.
12. The phrase is E. Auerbach's and is well supported in *Dante, Poet of the Secular World*, trans. Ralph Mannheim (Chicago and London, 1961).

language as upon any merely philosophical system. As soon, however, as we turn to Petrarch, this powerful balance is radically disturbed.

For, paradoxically, at the core of Petrarch's humanism is a profound mistrust or uncertainty about the value of this world and a profound apprehension of its mutability. As Kenelm Foster has written, 'it is hardly too much to say that Petrarch's religion was at bottom a cry to God prompted by fear and horror of death'.[13] In anyone but Petrarch it would be reasonable to associate such a view with the awful emphasis engendered by the Black Death upon the corruptibility of this world and the physical evidence of human decay. On such an understanding, the very precise view of sin which Dante developed – as a means of diagnosing, judging and rectifying the disorders of human existence – dissolves into a general terror or obsession with contamination, where remedies lie not so much in the careful discriminations of reason but rather in an acknowledgement that all human beings are dependent upon grace. Yet Petrach, while not immune from such attitudes, is far too complex a figure to describe in such large terms; and he (recognising the complexity of his own personality almost to the point of pride) derives his characteristic understanding from an inspection precisely of that personality rather than – as in Dante's case – from an examination of order and disorder in the external world. Judgement too, as Petrarch views it, is not as Dante understands it, primarily a matter of precise diagnosis, but rather a matter of guilt and shame. Petrarch's ethical responses are deeply personal and introspective. But they open the way for a new understanding of the psyche which is at times ascetically religious, at other times exuberantly confident that human beings (rich in talent and sensibility as Petrarch knows himself to be) can overcome the mutability of this world through the achievement of fame, literary glory and the contemplation of beauty.

To return now to Petrarch's *On His Own Ignorance*, the programme which Petrarch develops there in opposition to scholasticism depends upon a readjustment of the relations between will and intellect. 'It is better,' he declares, 'to will the good than to know the true':

13. Here and throughout on Petrarch, see K. Foster, *Petrarch, Poet and Humanist* (Edinburgh, no date), p. 147. Also Charles Trinkaus, *In Our Image and Likeness: Humanity and Divinity in Italian Humanist Thought*, 2 vols. (London, 1970). T. Bergin, *Petrarch* (New York, 1970); Maurice Bishop, *Petrarch and his World* (Port Washington, NY, 1973); H. Baron, *From Petrarch to Leonardo Bruni* (Chicago, 1968); N. Mann, *Petrarch* (Oxford, 1984); Marjorie O'Rourke Boyle, *Petrarch's Genius: Pentimento to Prophecy* (Berkeley, 1991). For a seminal reading of Petrarch's poetics see John Freccero, 'The Fig-Tree and the Laurel', *Diacritics*, 5 (1975), pp. 34–46.

Therefore the true moral philosophers and useful teachers of the virtues are those whose first and last intention is to make the hearer good . . . It is safer to strive for a good and pious will than for a capable and clear intellect. The object of the will, as it pleases the wise is to be good; that of the intellect is truth. It is better to will the good than to know the truth. The first is never without merit; the latter can often be polluted with crime and then admits no excuse.[14]

The danger in intellectual argumentation which Petrarch here identifies is that it should be indulged for its own sake and degenerate into mere curiosity, arid speculation or even pride in one's achievements. To avoid that, one must return to the primary motivations of the will, to ensure that its objects are good and that its energies are adequate. Internally, the mind will seek to re-establish a direct relationship with the God who originally willed its existence, while externally, in communication with other humans, the writer's task will be to speak heart to heart and stir in each reader a comparable love of the good and the truly beautiful. Thus in his philosophical writings Petrarch deliberately abandons formal argumentation – for 'in too much disputation truth is lost' – [15] and chooses instead (as will many of his successors in the Renaissance) to address his reader intimately in letters, orations, essays or, of course, lyric poems. Syllogisms and technicality of diction here yield to eloquence and persuasiveness of phrase. And in this regard, classic texts – slowly being rediscovered in their original form – were an essential resource, in that they provided rhetorical example and also a demonstration of how fame and eloquence, having endured through time, could still establish a heartfelt bond with the readers of later generations.

Now such a position represents a considerable departure from Dante's world where even pagan poets such as Virgil and courtly ladies such as Beatrice are portrayed as skilful dialecticians, advancing Dante's intellectual journey through technical argumentation. Yet the true interest and depth of Petrarch's work, especially in his poetry, lies in his realisation of how difficult it is to maintain a right direction in the will. In Dante's narrative, there is always someone to talk to (usually pictured as a distinct and historically located voice rather than a text), in search of support or authoritative guidance. The profoundly interior view which Petrarch cultivates reveals a mind teeming with undirected and self-generated pas-

14. Translation by Hans Nachod, in E. Cassirer, P.O. Kristeller and J.H. Randall, jr. (eds.), *The Renaissance Philosophy of Man* (Chicago, 1948), p. 101.
15. See *A Disapproval of an Unreasonable Use of the Discipline of Dialectic,* trans. Nachod, *The Renaissance Philosophy of Man.* E. Cassirer, op.cit., p. 134.

sions or cross-purposes. What is worse, the very instruments which Petrarch enlists to clarify and redirect the will may themselves prove delusive. For if beauty is in one sense a manifestation of order and harmonious relationship, beauty can also become an end in itself and thus deflect the mind from contemplation of God into an idolatrous concern with the images and artifices of this world. Likewise, if eloquence – taught supremely well by classical authors such as Cicero – can inspire even Christian generations, it can also degenerate into a trivial preoccupation with the superficialities, from a Christian point of view, of pagan practices or temporal reputation. The result is a spirituality which at its most fruitful generates a profound honesty of self-inspection. But there is the possibility of tragedy here, too, as the self is discovered to be poised between the contradictory claims of secular and divine goods; and for Petrarch the tragedy was in part a result of his cultural circumstances. Subsequent centuries were to applaud Petrarch for his devotion to the values of eloquence and beauty; and Petrarch seems half to have known that they would. Yet he himself was not free enough of earlier ethical schemes to pursue these values single-mindedly to their conclusion.

The tensions which Petrarch recognised in his own position are explored to their fullest extent – and characteristically left open – in his confessional work the *Secretum* where he imagines one version of himself (named 'Franciscus') in conversation with another version (named 'Augustinus') who attempts to wean his interlocutor from his devotion to poetry, to earthly glory and above all to his courtly lady, Laura. Here one sees evidence of an Augustinian strand of thought applied to practical moral questions which was to run through Renaissance humanism and would finally affect philosophers as distant as Calvin and Des Cartes.[16] In Augustine himself there is a 'radical reflexivity' which leads him constantly, in the *Confessions* and elsewhere, to direct the eye of inquiry away from the created world and inwards to the truth of the self which is knowledge of an unchanging God within us: 'Do not go outward; return within yourself. In the inward man dwells truth.'[17] This is echoed in Petrarch's own desire to rediscover himself – through the mist of distractions and doubt – in relation to God's creative will. Yet other – and, to Petrarch, equally potent – desires continually supervene; and even in his attempts to find a disciplinarian remedy for human passions he is not always able to sustain a fully Augustinian (or even Christian) position.

16. See Charles Taylor on Augustine's place in the history of 'inwardness', *In Interiore Homine*', *Sources of the Self* (Cambridge, 1989), pp. 127–58.
17. *De Vera Religione*, XXXIX, 72.

Throughout, he displays a concern if not precisely with argument and ratiocination then with a *chara* or 'rational exhilaration' which is Stoic in character; and, important as Stoicism itself will be in Renaissance thinking, it leads Petrarch himself into a dualistic desire to divide the spirit from the erring and corruptible body. Augustine would not sanction this. Nor would any Christian who, like Dante, believed in the ultimate unity of spirit and matter envisaged in the doctrine of the Resurrection of the Body, which (as *Inferno*, Canto VI, envisages) represents an ultimate return of the human spirit to a mode of bodily existence.

The implications of the *Secretum* are visible at every turn in the 366 lyric poems which constitute Petrarch's *Rime Sparse*. These are 'scattered rhymes' and there will be no attempt here at rational or even narrative order. Petrarch did in fact work unremittingly on the disposition of the poems in his collection; but the result is either to sharpen the conflicts in his position or else to associate the poet's psychic shifts with the patterns of temporal change, spelled out in the 365 days of a calendar year. Nor does Laura consistently offer to Petrarch the confidence in human nature which Beatrice offered to Dante. On the contrary, she is scarcely a presence at all in these poems; Petrarch's concern is constantly focussed upon himself in deciding whether his reaction to Laura is one of devout contemplation or of baneful obsession. Indeed, in the *Secretum* it is admitted that Laura is as much a word as a woman.[18] Through an endless series of puns, 'Laura' may be taken to mean 'breeze', 'gold', 'dawn' or, above all, the laurel crown that the poet has set himself to win. All of these attributes can be viewed negatively as objects which attract the misdirection of the will. Yet the same qualities and attributes may equally be celebrated as indications of the permanence which human beings can create for themselves through art and fame in the temporal life. This duality sets in motion the endless sequence of self-contradictions which Petrarch traces in the course of the *Rime Sparse*; and the process is one which disallows the attentions that Dante so conspicuously displays to the impact of another person upon the poet's own mind. Petrarch – who is any way inclined to dualism – rarely reaches outside himself to attempt even a fully descriptive account of the women he says he loves or of the natural but charismatic world which she inhabits.[19] Here, one is far from that strongly mimetic form of lan-

18. See *Secretum*, Book III. Cf. discussion of the representation of the Lady in lyric poetry below, p. 143.
19. Petrarch's *Trionfi* (written in *terza rima*) concern the varying 'triumphs' of Love, Shame, Death, Fame, Time and Eternity and also address these themes very directly.

guage which Dante cultivates in his use of the vernacular.

In this light, it is entirely characteristic that Petrarch should begin the *Rime Sparse* with a recantation which speaks of the 'brief dreams' which please the world and which clearly includes among such brief dreams the poems which are to follow in this collection.[20] Here before his collection has begun Petrarch has withdrawn into himself. The 'voi' to whom the poem speaks is undefined, a sounding board somewhere in posterity for Petrarch's complaints. Laura, unnamed, is gathered up into the experiences of shame and recrimination which produce the wrackingly self-obsessed eleventh line: 'di me medesmo meco mi vergogno' ('I for myself feel shame within myself'). Poetry itself becomes here an object of guilt, as Petrarch regrets the reputation his verses have won for him. Yet there remains still a reason to compose this poem of self-lacerating introspection. Here, encountering himself as he was and as he is, Petrarch enters the region of memory which for Augustine represents the soul's implicit knowledge of itself; and in the final line Petrarch arrives at what has been called the Augustinian proto-cogito of 'if I did not exist, I could not be deceived'.[21] Throughout, the poem, which 'weeps as it speaks', the verse has traced the oscillations and recriminations which constitute the Petrarchan self. And, finally, eloquence has its part to play in communicating the poet's understanding. For while eloquence may indeed be no more than one of the dreams 'which please the world', it serves here, without argument, to project the truth of its own inadequacies to any ear which can appreciate the finality and subtlety of the final cadence: 'che quanto piace al mondo è breve sogno': 'whatever pleases the world is a brief dream'.

The first major author to listen attentively to the Petrarchan voice was Boccaccio; and of the many paradoxes which traverse Petrarch's work, one in particular comes into focus as we turn to Boccaccio: namely, that, in abandoning the scholastic attempt to perceive rational connections between the created world and its creator, rationality itself was liberated and permitted to turn attention to the things of this world. Without suggesting any lack of religious faith on Boccaccio's part, the emphasis in Boccaccio's description of the world falls not upon the providence of its creator but upon the phenomena of change and generation – of Fortune and of Nature – in the earthly sphere. Boccaccio's concern is with the shifts of circumstance and of appetite which all

20. The full text of this sonnet can be found below, p. 120.
21. See E. Gilson, *The Christian Philosophy of Saint Augustine* (London, 1961), pp. 41–2.

human beings face in the course of a temporal life, and also with the responses which all human beings, regardless of class or gender, are able to make to these shifts.[22] One such response, as Boccaccio well knew, would have been Stoic detachment. But in the *Decameron,* at least, reason and will are replaced at the centre of human identity by a working wit or pragmatic intelligence which allows its possessor – whether merchant, trickster or wandering wife – to turn any vicissitude to his or her own advantage, or even *in extremis* to the defence of life itself.

Intelligence of this order can, as we have seen in the introduction, have social implications: the *brigata* of story-tellers, fleeing from the plague, are distinctly pragmatic in the way they construct a civil and civilised order in the face of natural disaster. And it is this that produces what has been described as Boccaccio's naturalism (which is to be distinguished as a concern with the underlying motives of human life from detailed realism). But the same form of intelligence could also be said to characterise the work which Boccaccio as author sets himself to perform. For if Dante relies to a high degree upon logic and Petrarch upon the cultivation of eloquence, then Boccaccio offers to Chaucer (who may resist it) a model in which the power of fiction – understood as both making and indeed as lying – is thoroughly investigated and enlisted for ultimately moral ends. Consider, for instance, the third story of the first Day: the Muslim Saladin, short of funds, thinks that he can pressurise the Jew Melchisidech into lending him what he needs by asking him an incriminating question – which of the three great religions of the world possesses the truth? Melchisidech evades the question by telling a story: a father has three sons and loves all equally but cannot express his love by any legacy since he has only one indivisible treasure, a ring – until, that is, he realises that by ordering two counterfeit rings to be made and then bequeathing these without revealing which is authentic and which false, he can achieve his purpose, despite the fact that his sons proceed to fight among themselves. Saladin is so impressed by the skill of the story that he refuses to prosecute his demands for money. At which Melchisidech himself now impressed by Saladin's goodwill lends the money anyway; and the two become close friends.

What is remarkable here is that fiction serves to release both Saladin and the Jew from the fixed habits of enmity to which their respective religions would have committed them. And this is achieved not through precept or, for that matter, through Petrarchan eloquence but through

22. See Aldo Scaglione, *Nature and Love in the Middle Ages* (Berkeley, 1963); R. Hastings, *Nature and Reason in the Decameron* (Manchester, 1975).

the illuminating power of wit. In itself, Melchisidech's story embodies an extraordinary realisation of the relativity of religious truths: a truth certainly exists, as does the true ring, but no one can tell that truth from its counterfeit. And so, one might conclude, there is no good reason to be at odds at all. But, so far from insisting upon this explicit conclusion, Boccaccio represents Saladin's intelligent appreciation of Melchisidech's no-less intelligent fiction as being itself the stimulus for the free and equitable friendship which arises between them. Story-telling, precisely by abandoning strict truth, produces its own higher morality.

The implications of the Three Rings story could be supported theoretically by reference to the *Genealogia Deorum*, where Boccaccio defends myth as a form in which an earlier − and even pagan − age can communicate with a later and Christian era.[23] There is also evidence here of the similarity which exists beneath the surface between Petrarch and Boccaccio in regard to their view of language; for both are capable of contemplating a world which consists rather of words and cultural traditions than immovable facts: where, for Petrarch, eloquence is the bond between human beings, fiction − as myth, 'making' or even, sometimes, as lying[24] − is for Boccaccio a comparably strong source of linkage.

Such notions as these hold much promise for future ages. But they also distance Boccaccio, as surely as they do Petrarch, from the Dantean world of fact, certain knowledge and definitive judgement. And Boccaccio is aware of this. It is true that (unlike Petrarch) Boccaccio makes frequent, explicit and usually respectful reference to Dante. Indeed, there are those who argue that Boccaccio's art is essentially medieval in character, and point not only to the structure of the Boccaccio's one hundred stories as a reflection of Dante's one hundred cantos but also maintain that the work is parallel to Dante's in moving systematically from the representation of absolute vice to the contemplation of perfect virtue.[25] Yet Boccaccio himself describes the *Decameron* as a Galeotto, employing the phrase which in *Inferno*, Canto V, is used to designate the pandering volume read by Paolo and Francesca in their illicit love affair. Moreover, as in the Three Rings story so throughout the *Decameron*, virtuoso liars tend to become unexpected heroes: Ceperello in Day One story one is described by the narrator as 'perhaps

23. This is available in a translation by Charles B. Osgood, *Boccaccio on Poetry* (New York, 1956). See especially Cap. XIV, pp. 42–52.
24. See Guido Almansi, *The Writer as Liar* (London, 1976).
25. See V. Branca, *Boccaccio: The Man his Works* (New York, 1976).

the worst man in the world' (and in Dante's scheme he would have been condemned without any 'perhaps'). Yet here both he and his stories are presented as pure fictions, releasing the reader from the need to arrive at any final judgement. This is not to suggest that Boccaccio (any more than Chaucer) is a cheerful amoralist. His understanding of social, intellectual and sexual *mores* is far too acute for any such accusation. Nevertheless, in most if not all of his tales, Boccaccio sees a positive, and indeed moral, value in the acts of creation, resolution and intelligent recreation which occur through fiction and even discerns a degree of essential humanity in the ambiguous responses which fictions can provoke. One of the main evils that the *Decameron* identifies is the evil of any tyrannical obsession with a single plan or role, whether that plan be expressed in discourse, in preconceived judgements or in other forms of social and sexual mastery. Wit – and the fictions exchanged in storytelling – are, time and again, brought forward in Boccaccio's work to achieve a release from such imprisonments.

It would be easy to conclude that, taken together, the writings of Dante, Petrarch and Boccaccio are evidence of a shift from Medieval to Renaissance modes of thought, whereby a world, sure and subtle in its dependence on established codes of thought and language, yields to another in which the terms of debate are constantly renewed; and readings of this sort have sometimes produced a debate as to whether Chaucer, in his turn, inclines to the Medieval or to the Renaissance model.[26] It is certainly worth noting that most Italians of Chaucer's period tended to follow Petrarch and Boccaccio rather than Dante, whose supremacy was not fully reasserted until the nineteenth and twentieth centuries. Chaucer, on the other hand, openly affirms his recognition of Dante's authority and shows a certain resistance to Petrarch and Boccaccio. As will be seen, Chaucer openly declares his affiliation with Dante while being cautious in his use of Petrarch's name. In regard to Boccaccio, while drawing more directly on Boccaccio's work than that of any other Italian, Chaucer never permits himself to use his name – as if there were something shameful about the association – whereas his debt to Dante and, to a lesser degree, Petrarch is firmly acknowledged. Yet to suppose that this justified a description of Chaucer as 'medieval' would seriously oversimplify the case, detracting

26. See, for instance, C.S. Lewis on the 'medievalism' displayed in *Troilus and Criseyde*, 'What Chaucer really did to *Il Filostrato*,' *Essays and Studies*, 17, (1932), pp. 56–75.

from the subtlety with which Chaucer interrogates the Italian tradition and the independence of his conclusions. As one turns now to consider in some detail Chaucer's reading of Italian texts, it will become obvious that, even in approaching Dante's *Commedia*, Chaucer is able to adopt a critical view, putting questions to the Dantean text which may well have been raised by his reading of Petrarch or Boccaccio.

DANTE AND CHAUCER: *THE HOUSE OF FAME* AND *THE CANTERBURY TALES*

Reference to Dante's poetry and, occasionally, to his theoretical treatises, occur at almost every stage of Chaucer's writing career.[27] It is, however, an early poem, *The House of Fame* (*c.* 1375), which suggests how well Chaucer knew the *Commedia* and how critical his use of Dante's example could be.

The House of Fame is an unfinished work and its dream allegory remains unexplained. Yet, on the evidence of recent studies,[28] there can be no doubt that Chaucer here reflects very deeply upon the linguistic, literary and philosophical foundations of his own art. In a dream, 'Geoffrey' visits the Domains of Rumour and of Fame: in the one he experiences the confusions that language can perpetrate; in the other he envisages the permanence of reputation which Fame can bestow upon poets and those whom poets celebrate. In a similar way, Chaucer, as poet, engages with both the potentialities and the relativities of the medium in which he is writing. On the one hand, his own poem ambitiously locates itself, through reference and allusion, in a tradition which embraces classical authors such as Claudian, Lucan and Statius and authors from the modern vernacular. On the other hand, the claims which Chaucer might wish to make on his own behalf as an 'authority' within that tradition are constantly questioned through the poet's comic portrayal of himself as the bewildered 'Geoffrey'; and the comedy of this

27. Arguments against any such statement have been voiced by Howard H. Schless in *Chaucer and Dante* (Norman, Okla., 1984). But see Winthrop Wetherbee, *Chaucer and the Poets* (Ithaca, 1984); Karla Taylor, *Chaucer reads the Divine Comedy* (Stanford, 1989); and most recently, Richard Neuse, *Chaucer's Dante: Allegory and Epic Theatre in The Canterbury Tales* (Berkeley, 1991).

28. See especially A.C. Spearing, *Medieval to Renaissance in English Poetry* (Cambridge, 1985), pp. 22–9, and D. Wallace 'Chaucer's Continental Inheritance: The Early Poems and *Troilus and Criseyde*',' contained in J. Mann and P. Boitani (eds), *The Cambridge Chaucer Companion* (Cambridge, 1986). Also S. Delany, *Chaucer's House of Fame: The Poetics of Sceptical Fideism* (Chicago and London, 1972).

portrayal begets a general tone of scepticism which, arguably, encourages the reader to inquire into the logical connections between the word (or the dream) and the world or Truth.

In speaking of fame – especially in relation to eloquence – Chaucer chooses a theme which is of central importance in the humanist thinking of Petrarch. Similarly, he would have found in Boccaccio an author who was notably (if often playfully) alert to questions of truth and falsehood. Yet it is through his reading of the *Commedia* that Chaucer seems to have focussed his intentions most clearly. In a general sense, Chaucer here extends the normal scope of a dream poem to include a visionary journey through the cosmos, and in that respect is clearly influenced by Dante. But there are more precise considerations than this. For not only are Chaucer's references to Dante drawn from all parts of the *Commedia,* they are also employed with a particularly strong sense of interpretative purpose. Within the space of seventy five lines in Book Two, Chaucer skilfully brings together widely separated verses – from *Inferno* II, *Purgatorio* IX and *Paradiso* I – to reveal what Dante, as author or as a character in his own poem, has to say on the question of Fame, tradition and authority. First impressions might suggest that Chaucer's aim was ironic or parodic; and certainly he will establish a position of his own against Dante's. Yet to a surprising degree he seems to have derived from Dante not only the essential themes of *The House of Fame*, but also an understanding of issues central to his own art – of comedy and of how to construct a comic persona.

It is in Book Two that Chaucer's protagonist, Geoffrey, dreams of the Eagle who is to accompany him in his pseudo-Dantean journey through the heavens. The Eagle stands at the heart of Chaucer's comedy, and characteristically begins its solemn task with, for the dreamer, a colloquial and all-too familiar 'Awake!', 'ryght in the same vois and stevene(*tongue*)/ That useth oon I koude nevene (*name*)' (*HF*, 561–3). Yet this same Eagle in *Purgatorio* IX has fallen upon Dante, while *he* dreams, with the silent power of Jove possessing Ganymede: in Canto IX an eagle as terrible as a thunderbolt, descends on Dante and lifts him to the sky.

For Dante, the Eagle is, among other things, an emblem of Imperial authority. And it is appropriate that this vision of authority should appear to him as it does, on the threshold of Purgatory: in *Purgatorio*, Cantos VIII and IX, Dante has just encountered the negligent rulers of medieval Europe who have refused to assume or acknowledge the legitimate exercise of power. Thus, in part, the dream of the Eagle is a dream of true justice, and no theme is more central to the *Commedia* than this. In Dante's view, the moral, intellectual, and spiritual life in all its aspects is founded on a love of Justice. So, when Dante's Eagle next appears, in *Paradiso*, its meaning extends beyond the political sphere to include a celebration of linguistic clarity and stability: the souls of the just who in *Paradiso*, Canto XVIII, form themselves into the shape of an Eagle before Dante's eyes initially spelling out for him the text, 'Love Justice': *Diligite Iustitiam* (*Par.*, XVIII. 91–3).

It is has been suggested that Chaucer, recognising in Dante a poet who spans Heaven and Hell,[29] either refuses, for his own part, to countenance such ambition or else implicitly deplores it. Certainly, in choosing for his domestic Geoffrey a guide of such cosmic magnitude as Dante's Eagle, Chaucer engages wryly enough not only with the authority of Dante's own text but also with the idea of authority on which the *Commedia* itself is in part constructed. There is here plainly an element of very daring burlesque; and the direct, often colloquial, language which Chaucer uses here in conjunction with a highly technical vocabulary makes, in *The House of Fame* as elsewhere in Chaucer, a considerable contribution to such effects of burlesque. Yet Dante – far more than Petrarch – could have taught Chaucer to speak directly and indeed to play registers of speech against each other. And to speak only of burlesque would be to underestimate the implications of Chaucer's comedy and to ignore the extent to which Chaucer may have responded to comedy as Dante himself had practised it in his own poem. For Dante, too, is capable of recognising a limitation in such authoritative principles as Justice, and he, too, can see the limits that lie around the aspirations to any comprehensive vision of universal order.

For in the first place, the authority of the Eagle, however central it might be, is not allowed in the *Commedia* to stand as an absolute: beyond all manifestations of rational justice, Dante recognises another power, the power of Divine Love, which is undoubtedly at one with Justice but which can also extend the implications of that principle or even overthrow the sovereignty of rational law. So the Eagle, particularly in *Paradiso*, Canto XX, can be seen not only as a symbol of Justice but also – by virtue of its association with St John – as a symbol of Revelation: in visionary love, the mind enters areas of knowledge which are beyond the grasp of laws and well-formed words. So, too, in the *Purgatorio*, while Dante dreams that he is being raised violently aloft by the Eagle, he is in fact being raised gently by St Lucy, the patron

29. See P. Boitani, 'What Dante meant to Chaucer', *Chaucer and the Italian Trecento* (Cambridge, 1983).

saint of light, acting not out of law but rather from an unaccountable love for Dante as an individual creature.

In the full perspective of the *Commedia* the implications of the interplay between Justice and Love are reflected in a variety of formal features. Dante at no point abandons the desire for comprehensiveness and clarity in his writing. But his text is also a text which can 'humble itself' as it recognises the greater validity of vision or seeks to represent the impact of spiritual love upon the individual; famously, the visual image in Dante's work carries as much meaning as the well-formed phrase, and the term 'comedy' indicates the extent to which the poet is prepared to allow – as Petrarch would not – a range of low or consciously 'humble' forms of speech, including on occasion, infantile forms, close to inarticulacy.[30]

A sustained example of this – which brings us directly to Dante's treatment of himself as persona and as poet within a tradition – occurs in the second passage to which Chaucer here alludes. In his immediate response to the Eagle, Chaucer cites the passage where Dante, for a first time in the *Commedia*, displays the radical intellectual humility of which we have been speaking. Thus when Chaucer declares his reluctance to respond to the Eagle: 'I neyther am Ennok, ne Elye/Ne Romulus, ne Ganymede (*HF*, 588–9), he is plainly extending the words in which Dante expresses his own unreadiness to journey into Hell when he declares that he is not 'Aeneas or Paul' who as heroes and saints were qualified to undertake such a venture (*Inf.*, 31–2).

As Chaucer recognises, there is a connection to be drawn between this passage and the *Purgatorio* dream: in both cases, Dante investigates the condition under which his destined journey is to take place. And in its narrative context, Dante's confession of humility not only involves a profound consideration of Fame but also, for a first time in the *Commedia*, institutes a dialectical opposition between Justice and Love.

In the first canto of the *Inferno*, Dante had been saved from the Dark Wood by the human representative of the Eagle, Virgil, whose *Aeneid* also dominates the opening book of *The House of Fame*. Dante's choice of Virgil as a guide is a remarkable assertion of his confidence in the capacity of rational justice, embodied in the Empire, to bring about spiritual solutions, and also of his trust in the rhetorical and culture resources of the Roman past. Virgil's assistance resides largely in his

30. See, for instance, his meeting with Beatrice in *Purg.*, XXXI. 13–15, where the Dante character cannot even utter the word 'yes' in audible tones. See also below, pp. 300–1.

'parole ornate' which, hoarse as they may have become (*Inf.,* I. 63), have still the power after thirteen centuries to stir a Florentine descendant from his torpor.

So far, Dante has appealed to the principle of Fame; and this appeal is corroborated when he associates himself with the great poets of antiquity in Canto IV. Indeed, in one respect, Dante makes the Roman qualities of the Eagle – especially the cult of Fame – one of the criteria of judgement in Hell. The first sinners that Dante encounters in Canto III are the *ignavi,* the apathetic who have left no mark as human beings on the memory of their fellows: Virgil contemptuously dismisses these sinners precisely because they have left no mark of fame on the world: 'Fama di lor il mondo esser non lassa' (*Inf.*, III. 49).

Now, there can be no doubt that Chaucer responds to this notion – as Petrarch also might have done. So, in one of the most seriously satirical and even judgemental passages of *The House of Fame,* he alludes to Dante's description of the apathetic angels who were 'neither rebels against God not loyal to Him' (*Inf.*, III. 37–8) when he makes those that 'ydel al oure lyf ybe' admit that 'We han don neither that ne this' (*HF,* III. 1732).

Yet none of this detracts from the profound sense of humility which the protagonists display in both Dante's and Chaucer's narrative. At the beginning of Canto II Dante, as character, is assailed by the sense of how absurd his journey into Hell must be, progressing into the dark with only the shade of a long-dead Roman to guide him. Virgil – whether as a man or as reason or as justice – cannot on his own bring Dante's journey to a successful conclusion. Rather, he must invoke a name which comes, like Lucia, from the realm of Love, the name of Beatrice. The protagonist begin to advance once more at the end of Canto II. But only after he has been encouraged by words – of a kind which have no place in Virgil's repertoire – drawn from the lexicon of vernacular love poetry, focussed upon the unheroic emotions of pity and images of tears (*Inf.,* II. 94–120).

It is only through a confession of dependence that the journey of Dante, as character, can proceed in its energetic pursuit of Fame. And this unheroic dependence in Dante no less than in Chaucer lies at the centre of the comedy which frequent surrounds the portrayal of the protagonist. There are many more moments of comedy in Dante's treatment of himself as character than is commonly realised;[31] and many of these are Chaucerian in their portrayal of the humiliations to which the

31. See, for instance, *Purg.*, XXI. 103, *et seq.*

eponymous character must submit. Yet the position defined by such comedy cannot be attributed only to Dante's fictive persona. Analysis would show that the questions raised by such episodes are almost invariably – as in *Inferno* II – questions of intellectual procedure or of judgement which the author, too, has to face in constructing his own poem. This is particularly clear in the third passage of the *Commedia* to which Chaucer refers. Chaucer's reference is one of a number of cases modelled on verses from the early *Paradiso* where the authorial voice, paralleling the voice of the protagonist in *Inferno* II, scrutinises the limits of its own linguistic competence and authority.

In the Proem to Book Two (ll. 523–528) Chaucer writes:

> O Thought, that wrot al that I mette,
> And in the tresorye hyt shette (shette = shut)
>
> Of my brayn, now shal men se
> Yf any vertu in the be,
> To tellen al my dreme aryght.
> Now kythe thyn engyn and myght! (engyn = skill)

But in *Paradiso,* Canto I, Dante invokes the god Apollo and far from asking to be raised above himself, seeks aid in the expression, simply, of what his mind has properly been able to carry back from the divine vision:

> Veramente quant'io del regno santo
> ne la mia mente potei far tesoro,
> sarà ora matera del mio canto.
> (Par., I. 10–15)

> (Truly as much of that holy realm as I can hold as treasure in my mind will now be the subject of my song.)

Dante here chooses to work within the confines of what mind and language are capable of attaining. And Chaucer shows his understanding of this implication by translating Dante's 'Apollo' into 'Thought'.

The principle of logical restraint is central to Dante's poetic theory and to his linguistic practice.[32] It is this which leads him as early as the *Vita nuova* to accept that while he can never say as much about Beatrice as she deserves, he will continue to speak of her – so that others should understand her effect on him – as clearly as he can without confusion or strain. The result is a clarity of speech which technically learns much

---

32. R. Kirkpatrick, *Dante's Paradiso and the Limits of Modern Criticism* (Cambridge, 1978).

from the Virgil as poet of the Roman Eagle while at the same time, in attempting to communicate of thoughts and feelings to a particular audience, resolutely acknowledges the danger of soaring 'so high that one should become base' (*VN*, 'Donne ch'avete . . . ' ll. 9–10).

At this point we return to Chaucer. For the implications of *The House of Fame* are by no means out of keeping with this conclusion. Connections have indeed been drawn between Chaucer's poem and Dante's principal statement of poetic theory, the *De Vulgari Eloquentia*, stressing that Chaucer shares with Dante an understanding of linguistic caution and artistic discretion which Dante recommends.[33] So Dante hears in the Italy of his day a Babel of warring tongues, uninformed by the craftsman-like care of the true poet while Chaucer – echoing Dante's entry into Hell – hears nothing but a jangling of tongues as he approaches the place of Gossip: 'Ne never rest is in that place/That hit nys fild ful of tydynges'(*HF,* III. 1954–60). But perceptions such as this lead neither Dante nor Chaucer to retreat from the vernacular into a Petrarchan world of monumental art.[34] On the contrary, each in his own way recognises, as Petrarch scarcely could, that voice ultimately is superior to text; and caution, discretion and humility in speech remain as important in moderating any inflated appetite for fame as in shaping the vernacular to the purposes of truth. For Dante is concerned in the *De Vulgari Eloquentia* to liberate the particular possibilities that lie in the vernacular as against the classical tongue; and the *Commedia* plainly takes far more risks with voice than the earlier tract, dramatising, for example, the disruptive outbursts of the damned and setting up a continual opposition between the regulatory and authoritative pronouncements of Virgil and the questioning and tentative voice of the Dante character. Discretion threads its way in the *Inferno* through release of mimetic energy and realistic dramatisation of tongues. In *The House of Fame*, Dante's own text becomes, so to speak, the authoritative Eagle: such an eagle is necessary if one is to avoid at one and the same time apathy and confusion of speech; and it is Chaucer's Eagle which elevates 'Geoffrey' while dissipating the rigidity of textual authority with its comic directness.

33. See James Simpson, 'Dante's *Astripeta Aquila* and the Theme of Poetic Discretion in *The House of Fame*', *Essays and Studies* (1986), pp. 1–17.
34. A complication here is that Chaucer's poem is an early work and the author's awareness of the limitations of his own technical skill must have led him to an awareness of the inadequacy of his own relatively clumsy couplets when placed alongside the fluent development of Dante's most sophisticated terzine. On the other hand, there is an awareness which runs through Chaucer (see below, on Petrarch p. 52) that his diction has always a native force and directness which he may not have found in Italian.

In practice and implication the differences between Dante's position and Chaucer's will not prove to be very great. One consequence is that both have a capacity for, in their diction, clear and well-organised speech. So at line 729 of Book Two the Eagle begins a philosophical exposition which undoubtedly owes much to Dante's *Paradiso*, Canto I, in the picture it draws of an Aristotelian cosmos where all things move to their proper end, insisting 'That every kyndely thyng that is/Hath a kyndely stede ther he/May bestin yt conserved be' and moves to that place by 'his kyndely enclynyng'. Here and elsewhere, Chaucer shares with Dante sufficient linguistic discretion and lucid technicality to translate such philosophy into vernacular English (witness the Nun's Priest's Tale). At the same time, both – with slightly different emphases – are able to see the limits of their own authority. So Chaucer can retire from the Dantean heights of scientific aspiration:

> 'Have y not preved this simply,
> Withoute any subtilite
> Of speche, or gret prolixite
> Of termes of philosophie,
> Of figures of poetrie,
> Or colours of rhetorike?
> Pardee, hit oughte the to lyke!
> For hard langage and hard matere
> Ys encombrous for to here
> Attones; wost thou not wel this?'
> And y answered and seyde, 'Yis.'
> (*HF*, II. 854–65)

The limit here is not, as it would be in Dante, what the human mind can bear in its encounter with divinity, but rather what, realistically, the human ear can tolerate. And that sense is one which penetrates the intervening discourse. Here Chaucer pictures a world of human words and voices sustained on the reverberation of sound, as if the solidity of the Dantean universe could dissolve into phonic multiplication. Dante's voice seeks to impel its reader in justice and love towards the otherness of God, constantly assuming authority – as any intelligent being is bound to do – but also, as a creature, constantly resigning authority in the face of its creator. In Dante's poem the defining and ever-desirable Other which impels the text is thought to be divine; in Chaucer, it is human voice and ear as the source and receptor of new tidings. Finally, it is appropriate that these tidings should not be known and that the poem should fall silent at the appearance of the Virgilian 'man of gret auctorite'. For sound will not cease to resonate, nor can it be stilled by authority. Yet this is not to end in chaos or in Babel. The poem concludes with the sense that truth will out beyond the limit of any written structure:

> That shal not now be told for me –
> For hit no nede is redely;
> Folk kan synge hit bet than I;
> For al mot out, other late or rathe. (rathe = early)
>
> (*HF*, III. 2136–39)

Intelligence here resides in seeing persons beyond the words they utter and trusting these folk – who are no authors – to be true.

As will be seen, the implications of Chaucer's early encounter with Dante's writing will be developed in the most ambitious work of his early maturity, *Troilus and Criseyde*. But even in *The Canterbury Tales*, Chaucer issues related to the question of authority continue to be associated with Dante.

First – and all too briefly – there is an allusion to Dante's writing which Chaucer audaciously ascribes to the Wife of Bath:

> But, for ye speken of swich gentillesse
> As is descended out of old richesse,
> That therfore sholdne ye be gentil men,
> Swich arrogance is nat worth an hen.
>
> (*WBT*, 1119–23)

This sentence directly echoes, in phrasing and theme, the fourth book of the *Convivio*. There Dante himself, making his earliest attempts to come to terms with Aristotelian ethics, offers his own version of the principles cultivated in the city humanism of the Florentine Republic: all human beings desire knowledge (*Con.*, I. i) and true nobility resides not in rank but in the pursuit of rational appetite.

In the mouth of the Wife, such a reference must at first seem like a final salvo in her sustained attack on bookishness. And so it is. But, as one found in considering *The House of Fame*, so here one should not underestimate how disconcerting Dante's own position can be: his argument, after all, is one which not only expresses the desire of an early bourgeoisie to free itself from feudal oppression but also enunciates the claim to intellectual independence which was to sustain Dante himself in exile. Superficially, the Wife's self-assertiveness is very different from that, surrounded as she is by the trappings of middle-class affluence and an aura of rapacious sexuality. Yet especially in her tale, the concern which the Wife enunciates – that consent not mastery should rule in human affairs – must, remotely, have its roots in the freedom that Dante claims.[35]

Nor is that all. For a full interpretation would quickly reveal an unlikely kinship between the Wife and Beatrice. If the Wife demonstrates the limitations of bookishness, then so in her own way does Beatrice: whether in the *Vita nuova* or in the *Commedia*, where Beatrice constantly eludes the preconceptions and expectations which literary tradition project upon her. So, as has been said, Beatrice's role in the *Commedia* is to reveal what the rational Virgil cannot reveal; and that revelation invariably involves a realisation of how intensely and joyously valuable human beings are. Dante himself ceases to be merely a scholar whenever he realises, through Beatrice, that human beings are, finally, to be loved not studied; and Beatrice in her often vertiginous effect upon Dante disallows any claim to authority which is not founded upon this understanding, as does the Wife of Bath.[36] Authority in both Dante and Chaucer resides upon an attention to the individual which admits the rational nature of that individual but also insists that one should contemplate, beyond rationality, the disconcerting singularity of persons.

Turning from a profound comedy of intellectual allusions to an equally profound tragedy, one finds that Chaucer, in the celebrated treatment of *Inferno* XXXIII which he offers in the Monk's Tale, continues to concern himself with episodes in which Dante has concentrated upon the limitations of linguistic authority. Tragic events by their nature resist representation.[37] And the events common to both stories are truly tragic: a

35. Cf. Chaucer 'moral balade' *Gentilesse* where 'vice' is seen as 'the heir to old richesse'. Also note that, considering the Wife of Bath's antipathy to Friars, a full account of the field of allusion would place the Loathly Lady motif in her tale against the Loathly Lady of Poverty whom Dante depicts in *Par.*, XI as an object of love for any true Franciscan.

36. The interpretation here is consistent with Carolyn Dinshaw's in *Chaucer's Sexual Politics* (Madison, Wis., 1989). Dinshaw draws a connection between the Wife's concern with the 'texture' of fabrics and the disruptive play of signifiers in her 'text'. One notes that Beatrice is herself closely associated with 'textures': the language in which Dante celebrates her is a vernacular, and he describes the effect of the vernacular, in terms drawn from the wool industry, as possessing qualities of, for instance, 'shagginess' and 'sleekness' (*De Vulgari Eloquentia*, II. vii). Like Beatrice herself, the signifiers of the Dantean vernacular are always likely to deliver more than a conceptual analysis can offer.

37. See recently on this ancient truth Elaine Scarry, *Resisting Representation* (Oxford, 1992).

father and his children are imprisoned and, after many months of captivity, are left by their captors to starve to death; painfully familiar as the situation must seem, it at once points to the primordial fragility of human beings in their dependence upon food, upon the good will of others, and upon the bonds of love that are tested *in extremis*.

Out of this situation, as Piero Boitani has shown in an incomparable essay,[38] Chaucer and Dante derive two radically different modes of tragic vision; and detailed analysis leads one to admit the validity of both. Here the concern is primarily with the attitude which Chaucer adopts to Dante's authority; and it is Chaucer himself who alerts us to this question when, at the conclusion of his tale, the Monk recommends that, for a full account of the story, one should turn to Dante 'who can it all endyte'.

We are, then, immediately faced with an apparent acknowledgement of Dante's superior authority. But what in fact has Chaucer left out? The story itself, though radically different in tone, is itself complete. It therefore seems likely that Chaucer is here referring to the frame of judgement which Dante constructs to reveal that the victim Ugolino is himself a traitor condemned to the lowest circles of Hell. The moral scheme which Dante has so authoritatively erected in the *Inferno* concludes with a vision of innumerable traitors, punished by confinement in the ice-bound lake at the bottom of Hell. For Dante, treachery is the worst of sins, partly at least because it subverts the rule of rational authority – as in the final cases of Brutus, and Cassius who raised their hand against Caesar. Against this, the Monk offers a moral vision in which human misery is seen as the consequence not of damnable vice but of the changes wrought by Fortune. The moral scheme is here conspicuously less complex than Dante's own. Indeed, one might argue that the Monk's voice, contrasted with Dante's, is itself meant to be condemned for over simplification; and in that regard it might be added that the concern with Fortune which is to become a familiar theme of later humanists is at one with an equally humanistic reverence, in the Monk's case, for literary prestige which displaces the agonisingly Christian engagement of Dante's text.[39] Be that as it may, the possibility remains that the abandonment of Dante's moral scheme is an instance of Chaucer's own authorial modesty, retreating here from the inhuman extremes of Dante's vision.

There can be no doubt that Dante offers a more complex vision than

38. 'Two Versions of Tragedy: Ugolino and Hugelyn', in *The Tragic and the Sublime in Medieval Literature* (Cambridge, 1989) pp. 20–55.
39. See also Coluccio Salutati on this episode, below, p. 88.

Chaucer chooses to pursue; and the complication extends beyond the sphere of moral judgement to that of characterisation, particularly in those sections of the *Inferno* – excluded from the Monk's Tale – in which Dante allows the traitor Ugolino to introduce his own story. In Dante's text, speech and authority are from the first painfully at issue. For where the Monk tells the whole tale and controls the scene with his authorial voice, Dante allows Ugolino to relate his own story. In Chaucer's version, Ugolino is the passive victim of violence and nothing is said about his involvement in the political violence of his own day. In Dante's version, Ugolino by his position in Hell is recognisable as the man who betrayed Pisa; and throughout, Ugolino's voice is indeed the voice of a traitor, marked with violence and manipulative skill. At the beginning of Canto XXXIII the mouth of this speaker is violently shown eating the brains from the head of Archbishop Ruggiero who had imprisoned him in the Tower of Hunger. The reason which Ugolino gives for telling the story at all is that he wishes, by the words he speaks, to defame his fellow traitor no less than to destroy him with physical violence. Ugolino's intentions themselves represent a malign act of judgement, and in that light, the Dantean scene reveals another tragic dimension: not only is the fundamental frailty of human beings demonstrated here but also the perversion of their highest faculties of speech and judgement. Ugolino's blood-stained and malevolent mouth incriminates the very pretension to truthful or authoritative utterance on which the *Inferno* itself has been constructed.

Such considerations profoundly modify the sympathy which at first it might seem natural to feel over the story of Ugolino's death. It is indeed notable that the same man who speaks so eloquently in his attempts to discredit his enemy was also – on his own admission – unable to express a single word of love or fellow-feeling and concern for his children in the Tower of Hunger. His silence in the face of their demands is repeatedly emphasised; treachery here emerges as a state of mind which denies any access to natural feeling.

But on precisely these points the tonalities of Chaucer's story are profoundly different. Here, Ugolino not only speaks but actually encourages physical proximity. In Dante's story, the sons throw themselves on the ground violently at right angles to their distant and still unspeaking father. In Chaucer's version, the sons slowly settle into Ugolino's bosom and kiss him as they die. Throughout, Chaucer's story is suffused with similar effects of pathos. And in aiming at such effects, Chaucer (or the Monk) also avoids the ambiguities which run through Dante's account and come to a climax in the final line of Ugolino's story. At this point, Dante's (already cannibalistic) Ugolino is shown groping over the dead bodies of his children and must finally be thought, as hunger overcomes pity, to have set his teeth into their dead flesh. Needless to say, this suggestion has no place at all in Chaucer's treatment.

A simple distinction between the tragic effects of these stories might ascribe the pity to Chaucer and the terror to Dante. The distinction, broadly, holds. But it can also easily obscure an important similarity between the two writers. For, whether in pity or in terror, the ultimate effect of both works is to concentrate attention on particularities of suffering and perversion; neither writer seems to suppose that these particularities can be reduced to simple explanation, to mere text or any kind of categorical judgement. Indeed in Dante's poem judgement finally resolves into the immediacy of pity. For his authorial response to Ugolino's tale is not to reassert the competence of his own moral vision but to summon an emotion which, while displaying overtones of anger, demands pity for the guiltless children of Ugolino. These children are picked out as the final object of attention; and if one doubted that Dante – contrary to his reputation for violent authoritarianism – placed a very high value on pity, it is enough, finally, to look in detail at the punishment he allots to the traitors in Hell. They are frozen in the permafrost of the last circle. But for that reason the tears they weep are constantly turned to ice in their eyesockets, forming there a 'crystal visor'. These may be tears of self-pity. But if the inhibition of tears is seen, by Dante, as a punishment, then it follows that the freedom to weep must in his view – in the poet's view – be a natural and profoundly desirable human capacity. Here Dante and Chaucer join as, beyond the confinement of words or the authority of judgement, they see pity as a fundamental mode of relationship between one human being and another.

CHAUCER AND PETRARCH

The questions, then, which Chaucer discovers in Dante's work begin with questions of intellectual authority, broadening to include questions which concern the perception of persons through judgement and through the emotions. On this latter point, it would have been entirely predictable that Chaucer should have looked to Petrarch for encouragement. Yet he does not. And now, as one begins to consider the particular use which he makes of Petrarch's writings, in the *Canticus*

Troili in Book One of *Troilus and Criseyde* and in the Clerk's Tale, it becomes apparent that he is critical enough both to identify and then largely to resist the characteristics in Petrarch's style – as well as in his thinking – which other writers would subsequently transform into a foundation for humanist study.

Two themes emerge from Petrarch's work, both of which offer an alternative to the emphases which Dante pursued: first, a profound concern with the will, particularly where the will is in contest with the emotions or passions; secondly, a concern with eloquence and with the fame that a poet – in the contemporary world as in the classical world – might win by his eloquence. Chaucer recognises this aspect of Petrarch's programme when in the Prologue to the Clerk's Tale his Clerk – or Chaucer himself – sets out to tell a tale drawn from 'Fraunceys Petrark, the lauriat poete . . . whose rethorike sweete/Enlumyned al Ytaille of poetrie' (ll. 31–33). Yet the lines of resistance which will be found in the tale itself have been anticipated already in the use he makes of Petrarch in *Troilus and Criseyde*.

The *Canticus Troili* is a translation of Petrarch's sonnet 'S'amor non è . . .', the first instance of many subsequent imitations of this sonnet.[40] Petrarch's sonnet exemplifies this poet's capacity both for moral debate and for psychological torment. Yet Chaucer, while rendering Petrarch's meaning very exactly, departs from the form of the original – translating the sonnet into a three-quatrain balade on the French model –[41] and also transforms its voice and implication.

Petrarch's poem is built around the 'contraries' of thought and emotion experienced by the lover. Such contraries were often to become formulaic in the work of Petrarch's imitators.[42] But in Petrarch's own sonnet they represent a subtle tracing of mutually destructive tendencies. The tensions of the poem are muted by Petrarch's characteristic pursuit of a certain refinement or – as it has been called – 'evasiveness' of diction. This 'evasiveness' restricts the use of concrete or unexpected turns of phrase. Yet for Petrarch evasion also proves to be a way of entering a purely mental area – unconfined and unshaped by empirical reality – which may, by turns, be terrifyingly vacant or a source of great liberation. Dante, it seems, can at need use any word in the language to define his purpose and to engage with or invoke historical realities – and clearly in this regard he has much to teach Chaucer. In Petrarch, the

40. See below, p. 116.
41. See below, p. 54.
42. See below, p. 119.

very intensity of his desire for lexical refinement runs in parallel with and sometimes counter to effects of moral intensity or inquiry.[43]

So Petrarch writes:

S'Amor non è, che dunque è quel ch' io sento?
ma s'egli è amor, per Dio, che cosa et quale?
se bona, ond' è l'effetto aspro mortale?
se ria, ond'è sì dolce ogni tormento?
S'a mia voglia ardo, ond' è 'l pianto e lamento?
s' a mal mio grado, il lamentar che vale?
O viva morte, o dilettoso male,
come puoi tanto in me s'io nol consento?
E s'io 'l consento, a gran torto mi doglio.
Fra sì contrari venti in frale barca
mi trovo in alto mar senza governo,
sì lieve di saver, d'error sì carca
ch' i' medesmo non so quel ch' io mi voglio,
e tremo a mezza state, ardendo il verno.

(If it is not love, what then is it that I feel? But if it is love, before God, what kind of thing is it? If it is good, whence comes this bitter mortal effect? If it is evil, why is each torment so sweet? If by my own will I burn, whence comes this weeping and lament? If against my will, what does lamenting avail? O living death, O delightful harm, how can you have such power over me if I do not consent to it? And if I do consent to it, it is wrong of me to complain. Amid such contrary winds I find myself at sea in a frail bark, without a tiller, so light of wisdom, so laden with error, that I myself do not know what I want; and I shiver in midsummer, burn in winter.)[44]

Here, even the definiteness of the individual 'I' seems progressively to disappear: there is no personal voice but rather a rhythm which shifts from constriction to desperate fluidity and brings into relief no picture of any actual emotional state but rather those verbs which suggest the possible modes of being and action: 'to be', 'to will', 'to be able'. Nor is there any woman represented here; the poem instead concerns a state of mind and confesses to an obsession with the experience of love which, disturbing as it already is, would be the more so if it proved to have no foundation in reality. Earlier poets would have used the sonnet form to

---

43. See G. Contini on *evasività*, as well as Dante's *'plurilinguismo'* contrasted with Petrarch's *'monolinguismo' Varianti ed altra linguistica* (Turin, 1970), pp. 169–92, also pp. 1–31.
44. Translation by Robert Durling, *Petrarch's Lyric Poems* (Cambridge, Mass., 1976). See also Peter Hainsworth, *Petrarch the Poet* (London, 1988) and his forthcoming Everyman edition (ed. and trans.).

debate such issues in an analytical way.[45] Yet in Petrarch even that minimal element of intellectual structure disappears or reveals its own
emptiness as the strong contrasts drawn, rhythmically, between 'bona'
and 'ria' dissolve into the formulaic contradictions of the second quatrain. The initial argumentation, with its scholastic terminology,
promises a rational structure. But the oxymora evade the grip of that
structure, and confirm in the end the very ambiguities of the condition
which the poem proposed to clarify: the concluding lines portray a will
which is paralysed, uncertain of any external object, unguided by the
discriminations of intellectual system and a prey to its own delicious
(and here, perverse) eloquence. So far from offering any conclusion, the
poem ends elegantly but painfully off-balance, as the participle 'ardendo'
projects the unresolved condition into a indefinite continuation.

Against this, consider Chaucer's version:

> If no loue is, O god, what fele I so?
> And if loue is, what thing and which is he?
> If loue be good, from whennes cometh my woo?
> If it be wikke, a wonder thynketh me,
> Whenne euery torment and adversite
> That cometh of hym, may to me savory thinke, (savory = pleasing)
> for ay thurst I, the more that ich it drynke.
> And if that at myn owene lust I brenne, (lust = wish)
> from whennes cometh my waillynge and my pleynte?
> If harme agree me, whereto pleyne I thenne?
> I noot, ne whi unwery that I feynte.
> O quike deth, O swete harm so queynte, (queynte = sly)
> How may of the in me swich quantite,
> But if that I consente that it be?
> And if that I consente, I wrongfully
> Compleyne, i-wis; thus possed to and fro, (possed = tossed)
> Al sterelees withinne a boot am I (stereless = rudderless)
> Amydde the see, bitwixen wyndes two,
> That in contrarie stonden evere mo.
> Allas! what is this wondre maladie?
> For hete of cold, for cold of hete, I dye.
>
> (*TC*, I. 404–20)

45. The earliest sonnets were written at the court of Frederick II in Sicily at the beginning of the thirteenth century. Far from being introspective they tended to be
epistolary works raising and responding to questions such as whether love, since it is
invisible, actually exists at all, and often written with a good deal of scientific interest
in psychological phenomena.

Taking this passage out of context, one might well think that it misses the subtleties of the original and falls victim to that weakness for the formulaic phrase which, in the future, was to afflict many of Petrarch's followers. The opening lines certainly bring the verb 'to be' into sharp relief. But Petrarch's concentration is quickly dissipated as the tight rhythms of the original – 'se bona' . . . 'se ria' – are replaced by the affective flourish of alliterations in lines 3 and 4. Debate is here transformed into emotional gesture; and Chaucer reduces the complex Petrarchan oxymora to a series of highly predictable oppositions. Finally, the open structure which Petrarch so movingly creates in the concluding line is lost as Chaucer gives to Troilus the entirely predictable, even histrionic, closure 'I dye', and thus destroys the syntactic variation between the first person indicative 'tremo' and the gerund 'ardendo'.

Yet such criticisms, of course, would miss Chaucer's point. For these lines – and their shortcomings – contribute directly to his characterisation of Troilus, and may, at a further remove, be seen as a parodic diagnosis of the intellectual and spiritual malaise which Chaucer has observed in Petrarch himself. Troilus in Chaucer's hands becomes a far more philosophical hero than the Boccaccian original. But in the *Canticus* his intellect is in the grip of a malady, a 'swete harm' arising as much from intoxicating phrases and mental languor as from moral confusion. His words thus reflect the *accidia* of which Petrarch accuses himself in the *Secretum*, a certain depression of the will or intellectual appetite, a frustration made worse by the wilful self-indulgence of that condition.

As part of a sequential narrative, the *Canticus Troili* carries implications quite different from its lyric original. For it is a part of Petrarch's malaise that his lyric poems do not fully belong to any such narrative structure but descend constantly into the intensities of the moment. Chaucer, however, as narrator is about to reveal the ironies of time and fate that bear down upon Troilus though they lie beyond the confines of his introspective horizon.[46] Standing back from the lyric moment of the *Canticus,* the authorial voice will shortly place Troilus in a scheme of continuing events and temporal repetitions: as chorus, Chaucer proceeds to comment on how Troilus is not saved even by 'blood roial' from the 'fyr of love' or from a submission to time which causes him to lose his 'hew' 'sixti tyme a day' (*TC* I. 444–48), and prays ('and wherefore God mi blesse') that he should be saved a similar fate. It is notable that a

---

46. See also below, pp. 143–4 on the structure of the *Rime Sparse* as rejecting the mixed form of prose and verse narrative exemplified in Dante's *Vita nuova*.

combination of lyric and narrative was available to Petrarch in the *Vita nuova* though he chose not to follow it. Chaucer, however, abandons the intensities of the Petrarchan lyric for the perspectives which Dante (and Boethius) had adopted in their combination of lyric and narrative modes.

Within *Troilus and Criseyde* there are many voices, as there are not in Petrarch's *Rime Sparse*. Some are lyrical, others are philosophical, colloquial or narrative. The perspective and at times the ironic objectivity which this encourages is wholly un-Petrarchan; and turning to *The Canterbury Tales* – where of course such voices are greatly multiplied – there is evidence that Chaucer understood very well how far he had departed from Petrarch's example. Here in the Clerk's Tale Chaucer takes as his primary source a story which Petrarch had translated into Latin from Boccaccio (and adapted with French inserts).[47] Yet not only does he shift the emphases which Petrarch had given to the story itself, but he also frames the tale with a prologue and an epilogue both of which throw a less than flattering light on Petrarch himself.

In the Prologue, the Clerk begins by claiming for himself, perhaps as a mark of scholarly kudos, the acquaintance 'at Padowe' with the 'lerned Clerk', Petrarch. Yet this celebratory move is at once qualified – as it will be again in the epilogue – so as to undermine any pretension of the kind which Petrarch himself might have encouraged to literary fame and immortality. In a harsh descent to realistic diction the Clerk declares that Petrarch 'is now deed and nayled in his cheste' (Clerk's Prologue, 1.29). So, too, the 'Envoy de Chaucer' – recalling that Griselda herself is now dead – encourages wives to disregard the example of her dangerously submissive patience and cultivate in defence of their interests not a high style but the crabbed eloquence of domestic nagging (Clerk's Tale ll. 1177–1211). Meanwhile, the Host's voice in the Prologue reminds us that this tale is part of the marriage debate, with its many competing voices, and proceeds to debunk the 'heigh style, as when that men to kynges write' (Clerk's Prologue, 1.18). On the whole the Clerk seems to consent to the Host's stylistic prescription, though he does smuggle into the prologue a rhetorical

---

47. See J. Burke Severs, *The Literary Relationships of Chaucer's Clerkes Tale,* Yale Studies in English, XCVI (New Haven, 1942). Also Anne Middleton, 'The Clerk and His Tale: Some Literary Contexts', in *Studies in the Age of Chaucer, II* (Oklahoma, 1980), pp. 121–50 and R. Kirkpatrick, 'The Griselda-Story in Boccaccio, Petrarch and Chaucer', in P. Boitani (ed.), *Chaucer and the Italian Trecento, op.cit.,* pp. 231–248.

periphrasis in which he records the high-sounding geographical description which Petrarch would have favoured.

The play of voices and intellectual levels which is anticipated in the Prologue continues into the tale itself where, without making any frontal attack on Petrarch, Chaucer subtly introduces and ultimately favours alternatives to his position. Thus, on the one hand, the tale is the product of excellent scholarly practice: Chaucer has collated a variety of sources and also shown a high degree of fidelity in his translation of Petrarch's Latin. On the other hand, the very structure of the tale smacks of the old-fashioned scholasticism which Petrarch sought to displace with his persuasive classical eloquence: in balanced form the Clerk counters the suggestion that clerks can never speak well of wives by telling a tale which does just that, while the epilogue concludes that good wives do not exist outside fiction.[48] Equally, as we shall see, the moral bearing of the story tends to favour a common-sense decency and moderation – expressed in relatively direct language – as against the elevated but extreme positions which Petrarch cultivates.

This is not of course to deny that Petrarch's version is a deeply serious piece of Christian morality. Petrarch has taken a story from Boccaccio's *Decameron* which, in staying close to its folk-tale origins, produces a brutal ambiguity of effect – and which is, if anything, intended to criticise the 'matta besitialitade', the mad inhumanity of the Marquis – and has deliberately attempted to elevate and clarify the aim of this text. Latin eloquence and Christian piety come together in Petrarch's narrative to resolve and close the issues which Boccaccio left open. Most notably – as Petrarch makes clear in his introductory Epistle – the story becomes instantly more comprehensible if it is read as an allegory, where the dreadful treatment which the Marquis of Saluzzo metes out to his wife Griselda can be taken as a figure for the education and ultimate rewards which God reserves for the patient soul. Petrarch certainly shows himself to be aware of the ambiguous responses which the story can evoke. But, in moving from the accessible if shifting medium of the vernacular (which is the linguistic medium associated with the ever-shifting Laura) into a stable and magisterial sphere secured by finely written Latin, his purpose is clearly to re-establish authorial control over this dangerous fiction.

48. See Helen Cooper, *The Canterbury Tales* (Oxford, 1991), p. 188.

Petrarch, however, while firmly holding to his allegorical scheme also expands the tale and finds room for many details which Boccaccio does not develop, for instance the wifely competence of Griselda. Chaucer avails himself of the narrative possibilities of such features and also attends to suggestions on points of detail taken from French versions of the Petrarch story. Yet Chaucer's treatment of detail leads to an understanding very different from Petrarch's own. For one thing the behaviour of the Marquis, so far from being seen as an expression of providential design, is thoroughly condemned by Chaucer (or by the Clerk).[49] A judgemental voice is heard in Chaucer's story and the Marquis is the target of judgement, so that, instead of Petrarch's celebration of a quasi-divine action, Chaucer envisages a direct opposition between the tyrannical ruler and the scholarly narrator: the Clerk is quite capable of seeing the behaviour of the Marquis as 'wicke' (Clerk's Tale, l. 785). The judgements, however, which the Clerk passes here are not supported by systematic argument but are comparable, in a quieter way, to the judgements which, in Dante's Ugolino-story, concentrate the emotional attentions of the on-looker. Here once more judgement becomes the agent of pity, demanding attention to the particularities of Griselda's case; and Chaucer carefully shapes the minutiae of Petrarch's story, especially in his representation of Griselda, so as to release this perception.

In Chaucer's story, Griselda is a figure whose character depends upon a saintly strength of will: to a greater degree than in Petrarch's version, Chaucer's Griselda actually accedes to the Marquis's intentions. In the *Decameron* such behaviour might well have seemed perverse. Boccaccio's Griselda remains inhumanly silent throughout her ordeal; she is as extreme in her behaviour as her husband is in his, and may indeed seem to collaborate with him in his violent plan. Yet Chaucer, while acknowledging the heroism of Griselda, finally speaks a language of perceptions and emotions rather than of moral diagnoses. The Clerk's Tale invites the reader to appreciate the ordinary humanity of Griselda; she is a competent women whose skill in political management is described too precisely to be reduced to allegory. In no way is she the lonely cypher that Chaucer would have found in Petrarch. On the contrary, the lesson which Griselda's fate enunciates is that the power of the will should never be employed capriciously but must always be used in the furtherance of consent between one person and another.

49. See David Wallace, *Chaucerian Polity: Absolutist Lineages and Associational Forms in England and Italy* (Stanford, forthcoming).

This is a practical lesson, in harmony with the marriage-debate to which the Clerk's Tale belongs. But even this is finally less significant than the emotional colour which Chaucer's story generates. Chaucer's Griselda expresses emotions which are to be found in neither Petrarch nor Boccaccio. More importantly, she is perceived as a focus for the feelings of others, who include both the teller of the tale and, apparently, the ideal reader. This is no lonely figure poised against her own isolation as in Petrarch, but one who – however much overcome by the power of the Marquis – is capable of looking outward to other human beings as the proper object of moral attention.

It is consistent with this emphasis that Chaucer's narrative strategy should differ from Petrarch's in encouraging a close and emotionally committed response from its reader. Relying upon a certain theatricality of attention, Chaucer's narrative demands that the reader look with close concentration at the actions of the two central figures. Such looking requires that judgements should not so much be voiced in any systematic way but rather be felt in pity on the nerves.[50] Where Petrarch is concerned to read the situation as a spiritual text, Chaucer depicts a situation which is in its literal sense unspeakably cruel and demands a sympathy akin to that which theatrical tragedy generates.

This is particularly noticeable in the first meeting of Walter and Griselda. Here Petrarch is insistent that the Marquis himself possess a certain *acer intuitus* – sharpness of insight – which enables him to see the virtues of the peasant girl and not be distracted by youthful lust. In Chaucer's version Walter eventually learns to exercise such insight. But initially his response is quite different: his first approach is characterised by an aggressive and acquisitive glance. As he goes out hunting, he sees Griselda from the saddle as if she herself were his prey: 'Upon Grisilde, this povre creature,/Ful ofte sithe this markys sette his ye/As he on huntyng rood paraventure' (Clerk's Tale, ll. 232–4); likewise, his decision to take her as his bride is depicted as a brutal casting-up, which, once her merits have been catalogued, leads him to the conclusion 'that he wolde/Wedde her oonly'. Sympathy for the Marquis is very limited in Chaucer's tale – as, of course, it is not in Petrarch's – for at every stage the Marquis exemplifies an attitude of mind, and of eye, directly opposed to that which the teller of the tale is seeking to develop in his audience.

As for Griselda herself, she is evidently more self-possessed in the

50. See Elizabeth Salter, 'Chaucer: The Knight's Tale and the Clerk's Tale', *Studies in English Literature,* V (1962).

Clerk's Tale than Petrarch makes her. Yet there is, strikingly, no attempt to endow her with inwardness or to trace the fluctuation of her feelings. To that degree she is absent; and it is this 'absence' of Griselda in Chaucer's treatment which determines a reading style, demanding of the reader precisely that sharpness of insight which the Marquis possesses in Petrarch's version. Within the story itself, such a response is depicted in the choric reactions of the Marquis's subjects who, for instance, at line 897 follow Griselda 'wepyng in hir weye' when she returns in disgrace to her father's house: their tears themselves mark the track she herself, unweepingly, is treading. So the 'absence' of Griselda is no Petrarchan evanescence or lyrical desire for spirituality; on the contrary, she occupies a public space and invites, by her very humility, the precise knowledge that 'pitee' can produce.

This reading is confirmed if one turns finally to the figure of the Clerk. Throughout the tale the Clerk stands in close correspondence to Griselda. It has been noted that there was, in Chaucer's time, a commonplace parallel to be drawn between clerkly and virginal modesty;[51] and just as the Marquis's hunting glance falls upon Griselda, the rapacious eye of the Host has fallen upon the absence of the Clerk (as elsewhere it does upon Chaucer), drawing him, as Griselda was drawn, into unexpected prominence. But within the tale the Clerk quickly re-establishes – against hosts, hunters and even allegorists – an alliance with the figure of Griselda, asserting her merit not by any scholarly power of interpretation or moralisation but rather by the 'sharp insight' which leads him to respond continually to her unspoken demands. Moral vision here resides not in the enunciation of principle but in a specificity of response which texts and language can never fully express.

CHAUCER AND BOCCACCIO

The *Decameron* was the ultimate source for Petrarch's Griselda fable. Chaucer seems not to have known that. Nor can it be said with any certainty that Chaucer had read the *Decameron*, though it seems quite likely that, while in Italy, he would have encountered extracts of the work, either in circulation or in oral performance. In *The Canterbury Tales* there are at least six stories which have analogues in Boccaccio's collection; and there is no precedent apart from the *Decameron* for the

---

51. See Helen Cooper, *The Canterbury Tales,* op.cit., p. 185.

use of an authenticating device such as the plague or a pilgrimage to frame a collection of short stories.[52]

On the whole, however, the differences between the *Decameron* and *The Canterbury Tales* are more instructive than the similarities. A full investigation of these differences would contrast the implications, in regard to symbol and suggestion, between Boccaccio's settings, which characteristically include the idyllic garden of the *brigata* and the townscape of many of the stories they tell, with Chaucer's representation of a journey which moves, ambiguously perhaps, between tavern and shrine under the stimulus of a spring-time urge to travel. Such an investigation would compare, in Chaucer's case, an understanding of human beings which demands that prologues and epilogues should be written to characterise the voices of particular tellers with another, in Boccaccio's case, where narrative voices merge in an anonymous chorus and where (usually to the disappointment of the English reader) there is no equivalent of the General Prologue to particularise the dress, manner and rhetorical resources of the story-tellers. Finally, one would have to consider the distance that arises between an author such as Chaucer who creates an authorial voice which acts and interacts with the voices of the tellers and another such as Boccaccio who preserves a high degree of anonymity, as if his stories were the product of the civic group itself rather than of an individual.[53]

If, however, one turns directly to those works where Chaucer did, without doubt, draw upon Boccaccio, it is possible to follow in some detail the paths which, while initially parallel, lead the two authors to their eventual divergence. These works – the *Filostrato*, the *Filocolo* and the *Teseida* – were all the product of Boccaccio's early years in Naples. They were thus written in a courtly and monarchical ambience similar to that which Chaucer would have known in Richard II's England; Naples was in Boccaccio's time ruled by Angevin Kings, and for that reason the influence of French culture would have been even stronger there than it was in England. But just as Boccaccio in the writings of his

52. See Helen Cooper on framing devices in *The Structure of the Canterbury Tales* (London, 1983). For the subsequent history of framing devices in the sixteenth-century novella, see below, pp. 227–8.

53. Translations of Chaucer's sources in Boccaccio's minor works are available in a (selective) edition by N. Havely, *Chaucer's Boccaccio* (London, 1980); see also H.M. Cummings, *The Indebtedness of Chaucer's Works to the Italian Works of Boccaccio* (Cincinnati, 1916; repr. New York, 1965). An expanded version of the account above is to be found in R. Kirkpatrick, 'The Wake of the Commedia', in P. Botaini (ed.), *Chaucer and the Italian Trecento*, op.cit., pp. 201–230.

Neapolitan period sets himself to emulate and to advance beyond the French model, so Chaucer, taking encouragement from Boccaccio's example, seems also to have realised that he was free to outdo or modify the Italian example no less than the French.[54] He comes to Boccaccio's writing at the height of his own maturity, especially in *The Canterbury Tales*. And certainly he displays a remarkable willingness to depart from the Italian original in point of detail and implication. In Boccaccio, Chaucer would have found an acute understanding of the ways in which social groups construct their own identities; and in *The Canterbury Tales* he too is concerned with the means by which the pilgrims come to form a community, even if in choosing the Dantean image of a journey to express this process of social formation he moves away from the relatively static and confined model suggested by Boccaccio. In Boccaccio, too, he would have discovered a profound interest in how literary works can reflect and develop the codes by which a social order operates. But his attitude to social groups and to the individuals which belong to them remains his own, as does his understanding of the codes by which such groups live and within which he himself as poet writes.

Boccaccio's prose *Filocolo* provided material for the Franklin's Tale (though Boccaccio retells the tale in the *Decameron*, Day Ten), and was written when Boccaccio was little more than twenty years of age. This is an ambitious version of the French romance *Floire et Blancheflor* relating the adventures of two long-separated lovers as they seek to be reunited. It is notable that Boccaccio begins by associating himself as closely as possible with the Angevin court. He retells the history of the dynasty, and speaks of his own courtly devotion to Maria, whom for the sake of his fiction he regards as the natural daughter of King Robert. Love here, as in the prefaces to all the minor works, is seen as the precondition and stimulus to literary achievement: not only does Boccaccio attempt to show that Italian is the equal of French, he also includes sustained allusions to classical literature and mythology, particularly to Ovid. The book is clearly intended as a display of prowess; and to that extent Boccaccio does create an authorial persona, though a persona which is significantly different from Chaucer's, where timidity in love and speech is emphasised.

Yet the authorial voice of Boccaccio's proem does not enter into the narrative itself. This is particularly noticeable in the Book IV where the

54. Throughout, see David Wallace, *Chaucer and the Early Writings of Boccaccio* (Woodbridge and Dover, New Hampshire, 1985).

source of the Franklin's Tale is to be found. Here, anticipating the *Decameron*, Boccaccio consigns a sequence of tales to a group of narrators gathered in a courtly garden of love. But, different as this will prove to be from Chaucer's procedure, it is also different from Boccaccio's own in the *Decameron*.

The tales told here all concern the moral entanglements that love can lead to. Yet the *Filocolo*, unlike the *Decameron*, treats each episode as a test case, to be analysed and judged in the perspective of the courtly code. In the *Decameron*, the audience, though similar in its cultural formation, rarely arrives at moral conclusions. Instead, Boccaccio stresses the diversity or ambiguity of its responses, as if it were the function of narrative rather to animate than to resolve discussion.

In the *Filocolo*, any such ambiguity tends to be authoritatively suppressed. So, in *Filocolo*, IV,[55] a married woman, distracted by the unwanted attentions of a lover, sets the lover a seemingly impossible condition for her compliance which requires (as also in the *Decameron*, Day Ten story five, though not in the Franklin's Tale), that a summer garden be made to flower in winter. When the task is performed, through the assistance of a magician, the dilemma which the lady faces is only resolved by the magnanimity of the three male protagonists – husband, lover and magician – who, in turn, protest that the vow must be kept, that, after all it need not be kept, and that due payment need not be made. In the *Decameron* this contest in generosity provokes a debate – 'too long to tell' – which is concluded by the Lady Fiammetta who declares that disputation is appropriate rather to Schools than to present playful circumstances. In the *Filocolo*, however, the Lady who rules the proceedings insists that judgement must be made; and – in the course a discussion which is recorded in full – she will tolerate no dissent. Moreover, her judgement, while eclipsing that of her male disputants, falls decisively in favour of the husband: the wife had no independent right to make a vow at all, while the husband, in demanding that she should, was in fact prepared to sacrifice the greatest thing he possessed: the honour of a chaste wife.

As soon as Chaucer's Franklin begins to speak, much proves to have changed, not only in the detail and emphasis of the story itself but also in the way it is framed and presented to its audience. The Franklin's Tale is located within a continuing discussion of marriage and mastery.

---

55. References to '*Tutte le Opere di Giovanni Boccaccio*' a cura di Vittore Branca (Milan, 1967), Vol. I, pp. 395–405.

Yet the questions raised by this discussion continually touch upon matters, particularly of sexual politics, which are kept firmly at bay in the
formal and well-regulated proceedings of the *Filocolo*. As always, the
narratorial voices in *The Canterbury Tales* are diverse, often disruptive,
inclined less to debate than to competition. It is notable, though, that
the peculiar characteristic of the Franklin's own voice is a concern with
moral issues which matches the *Filocolo* in intensity while, at the same
time, altering the character of the code within which these issues are
examined. It might indeed be suggested that the Franklin is a *parvenu*,
seeking prestige from the chivalric conventions displayed in the
source.[56] Yet this would do less than justice to Chaucer's own recasting
of the original, and would cloud a further debate which Chaucer seems
here to have created within the Franklin's own psyche between the
conventional virtues of honour and magnanimity and the deeper claims
of 'trouthe' and freedom.

Within *The Canterbury Tales*, the Franklin's voice – marked throughout by age and experience – follows on from, and contrasts with, the
enthusiastically chivalric voice of the Squire. Likewise, in relation to its
source, the tale prefers a male – even patriarchal – voice as arbiter to
that of a courtly queen. But the voice also displaces the bookishness of
the Boccaccian original with acerbic appeals to common sense which
could easily betoken a cynicism towards all kinds of code – whether of
love, learning or literature – were it not that this scepticism appears, as
the tale proceeds, to release a steady and unsophisticated admiration for
the moral decencies of which human beings are capable. A consequence
of this shift is seen in the treatment of the woman at the centre of the
story. In the *Filocolo* she provides little more than an occasion for the
moral heroics of the male protagonists and for the debating points of the
courtly audience. In Chaucer's version, Dorigen is freed from this conventional circumscription and allowed to stand as the moral focus of the
Franklin's attention.

The characteristics of the Franklin's voice and Dorigen's position in
Chaucer's story are articulated through a series of alterations to the
Filocolo story. First, retreating from the Mediterranean ambience of
Boccaccio's romance, Chaucer identifies his story as a Breton Lay, and
locates it against a bleak seaboard terrain. Implicit in this move is the
same mistrust of sophistication which leads the Franklin to disavow any
poetic inspiration or knowledge of Cicero – where Boccaccio evidently

56. See A.C. Spearing in his edn of the Franklin's Tale (Cambridge, 1976).

relishes his own eloquence – and to claim knowledge only of such 'colours' as 'growen in the mede' (FT, 723). At the same time, the shift also allows a strong psychological interest to develop around the figure of Dorigen. The rocks of the sea-shore become to her the focus of obsessive attention: while her husband is single-mindedly pursuing his own kind of honour in battle overseas (FT, 811), Dorigen laments the possibility that he will be ship-wrecked on his travels. Thus when Dorigen, in Chaucer's version, demands that her lover should remove the rocks from the sea, the motive is not merely to devise an extravagant impossibility, but also serves – with a great increase in both irony and pathos – to express her overwhelming concern for her husband, while simultaneously exposing herself to moral danger. At lines 865 to 893 Chaucer attributes to Dorigen, in her chilly landscape, a serious reflection upon the uncertainties of the temporal world and the steadfast hand of Divine Providence, until, pestered by Aurelius, she abandons the religious gravity of such a stance, allowing a distraught psychological caprice to express itself in her brush-off line.

Just as the soberly Christian Dorigen would not expect magic to affect her case, so – in close conjunction with her – the voice of the Franklin is never more sceptical than in his dealings with the magical apparatus of the story. But, as author, Chaucer has himself made significant alterations on this front. For at the centre of the *Filocolo* story (though subsequently excised from the *Decameron*)[57] there stands a flamboyant evocation of the magic which allows the promise to be fulfilled. Referring extensively to the incantations of Medea in Ovid's *Metamorphoses*, VII, Boccaccio introduces a macabre and detailed evocation of primitive ritual (which itself is quite out of keeping with the cool analysis offered by the Queen at the conclusion of the story): Tebano, the Theban necromancer, enlisted by the lover, strips off his clothes and shoes, letting his hair spread out over his naked shoulders (*Fil.*, 399); and, having turned three times to the stars with open arms, he kneels on the ground to invoke darkness and the powers of Hecate. Then 'faster than any bird that flies a chariot appears drawn by two dragons' (*Fil.*, 401), Tebano mounts and flies off in search of the flowers he has promised to produce, traversing 'Spain, Crete, Pelion, Ocris and Ossa, Mount Nero, Pacchino, Peloro and Appennino'.

Against this Ovidian extravagance, the mechanisms of magic which Chaucer describes are scarcely magical at all, and far from being suffused

57. And also excised from Havely's otherwise useful translation op.cit.

by the literary excitement of Boccaccio's passage, are dominated by the decidedly anti-intellectual voice of the Franklin who insists that such wicked folly in our eyes is not worth a fly 'for hooly chirches feith in our bileve/Ne suffreth noon illusioun us to greve' (FT, 1133). With a weary realism, the Franklin allows that the magician by his 'japes' did manage for a week or two to make it 'seem' that the rocks had disappeared (FT, 1296). Through the Franklin, then, Chaucer engages with the dangerous display of intellectual hocus-pocus in which Boccaccio had taken so much pleasure, only to reject it. But in place of that there enters a moral realism, which again has no counterpart in the highly intellectual debate of the *Filocolo*:: in human beings themselves there is a truth which reveals itself, without recourse to any kind of magic, in the freedom to produce unexpected acts of kindness and generosity. Notably, even the husband Arviragus is here allowed to exemplify this. In the *Filocolo* the husband had been motivated overtly by a sense of honour which demanded that promises should be kept, even though, as he adds, rather chidingly, foolish vows should not be made in the first place. Dubious as this proposition itself is, it becomes the more so when one finds that the husband was secretly frightened of the power of the necromancer. But Chaucer's Arviragus is deeply concerned that the wife should maintain her own 'trouthe'(FT, 1478). Thus on returning from the pursuit of 'worship'(FT, 811) in battle, the husband finds Dorigen in a state of anxiety which is the greater in that her mind has tended to run frenetically upon literary examples of chastity (FT, 1367, *et seq.*). But the level immediately returns to that of practical and considerate domestic conversation (FT, 1467), in which the husband, weeping, arranges for the protection of Dorigen's honour and (as he does not in Boccaccio) for the safety of her person. At this point the Franklin's voice enters (FT, 1493, *et seq.*). And while the Franklin is prepared to admit that the husband's behaviour might seem reprehensible (thus changing the original topic of debate from praise to blame), he is not really interested in debate at all. Here, for once, he alerts the reader to the workings of his own narrative, to suggest that his story will deliver a conclusion beyond the expectations of judgement. The surprise of course lies in the generosity which each of the protagonists proceed to display when confronted, as the husband was, with the 'trouthe' of the situation. Even the clerkly magician (whose reputation earlier had been so vigorously attacked) is allowed to enter into this reciprocation, as he contemplates (FT, 1608) the spectacle of how 'everich of yow dide gentilly til other'. The tale ends with an inquiry: 'Which was the moste free, as thinketh yow' (FT, 1622). But this does not seem intended to raise those invidious questions of judgement which the *Filocolo* was primarily concerned to pursue. The brusque conclusions offered by the Franklin himself, as he retires from the literary competition, points to truths which cannot be contained within the codes of literary or social expectation.

In the Franklin's Tale, Chaucer depicts a possible escape from the codes and conventions which his Italian original revealed to him. In the Knight's Tale, Chaucer engages with a similar question. But here, in a narrative where the inevitabilities of fate are frequently invoked, the characters appear as victims also of the social principles, whether amorous or military, which underlie their own existence. In this regard, the Knight himself, as Christian teller of a tale set in pagan times, is shown to be under stress. The Knight in the General Prologue had stood as the lynchpin of the hierarchical social code on which, to some degree at least, the world of *The Canterbury Tales* is constructed. Yet when the tales get under way, threats immediately arise against the code he represents, as the drunken Miller assails it in the next tale; and even within the Knight's own tale, there are aspects of the voice and narratorial posture which Chaucer attributes to him that complicate (as comparison with Boccaccio's version will show) any simple reaffirmation of his authoritative position.[58] The language of story-telling proves to be a dangerous world for a knight to enter.

It is, of course, not always easy to decide what should be attributed to the voice of the teller and what to the voice of the author himself; and though I shall claim – more vigorously than some might – that the voice of the Knight has its own recognisable characteristics, one may nevertheless begin with the authorial decisions which Chaucer himself seems to have made in choosing and emending a Boccaccian text for use at the head of *The Canterbury Tales*. In settling upon a treatment (possibly already completed) of the verse *Teseida* he matched himself against a work which, in literary terms, had distinctly military ambitions. In the *Teseida* the aspirations characteristic of Boccaccio's Neapolitan period, led the author to attempt to fill a *lacuna* in the Italian literary tradition. For, as Dante had noted, there was no example of war poetry in the Italian vernacular.[59] In response, Boccaccio took a theme from Statius's *Thebaid*, (making confident reference in passing to the Oedipus legend and to Ovid and Lucan; moreover, on the pattern of Virgil's *Aeneid*, he divided his work into twelve (extremely lengthy) books. Then, lest the epic

---

58. Lee Paterson, *Chaucer and the Subject of History* (London, 1991).
59 See the discussion that begins in Dante, *De Vulgari Eloquentia*, II. iv.

dimensions of his story should pass unnoticed, Boccaccio proceeded to write a series of prose annotations (which Chaucer may or may not have known) emphasising his own literary purposes and the Christian bearing of the pagan tale. And these notes are just one of a number of features which serve to modify the military subject. Here, for instance, as in the *Filocolo*, the ostensible motive for composition is to display intellectual daring in the eyes, this time, of a flinty-hearted lady. Furthermore, each book of the *Teseida* is introduced by a sonnet rendering into a lyric summary the epic events and arguments that follow; and correspondingly the style of narrative not only draws on the highest registers of lyric and military writing, but also owes much, including its stanza form, to the *canterini* – popular tellers of brisk uncomplicated tales.

A century and a half after the *Teseida,* Ariosto and Tasso were to fulfil triumphantly Dante's demand for a military style;[60] and in doing so they would develop a genre, the epic romance, which – containing a mixture of elements similar to the *Teseida* – exerted a notable influence on Sidney and Spenser. But Chaucer, so far from anticipating such developments, sets out to clarify, abbreviate and in places to reorganise Boccaccio's narrative with the aim, it appears, not of enacting a theoretical conception of genre but rather of creating a structural pattern richer, internally, in balances and cross-reference than Boccaccio's, and more concentrated in its focus upon the implications of the original story.

At the same time, the emphases which Chaucer introduces here, so far from clarifying the work as Boccacio's *marginalia* and lyrics profess to do, render the Knight's Tale far more disconcerting than any tale of love, war (or even scholarship) could ever be. Specifically, Chaucer strengthens the depiction of the pagan world and then proceeds – as he had already done in *Troilus and Criseyde* – to scrutinise this world from a Christian stand-point. But even this scrutiny is not secure. The tale recognises a need for Christian solutions in the pagan world; yet the voice of the Knight, veering constantly towards Christian vocabulary, never arrives at confident expression of that creed. In place of the often lyrical and always leisurely tenor of Boccaccio's text, Chaucer substitutes an intensely tragic perception of the instability and even malignity of a world in which there are no Christian certainties.

Technically, one of the devices which Chaucer – considered as primary narrator – employs to abbreviate and intensify Boccaccio's text, is *occupatio*, whereby the author, or arguably the fictional teller, is seen to mark the excisions made in Boccaccio's text by claiming that he will not

60. See below, Chapter 4.

attempt to communicate all that might be said on this or that subject, while tending on the whole to do precisely that. One might say that there was a military forthrightness about this, appropriate to the voice of the teller, were it not that many of the major omissions from Boccaccio's text are actually omissions of military material. When the need arises, as in Part III, Chaucer's Knight can speak of battle with graphic and often tragic force. But there is no sense that the Knight is as enthusiastic about military set-pieces as Boccaccio is in his *Filocolo*. The Knight's Tale, failing to establish a firmly Christian perspective, also denies itself any primitive attachment to the military code.

The most striking example of narratorial silence in The Knight's Tale – and of its stylistic and thematic consequences – involves an almost total excision of the first two books of the *Teseida*, where Boccaccio describes Theseus's victory in war as well as in love over the Amazonian 'regne of femynye'. Boccaccio in his notes declares that he deliberately included this episode for reasons of literary curiosity: Amazons, 'being strange to the reader', make for good reading. In any case, Boccaccio, as the *Decameron* demonstrates, never baulks at situations in which power and sexuality are the issue. Chaucer, however, allows his Knight to suppress suggestions of sexual danger, as if – at least on one interpretation – he were attempting to preserve distance and authority in the face of these disruptive considerations. To that degree, there is already a degree of instability in the Knight's position. At the same time, the excision ensures a rapid concentration of attention on the central question of Palamon and Arcite. The Knight's Tale deliberately subordinates the military theme to a theme of love, in regard both to Emily and to the friendship between her two lovers. Having chosen this as his focus for the opening movement of his narrative, Chaucer proceeds to create both by narrative organisation and by the local effects of his poetry a peculiar intensity of uncomforted, even tragic, seeing.

So, for instance, in Boccaccio's prison scene, Chaucer would have found a passage which, in diction and in its presentation of psychology, amounted to a highly lyrical play upon the conventions of love suffering; and much of the art here lies in the fact that both of the imprisoned lovers could sing, as it were, the same familiar song. The scene is suffused with atmospheric aura of a lover's dawn song, as Emily is seen first through a little window ('una fenistretta'), walking in a garden which is illuminated only by the *chiaroscuro* of the early hour: the day is 'scuretto' (still rather dark). The lover responds with a sustained gaze, expressed in a participle – 'rimirando' – and immediately resorts to the language of adoration, murmuring to himself 'Quest'è di paradiso' (*Tes.*, III. 10-13). Notably, however, he is composed enough to invite his companion to share the scene with him, and – long before any quarrel breaks out – the two descant together in comparable terms on the distant and unattainable vision:

> E ritornato dentro pienamente
> disse: – O Palamon, vien a vedere
> Vener è qui discesa, veramente
> (*Tes.*, III, 10–13)

(And gazing fixedly at her, he said to himself: 'She is from Heaven!'. Then returning inside he said: 'O Palamon, do come to see. Truly Venus has descended to this place.')

Yet Chaucer has derived from this situation a scene of extraordinary tension in which the courtly conventions underlying Boccaccio's scene themselves become the source of a quarrel: when Arcite hears Palamon claim that he has seen an angelic vision, he argues his superior claim in that he loves Emily as a woman not as an apparition. To emphasise this immediately lethal dissension, Chaucer has changed both the narrative and linguistic structure of the original. So, in the *Teseida* it is Arcite who in fact first sees Emily. Chaucer, by making Palamon the first, prepares for the chiasmic formula which governs the tale, whereby Arcite, coming second, may temporarily win Emily through military violence while Palamon, loving her first, is also allowed to love her last. As for language, Chaucer breaks completely with the lyricism of Boccaccio's treatment. In the Knight's Tale, Palamon begins restively scanning the horizons which he cannot reach, being impeded not merely by a 'finistretta' – through which, as Boccaccio's hero does, he might thrust forth his head into the dawn air – but by a brutal iron grill. And Chaucer's Palamon does not initially speak of Emily in lyrical terms as a goddess, but rather – jangling in every nerve of his hitherto listless body – expresses an agonised awakening to a new life with the inarticulate 'A!':

> And to himself compleyninge of his wo;
> That he was born, ful ofte he seyde, 'allas!'
> And so bifel, by aventure or cas,
> That thrugh a wyndow, thikke of many a barre
> Of iren greet and square as any sparre,
> He cast his eye upon Emelya,
> And therewithal he bleynte and cryde, 'A!'
> (KT, 205-219)

The implications of such changes to the *Teseida,* which could be paralleled throughout the Knight's Tale, are seen particularly clearly in its concluding episodes, where the story demands that supernatural or religious machinery should be introduced and, finally, that the author should declare his philosophical hand in some meditation on the text he has written.

In the *Teseida,* the pagan gods are introduced with a fine flourish to oversee the fated end of the quarrel between Arcite and Palamon. This allows Boccaccio the opportunity to add mythological reference to his, already very various, stylistic palette. And Boccaccio's gods proceed to perform with a correspondingly high degree of eloquence and, indeed, unanimity. There is here no more of a quarrel among the gods than there was initially between the two rival lovers. Mars has his favourite, as Venus has hers; but both can agree upon an equitable disposition of spoils, so that when Mars has triumphed through Arcite's victory, he submits graciously to Venus's claims on behalf her own devotee: ' "My friend," he said, "you speak the truth. Now do what you will" ' (*Tes.,* IX. 3). A similar sense of cool harmony governs the remaining phases of the tale. These phases are extremely protracted but their length allows Boccaccio to try his hand at yet more literary genres and effects. These include the ritual solemnisation of Arcite's death, with its picturing of pagan practices. But Boccaccio also finds space to open a perspective above and beyond the horizons of pagan mythology. His conclusion – with an obvious allusion to the *Somnium Scipionis* motif drawn from Cicero – shows Arcite after death rising to the heavens and looking down in contempt upon the vanity of the earthly sphere. Religious experience, from the most pagan to the Christian, constitutes Boccaccio's subject matter. The interest, however, lies not in any philosophical investigation but rather in the author's intellectual virtuosity and in the play of art which draws into exuberant harmony the codes, conventions and literary allusions which underlie his own – and the reader's – literary culture.

But Chaucer, as by now one should expect, is far more troubling. Significantly, it is Chaucer who omits the consoling *Somnium Scipionis* motif which he had himself used in the conclusion of *Troilus and Criseyde.* And this omission is indicative of an ending which allows no comfort to be taken in the metaphysical perspectives which it opens up. The pagan gods in the Knight's Tale are themselves in a state of disturbance and tension. Here, most importantly, Saturn is the ultimate court of appeal; and while Saturn seems to be applauded by the voice of the

Knight as a fountain of ancient wisdom, it is impossible to forget that he is an old and displaced authority who, by his own confession, is the ruler of murder, mayhem and violence. The premature Baroque of Boccaccio's narrative has no more a place here than the menacing 'smilere with the knyf' in Boccaccio's account of the Temples. Thus, where it is Venus in the *Teseida* who brings about Arcite's fatal fall, Saturn in Chaucer's account is the prime mover, enlisting the agency of Pluto, another dark god, to do so. And this emendation prepares for the extraordinary increase in visual intensity which Chaucer musters in dealing with Arcite's death. Here, Boccaccio begins with an invocation to the Furies and thus – by way of literary allusion – to the classical machinery of tragic fate, whereas Chaucer focusses starkly on the moment at which the sinister Pluto unhorses Arcite. So, too, where Boccaccio, instead of concentrating on Arcite's wound, diverts attention to the operatic lamentations of the courtly audience, Chaucer – with alliterative power and Dantean command of the precise image – accelerates into a focus upon the wound itself:

> Out of the ground a furie infernal sterte,
> From Pluto sent at requeste of Saturne,
> For which his hors for fere gan to turne,
> And leep aside, and foundred as he leep;
> And er that Arcite hat taken keep,
> He pigte hym on the pomel of his heed,
> That in the place he lay as he were deed,
> His brest tobroken with his sadel-bowe.
> As blak he lay as any cole or crowe,
> So was the blood yronnen in his face,
> Anon he was yborn out of the place,
> With herte soor, to Theseus paleys.
>   (KT, 2684–2695)

As to the conclusion of the tale, the Knight is left to find a moral language which can adequately contain the tragedy he has evoked. But, lacking the *Somnium Scipionis*, it is doubtful whether he succeeds. There is ritual here in the funeral celebrations; there is even – as there is not in Boccaccio – a diplomatic marriage arranged by Theseus to tie the uncomforted strands together. Indeed, in these final passages, Theseus looks increasingly like the Knight's chosen centre of authority. Yet if he is, the great speech on the 'feire cheyne of love' must itself be seen less as an authoritatively final conclusion than as dramatic feature, modified by one's understanding of context and of the position occupied by the speaker. Here Boccaccio had written a great elegiac hymn to the transience and mutability of earthly things (*Tes.*, XII. 3–7); and against this Chaucer increases the technical and philosophical character of the speech, drawing on reminiscences of Aristotle, Aquinas and Dante. Yet the speech never quite settles into that fully Christian mode which, as will shortly be found, had been a part of the conclusion in *Troilus and Crisyede*. We are left with a scene dominated by the social and political authority of Theseus and yet bereft of any confident sense that the codes employed in that scene can be traced to a metaphysically absolute point of attachment. There is, equally, little sense that such codes can be employed with the aesthetic enthusiasm which Boccaccio had displayed.

TROILUS AND CRISEYDE

In the Proem to Book Two of *Troilus and Criseyde,* lines 22 to 28 Chaucer writes:[61]

> Ye knowe ek that in forme of speeche is chaunge
> Withinne a thousand yeer, and wordes tho
> That hadden pris, now wonder nyce and straunge
> Us thinketh hem, and yet thei spake hem so,
> And spedde as wel in love as men now do;
> Ek for to wynnen love in sondry ages,
> In sondry londes, sondry ben usages.

These lines express an interest in linguistic mutability which Chaucer shares with all three of his Italian mentors. Dante began the *Convivio* by lamenting the changeability of vernacular languages, went on to seek remedies in the *De Vulgari Eloquentia* and decided finally in *Paradiso*, Canto XXVI, that it was entirely natural and proper that the vernacular should change according to the dictates of human reason. In Petrarch's case, the 'varying style' of his poetry represents in part an attempt to develop a form of expression which could reflect the fluctuations of emotion and conscience,[62] though this same attempt also alerted Petrarch to the insufficiencies of vernacular speech and led him to value

---

61. For *Troilus* see B.A. Windeatt, *Troilus and Criseyde: 'The Book of Troilus' by Geoffrey Chaucer* (London and New York, 1989*).* See also Giulia Natali, 'Boccaccio's *Filostrato*', Karl Reichel, 'Chaucer's *Troilus*: Philosophy of Language', Jill Mann, 'Shakespeare and Chaucer: What is Criseyde Worth?', all in P. Boitani (ed.), *The European Myth of Troilus* (Oxford, 1990). Also Morton W. Bloomfield, 'Distance and Predestination in *Troilus and Criseyde*', PMLA, LXXII (1957), 14–26; Jill Mann, 'Troilus' Swoon', *Chaucer Review* 14 (1980), pp. 319–35.
62. See below, p. 120 for the opening sonnet of the *Rime Sparse*.

at a higher rate the works which he wrote in the supposedly permanent language of Latin. Boccaccio's Epilogue to the *Decameron* boldly admits that words have an arbitrary rather than an intrinsic relationship to objects and then asserts that, for this reason, all words – however gross in suggestion – can be used freely and without shame as the instruments of human intelligence.

It is perhaps predictable that the modern reader should be receptive to these aspects of medieval theory: recent criticism of all kinds, recognising the arbitrariness of language, has been especially attentive to the shiftingness of texts or cultural codes and conventions. Characteristically, there is an inclination now to see literary works as the product of an intertext, generated by tradition or convention, and to doubt whether an author can ever be thought to stamp his own intentions or personality on the written page. One is encouraged to speak of texts producing texts rather than of writers producing authoritatively finished 'books'. It is no less predictable that considerations of this sort should also have arisen in the early years of the vernacular tradition. The writers under consideration in this chapter were all, perforce, experimentalists in their use of an untried idiom while the generative function of 'intertextuality' displayed itself in the practices of translation and imitation. Yet of course there were emphases and directions in the writing of the period which differ considerably from those which have arisen in modern theory. In particular, the image of the book itself came to express during the Late Middle Ages a philosophical confidence in rational order and, increasingly, stood as a definable and lasting monument to authorial achievement.[63] Equally, the possibility was developing – encouraged by the growth of libraries and scholarly practice – of inspecting the 'sondry usages' of 'sondry landes and sondry ages'. This could lead, as Chaucer's words tend to suggest, to a recognition – which the modern relativist might reject – of a common or universal humanity expressed in, say, the impulses of sex and love.

These linguistic and literary considerations reflect some of the larger philosophical and theological questions which emerged in the course of the thirteenth and fourteenth centuries. Up to a point, Dante could regard the created universe as itself a book to be read with the aid of logical analysis. But a recognition of the shifting nature of human language could also lead to what has been called a 'sceptical fideism', in

---

63. The classic statement of this position – which I would contest in its application to Dante – is to be found in E.R. Curtius, *European Literature and the Latin Middle Ages*, trans. Willard R. Trask, Bollingen Series XXVI (Princeton, 1967), p. 326, *et seq.*

which confidence in the apparatus of logic interpretation was under-
mined and replaced by an emphasis upon faith as the bond between the
human spirit and its Creator. Such scepticism could be liberating in that
rational inquiry now turned its attention to the sphere of human nature
and human tradition. But the search for an absolute faith in God could
also exacerbate the awareness of how mutable and insecure were the
things of this world. Fortune looms larger in the minds of Petrarch,
Boccaccio and Chaucer than it does in the mind of Dante. Introspection
likewise reveals the vagaries of emotional processs. And Time – as that
which simultaneously erodes the permanence of human beings and challenges the artist to create, through art itself, a secular permanence –
becomes a constant theme.

In *Troilus and Criseyde,* Chaucer gives his most comprehensive account
of issues such as these, while testing himself more extensively than in any
other work against all three of his of his Italian predecessors. Here, as in
the Knight's Tale, Chaucer starts from one of Boccaccio's earliest works,
Il Filostrato, and certainly seems to have recognised the originality of
Boccaccio's narrative technique. In place of the lengthy and involuted
story-lines of the Romance form, Boccaccio had written a work which
pursues a single, unified action, concentrated upon the developing
responses of his protagonists to their tragic love affair. Chaucer follows
the same action and, indeed, in regard to characterisation, greatly increases Boccaccio's effects of concentration: in *Il Filostrato* as in the *Decameron*,
Boccaccio is more concerned with the public surface of character, represented in the great verse-arias which the author ascribes to his
protagonists, than in introspection or minute observation. Chaucer is, in
this regard, evidently more detailed and searching in his view of character
and of dramatic voice. At the same time, in regard to thematic scope,
Chaucer also expands upon Boccaccio's original. There is a case for saying that Dante has inspired him to attempt a work as monumental and
comprehensive in its philosophical range as the *Commedia* itself.[64] Indeed,
Chaucer's pointed refusal to name Boccaccio as his source – preferring to
invent a pseudo-classical authority, 'Lollius' – may itself be seen as evidence of a certain pretension or else as an unwillingness to associate with
a less than worthy example. Be that as it may, the many craftsman-like
shifts that Chaucer introduces in his reading of the original introduce,
certainly, a far greater sweep of philosophical consideration than
Boccaccio had displayed in the characterisation both of Troilus's voice

64. See Piero Boitani, 'What Dante meant to Chaucer', in Boitani (ed.), *Chaucer and the
Italian Trecento*, op.cit.

and of the authorial stance.[65] In such developments not only does Chaucer add a dimension of intellectual heroism to the work but also shows as profound an understanding as might be found in Dante or in Petrarch of the differences between the resources of classical culture and those of a Christian author in the examination of questions pertaining to the interior life, to Time and to Providence.

It is impossible here to conduct a full study of the *Troilus and Criseyde*. Yet many of the questions which the poem at large has addressed on both a literary and philosophical front are brought into focus by the strangely extended and often contradictory sequence of conclusions which Chaucer offers in the last eighty lines. Here, 'the sense of an ending' – involving both philosophical purposes and literary ambition – is highly problematical. The notion of a 'book' itself is put to the question, along with Chaucer's own claims to ethical and literary authority; and the question reveals a set of alternative positions each of which in turn can be associated with views which Chaucer would have discovered in Boccaccio, Petrarch and Dante.

The sequence begins with stanzas at ll. 1772 – 'Biysechyng every lady bright of hewe . . . ' – and ll. 1786 – 'Go litel book . . . ' – which in two ways mirror Boccacio's literary position. First, in identifying the book itself as a book of love, and in asking indulgence of the lady reader, Chaucer locates his work within a sphere which Boccaccio made his own when he spoke, in the *Proem* of the *Decameron* as an entertainment for the lady reader. Here, Chaucer momentarily glances at the notion that literature may be a pastime, remote from the severe concerns of judgement or battle and answerable only to the subtle jurisdiction of 'every gentil womman'. It is a 'litel' book on this view, and even in some sense a disposable work which can be bidden to 'go'. Correspondingly, in the course of *Troilus and Criseyde* one of the many voices which Chaucer creates has been that of Pandarus. This is a voice, frequently, of gossip, anecdote and prattle, a Boccaccian voice which responds pragmatically to shifting circumstance and seeks to construct a story in which the appetite for entertainment, on a sexual as well as an imaginative level, can be unashamedly satisfied.

On the other hand, Chaucer's book simultaneously places itself within the great tradition which derives from the classics and not only pleads

---

65. A particularly good example which can be studied closely in Windeatt, op.cit., is at the end of the fifth book where it is particularly noticeable how Chaucer rearranges Boccaccio's text – which ascribes to Troilus an extended monologue – so as to allow an interplay between the authorial voice and that of the protagonist.

with ladies for indulgence but also 'kisses the steps' (*TC*, V. ii. 1791) of the great male writers who define the growing consciousness of literary ambition – Virgil, Ovid, Homer, Lucan and Statius. The claim is made with a protestation of modesty. But it also echoes Dante's desire, as expressed in *Inferno,* Canto IV, line 94, to be numbered among the school of ancient poets and subsequently leads to a fear – of a kind which the scholarly conscience of a Petrarch might have echoed – that the evident mutability of language might damage such claims if the text falls into the hands of incompetent scribes. There is an evident and threefold tension here: a new conception of literature as an entertaining fabric of lightly shifting voices contrasts with an ancient but newly revived aspiration to authority and permanence which is threatened by the innate mutability of the medium in which such monuments are to be constructed.

But these warring conceptions have an ethical as well as a literary implication. For the poet's simultaneous awareness of how transient his medium was and how great were his own ambitions might easily have led to the twofold retraction which is an ever-present spectre in Petrarch's poetry.

In this respect the palinode – 'O yonge fresshe folkes . . . ' (*TC*, V. ii. 1835) – may well be taken to reflect that penitential sense which under-lies all Petrarch's vernacular works of the vanity of human achievement in a mutable world. The voice here is more colloquial and direct than Petrarch's ever is. But in these lines there comes to a climax the concern with questions 'of will, of intention, of choice, motive and result' which have been said to characterise the philosophical programme of *Troilus and Criseyde.*[66] Throughout, Chaucer has displayed that same interest in conflicts which Petrarch investigates in the depiction of his love for Laura. Indeed, on a (reductively) Augustinian view,[67] Chaucer's portrait of Criseyde could be taken to express a characteristically Petrarchan ter-ror over emotional idolatry; and the palinode, on that view, would turn aside, as Petrarch eventually does, from the snares of vernacular litera-ture and its unremitting obsession with human love. But in Petrarch the classical world itself could be a 'Laura', an imaginative and cultural dis-traction from wholehearted Christian devotion. And Chaucer, too, registers this danger in lines 1849–1855, distancing himself from the cul-ture 'of Jove, Apollo and of Mars of swich rascaille', which earlier in

66. Delany, op.cit.
67. As, for instance in D.W. Robertson jr., 'Medieval Doctruines of Love', *A Preface to Chaucer: Studies in Medieval Perspectives* (Princeton, 1962).

the poem he had been at pains to evoke with such precision. The alternative offered here is a devotion, which Petrarch would have understood, to the 'sothefast' Christ (*TC*, V. ii. 1860); and this devotion also involves – as it does in Petrarch's many didactic epistles – the establishment of a coterie of sober male figures, including 'moral Gower' and 'philosophical Strode' who can be trusted to read the book in a spirit not of flighty exhilaration but of scholarly interest and Christian meditation.

Yet in the last stanza of all, the affiliation which Dante claims is not with Gower, Strode or even Petrarch, but with Dante; and the philosophical and Christian sympathies which are revealed here move, as by now one should expect, into an area quite different from that which Petrarch had made his own. Nor does Chaucer here emphasise those aspects of Dante's work which speak of literary and intellectual authority. On the contrary, as in *The House of Fame*, Chaucer here associates with the Dante who understands or even rejoices in the limitations of literary and philosophical categories and discovers a reconciliation between human and divine love. For when Chaucer speaks to God as

> Thow oon, and two and thre, eterne on lyve,
> That regnest ay in thre, and two and oon.

he exactly renders Dante's original:

> Quell'uno e due e tre che sempre vive,
> e regna sempre in tre e 'n due e'n uno.
>
> (*Par.*, XIV. 28–29)

Context here is significant: Dante is, at this point, close to the conclusion of an episode in which he has celebrated the achievements of those Christian philosophers, such as Aquinas and Boethius, who had pursued a rational understanding of divine wisdom as expressed in the created world. It is characteristic of Dante that he should rejoice in the capacity of the human mind to appreciate the geometry which underlies the order of creation. But now the philosophers contemplate the Trinity, which is the ultimate principle of Christian order constituted, beyond reason, in the personal will and love which God experiences for his own infinite existence. At this point the rationality of number and geometry dissolves. In Dante's lines – as Chaucer faithfully records – number loses its sequential regularity and, in a movement expressed by a lyric gracefulness of verbal rhythm, circles back upon itself as 'one, two, three' becomes 'three, two, one'. There is here no Petrarchan regret over the ambitions of the rational mind. There is, however, a realisation that beyond the legitimate aspirations of reason – in an area frequently revealed to Dante by his unambiguous love of Beatrice – an ultimate understanding is possible which can only be achieved through a devotion to God as a true person. So, too, for Chaucer, order finally resides in a recognition of truths which admit the validity of books and texts but also recognise that all human constructs must pass away to enable a higher understanding in love of a God who is a person and who creates the human person itself as a worthy object of contemplation. Dante may confidently proceed to evoke, as Petrarch could not, the doctrine of the resurrected body, as a guarantee of human identity and to depict his own encounter with God as the contemplation of the human countenance of the Deity. Chaucer will not attempt this. But throughout his work there will be a willingness to look with ironic detachment at the achievements of human reasoning – whether in the figure of Troilus or of Chaunticleer – and to avoid the desperations that afflict Petrarch through an unwavering interest in the specific details and differences of the voices that lie beneath such reasoning. There is a faith here not only in God but also in the personal presence of human beings themselves which Petrarch could not share. For him, as for many a modern deconstructionist, the self is a text always at the mercy of linguistic mutability; and in many respects the age which Petrarch's thinking was to inaugurate also abandoned the doctrines and the imaginative concentration on particulars which Dante and Chaucer shared. But at the end of this period Shakespeare emerges, reasserting in his own dramatic form the beliefs which had been submerged under the bookish passions of the Renaissance.

Chapter 2

Education and Politics, 1350–1550

INTRODUCTION

When Italian intellectuals of the late fourteenth century turned their eyes to England, they commonly expressed horror at the backwardness and insularity of the culture they saw there. To Petrarch the country was a remote and uncultivated region on the edges of civilisation, 'surrounded by the perpetual collision of the surrounding seas'.[1] In a similar vein, Benvenuto da Imola – a fourteenth-century commentator on Dante's *Commedia* – could speak of the intellectual 'spiders' who inhabited the British Isles.[2] This is a telling comment. By 'spiders' Benvenuto draws attention to the prevailingly scholastic character of learning at Oxford where the tightly woven webs of Aristotelian logic which Petrarch had sought to clear away in his *On His Own Ignorance* still provided the frame and method for study. In Italy by Benvenuto's time in the mid-fourteenth century, an alternative and – to the Italians at least – superior form of learning had begun to establish itself.[3]

Already Italian thinkers could speak of how the arts were 'awakening' from a thousand years of slumber,[4] and were seeking the roots of their culture in the classical past. In the course of the fifteenth century, this awakening – which now one describes as the Renaissance – in associa-

---

1. *Rerum familiarum libri.* I. 7, cf. I. 12. These letters are available in a translation by Aldo S. Bernardo, 3 vols (Albany New York, 1975–85).
2. Quoted from B.L. Ullman in 'The Origins of Italian Humanism', in *Studies in the Italian Renaissance* (Edizioni di Storia e letteratura, Rome, 1955), p. 29.
3. Benvenuto da Imola (*c.* 1338–87) composed not only a famous commentary on Dante's *Commedia* but also commentaries on works by Virgil, Lucan and Seneca.
4. See especially, E. Panofosky, *Renaissance and Renascences in Western Art* (London, 1970).

tion with the development of scholarly humanism affected the whole of Europe, stirring the cobwebs even in its most insular corners.[5]

It was once possible to discuss the Renaissance with unambiguous enthusiasm. Renaissance humanism, one learned, offered, in place of 'cramping medievalism', a 'larger and fuller life' to the individual;[6] and in 1868 Jacob Burckhardt concluded his study of the period with a celebration of the theism which led European culture out of the medieval 'vale of tears' and prepared for the modern world:[7]

> The soul of man can by recognising God draw Him into its narrow boundaries, but also by love of Him expand into the Infinite . . . One of the most precious fruits of the knowledge of the world and of man here comes to maturity, on whose account alone the Italian Renaissance must be called the leader of modern ages.

Recently, however, critics have approached the period with more misgivings. We have already seen that, as humanism began to make its mark, Chaucer had his own suspicions of Petrarch who may well be regarded as the founder of the movement. It is especially important, in assessing the transmission of Renaissance humanism to England, to emphasise the ways in which the Burckhardtian view has been modified.

First, the continuities between the Medieval and the Renaissance worlds seem now to have been stronger than was once supposed.[8] The terms 'Middle Ages' and 'Renaissance' were terms devised polemically by the later age to assert its own prestige. But the questions stimulated, say, by scholastic theology continued to be asked (even if the form and methods of inquiry changed);[9] and while the character of Christian spirituality altered, it was always possible for a reformer such as Savanarola to resuscitate the pieties of earlier centuries. In England, native traditions of thought are by no means abandoned by later thinkers. Certainly, in regard to the questions of language – which, as will be seen, is an area of central concern in the period – English intellectuals such as Sir Thomas

5. Peter Burke gives a useful list of scholars travelling in Italy in 'The Spread of Italian Humanism', in Anthony Goodman and Angus Mackay (eds.), *The Impact of Humanism on Western Europe* (London and New York, 1990), pp. 1–22. See also Anthony Grafton and Ann Blair (eds.), *The Transmission of Culture in Early Modern Europe* (Philadelphia, 1990).

6. Cf. W. Boyd and E. King, *The History of Western Education* (London, 1921; 1969), p. 138.

7. Jacob Burchkhardt (originally published 1868), quoted here from *The Civilization of the Renaissance in Italy*, trans. S.G.C. Middlemore (London, 1965), p. 341.

8. See Walter Ullman, *Medieval Foundations of Renaissance Humanism* (London, 1977).

9. See Charles Trinkaus, *In Our Image and Likeness: Humanity and Divinity in Italian Humanist Thought*, 2 vols (London, 1970); also his *The Poet as Philosopher: Petrarch and the Formation of the Renaissance Consciousness* (New Haven, 1979).

Elyot resist or modify the linguistic prescriptions emanating from Italy in the light of English usage; and no comparison of England and Italy in the age of Shakespeare would be accurate unless it admitted the wide difference in linguistic character between the two cultures.

Secondly, there can be no suggestion that Renaissance humanism, as it spread throughout Europe, communicated any unified philosophy or systematic account of human characteristics. It is true that, by 1486, Pico della Mirandola could compose an oration 'On the Dignity of Human Nature';[10] and this resonant title (which could be matched by others polemically opposed to any supposedly medieval obsession with human misery) introduces an attempt to demonstrate the 'reciprocal affinities' (op.cit., p. 249) which can be observed in human beings of whatever place and whatever time. But the viewpoint adopted in Pico's inquiry was distinctly that of a European intellectual aristocrat; and such a viewpoint implies not only a simplification of human nature itself, but also a simplification of the diversity of interests and modes of inquiry which were cultivated in the course of the fourteenth and fifteenth centuries. In terms of intellectual field, many lines of inquiry – in literature, archaeology, philosophy and, eventually, science – developed independently, at different speeds and in different parts of Italy. These concerns could at times be harmonised and did produce the occasional 'Renaissance Man', whose talents lay across the spectrum of intellectual possibilities. Yet the same diversity of concerns could also produce competing emphases. And in England the visionary claims of Pico seem largely to have been resisted in favour of a particular application of his thought to spheres such as literature, politics and education. Similarly, the tempo at which humanism developed and its characteristics from place to place were significantly different. In Italy itself, Florence, Venice and Rome (among many others) all developed at different stages and in different ways, as is evident simply from the history of architectural and visual styles in each of these three cities. But differences of this sort become even more acute when one considers that in Northern Europe the Renaissance largely coincided with the Protestant Reformation. In conjunction with the Reformation, forms of 'Northern Humanism' had developed, more bourgeois in their educational character than courtly Italian Humanism and somewhat more practical in their

---

10. So Giannozzo Manetti (1396–1459) could deliberately compose his treatise *De Dignitate et excellentia hominis* (*On the Excellence and Dignity of Human Beings*, Basle, 1532) in direct opposition to the treatise *On the Misery of Man* by the thirteenth-century Pope Innocent III – and in due course his work was condemned by the Index.

aim.[11] Thus in England, Erasmus was probably as influential as any single Italian thinker. Eventually, as Protestantism developed, the past age which the scholar and humanist sought to 'awaken' was as likely to be the age represented by the Scriptures as that discovered in the classics. It is nevertheless true that Protestants as late as the seventeenth century could recognise the merits of Petrarch as an intellectual model and enlist him in the cause of reform.[12]

Thirdly, as has already been suggested,[13] humanism was from the first connected closely (if tacitly) with the political development of the cities and courts where the earliest humanist thinkers flourished. In retrospect, the magnitude of achievement in the art and literature of the period can lead one to suppose that the works were produced, independent of historical context, in pursuit of some early notion of art for art's sake. The connoisseurship of Renaissance patrons may, at the time, have done much to encourage such an interpretation. Yet painting, sculpture and literature were, for the most part, courtly luxuries and in a modern perspective can often be seen as components in a programme of propaganda.[14] The subtler connections between power and imagination may still await the analytical attention of modern historicists. But the humanists themselves must in many cases have seen quite clearly the implications of their own activities, and need not by any means have been embarrassed by their own alliance with politics and power. The diffusion of humanist practice throughout Europe was to a degree brought about by a recognition among princes, diplomats and educationalists that the new studies developed in Italy might be of advantage to them in pursuing a social or political agenda. English travellers to Italy – from the earliest such as Tiptoft to Tudor courtiers such as Wyatt and Surrey, and Elizabethans like Sir Philip Sidney – were all able to adapt their experience of Italian humanism to courtly as well as to intellectual and artistic purposes.

Such qualifications as these are not meant to discredit the excitement which most travellers experienced on encountering Italy in the fourteenth and fifteenth centuries. Yet, arguably, this excitement derived less from some romantic vision of intellectual liberty than from a direct

---

11. For a detailed discussion of the relationship between humanism and reform – which advises against too sharp a distinction between the 'northern' and Italian forms of humanism – see Peter Matheson in *The Impact of Humanism on Western Europe* (London and New York, 1990), pp. 23–42.
12. For a discussion of the use which English thinkers made of Petrarch in this regard, see David Norbrook, *Poetry and Politics in the English Renaissance* (London, 1984).
13. See above, pp. 17–22.
14. See Lauro Martines, *Power and Imagination: City States in Renaissance Italy* (London, 1980); also his *The Social World of the Florentine Humanists* (London, 1963).

encounter with, so to speak, a technological revolution. There were, of course, notions of liberty available – in a political as well as a metaphysical sense – often cultivated in republican circles of Florence and Venice; and eventually thinkers such as Vasari were to speak as if inspired by some conception of historical progress.[15] Yet it was not the great idea of progress that proved to be important, but rather the development of appropriate and ever more sophisticated techniques in the arts and in intellectual procedure. To a high degree, the great achievements of subsequent ages were all built around the development of scholarly practices which insisted upon a precise knowledge of the past and upon its precise application to the present.[16] This is exemplified by the technical developments that artists such as Donatello made through an increasingly informed understanding of classical statuary. But in the literary sphere it was Petrarch who began this process by insisting, as we have seen,[17] upon an exact attention to Latin style. Such attention involved a move away from the 'barbarity' of medieval Latin; and the figures to be examined in this chapter all helped to develop a curriculum which, beginning with a thorough education in the classical languages, eventually extended into the fields of history, philosophy and artistic practice.

It should be noted that for a considerable length of time, there was little literature written except in Latin;[18] and to that extent Renaissance humanism is responsible for distracting Italian writers from the vernacular example of Dante and English writers from the example, if not of Chaucer then of other potent contemporaries such as Langland. But in the long run, as we shall see in later chapters, the processes of linguistic imitation – which in England meant as much the imitation of Italian as of classical texts – did not necessarily lead to a stifling of the vernacular impulse, but, arguably, enriched its range and rhetorical competence. In the present chapter I shall be concerned with the ways in which classical influences developed in Italy until their complex flowering in Ficino, Castiglione and Machiavelli, and to the ways in which the travellers, scholars and courtiers, such as John Free, John Colet and Sir Thomas Elyot, ensured that England received the intellectual technology of linguistic and editorial study.

15. See 'The Renaissance Idea of Progress', in P.O. Kristeller (ed.), *Renaissance Essays* (New York, 1962).
16. See P.O. Kristeller, *Renaissance Thought* (New York, Harper Torchbooks, 1961) and *Eight Philosophers of the Renaissance* (Stanford, 1964).
17. See above, p. 32.
18. On Latin influences on the literature of the period see Robin Sowerby's *The Classical Legacy in Renaissance Poetry* (London, 1994).

THE ITALIAN EXAMPLE: COLUCCIO SALUTATI AND GUARINO

Of the many figures who might stand as representatives of early Italian humanism, two in particular demonstrate its characteristics in regard both to intellectual technique and to the politics of the period.

The first is Coluccio Salutati,[19] who was Chancellor of the Florentine Republic between 1375 and 1406. Coluccio is among the earliest to speak of an awakening in literature, and his political writings are not only among the first manuscripts which Duke Humphrey bequeathed to Oxford University but they also found their way into the original library of King's College, Cambridge.[20] The second is the educationalist Guarino (1374–1460)[21] who, in 1429, set up school in Ferrara under the patronage of Niccolò d'Este. It was this school which seems especially to have attracted Oxford scholars, drawn to Italy no doubt under the stimulus of Italian books in Duke Humphrey's Library and by the increasing numbers of scholarly Italians who visited England.

As we have seen, the Florence to which Coluccio Salutati came in 1375 had, for at least a hundred years been developing an early version of humanist practice.[22] Coluccio's remote predecessor in the governmental office of Chancellor was Brunetto Latini; and since Brunetto's time, not only had civic and secular interests come to be recognised in the establishment of a university in the city but Dante, Petrarch and Boccaccio had also by now made their contribution.

Coluccio, as a notary, had himself been trained in the law schools of Bologna, and his legal reputation had secured for him, before his arrival in Florence, a series of posts in other Tuscan cities. Coluccio's mobile career involved periods of unemployment (or *otium*), during which he was able to pursue his literary and philosophical interests (at least one

---

19. On Coluccio, see Trinkaus, op.cit., also Ronald G. Witt, *Hercules at the Crossroads: The Life, Works and Thought of Coluccio Salutati* (Durham, NC, 1983).
20. See B.L. Ullman, *The Humanism of Coluccio Salutati* (*Medioevo e Umanesimo*, Vol. 3 (Padua, Editrice Antenore, 1963), p. 280. For Duke Humphrey, the brother of Henry V, see p. 22. See K.B. McFarlane on the book-collecting habits and the Italian affiliations of the Lancastrians, *England in the Fifteenth Century: Collected Essays* (London, 1981).
21. Generally on education see Paul S. Grendler, *Schooling in Renaissance Italy: Literacy and Learning 1300–1600* (Baltimore, 1989). See also Anthony Grafton and Lisa Jardine, *From Humanism to the Humanities: Education and the Liberal Arts in Fifteenth- and Sixteenth-century Europe*, (London, 1986).
22. See above, *Intro.* p. 36.

modern critic can regard him as a finer philosopher than Petrarch),[23] and was likewise in a position to cultivate a wide circle of literary acquaintances, so that, on his arrival in Florence, he was already the correspondent and friend of Petrarch and of Boccaccio. From that point on, Coluccio used his public influence to foster the growth of literary scholarship, showing concern not only for connoisseurship but also for the practical development of scholarly method. Where Boccaccio had brought a Calabrian to Florence as a teacher of Greek, Coluccio obtained a salaried position for Chrysoloras,[24] who was subsequently to play a prominent part in the promotion of Greek studies. In addition, Coluccio was a great searcher-out of books, exploiting fully the international network of Florentine economic and diplomatic connections; and he showed an advanced sense of the library, as a place where scholars could compare multiple copies of a work and establish reliable texts. He was himself an editor and orthographer, concerned with the detail of Latin usage: the relative merits of singular and plural forms of the second person were, apparently, as important to him as 'she', 'he' or 's/he' have become in recent years.

Coluccio's own writings mainly concern politics – both practical and theoretical – or matters of education, and they are usually cast in letter form. It is notable that these letters bear the marks of Brunetto's prose style, and to that degree they remain within the medieval sphere. Yet it is also characteristic of Coluccio as a humanist that his thought should be expressed, as was Petrarch's, in a form which sought to move the reader by eloquence or intimacy of appeal rather than by formal argument. There is ample evidence of the impression that these letters made. In England it is recorded that a courtier of Richard II admired the force of Coluccio's phrasing; and there is in his words a pale echo of words uttered by the Milanese tyrant Visconti who declared that a letter from Coluccio was worth a thousand mounted warriors. Even as late as 1550, Coluccio's prose could be praised for 'spreading sound opinions drawn from every source and displaying the brilliancy of ancient eloquence'.

Such comments are classic indications of the prestige and political impact that, subsequently, many humanists were to command. Yet Coluccio not only writes in response to political exigency but also displays a well-developed sense of scholarly detachment as, for example, in the critical assessment of source material; and even if political considera-

23. See Trinkaus, op.cit., p. 212.
24. See G. Cammelli, *I dotti Bizantini e le origini dell'umanesimo; Manuele Crisolora* (Verona, 1941).

tions can be discerned obliquely beneath his theoretical writings, these writings also bear witness to the vigorous pleasure which their author took in academic debate.

This pleasure can be observed in an otherwise highly problematical work, Coluccio's *De Tyranno*.[25] This treatise grew out of a long tradition of medieval works that defined – and criticised – tyranny as the arbitrary exercise of power,[26] and that tradition was, of course, essentially in harmony with Florentine ideology, which increasingly in the fourteenth century contrasted its own political character with that of Milan, ruled by the tyrannous Visconti. At the same time, where in the late Middle Ages, thinkers had tended to applaud the justice of the Roman Empire as a check upon disorder and tyranny, the dominant note in the political thought of the early Renaissance was a devotion to Ciceronian ideas of the Republic.[27] Coluccio himself argued elsewhere that Florence had been founded not under the Empire but under the Republic.

For all that, in *De Tyranno* the republican Chancellor avoids any predictable attack on tyranny. Rather, he takes up a topic of debate from the classical past and – walking a very fine line – sets out to argue that the murder of the autocratic and conceivably tyrannical Julius Caesar was an unjustifiable act. Thus, the Roman people could be said *de facto* to have accepted Caesar's rule. Indeed, Caesar's assassins, once in power, retained, as though legitimate and necessary, institutions which he himself had introduced. In any case, Coluccio argues, there is 'no greater liberty than obedience to a just Prince'.

Considering that over a period of some four years from 1378 Florence had been threatened by the Ciompi rebellion,[28] there may be pragmatic reasons for Coluccio's insistence on the value of strong central rule. Yet political pragmatism is allied here (not for the last time) with academic debate. The work is a letter in response to a scholarly inquiry; and Coluccio meets his correspondent not with scholastic arguments but rather, given a certain academic asperity, with a cool assessment of evidence and probability and a persuasive eloquence of style. The debate

25. A translation is available (along with other treatises on tyranny) in Ephraim Emerton, *Humanism and Tyranny: Studies in the Italian Trecento*, (Cambridge Mass., 1925), pp. 25–116. For the place of this work in the development of civic humanism, see A. Rabil (ed.), *Renaissance Humanism: Foundations, Forms and Legacy*, Vol. I (Philadelphia, 1988).
26. Here and throughout see Hans Baron, *The Crisis of the Early Italian Renaissance*, op.cit., *passim*.
27. See Richard Tuck, 'Humanism and Political Thought', in Goodman and Mackay, op.cit., pp. 43–65.
28. See above, p. 17.

soon broadens in fact to include a particularly eloquent disputant from the past, Cicero himself. For while Coluccio maintains that he has the utmost respect for Cicero as orator and philosopher, he does not hesitate to register profound disagreement with Cicero's Republican sentiments. The desire to 'speak with the past' – and indeed to argue with it – has already been born.

The most striking aspect of *De Tyranno*, however, is its conversation with the recent rather than the distant past. The question which provokes Coluccio's exposition concerns the legitimacy of Dante's decision in *Inferno,* Canto XXXIV, to put Brutus and Cassius as traitors in the jaws of Satan. Paradoxically, Coluccio seems prepared to abandon the high principles of Florentine republicanism in order to defend the prestige of a fellow-Florentine cultural hero – who was himself by no means a republican. In doing so Coluccio reveals an ability to reflect both Medieval and Renaissance tendencies of political thought.

On the one hand, he unequivocally accepts Dante's position that Providence is expressed in the punishment of Brutus and Cassius; and such an opinion, while understandable in a exile seeking assurances of political order, sounds anachronistic in the mouth of an early humanist. On the other hand, nothing could be more humanist than the tone and form in which this argument is cast. Dante himself, facing a political position of which he disapproved, would either have turned to the logical constructions of the *De Monarchia* or else to the violent and polemical judgements of the *Inferno*, where even Brunetto Latini is condemned to Hell. Coluccio, instead, maintains the pleasures of civilised debate as well as his objectivity, and will have none of this. Even when writing of the conspirators, he is prepared to say in measured terms, which seek to highlight issues of nobility and glory:

> I am not blaming them for their proud spirit in refusing to tolerate a superior – or even an equal. I will not blame them for their ambition in hoping for honours and desiring to be counted among the leaders of the Roman Senate and people. This was the glory they worked for, but these are things not to be gained by parricide, by criminal practices, by pride and ambition. True glory is the offspring of true virtue and is only found in a reputation for true virtue.

The issues raised by Coluccio, in regard to the relations of Empire and Republic, will run through the Renaissance until they arrive, however remotely, at Shakespeare's *Julius Caesar*. There may be a hidden agenda here. After all, in terms of practical politics, the Medici were shortly to rule republican Florence by a policy of double-think which Coluccio almost anticipates in his defence of Caesar's *de facto* legitimacy. Yet if that is the agenda, it is only very remotely addressed. More directly, one sees here – from the disinterested pleasure which Coluccio takes in literary discussion – an attitude which is immediately consistent with his educational writings. Coluccio is among the first to demand that literature should be admitted at the core of any educational curriculum: Christians, he insists, should not fear literary works – even if written by pagans – and the enjoyment which literature offers can be regarded, in Coluccio's view, as a means of securing the attention, interest, and goodwill of the student.

It is a comparable belief in the value of literary pleasure which, increasingly, stands at the centre of educational practice in the humanist period. Teachers such as Pietro Paolo Vergerio,[29] with whom Coluccio corresponded, expected the child to be surrounded by influences which would promote a love of virtue. It was, for instance, important in Vergerio's opinion that a pupil should be educated in a noble city which provided daily illustrations of the glorious achievement in art and civic enterprise: but the literature and history of Rome would provide an intellectual equivalent to such direct experiences.

The novelty in this approach – and presumably its initial appeal – lay in a concern to elicit from students their natural propensities for virtue in command of themselves rather than providing, as scholastic training would, the intellectual instruments for an inquiry into God and the world which God had created. To that end, games, dancing and gymnastics could all have their place in the humanist syllabus. But a further end was also in view, which was the inculcation of habits of virtue which would eventually contribute to the good government of the realm. Vergerio in developing this view draws strongly on Quintilian,[30] translating and commenting on his treatise, *The Education of an Orator*. But the same purpose is powerfully reflected in a letter which Guarino wrote to a pupil who had made a name for himself as military governor of Bologna:

29. Born Capodistria 1370, died in Hungary 1444, in the service of King Sigismund.
30. The works of Marcus Fabius Quintilianus (AD 36–95) had been known in fragmentary form – as texts concerning education, ethics and rhetoric – throughout the Middle Ages. But the whole text of his *Institutio oratoria* was not discovered until 1416. Quintilian had written out of respect for Cicero and with a strong desire to remedy what he saw as the degeneracy of Latin rhetoric and to connect education with moral virtue.

I understand that when civil disorder recently aroused the people of Bologna to armed conflict you showed the bravery and eloquence of a soldier as well as you had previously meted out the just sentence of a judge . . . You owe therefore no small thanks to the Muses with whom you have been on intimate terms since your boyhood and by whom you were brought up. They taught you how to carry out your tasks in society. Hence you are living proof that the Muses rule not only musical instruments but also public affairs.

(*Epistolario*, Vol. I, p. 263)

The introduction to the Muses which Guarino offered could take as long as six years.[31] Elementary courses would stress proper pronunciation of Latin and public reading. Only then would a study of texts be introduced. This would concern both the analysis of syntax, and the provision of as much historical, geographical and mythological material as was necessary for general understanding. Much emphasis here would be placed upon training of the memory. In the third stage, pupils were taught to write Latin after the pure styles of Virgil and Cicero. In the final stages of the course, when the possibility of rudimentary error had been eliminated, the writings of the student would be expected to be rich in allusion to a wide range of Latin authors and to demonstrate a grasp of the information which had been gleaned from the reading of these authors.

The teaching methods employed at the time do not at first sight seem to have been designed to draw out the best from such a curriculum. Although students were expected to make notes and assemble their own examples, the teacher himself occupied a dominant position and can be found – for example in the manuals written by Guarino's son – wringing every last particle of information from a single word in a way which would eventually seem fatuous even to Renaissance itself (as, for instance, to Shakespeare in *Love's Labour Lost*): as, for example, when the word '*Impediti*' becomes the subject of a lengthy exposition:[32]

'being kept busy', plural form, literally meaning *we are kept busy*; this is more elegant than the singular and was an attempt to avoid seeming arrogant; for the ancients considered it more humble to speak of oneself in the plural than in the singular.

Yet even such pedantries can be impressive in the mouth of a charismatic teacher. And the ultimate goal of the linguistic programme (as when a

31. For an admirably sceptical account of this syllabus see A. Grafton and L. Jardine, op.cit., ch. 2.
32. See notes from introductory lectures, quoted Grafton and Jardine, op.cit., p. 18.

music teacher insists on the regular practising of scales) was to promote the fluency and freedom of expression which apparently served Guarino's pupil so well in the square at Bologna. It would be anachronistic to expect, in the idiom of nineteenth- or twentieth-century educational philosophy, any liberation of the 'whole personality' in such a scheme. Yet the humanists were confident that acquaintance with Roman conceptions of glory and virtue would provide a highly developed vocabulary through which the individual might articulate – or construct – a public persona.

TWO ENGLISH HUMANISTS: JOHN FREE AND JOHN TIPTOFT

In the course of Guarino's long career, his reputation spread throughout Europe, drawing students from all parts of Europe, no less from Hungary than from England.[33] By the 1440s a small but influential stream of churchmen and aristocrats had begun to make their way to Italy. Two of these are of particular interest, John Free (1430?–65) the scion of Bristol merchants and John Tiptoft (1427–70), Earl of Worcester who in the course of a long and tumultuous career, which ended in execution, occupied some of the highest offices in the land, including – under Edward IV – that of Lord High Constable and also Lord Treasurer of England. Free was eventually to be appointed secretary to Tiptoft; and their relationship illustrates a form of patronage that would become common between humanists in the period. But the career of each, independently, also deserves attention as an indication of the range of interests that Guarinian humanism was able to satisfy.

Like Tiptoft, Free had been a member of Balliol College, Oxford, and attained a fellowship there. The Oxford syllabus had begun to admit – alongside the study of Aristotle – a degree of attention to Cicero, Ovid and Virgil.[34] In Ferrara, however, where Free arrived in 1456, literary and linguistic study was already a central feature of public as well as of educational policy. The ruler of Ferrara, Borso d'Este (who is sometimes regarded as a Machiavellian *avant la lettre*) could also arrange performances of Plautus's comedies, playing to as many as 10,000 people.[35]

33. See especially. R. Weiss, *Humanism in England During the Fifteenth Century* (Oxford, 1948).
34. For Free and Tiptoft see R. J. Mitchell, *John Free: From Bristol to Rome in the Fifteenth Century* (London, 1933) and *John Tiptoft: 1427–70* (London, 1938).
35. See L. Muratori, *Rerum Italicum Scriptores*, Vol. XXIV, part vii.

Free himself appears to have taken enthusiastically to literary study. When, in an early letter, he records the death of the great humanist Lorenzo Valla, his grief is reserved above all for the loss of an exemplar of elegant Latinity. It appears that in 1457 Free began the study of Greek; and in 1458, he left Ferrara for Padua to pursue a course in medicine. It was here that he met the Earl of Worcester, and one of his first secretarial acts seems to have been to compose a letter accompanying a gift of books – including such advanced authors as Lucretius and Tacitus – from Tiptoft to Corpus Christi College, Oxford.

The style which Free displayed in the Corpus Christi letter was mature and professional. His skill in this regard presumably accounts for his subsequent acceptance in Rome. Though arriving as a qualified physician, Free was to work, effectively, as a papal courtier; and immediately before his death, he received the promise of the Bishopric of Wells.[36] By this time – rejoicing in the humanist name, 'Phreas' – Free had begun to make Latin translations from the Greek. His professional concerns are fully illustrated when he dedicates to Tiptoft his translation of that 'great work of learning', Synesius's treatise *In Praise of Baldness*. The humanist here speaks with a chivalric daring and zest of the problems he has set himself to solve:

> The books [Synesius] wrote bristle with so many thorny problems that I rather doubt whether any other volumes by Greek authors can compare with them in intricacy of subject matter or obscurity of style. No one – so far as I know – has ever been found to touch this author's work.

The same dedication eulogises Tiptoft, in words borrowed from Pope Pius II, as uniquely comparable 'in character and eloquence with the most illustrious Emperors of Greece and Rome'. In Free's own opinion Tiptoft does not take second place 'even to Alexander the Great of Greece'. To those, however, who were not humanists, such as John Rastell, Tiptoft's exercise of power when in office more properly entitled him to be called the 'Butcher of England'.[37] The paradox which this discrepancy of opinion suggests was by no means uncharacteristic of the relationship between humanism and politics in the period.

On the one hand, Tiptoft – having family associations with the Houses of both York and Lancaster – may first have gone to Italy to avoid unreconcilable allegiances during the Wars of the Roses. And a

36. Cf. the career of John Gunthorpe (died 1465) who did become Bishop of Wells after his visit to Italy. See R. Weiss, *Humanism in England during the Fifteenth Century* (Oxford, 1948).
37. See John Rastell (died 1536) *Pastyme of People,* first printed in 1529.

directly political product of his travels seems to have been a conception of his role as Lord Constable that combined Roman Law (which allowed, as the Common Law did not, the use of torture in the extortion of evidence) with a Machiavellian appreciation of political ruthlessness. It appears, for instance, that he had sought to displace the common law with sentences which involved the impaling as well as the hanging, drawing and quartering of mutineers.[38] Eventually, at his execution in 1470 – when, as Geoffrey Hill records in *Funeral Music,* Tiptoft asked to be executed with three strokes of the axe in honour of the Trinity – the crowd 'all cried out that he must die, for he had introduced the law of Padua where he used to study'.[39] It may have been no mitigation that he was accompanied at his death by an Italian priest.

For all that, Caxton can speak of Tiptoft as warmly as John Free had done, seeing him as the 'Earl of Worcester . . . to whom I knew none like among the lords of the temporality in science and moral virtue'. And it was with Caxton that Tiptoft published his own humanist writings, a volume of Cicero's *De Amicitia* and a translation of Buonaccorso da Montemagno's *Controversia de Nobilitate,* rendered as *The Declamation of Noblesse.* This latter work involves a long and unresolved debate between two suitors for the hand of a certain Lucrece on the nature of nobility – as to whether it derives from blood and riches or from personal worth. Here, whatever his political temper, the scholarly Tiptoft can eloquently voice the claims of merit against those of rank when he writes:

> Nevertheless, the sum of all my labours hath rested in this, to be a curious searcher for our public weal, merry at home, laborious outward, busy to attain science, piteous of them which had necessity . . . By the which I have judged myself to attain best noblesse, and I have trowed by these virtues to polish my courage and to make it more worshipful . . . Where didst thou anything in thy days that thou canst rehearse? Where by thou wouldst claim or challenge worship or noblesse? Wherever received our city any benefit by thee, or anything of laude [praise][40]

A SECOND PHASE OF HUMANISM: PHILOSOPHY AND GREEK IN ENGLAND AND ITALY

Pope Pius II, hearing an oration delivered by Tiptoft (which John Free had probably helped to compose), is said to have wept, realising that

38. See Mitchell, p. 203 and Einstein, p. 314.
39. Calendar of the Patent Rolls, 1461–7.
40. See Mitchell, op.cit., p. 236.

now even an Englishman could speak with proper eloquence. Before the next century was out, men such as Linacre, Colet and Grocyn could be accepted in Italy without astonishment. But by this time humanist studies had themselves entered a new phase.

In the first place, it seems that the scholar was now free to move beyond the sphere of teaching and textual criticism into the central areas of philosophical and theological debate. Notably, Lorenzo Valla (1407–57),[41] set out, philosophically, to reform the logic of Aristotle by an appeal to actual usage in language. He also applied philological methods to scriptural study in a way which won the approval of Luther and suggests the connection between humanist practice and the advance of the Protestant Reformation.[42] Famously, in 1440 Valla disproved, on purely stylistic grounds, the authenticity of the Donation of Constantine. Since the time of Constantine the Great, the Church had claimed that the Emperor had endowed it with riches and temporal power, asserting that this justified the dominion which the Church increasingly exercised in the political affairs of Europe. A textual scholar had shown convincingly that the claim was false; on stylistic grounds Valla demonstrated that the document of donation must itself be a forgery.

At the same time, humanists began to develop their own forms and schools of philosophy. The emphases and tendencies they pursued were manifold.[43] But among the most influential was the Neo-Platonism which came to be cultivated under Medici patronage in the so-called Florentine Academy. In the Middle Ages, Neo-Platonism – deriving from the interpretations which Plotinus placed upon Plato's writings – had been subtly combined with Aristotelian thought to provide a Christian metaphysic and cosmology which Plato himself would certainly not have recognised.[44] But the advancing study of Greek made it possible to return to the authentic words of Plato and Plotinus. The

---

41. P.O. Kristeller on Valla in *Eight Philosophers of the Renaissance* (Stanford, 1964), pp. 19–36.

42. Cited by Luther for his discussion of Sacrament of Penance (see Trinkaus, op.cit., p. 576)

43. For the diversity of philosophical schools in the Renaissance see the Charles B. Schmitt and Quentin Skinner (eds.), *Cambridge History of Renaissance Philosophy* (Cambridge, 1988).

44. E.R. Dodds' introduction to S. McKenna's translation, *Plotinus: The Enneads* (London, 1962); also P. Boyde, *Dante, Philomythes and Philosopher* (Cambridge, 1981), pp. 172–201.

foremost philosopher of the academy was Marsilio Ficino who had translated both of these philosophers.[45]

In a letter to Lorenzo de' Medici Ficino declares that the purpose of his philosophy is 'to reinforce the worship of God and to bring about a new understanding of the nature of man'. To see how he attempted this reconciliation, it is worth quoting at length from another of Ficino's many letters – not least because, even in translation, the richness of its style immediately suggests an advance upon the work of early humanists:[46]

It was the chief work of the divine Plato, as the dialogues of Parmenides and Epinomis show, to reveal the principle of unity in all things, which he called appropriately the One itself. He also asserted that in all things there is one truth, that is the light of the One itself, the light of God, which is poured into all minds and forms, presenting the forms to the minds and joining the minds to the forms. Whoever wishes to profess the study of Plato should therefore honour the one truth, which is the single ray of the one God. This ray passes through the angels, souls, the heavens and other bodies. As we discussed in the book on love, its splendour shines in every individual thing according to its nature and is called grace and beauty; and when it shines more clearly, it especially attracts the man who is watching, stimulates him who thinks and catches and possesses him who draws near to it. This ray also compels him to revere its splendour more than all else, as if it were a divine spirit, and once his former nature has been cast aside, to strive for nothing else but to become this splendour. This is plainly because the lover is not content with the sight or touch of the beloved and continually exclaims, 'I do not know what this man has that sets me on fire, nor do I understand what I desire'. The soul consumed as by the divine brilliance which shines in the beauteous man as though in a mirror, is seized unknowingly by that brilliance and is drawn upward as by a hook, so that the soul becomes God. Then must a man be considered mad as well as miserable, who, whilst called thus to the sublime through vision, plunges himself into the mire through touch. Although he could become God instead of man by contemplating the divine through the human beauty, from man he returns to beast by preferring the physical shadow of form to true spiritual beauty.

45. Ficino (1433–99) enjoyed the patronage of Cosimo de' Medici from 1462, became a priest in 1472 and continued his work of scholarship and translation, principally under Lorenzo the Magnificent, until the overthrow of the Medici in 1494. His most independent work of philosophy was the *Theologica Platonica de immortalitate animae* (*Platonic Theology Concerning the Immortality of the Soul*), but he also wrote commentaries on Plato and Plotinus and took a keen interest in both astrology and magic.

46. Translated from *The Letters of Marsilio Ficino*, ed. P.O. Kristeller (London, 1975), pp. 84–5.

Ficino here pictures a universal system of correspondences and proportion. The enlightened mind responds to this system not in reason but in ecstatic love of beauty and order; and in doing so, it begins to rise, in contemplation, through admiration of the material world to a vision of the very principle of order and beauty which is expressed in the Unity of God.

The implications of such thinking resonate throughout the Renaissance – from Castiglione, to Michelangelo to Edmund Spenser – and are likely to re-emerge whenever thinkers look for a mystical connection between the beauty of created objects and the order of their creator.[47] Yet such a philosophy also had a peculiar suitability to the time and place in which it was conceived. There is here, for instance, an overwhelming sense of the luxury and plenitude of creation which fits well with the patronage and political munificence that formed its background.[48] Equally, this is a philosophy designed to appeal to the elite; only those of particularly refined and elevated perceptions will be able to rise up in contemplation of beauty. Thus many forms of Renaissance art, especially emblematic art, can be seen as a test or initiation rite through which the chosen must pass, abandoning mundane rationality in seeking a superior mode of perception: 'for when the [the mind] loses its reason by becoming drunk with nectar, then it enters into a state of love, diffusing itself wholly into delight; and it is better for it thus to rage than to remain aloof from that drunkenness.'[49]

Such appeals to the exquisite, however, should not obscure the influence of Neo-Platonic thought in a wide variety of sometimes conflicting areas. On the one hand, this philosophy is itself the justification of a delight in physical beauty which – in significant contrast to the *taedium vitae* which Hamlet expresses in his speech 'What a piece of work is a man' – could lead Ficino to a triumphant celebration of the human form, 'erect, looking to heaven, because the finer elements of fire and air have a greater part in us than in other creatures'. On the other hand, the God that the Neo-Platonist seeks always lies hidden beyond the mind that seeks it in a way which encourages that mind to a leap of faith.

47. See Charles Taylor, *The Sources of the Self: The Making of Modern Identity* (Cambridge, 1989), pp. 250–1.
48. See Trinkaus op.cit., Vol. II, pp. 491 and 493.
49. See especially Edgar Wind, *Pagan Mysteries in the Renaissance* (London, 1958; Penguin 1967), p. 60.

A similar confidence – and ultimately faith – is expressed and developed by Ficino's younger associate Pico della Mirandola[50] whose account of Creation involves the vision of a God who, reserving no specific attribute for the human being, places it at the centre of the universe and endows it with the capacity to make of itself what it wills:

> The nature of all other beings is limited and constrained within the bounds of law prescribed by Us. Thou, constrained by no limits, in accordance with thine own free will, in whose hand We have placed thee, shalt ordain for thyself the limits of thy nature. We have set thee at the world's centre that thou mayest from thence more easily observe whatever is in the world. We have made thee neither of heaven nor of earth, neither mortal nor immortal, so that with freedom of choice and with honour, as though the maker and moulder of thyself, thou mayest fashion thyself in whatever shape thou shalt prefer.[51]

Out of context, there are implications here which might easily lead to the over-reaching and self-affirmation so characteristically cultivated in latter-day myths of the Renaissance; and certainly Pico's emphasis on human creativity and self-fashioning reflects essential features of Renaissance thought. Yet Pico, on closer examination, is speaking of a capacity which human beings have, not to transgress, but to stand at the centre of the cosmic order and create syntheses from its many manifestations. It is this interest in synthesis that underpins Pico's particular contribution, which advances beyond Ficino particularly in the development of a 'poetic theology'.[52] Unlike Ficino, Pico looked not only to Greek but also to Hebraic texts and to the Cabbala; for in these he saw the possibility that wisdom, as created by human beings, would be passed down through all ages in the traditions of thought which the scholar was now in a position to fathom.

Though English humanists of the early sixteenth century rarely command the eloquence of a Ficino or a Pico, some were nevertheless accepted into the Medici circle (as for example Lineacre in his association with the great teacher Poliziano). And, in a manner which reflected the especial characteristics of Northern Humanism, John Colet in particular could range over the whole area of humanist study, in regard not

---

50. Pico (1463–94) was a Lombard of aristocratic birth who, after pursuing his studies of philosophy in Ferrara, Padua Florence and Paris, came under the protection of Lorenzo the Magnificent.
51. Trans. P.O. Kristeller, in E. Cassirer (ed.), *The Renaissance Philosophy of Man*, op.cit., pp. 224–5.
52. See Wind, op.cit., pp. 17–25.

only to its educational implications but also to its philosophical and religious significance.[53]

As the founder of St Paul's School, Colet expresses, in powerfully demotic English, the essential demand of the humanist for pure Latinity when he banishes from his school 'all barbary, all corruption . . . all such abusion which more rather may be called blatterature than literature'.[54] Yet it is with a comparable vigour of intellect that the young Colet had engaged in correspondence with Ficino, pursuing a philosophical contempt for Aquinas and Aristotelian scholasticism. Thus he is quickly led to embrace the Platonic assertion that there must exist divine *invisibilia* corresponding to all visible things in the world.[55] But this leads on directly to a recognition, compatibile with the most generous conceptions of the Neo-Platonists that:

> We can enjoy the divine mind through various ideas and seek it through various traces . . . God so disposed the intellectual eyes and tendencies of the various souls in different manners, in order that we may approach the different possessions of the manifold goods by different paths.

There is here the beginning of a more overtly Christian tendency than one finds in Ficino; and Colet will never go so far as to admit, as the Platonic Ficino did, that the soul enjoyed any pre-existence. But he is prepared to see the structure of the world as we know it in terms which are wholly at one with Pico della Mirandola's synthesis. The elaborate parallel which Pico developed between the macrocosm and the microcosm is clearly reproduced in Colet's view of man as 'to such a degree a composite being that we may consider him the child of the whole universe, corporeal and incorporeal'. Coming even closer to Pico, he declares:

> Man is an epitome of the whole universe resembling in his spiritual faculties the nine orders of angels; and it follows, that he will resemble the heaven in the more refined part of his body, and the sublunary world in the lowest part.

One need not stress how deeply these notions enter the Elizabethan view of the world.[56] One notes, however, that here, even without the

---

53. On Colet, see Leland Miles, *John Colet and the Platonic Tradition* (London, 1962); S. Jayne, *John and Marsilio Ficino* (Oxford, 1962), and E. Cassirer, *The Platonic Renaissance in England* (Edinburgh, 1953). Also A.C. Spearing, *Medieval to Renaissance in English Poetry* (Cambridge, 1985). For a view which emphasises Colet's hermeticism see John B. Gleason, *John Colet* (Berkeley, 1989).

54. See Miles, op.cit.

55. Miles, op.cit., p. 19.

56. A.O. Lovejoy, *The Great Chain of Being* (Cambridge Mass., 1936).

expansiveness of Neo-Platonic rhetoric, there is an attempt to provide an alternative to scientific particularity of observation – whether Aristotelian or Baconian – whereby the created world may be read for its mystic rhetoric of cosmic correspondences.

MACHIAVELLI AND CASTIGLIONE

In both England and Italy, the educational programme of early human-ism laid the foundation, as later chapters will show, for vernacular literature in all genres. But the resilience and adaptability of humanist thinking in the practical sphere are shown at the beginning of the fif-teenth century by the way in which two figures, Castiglione and Machiavelli, responded to the great political changes which began with the sixteenth-century invasions of Italy.[57] In the course of the early six-teenth century, the cities of Italy rapidly lost their former independence, while England – with the end of the Wars of the Roses and the accession of Henry VII – was quick to establish itself as a nation-state. Yet in their different ways both Italy and England were able to find material in both Castiglione and Machiavelli which answered to the needs of their new circumstances. The period, one notes, was also one in which printing assisted the dissemination of ideas, with results which – in the case of England – will soon be apparent from the writings of Sir Thomas Elyot.

Il Cortegiano, having been published in 1528, appeared in an English version by Sir Thomas Hoby in 1561 as *The Book of the Courtier.* Castiglione had himself made a diplomatic visit to England in 1506 to receive the Order of the Garter on behalf of Guidobaldo, Duke of Urbino; and subsequently, his writings were to stimulate an interest in courtly (and, by implication, diplomatic) behaviour which would also produce, in the course of the century, translations not only of the *Cortegiano* itself but also of etiquette books by authors such as Stefano

---

57. Castiglione (born at Casatico near Mantua 1478, died in Toledo, Spain 1529) pursued a diplomatic career, initially in the service of the Dukes of Urbino. The first version of *Il Cortegiano* was completed in 1516. A final version was completed in 1527 and was published in Venice by Aldo Manuzio in 1528. Other works include the pastoral *Thyrsis.* Machiavelli (born Florence 1469, died near Florence 1527) was employed in his early years as secretary to the committee in charge of military and diplomatic affairs. But falling under suspicion of anti-Medicean activities, he was dismissed from office in 1512 and never regained any governmental position. Living in seclusion near Florence, he composed several comedies, including the *Mandragola* (see below, pp. 207–11) as well as works of political theory and history. Only the *Mandragola* and *The Art of War* were published in his own lifetime. *The Prince* was not published until 1532.

Guazzo and Giovanni Della Porta.[58] As for Machiavelli, it seems likely that Thomas Cromwell possessed certain of Machiavelli's writings in manuscript before they appeared in printed form in England.[59] Editions and translations of *The Prince* were slow to appear in England, though the reputation of the book preceded it. It may be that a full appreciation of Machiavelli's political philosophy was not achieved until the mid-seventeenth century.[60] But Machiavelli's arguments for strong absolutist rule – which were probably engendered in the first place by his recognition of the development of nation-states, particularly in France – was bound to be sympathetic to certain Tudor ears, or else would have stimulated strong resistance. By the end of the century there were not only translations but also Italian-language editions of Machiavelli's work available in England, issuing from the English publishing house of John Woolfe.[61]

At first view, Castiglione and Machiavelli stand in marked contrast. Castiglione begins the *Cortegiano* in a vein of nostalgia, as courtiers from the recent past are shown gathering for four evenings of conversation at the court of Urbino to debate, often light-heartedly, what the qualities of the perfect courtier might be. The book also ends on an elegiac note: momentarily, the discussion described in the last book has produced an ecstatically Neo-Platonic account of spiritual love and beauty; but the ecstasy fades as the dawn of a new day filters through the palace windows. In contrast, Machiavelli is concerned not with a passing age but rather with the present or the future, and with the stratagems that any new prince (or usurper) might adopt in attempting to establish himself in his realm. In the words of Thomas Cromwell, Machiavelli's thinking 'is more useful than the dreams of Plato'; and Francis Bacon, similarly, will praise Machiavelli for the empiricism which led him to describe 'men as they are, not as they ought to be'.[62]

---

58. See J.L. Lievsay, *Stefano Guazzo and the English Renaissance* (Chapel Hill, 1961).
59. See Einsten, op.cit., p. 292, who also records the violently antagonist reactions of Cardinal Reginald on yielding to Cromwell's suggestion that he should read Machiavelli.
60. See Felix Raab, *The English Face of Machiavelli* (London, 1964), esp. p. 77, *et seq.*
61. See George Watson, 'Machiavel and Machiavelli', *Sewanee Review* 84 (1976), 630–48. Also A. Gerber, 'All of the Five Fictitious Italian Editions of Machiavelli Printed by John Woolfe of London (1584–1588)', *Modern Language Notes XXII* (1907). See also F. Raab, *The English Face of Machiavelli* (London, 1964).
62. See Cromwell in correspondence with the anti-Machiavellian Cardinal Pole in *Epistolae Reg. Pole,* 1744, p. 151. For the very close connections between Bacon's thinking and Machiavelli's in 'attempting to achieve development in the face of historical degeneration', as demonstrated both in *The Advancement of Learning* and in *The New Atlantis*, see Charles Whitney, *Machiavelli and Modernity* (New Haven, 1986), p. 197; also L. Jardine, *Francis Bacon: Discovery and the Art of Discourse* (London, 1974).

Two aspects of Renaissance thought, then, seem to be expressed and counterpoised in Castiglione and Machiavelli – the one seeing truth as the contemplation of an ideal pattern, the other seeking it in the observation of the world as it is. Yet it would be misleading to express the difference between Castiglione and Machiavelli simply in these terms.

For one thing Castiglione was conspicuously a more successful politician than Machiavelli. Where Machiavelli suffered torture, disgrace and neglect, Castiglione not only found that his books were placed – alongside the Bible – at the bedside of the Emperor Charles V, but he was also deeply enough involved in the politics of his time to be blamed personally by the Pope for the Sack of Rome (and yet still within months of his death to be promised a cardinalship).[63] Conversely, it would be a mistake to underestimate the depth of Machiavelli's humanist formation, the height of his principles or the vigour of his concern over liberty and human dignity. Even his personal habits are said to have displayed a scholarly fastidiousness which led him to wash and ceremonially re-clothe himself before he entered his study, to commune with classical texts.[64]

To engage more closely with these parodoxes, consider first Machiavelli's political philosophy.[65] At the centre of Machiavelli's thought is a conviction that human beings are corrupt:

> One can make this generalisation about men: they are ungrateful, fickle, liars and deceivers, they shun danger and are greedy for profit.   (Prin., XVII)

What is more, Machiavelli also believes that at least one half of human life is governed by Fortune or by changing circumstance (*ibid.*, XXX). This at first sight represents a cynical reversal of the confidence in human nature which Renaissance thinking is often thought to encourage. Yet Machiavelli is no cynic, even though his own experience of political life might easily have made him one. On the contrary, his concern is to find ways of countering – or else, more subtly, of employing to good effect – the corruptions which he has observed in human conduct. His aim is to show how political communities can be formed which – recognising, as a matter of fact, what human nature is truly like

63. See Trafton in Hanning and Rosand, *Castiglione* op.cit. p. 157
64. See for a development of this positive evaluation Sebastian della Grazia, *Machiavelli in Hell* (London and Hemel Hempstead, 1989).
65. For Machiavelli see especially Quentin Skinner, *Machiavelli* (Oxford, 1981) and his chapter 'Political Philosophy' in *The Cambridge History of Renaissance Philosophy*, op.cit. See also J.R. Hale, *Machiavelli and Renaissance Italy*, revised edn. (London, 1972); S. Anglo, *Machiavelli: A dissection* (London, 1969) and Sebastian de Grazia, op.cit.

– may still protect the liberty of the state and express the desire which human beings legitimately have for glory.

Machiavelli in this light may rightly be said to concern himself with virtue. But his understanding of virtue – or *virtù* – involves a radical redefinition; and, like any good humanist, Machiavelli returns to the classical world for enlightenment: the word 'virtù', as Machiavelli uses it, is etymologically connected to the Latin 'vir' – 'man' – and is intended to refer to qualities of manliness, courage and prowess. On this understanding, corruption is not at all a matter of unprincipled behaviour but rather one of apathy. In the face of changing circumstances, and particularly in the face of political danger, a 'virtuous' response will above all be an energetic response. So, in one of many images which he chooses to represent this view, Machiavelli applauds the political vigour of Pope Julius II, whose actions have demonstrated that we need not in the end be passive or feeble and that we are not at the mercy of Fortune:

> I hold strongly to this: that it is better to be impetuous than circumspect, because Fortune is a woman and, if she is to be submissive, it is necessary to beat and coerce her. Experience shows that she is more often subdued by men who do this than by those who act coldly. Always being a woman, she favours young men, because they are less circumspect and more ardent and because they command her with greater audacity.
>
> (*Prin.*, XXV)

The god Hercules won his own godhead by the powers he displayed in his twelve labours; and the figure of Hercules was widely used in Renaissance celebrations of heroic power.[66] Boccaccio, too, had already pictured how a capacity for pragmatic action could lead to success, commercially or sexually, against Fortune. In Boccaccio, as in Machiavelli, Fortune is no metaphysical principle but a secular power of history or circumstance. Yet in spite of these antecedents, it is not surprising (even, or especially, on a modern view) that Machiavelli's unabashed praise of political virility should sound offensive and disconcerting.

Effectively, *virtù* is a willingess to act in the political sphere according to the demands of the moment. Moral principle might be – though need not necessarily be – an impediment to such action. And so might any preconceived attachment to political precedent. Implicitly,

---

66. See E. Cassirer, *The Individual and the Cosmos in Renaissance Philosophy*, trans. Mario Domandi, (New York, 1963; originally published as Vol. X in *Studien der Bibliothek Warburg*, Leipzig and Berlin, 1927).

Machiavelli's thinking takes issue with a whole tradition which assumed broadly that political behaviour could be governed by moral considerations. Dante, for instance – though as contemptuous of apathy as Machiavelli is – nevertheless based his political remedies on a belief in absolute or divinely sanctioned justice, and produced a theory in *De Monarchia* which depended heavily upon scholastic arguments of an Aristotelian cast. Neither the humanist nor the pragmatist in Machiavelli could have assented to that. In like manner, he also set himself against his fellow humanists who, by Machiavelli's time, had allowed an unquestioning complacency to settle over their use of terms like 'freedom' and 'glory'. Laudable as these words might sound in the mouth of Bruni, they could easily be seen, on a Machiavellian view, to have clouded the political mind at a time when, with the invasions of Italy, *realpolitik* should have been the order of the day.[67] On this count, Machiavelli may even be at odds with his friend and fellow historian Guicciardini; for where Guicciardini's writings,[68] representing the tragedy of Italy, counsel a certain worldly wisdom – which does indeed come near to cynical passivity – Machiavelli constantly prefers to unsettle the mind of his reader, demanding new thought and new definitions appropriate to new occasions:

> These princes of ours whose power had been established many years, may not blame fortune for their losses. Their own indolence was to blame, because . . . having never imagined when times were quiet that they should change (and this is the common failing of mankind never to anticipate a storm when the sea is calm), when adversity came their first thoughts were of flight not of resistance.
>
> (*Prin.*, XXIV)

Machiavelli, then, attempts to distinguish power from morality – or at least from morality in its most obvious aspect; and one of his contributions to intellectual history is, of course, to have made possible the sociological study of power as a phenomenon independent of individual moral considerations.[69] It needs to be emphasised, however – in view of Machiavelli's reputation – that in *The Prince* his concern is specifically not with private morality but with the good of the public realm. Thus he, no more than any of his republican forebears, desires to promote tyranny; and Machiavelli opposes the capricious or self-seeking use of

---

67. See Gilbert, *Machiavelli and Guicciardini,* (Princeton, 1965).
68. See above, Introduction p. 20.
69. For Machiavelli and the private conscience, see below, pp. 207–11 on the *Mandragola*.

power in his portrait of Agathocles (*Prin.*, XXX). The new Prince must abandon complacency and the luxuries of moral self-approbation, cultivating, in the interests of his realm, a constant and 'virtuous' vigilance: at all times, even out in the country, the Prince will be inspecting the landscape with a strategic eye for military weak points and defences (*Prin.*, XIV). The populace, too, – enlisted perforce in a militia – will continually be made to realise the stake which they have in the survival of the commonwealth. *Virtù* will be required of the people no less than of the Prince.[70]

It remains true that the line to be drawn here is disconcertingly fine, as seems to have been particularly apparent to Machiavelli's Elizabethan readers.[71] On the one hand, Marlowe in picturing the Jew of Malta contemplates, with some relish, the consequences which follow when Machiavellian principles are translated from the public to the private sphere. Marston, too, in his *Sofonisba*[72] can speak of the ruthless politician using men in practice 'like wedges to drive each other out'. On the other hand, in *Tamburlaine* Marlowe portrays the imaginative energy that may be released through the apparently amoral practices of the new prince.[73] So, too, Marston in *Sofonisba* gives a particularly subtle account of the Machiavellian argument when, in Act II. i. ll. 58–9, an argument is proposed which envisages the political necessity of treacherous acts: just as in all medicines there is an element of poison, so in all political remedies there is dishonesty – 'And if it be sometimes of forced use/Wherein more urgent than in saving nations' (ll. 58–9) – to which the only response is a high-minded and all too easy retreat into the luxurious confines of conscience – 'our vow, our faith our oath, why they're ourselves' (l. 83). As for Shakespeare, he may in *Macbeth* display the tragedy of a conscience lost through the temptations of political action, but he is equally sensitive in *Measure for Measure* and *The Tempest* to the complications which arise through the abdication of political power.

It is perhaps the delicacy of such distinctions that makes Machiavelli's work inherently dramatic, as if it were through effects of dramatic

---

70. This is especially emphasized in the *Discorsi*.
71. For a modern view of these issues see Bernard Williams, 'Politics and Moral Character', in *Moral Luck* (Cambridge, 1981), pp. 54–70, where, conflating Plato and Machiavelli, he produces the question 'How can the good rule the world as it is?', p. 66.
72. See below, p. 270.
73. See Antonio D'Andrea, 'Giraldi Cinthio and the Birth of the Machiavellian Hero on the Elizabethan Stage', in *Il Teatro italiano del Rinascimento* a cura di Maristella de Panizza Lorch (Milan, 1980), pp. 605–18.

surpise and complexity that Machiavelli could most effectively stir the *virtù* of his reader. Consider, for instance, his disconcertingly theatrical account of Cesare Borgia and Rimirro d'Orca in Chapter Seven of *The Prince*. Cesare Borgia, the illegitimate son of Alexander VI annexes Cesena. The realm has been hitherto plagued by lawlessness, to the detriment of its citizens, and Cesare Borgia's first act is to restore good order by appointing a hard man, Rimirro d'Orca, to persecute the local brigands. The citizenry are delighted, until Rimirro's cruelty threatens their own interests, at which point, Rimirro is himself discovered in the city square dissected neatly in two, with a bloody knife and an executioner's block beside him. By these means social order is re-asserted, and even, ironically, a certain moderation, in that the extremes of Rimirro's behaviour are curbed by Cesare's 'virtuous' action. But simultaneously of course this action also reasserts the secret power that Cesare wields in his constant battle against changing circumstance.

Terror, then, has it uses and also displays – at least at a distance – a capacity for a certain histrionic wit. But in regard to theatricality, Machiavelli's view of human action shares a great deal with Castiglione's. For both carry to a conclusion the early humanist realisation that the social world is ours to construct for ourselves through rhetoric and debate. The sphere of Castiglione's theatricality is that of courtly performance.[74] Yet even the courtier whom Castiglione sets out to fashion – endowed with all his courtly graces – will prove to have a political role to perform.

Prose style, in Castiglione's case, as in Machiavelli's, says a good deal about the man and his intellectual purposes. However, where Machiavelli's writing aims deliberately to disconcert, Castiglione displays a continual desire for balance; even when he is dramatising the cut and thrust of debate, Castiglione, by the poise of his descriptions, reminds his reader that a middle way is possible, and rarely allows any final opinion or recommendation to be voiced. In this vein, the work opens with

74. See Wayne Rebhorne, *Courtly Performances: Masking and Festivity in Castiglione's Book of the Courtier* (Detroit, 1978). Also for Castiglione see J.R. Woodhouse, *Baldassare Castiglione: A Reassessment of The Courtier* (Edinburgh, 1978); R. Hanning and David Rosand (eds.), *Castiglione: The Ideal and the Real in Renaissance Culture* (New Haven and London, 1983), p. 51; Joseph D. Falvo, *The Economy of Human Relations: Castiglione's 'Libro del Cortegiano'* (New York, 1992), and Virginia Cox, *The Renaissance Dialogue* (Cambridge, 1992). Also, Virginia Cox (ed.), *Castiglione's Book of the Courtier as Translated by Sir Thomas Hoby* (London, 1994).

a lightly idealised account of Urbino – which prefers to see the city as a microcosmic centre of civilisation rather than to record its recent history during which the city, as a pawn in Papal politics, had been briefly taken over by Cesare Borgia.[75] Similarly, Castiglione's cast of courtiers – among whom there is at least one double murderer, Francesco Maria della Rovere – lose the rough edges of their historical reality as they participate in the fluent choreography of Castiglione's prose. There is, too, an apparent absence of any strongly authoritarian voice here: the great Federigo da Montefeltro is long dead, the present ruler of Urbino is absent, and even Castiglione is, supposedly, away in England at the time of the discussions. Yet power passes to surrogates – the Duchess and her own spokeswoman Emilia – who are adept at maintaining a subtle, indeed scarcely visible control over any subversive or immoderate tendencies in the discussion. And her purpose in setting up the discussion is to ensure that certain topics which might have produced immoderate discussion should not be countenanced: in choosing a topic for playful discussion, it would not, for instance, do to consider why women prefer serpents to rats nor to invite confessions as to what forms of vice, virtue or madness one would like to see in a lover. Topics as risqué as this occasionally threaten to surface. But it is one of the functions of the civilised humour which Castiglione discusses in Book II to defuse such situations; and every discussion, however impassioned, is punctuated and appeased by an urbane smile.

As Cesare Borgia maintained order through his surrogate Rimirro d'Orca, so from the outset in the *Cortegiano* the courtly balance is sustained against a background of unnameable power. This is the condition of the game which the courtiers are to the play: the courtiers set themselves to consider the qualities of a perfect courtier but there is little sense that they ever could, or even intended, to arrive at an authoritative definition.

Yet the choice of subject is far from negligible, and the game-playing itself, though practised here in the rarified atmosphere of a Renaissance court, has far-reaching implications. For Castiglione's work investigates

75. Though a small and provincial city, Urbino had come into prominence under the Montefeltro dynasty, especially when its alliegances around 1400 shifted towards alliance with the Papacy. The Ducal Palace of Urbino where the *Cortegiano* is set is a peculiarly powerful symbol of the achievements of the Montefeltro rulers. Built principally by Duke Federigo (1444–82) – who is known from portraits by Piero della Francesca – the castle reflects his tastes and abilities as a patron of the arts; and traditions of patronage were continued by his ailing son Guidobaldo (1482–1509). Louise George Clubb speaks of the Utopian elements of the *Cortegiano* in Hanning op.cit.

attitudes and responses which may well be thought characteristic of all groups and all forms of communal behaviour.[76] Castiglione may not go very deeply into the psychology of the individual but he does develop, so to speak, an early form of game theory in which he registers the shifts, turns, accommodations and sleights of hand that, in practice, always seem to be necessary for the smooth operation of any community. Even when Castiglione is at his most Utopian, the demands which he makes upon human beings reflect far more accurately the recognisable characteristics of human nature than those to be found, say, in More's totalitarian Utopia.

At the centre of Castiglione's theory – developed early in the discussion – is the notion of *sprezzatura*: this is the quality which the courtier will display in all the manifold activities which he undertakes. One might translate this term as 'nonchalance'. Yet, significantly, the word itself – which is a neologism – is never explicitly defined in Castiglione's own text. Instead, as with Machiavelli's *virtù*, a sense of the word develops from its use in context. There is indeed some case for saying that a clear definition was never intended. *Sprezzatura* is the quality of the courtier; those who are themselves courtiers can recognise it when they see it, and would neither wish nor be able to divulge the formula to those outside their circle.

There are conceivably sinister implications here which multiply as one examines the various elements of concealment that seem to be involved in the cultivation of courtly arts. Yet all groups have their secret codes; and the pursuit of *sprezzatura*, seen in its positive light, is a way to ensure confidence and self-possession in the performance of the rituals which the courtly tribe identified as central to its own existence. So in Book I it becomes apparent that the whole range of courtly activities can be performed either with or without *sprezzatura*, and that any overzealous display of art will be condemned as ridiculous affectation. Thus (using the Tudor translation by Hoby, where *sprezzatura* is rendered as 'recklessness' or, here, as 'dis-gracing'):

> And even as the bee in green meadows fleeth always about the grass, choosing out flowers; so shall our Courtier steal his grace from them that to his seeming have it, and from each one, that parcel that shall be most worthie thy praise. And not to do as a friend of ours, whom you all know, that thought he resembled much Ferdinand the younger of Aragon, and regarded not to

76. On the appropriateness of game theory to the study of these texts and also *passim* on Hoby, see Frank Whiggam, *Ambition and Privilege: The Social Tropes* (Berkeley, 1984).

resemble in any other point, but in the often lifting up of his heade, writhing therewithal a part of his mouth, the which custom the king had gotten by infirmity . . . But I, imagining with my self often times how this grace commeth . . . finde one rule that is most general . . . And that is to eschew as much as a man may, and as a sharpe and dangerous rocke, too much curiousnesse, affectation) and (to speake a new word) to use in everything a certain disgracing [sprezzatura] to cover art withall, and seeme whatsoever he doth and saith to doe without paine, and (as it were not) minding it.

(Cort., I)

On this view, *sprezzatura* is an art – born of observation and graceful exercise – which avoids any impression of artfulness or effort. In common with the early educationalists, Castiglione looks for the development of the public self in a wide variety of activities. Yet in all of these he recognises that the self, far from seeking aggrandisement or even undue notice, can best comport itself in public with a moderation, poise and restraint – akin, one might say, to that which Castiglione himself shows in his prose style.

Understood in this sense, *sprezzatura* will be a quality observable in all aspects of Renaissance thinking. For instance, in the sphere of the visual arts, Michelangelo will be credited with the peculiar grace that allows him to tackle momentously difficult projects and yet to achieve his end without apparent labour.[77] At the same time, the notion has a particular application in the political arena, where *sprezzatura* quickly reveals its kinship to the pragmatic *virtù* which Machiavelli recommends. For clearly there is an element of dissimulation and even self-promotion involved in the practice of *sprezzatura* – however much Castiglione may try to distinguish it from 'affectation'. The adept will only *seem* to be working without exercise or forethought, and will certainly make sure that his display of courtly arts will catch the eye of his prince.

In its political aspect, *sprezzatura* can rightly be regarded as a technique for 'survival at the Renaissance court',[78] as it might be in any other organisation. And when one recalls that the courts of the period, whether in Italy or England, were increasingly absolutist or despotic there is reason to emphasise the practical value of the quality. Yet for the same reason, *sprezzatura* in a courtier – like *virtù* in a Prince – may have been a practical means to promote the best ideals of the court. This

---

77. See David Summers on 'grace' and 'difficulty' in *Michelangelo and the Language of Art* (Princeton, 1981). Vasari in his *Life of Giotto* speaks of the skill which allowed Giotto to depict agonised figures 'writhing with the 'greatest grace in the world'.
78. See Woodhouse, op.cit., *passim.*

certainly is the application which Castiglione stresses in the first half of the fourth book of the work. For here Castiglione makes it clear – with a pragmatism deriving no doubt from his own diplomatic experience – that in the circumstances of an absolutist court the only chance of recommending any particular course of action might well have been to find the appropriate occasion – be it in a dance or out hunting or in a light-hearted discussion – to catch the ruler's eye and take the occasion to promote a favoured course of action.

Here again the possibility of flattery or self-interest is at once apparent. But Castiglione is explicitly opposed to tyranny; and it is at this point that the final sequence of the fourth book comes into its own. The first half of Book IV is distinctly Aristotelian in its careful attention to the realities of political life. But the second half is Platonic in attempting to reveal an ideal order of love, beauty and truth. It is a sign of Castiglione's philosophical pretensions that he should seek to establish a balance between these two approaches. But it is also essential to his outlook that the measure and devotion to truth which the courtier observes – and the grace which he exercises – should be seen to derive from his love of the ideals which neo-Platonists such as Ficino had so strongly emphasised. So Bembo,[79] approaching his conclusion in Book IV, declares:

> Therefore vouchsafe (Lord) to hearken to our prayers, pour thy self into our hearts, and with the brightness of thy most holy fire lighten our darknesse, and like a trusty guide in this blind maze show us the right way.

It is true that, at the conclusion of this speech, Bembo is plucked down from his ecstatic heights by a gently mocking tug on his sleeve: characteristically, Castiglione avoids extremes and reasserts good measure even where virtue is the issue. Yet he also affirms in this conclusion that, as well as the unnameable powers of the political world, there is an unnameable virtue which may give direction to all that is done in the illusory sphere of brute reality.

HOBY, ELYOT AND THE ITALIAN TRADITION

It is customary to enquire whether Castiglione's *Cortegiano* can be considered an etiquette book. There is no doubt that the book was so

79. Historically, Bembo (1470–1547) built an illustrious career on his literary talents, especially as secretary to Pope Leo X, and became the leading authority of his day on matters of linguistic usage. See below, pp. 117–18.

considered by a good many of its original readers in England, and for that reason took its place alongside other Italian books which dealt with such aspects of courtly behaviour as dancing, duelling and toxophily. As late as 1581, Sidney can suggest that one reason for learning Italian is to acquire a true appreciation of horsemanship from Pugliese's work (*Apology*, p. 2); and the effectiveness of such reading – facilitated now by the dissemination of printed copy – is underlined by those contemporary aristocrats who complained that the secrets of courtly behaviour were now too easily available to the *parvenu*. At the same time, Shakespeare in *Romeo and Juliet* could put his reading of the manuals to theatrical use. When, depicting Mercutio's death in a bungled duel, he reflects the warnings uttered by Italian swordmasters against arbitrary intervention in a sword-fight. Likewise, Touchstone's catalogue of 'lies direct' and 'quips modest' in *As You like It*, V. iv. 64, reflects a mock-Italian sense of punctilio.

Yet there is much in the *Cortegiano* which resists direct application: if *sprezzatura* is to be learned at all, then it will be learned not as a precept might be, but rather as an exercise in style or skill. As with the best representatives of Renaissance thinking, Castiglione – like Machiavelli – is concerned to elicit an appropriate response, by eloquence and example, rather than to impose a rule. The question now is whether English writers of the period understood this or not.

From the preface to his translation, it seems that Sir Thomas Hoby,[80] understood very well indeed. Certainly, in his view, the *Cortegiano* will serve as an invaluable *vademecum* for persons of all ranks, at every stage in their lives, offering them 'an encouragement to garnish their minds with moral virtues, and their bodies with comely exercises'. But Hoby recognises that the action of the book will be oblique. To 'Princes and great men, it is a rule to rule themselves that rule others' and can effectively be such because it slips under the defences of arrogance or censorship: the ruler will find there 'such matters that friends durst not utter unto kings'. Hoby also recognises that the *Cortegiano* is a dialogue and that, in being so, avoids the rigidities of direct statement:

> Both Cicero and Castilio profess they follow not any certain appointed order of precepts or rules, as is used in the instruction of youth, but call to rehearsal matters debated in their time to and from in the disputation of most eloquent men and excellent wits in every worthy quality.

80. Sir Thomas Hoby (born Leominster 1530, died Paris – as ambassador to France – 1566) travelled to Italy twice, attended the University of Padua in 1547 (where a group of exiles from Mary Tudor's Catholic England had gathered) and later travelled as far as Sicily and Calabria. He was of a firmly Protestant background and was knighted by Elizabeth I.

Turning, however, from translation to the interpretations found in Sir Thomas Elyot's work, it is striking that there is no acknowledgement here at all of the debate element in Castiglione's work or any attempt to reproduce it formally in his own. Elyot had many opportunities to enter into debate as he read in preparation for his book. Although Castiglione is acknowledged to be one of his main sources, it is by no means the only one: as well as drawing upon other writers of conduct books such as Pontano and Palmieri, Elyot seems almost certainly to have read – and disagreed with – Machiavelli. Yet the work does not portray or allow dissension. In a contrast suggested by Sir Francis Bacon, Elyot's work is cast in 'a magisterial mode which demands a simple consensus' whereas the *Cortegiano* is written in an 'initiative' mode which, in laying bare the stages by which those conclusions were reached, offers the readers 'a thread on which to spin an original next work of knowledge'.

Sir Thomas Elyot – who lived between 1490 and 1546, and whose importance is recognised by T.S. Eliot when he claims him as a remote ancestor – was formed intellectually at the Inns of Court,[81] which at that time provided a preparation for the monarchical as well as the legal courts. Elyot was to spend his life on the fringes of the Henry VIII's court – where he was adept enough to survive when the heads of more eminent associates were rolling. Indeed, it was here, probably, that he acquired copies of Castiglione and Machiavelli from Thomas Cromwell. At the same time, the Inns were rapidly becoming centres of humanist study, as later they would be of literary experimentation; and though Elyot continued to practice law as well as courtliness, his humanistic works show a good deal of intellectual ambition. They include renderings from Boccaccio of at least one high-minded – though inherently mysogynistic tale – as well as a translation (1534) of Pico della Mirandola's *The Rules of a Christian Life*. In regard to the English language, Elyot showed great interest, as did his Italian mentors, for the development of his own vernacular.[82] He produced dictionaries and, in the course of writing *The Book of the Governor*, experimented with neologisms to expand the scope of his native language. Notably, it is Elyot

---

81. For Elyot see John M. Major's abridged version, *The Book Named the Governor* (New York, 1969) and also his *Sir Thomas Elyot and Renaissance Humanism* (Lincoln, Nebraska, 1964); also P. Hogrefe, *Life and Times of Sir Thomas Elyot, Englishman* (Iowa, 1967). Also Leslie C. Warren, *Humanist Doctrines of the Prince from Petrarch to Elyot* (Chicago, 1939).
82. See below pp. 117–18.

who introduces the word 'democracie' into English, though the sense in which he uses it is pejorative.[83]

In the *The Boke Named the Governor*, Elyot displays some of the Utopian aspirations of Sir Thomas More, but he is primarily concerned with pragmatic questions of education and in particular with the education of gentlemen. His aim is to see that those who are fitted for rule by birth, should be trained well enough to contribute in a practical sense to the government of their country. Elyot in fact never completed the educational part of his programme. It seems likely, however, that he intended to conclude his book, following Castiglione's model with an examination of how the 'governour' would proceed to act in the political sphere.

Like Coluccio and subsequent humanists, Elyot seeks to develop the inherent talents of each pupil and indeed notably insists that 'we should strive not with the universal nature of man, but – that being conserved – let us follow our own proper natures' (op.cit., p. 14). Similarly, he places literary study close to the centre of this development, reproducing an argument for literary study which traversed the Renaissance from Boccaccio to Sidney to the effect that, in ancient times, poetry was held in highest esteem – since 'all wisdom was supposed to be therein included' (op.cit., p. 113). Thus – in an example which seems to portray the reverse of Prospero's experience in Shakespeare's *The Tempest* – Elyot speaks of an exiled king who bided his time as a humble teacher of literature and thereby so impressed his subjects that they restored him to his realm (op.cit., p. 67). But literature is not Elyot's only concern. In common with Castiglione, he recognises that a wide variety of exercises are needed if the proper nature of the individual is to be expressed:

> For how many men be there that, having their sons in childhood aptly disposed by nature to paint, to carve, or grave, to embroider . . . but that as soon as they espy it, they be therewith displeased, and forthwith bindeth them apprentices to tailors, to weavers, to tuckers and sometime to cobblers?
> (*Gov.*, p. 121).

Notably, Elyot reprimands the English for their particular repressiveness in this regard; and he seems happy to recognise that Italy will serve well as a model in the cultivation of individual talents. Yet on matters of public policy, Elyot, in common with, say, Ascham can also at times express considerable reserve about things Italian. In particular, he speaks

---

83. The *Oxford English Dictionary* attributes the word to Elyot in 1528.

of the parlous state of certain Italian republics such as Venice and Florence, and significantly insists upon the better government of those states which are autocratic (*Gov.*, p. 55).

With this, there is revealed an aspect of Elyot's work which seems to enter, without ever daring to admit as much, into silent debate with Machiavelli. As a relatively successful attendant at Henry VIII's court, Elyot must have had some first-hand knowledge of *realpolitik*. And at the centre of his work, one discovers a vision of a stable, hierarchical order which although at first resembling the ideal order envisaged by the Neo-Platonists, quickly if obliquely reveals an application all too well suited to an absolutist regime. Famously, Elyot requires his reader to contemplate the order and observable degree of all things in the Universe:

> In everything is order; and without order may be nothing stable or perma-
> nent; and it may not be called order except it do contain in it degrees, high
> and base, according to the merit or estimation of the thing that is ordered.
> Now to return to the estate of mankind, for whose use all the said creatures
> were ordained of God, and also excelleth them all by prerogative of knowl-
> edge and wisdom, it seemeth that in him should be no less providence of God
> declared than in the inferior creatures but rather with a more perfect order and
> disposition. And therefore it appeareth that God giveth not to every man like
> gifts of grace or of nature but to some more, some less, as it liketh his divine
> majesty.
>
> (ibid., pp. 44–5)

The passage then concludes with a confident vindication of the princi-ple of reputation or 'estimation' which insists that it is reasonable for just authorities 'to be set in a more high place than the residue, where they may see, and also be seen'.

The implications of Elyot's position are revealed in Shakespeare's *Troilus and Cressida*. For it is this passage which Shakespeare probably used as a source in picturing how the machiavellian Ulysses attempts to make Achilles return to fight against Troy (Act I. iii. 83–124). For Elyot, as for Ulysses, reputation and estimation are the real guarantees of order in this world. Neither Machiavelli nor Castiglione would have disagreed with this view: the Renaissance world in its social aspect is constructed out of opinion. Yet it seems unlikely that Elyot understood what he was saying in this regard. His concern seems to be to project a supposedly natural picture of orderly authority more in keeping with the presuppositions of the Wilton Diptych than, so to say, the dynamic relativities of the mid-sixteenth century.

In a similar way, Elyot roots his perception of order in a homeliness of imagery – as if order could truly be observed everywhere – quite unlike the courtliness of Castiglione's style:

> and where order lacketh, there all thing is odious and uncomely. And that we have daily experience, for the pans and pots garnisheth well the kitchen, and yet should be to the chamber none ornament.
>
> (ibid. p. 47)

There is nothing here of the grace and illuminated abstraction which Castiglione commands when he speaks of 'the indistinct beauty of the highest good which with its light calls and pulls all things to itself beauty' (*Cort.*, IV LXIX). On the other hand, Elyot in such passages does make clear that he is writing not simply for a small Italian court[84] but for the local and provincial esquires who, in a unified country, will play their part in the conduct of national affairs. There is a confidence here of order in all things which, if suspicious to the sophisticated eye – whether Italianate or modern – exactly registers the pretensions of Tudor absolutism.

The same understanding, finally, controls Elyot's celebrated account of dancing, that most courtly of activities offered in Book I of *The Governor* chapters 20 to 22. For while Elyot allows the educative value of this pursuit, dancing for him – as for his descendant – is important because it signifies matrimonie and – 'if you do not come to close' –[85] seems to be as much a part of the muddy field of nature as it is of the court. Dancing itself is an expression of order and, for Elyot, of moral order. Therefore, when we begin to dance we touch the ground three times out of reverence for the Trinity; and in a dance, we see fully the supposedly natural categories of male and female, the male being always 'fierce, hardy and strong' and the woman 'timorous, mild and tractable':

> Wherefore when we behold a man and a woman dancing together, let us suppose there is to be concord of all the said qualities being joined together . . . And in this wise fierceness joined with mildness maketh severity; audacity with timorosity maketh magnanimity; willful opinion and tractability . . . maketh constancy . . . These qualities, in this wise being knit together and signified in the personages of man and woman dancing, do express or set out the figure of very nobility, which, in the higher estate it is contained, the more excellent is the virtue in estimation.
>
> (*Gov.*, pp. 164–5)

84. I am indebted to Virginia Cox for the suggestion that Castiglione – though setting his work in such a court – may from the first have intended to speak to an international audience.

85. T.S. Eliot, *Four Quartets*.

On such a view dancing may be emblematic of virtue – and of prudence (*Cap.*, 22). Yet there is little room for *sprezzatura*:

> Now because there is no pastime to be compared to that wherein may be found both recreation and meditation of virtue, I have, among all honest pastimes wherein is exercise of the body, noted dancing to be of an excellent utility, comprehending in it wonderful figures (or, as the Greeks do call them, *ideae*) of virtues and noble qualities; and especially of the commodious virtue called prudence.

> (ibid.)

A few years later, Sir John Davies in his poem 'Orchestra' (1594) will turn the dance wittily into an image of mystic participation in the cosmic order.[86] Spenser, too, representing the height of Courtesy in Book Six of *The Faerie Queene*, will see the dance as a point of connection between earthly and heavenly order; and the inspiration for this elevated vision will lie in the writings of Pico and Ficino. Elyot himself, for all the stolidity of his own performance, can be credited at least with having introduced the imagery and political seriousness of Italian thought into the cultural soil of England.

---

86. On Davies see James L. Saunders, *Sir John Davies* (Boston, 1975). On dance as a mystic symbol see Frances A. Yates, *The French Academies of the Sixteenth Century* (London, 1947).

Chapter 3

Humanism and Poetry

INTRODUCTION

In *The Arte of English Poesie*, George Puttenham speaks of how 'travellers to Italy tasted the sweet and stately measures of the Italian poesie as novices newly crept out of the schools of Dante, Ariosto and Petrarch'.[1] These words point to an apprenticeship which English writers were eventually to serve in all genres, epic, comic and narrative as well as lyric. It was, however, through lyric poetry that humanism which, initially, concentrated its attention upon classical texts began to contribute actively to the development of vernacular literature. As early as 1426, some enlightened piece of bookmanship had brought a copy of Petrarch's poems to the library of Peterhouse at Cambridge;[2] and though the translation of Petrarch's 'S'amor non è . . . ' in Chaucer's *Troilus and Criseyde* seems not to have set an immediate trend, the poem was much favoured by early sixteenth century poets and in 1582 a later Petrarchan, Thomas Watson, cites Chaucer's version as a precedent when composing his *Hekatompathia*.[3] In the sixteenth century, Petrarch's poetic influence was by no means constant. For instance, it falls into a trough between 1540 and 1580. There were also many English writers

---

1. G.D. Willcock and Alice Walker (eds.) *The Art of English Poesie* (Cambridge, 1936), p. 60.
2. See Einstein, *The Italian Renaissance in England* (New York, 1902), p. 54.
3. See throughout George Watson, *The English Petrarchans: A Critical Bibliography of the Canzoniere* (London, Warburg Institute Surveys III, 1967); J.W. Lever, *The Elizabethan Love Sonnet* (London, 1956); Thomas M. Greene, *The Light in Troy: Imitation and Discovery in Renaissance Poetry* (New Haven and London, 1982); Thomas P. Roche jr., *Petrarch and the English Sonnet Sequence* (New York, 1989); D.G. Rees, 'Italian and Italianate Poetry', in *Elizabethan Poetry*, J.R. Brown and B. Harris (eds.), (London, Stratford-upon-Avon Studies 2, 1960). Anthony Mortimer, *Petrarch Canzoniere in the English Renaissance* (Bergamo, 1975) provides texts of both English and Italian precedents, as does Stephen Minta for both French and English petrarchans in *Petrarch and Petrarchism* (Manchester and New York, 1980).

who would echo Chaucer's suspicion of the 'long-deceased' Petrarch; and, throughout, the native tradition, in regard to metre and diction, would often resist the introduction of Italianate examples. Nevertheless, by the early decades of the sixteenth century in England there were many others who speak, in humanistic vein, of the triumph that literary fame can enjoy over mere mortality. So an anonymous entry in Tottel's *Miscellany* (ed. Rollins I, p. 169) may well end by affirming the superior beauty of his English Lady over Petrarch's Laura; yet he resonantly begins in praise of Petrarch himself as 'head and prince of poets all/whose lively gift of flowing eloquence/well may we seek'.

For Surrey, Petrarch stands as a modern equivalent of Virgil or Cicero;[4] and it was through the influence of Petrarch and other Italian writers, that English poets began to seek an alternative to the diction and forms of verse which they had inherited from Chaucer. Of course, the language of Donne, Marlowe and Shakespeare cannot be explained by reference only to the Italian model. Yet, considering that even the blank verse line – as used in Milton's epic poetry – had its origins in Trissino's experiments at the beginning of the sixteenth century,[5] the stimulus which Italy provided to technical innovation, albeit in the face of resistance, cannot be disregarded.

In Italy itself, the reflection upon technical questions which Petrarch had initiated and which was subsequently encouraged by the emphasis given by humanists to literary study, began to display itself in the development of theoretical as well as practical considerations of literary form. Critics such as Scaliger (1484-1525) and Castelvetro (1505-71)[6] were to provide the foundation for the literary criticism of Puttenham, Fraunce and Sidney.[7] In its theoretical form this critical movement owed much to the rediscovery of Aristotle's *Poetics*. But at the outset, the debate was located – at a point of intersection between literary, linguistic and social concerns – in the Italian *Questione della lingua*, which concerned the appropriate form for written Italian throughout the peninsula. A tendency to academicism began here, and found no exact equivalent in England. But Sir Thomas Elyot is one among several thinkers who seems to have been influenced by this debate as it appears

4. See Emrys Jones, *Henry Howard Earl of Surrey: Poems* (Oxford, 1964), pp. xx–xxi.
5. See P. and J.C. Bondanella, *Macmillan's Dictionary of Italian Literature* (London, 1979), p. 521.
6. For Castelvetro, see below, pp. 200–1.
7. See Bernard Weinberg, *A History of Literary Criticism in the Italian Renaissance*, 2 vols. (Chicago, 1961).

in Castiglione;[8] and a comparable influence upon literary practice throughout Europe makes the *Questione* worth examining.

On one side of the controversy were figures such as Bembo – who last appeared as a proponent of Neo-Platonic thought in Castiglione's *Cortegiano* –[9] arguing that a literary language must take posterity as its audience and that, seeking an enduring fame, the literary author must write in the prestigious idiom of the Tuscan classics – by which Bembo meant in part Dante, who initiated the debate in *De Vulgari Eloquentia*, but more especially the elevation and polished eloquence of Petrarch and Boccaccio. The other side – represented by, among others, Castiglione himself – was pragmatic, allowing more wide-ranging usage and permitting words to be chosen according to the literary instincts and tastes of the writer.

On the whole, Bembo's school prevailed; and his concern with formal refinement helped to encourage developments of Petrarch's language – often in association with music – in a courtly direction unknown to Petrarch himself.[10] But the sonnet was the main beneficiary of Bembo's victory. The sonnet form had been devised in Sicily in the early thirteenth century, and was originally used in debates about questions of love, for instance in epistolary debates. In Dante's view, the sonnet was greatly inferior to the longer and metrically far more complex *canzone*. Petrarch himself had written *canzoni* – and generally had expressed reservations about the validity of vernacular verse forms, which he describes disparagingly as 'scattered rhymes' in the introduction to his sonnet sequence. But the *petrarchisti* would rarely share these doubts and, alongside the sonnet, confidently developed many other vernacular forms of lyric verse, including madrigals, *frottole*, and *strambotte*.[11]

The poetry of petrarchism is by no means identical in effect or implication to Petrarch's own poetry. Nor is it as static or backward-looking a phenomenon as sometimes it is thought to be. In Italy itself, writers

8. See above, p. 109.
9. See above, pp. 51–60.
10. See John Stevens, *Music and Poetry in the Early Tudor Court* (London, 1961), esp. pp. 280–2.
11. Such forms tended to be of popular origin, refined and polished for courtly use. The basic structure of the *madrigal* was two connected stanzas of three eleven-syllable lines – rhyming ABC ABC – with a final couplet of eleven-syllable lines, rhyming DD. The *frottola* was a form involving wordplay, word-capping and the accumulation of lexical extravagance in a generally irregular metre: a basic pattern is AAB/ BBC/CCD, etc. The *strambotto* was a love poem meant to be set to music. Metrically, it is based on an eight eleven-syllable stanza, rhyming (in Sicily) ABABABAB, or (in Tuscany) ABABCCDD. Six-line variants can be found.

who were not Tuscan began to appear such as the Neapolitan Sannazaro,[12] while the Florentine Michelangelo could resort in the diction of his *rime* to his much admired Dante as well as to Petrarch.[13] In an extreme form, reactions in Italy as well as in England could lead to an anti-petrarchism represented, for instance, by Aretino, who will appear later as an author whom Wyatt consulted. Yet petrarchism had become so deep-rooted that the language in which the anti-Petrarchan position was voiced was frequently that of Petrarch himself. In any case, Petrarch's example was powerful enough to generate divergent developments, whereby some poets, such as Cariteo, pursued the moderate and restrained line of Bembo, while others, such as Serafino,[14] developed a latent vein of extravagance in the Petrarchan conceit, which allowed, for instance, that figures and tropes – fires, bonds and arrows – should be treated as if they were literal references.[15] Other important developments involve the heroic sonnets of Della Casa and Tasso.[16] Historians – and some contemporaries, too – may at times speak of petrarchism as a 'psychotic epidemic' which spread a contagion of 'icy fire' throughout Europe.[17] But such judgements should not obscure the originality and diversity of petrarchism itself, nor lead one to suppose that petrarchism invariably obliterated the spiritual and moral discoveries which lay at the heart of Petrarch's own poetry.[18]

However complex petrarchism might prove to be, the need for tech-

12. See below, pp. 145–54.
13. For a translation of Michelangelo's poetry see J. Tusiani, *The Complete Poems of Michelangelo* (London, 1961). On his poetry R.J. Clements, *The Poetry of Michelangelo* (London, 1966). See also C.J. Ryan (Edinburgh, forthcoming) and new translation in an Everyman edition.
14. Cariteo was the academic nickname of Benedetto Gareth (born ?1450 Barcelona, died Naples 1514), who was a court poet to the Aragonese rulers of Naples. Serafino (1466–1500) was a singer, lutanist, composer and poet who died in the service of Cesare Borgia.
15. It is this development which allows Donald Guss in his excellent *John Donne, Petrarchist* (Detroit, 1966) to claim that Donne descends from a Petrarchan line. There is unfortunately no space to pursue this suggestion in the present volume.
16. On the influence which this form had on Spenser and Milton see, respectively, J.R. Lever, *The Elizabethan Love Sonnet* (London, 1956), pp. 92–138, and F.T. Prince, *The Italian Element in Milton's Verse* (Oxford, 1954).
17. Leonard Forster, *The Icy Fire: Five Studies in European Petrarchism* (Cambridge, 1969), p. 61. See also Bruno's dedication of the *Eroici furori* to Sidney.
18. An important feature in the development of Petrarchism is the great wealth of commentaries that went with the movement from manuscript to printed book: an excellent discussion is contained in Roche, op.cit., pp. 000. In the commentary of Velutello, for instance, it is notable that emphasis is given to the historicity of Petrarchan's experience rather than to the moral and spiritual dimensions of his writing. See also P. Thompson, 'Wyatt and the Petrarchan Commentator', *Review of English Studies*, (1959), pp. 225–33.

nical schooling in vernacular verse can at once be illustrated by placing a poem which Bembo discussed with admiration in his *Prose della volgar lingua* (Venice, 1525) alongside an English version from Tottel's *Miscellany*:[19]

Voi ch'ascoltate in rime sparse il suono
di quei sospiri ond'io nudriva 'l core
in sul mio primo giovenile errore
quand'era in parte altr'uomo da quel ch'i'sono,
del vario stile in ch'io piango et ragiono
fra le vane speranze e 'l van dolore,
ove sia chi per prova intenda amore,
spero trovar pietà, non che perdono.
Ma ben veggio or sí come al popolo tutto
favola fui gran tempo, onde sovente
di me medesmo meco mi vergogno;
et del mio vaneggiar vergogna è 'l frutto,
e 'l pentersi, e 'l conoscer chiaramente
che quanto piace al mondo è breve sogno.

                                                    (*RS*, I)

(You who hear in scattered rhymes the sound of those sighs that were my heart's food at the time when I first went astray in youth, when in part I was another man from what I am now: for the varied style of my weeping and speaking, varying between vain hopes and vain sorrow, where there is any one who knows by experience what love is, I hope to find both pity and pardon. But now I see how for long I was the talk of the crowd, so that often I am filled with shame at myself, which shame is the fruit of folly, and repentance, and the clear knowledge that all that gives pleasure in this world is a brief dream.)

You that in play peruse my plaint and read in rhyme the smart,
Which in my youth with sighs full cold I harboured in my hart,
Know ye that love in that frail age, drave me to that distress,
When I was half an other man, then I am now to guess.
Then for this work of wavering words where I now rage, now rue,
Tossed in the toys of troublous love, as cares or comfort grew,
I trust with you that loves affaires by proof have put in ure:
Not onely pardon in my plaint, but pities to procure.

---

19. References to Tottel's *Miscellany* are to the revised edition by Hyder Edward Rollins (Cambridge, Mass., 1965), 2 vols. See also Rollins' edition of *The Phoenix Nest* (Cambridge, Mass., 1931).

For now I wot that in the world a wonder have I be,
And where too long love made me blinde, too late shame makes me see.
Thus of my fault shame is the fruite, and for my youth thus passed
Repentance is my recompence, and this I learne at last.
Looke what the world hath most in price, as sure it is to keep,
As is the dream which fancy drives, while sense and reason sleep.

(Tottel, ed. Rollins I, p. 219)

The comparison at once reveals areas where – particularly in regard to 'pure verbality', in 'balance, parallelism, antithesis and pleasurable asymmetry' –[20] English had a good deal to learn from Petrarch. Classical literature could teach some of this. But in place of the periodic Latin sentence, Petrarch achieves a liberation of vernacular resources, showing a great sensitivity to the interplay between syntax, caesura, and rhythm, to the variations introduced by enjambment and to the contrasts that are possible in a sonnet between the octet and the sestet. Through the rhyme scheme, 'core' here is suggestively associated with 'errore', while even the plain word 'sono' ('I am') rhymes with 'suono' ('sound') to raise a haunting suggestion that the self of the poet is, after all, no more than a sound. Alliterations and variations in Petrarch do not merely create aesthetic and organisational patterns but also produce an insistent emphasis upon notions of shame and self-hood. So 'Ma' – 'but' – introducing the sestet also introduces a change of emotional focus, from the pity evoked in public to the inner pain and recrimination that the poet himself must feel. Then finally syntax, enjambment and verse form conspire to produce – as so often in Petrarch – a painfully shaded and inconclusive last line: knowledge is achieved, and clear knowledge at that, but as the line break articulates the sentence – preparing for the conclusive dependent clause – so it introduces an ironic emphasis whereby the knowledge attained is seen to be the knowledge of how all human attainment in art or intellect is no more than a brief dream.

In technical terms, the English translation fails at all these points. Yet in regard to theme and thought, this version also takes serious account of the penitential purposes of the original; and in that regard it is truer to Petrarch than many which treat their exemplar simply as a love poet. The simplicity of the translator's language underlines a concern – always present in Petrarch's own poetry – over the Christian implica-

20. Emrys Jones, op.cit., p. xvii.

tions of words such as 'shame' and even 'love' itself which the lover might also employ to express a sexual experience. For Petrarch, indeed, the very effects of beauty which he seeks in his own poetry can be a source of spiritual recrimination. And while for most petrarchans the linguistic and aesthetic brilliance of Petrarch's poetry seems to have disguised this aspect of his work, the conflicts are always likely to surface when a translator treats the language of desire – of will, choice and mental direction – with the austerity that Petrarch himself can command.[21] Shakespeare might eventually pun in his sonnets on the sexual implications of the word 'will'; but a petrarchan who understood Petrarch's own Christian purposes might well be acutely aware of the moral implications hidden beneath the sexual surface. Thus, in a rather brutal form, the protestant Harington – whose son will appear in the next chapter as the translator of the *Orlando Furioso* – finds a sectarian and even political ally in Petrarch when he identifies Petrarch's 'Fiamma dal ciel su le tue treccie piove' (*Rime Sparse*, CXXXVI) as a virulent attack on the idolatry of the Catholic Church, the 'Whore of Babylon':[22]

> Vengeance must fall on thee, thou filthy whore
> Of Babylon, thou breaker of Christ's fold,
> That from acorns and from the water cold
> Art rich become with making many poor.

The danger of idolatry is constantly acknowledged in Petrarch's poetry alongside his equally constant devotion to the beauty and dignity that can be discerned in the products of human nature and human art. That devotion itself would inspire considerable confidence in subsequent writers of the High Renaissance, particularly when it was associated with the development of Neo-Platonic philosophy which also, as we have seen, placed a high value on beauty; and connoisseurs of art and of courtly performance would quickly adopt words such as 'grace' to their particular secular uses. But more attentive writers were

21. See the Hill MS translation of *Rime Sparse*, CCCLXV, Mortimer p. 105, as an example of penitential petrarchism.
22. George Watson insists that one should view Petrarch as a Catholic, especially in his devotion to the sainthood of Laura, which is stressed, after her death, in the second half of the *Rime Sparse*. These elements are there especially in the second half of the book, but they did not deter Protestant thinkers from finding merit in Petrarch's artistic achivements and anti-papal polemic. See David Norbrooke, *Poetry and Politics in The English Renaissance* (London, 1984).

also able to discover the tensions inherent in Petrarch's initial project, as for instance Michelangelo whose petrarchanism is part of his terrible wrestle with material nature.[23] In England too there could be a development of the Neo-Platonic themes intrinsic to the Petrarchan position, as for instance in the opening of Spenser's *Hymne of Heavenly Beauty*:[24]

> Rapt with the rage of mine own ravisht thought,
> Through contemplation of those goodly sights,
> And glorious images in heaven wrought,
> Whose wondrous beauty breathing sweet delights,
> Do kindle love in high conceited sprights:
> I fain to tell the things that I behold,
> But feel my wits to fail, and tongue to fold.

Yet the petrarchan movement had acquired by Spenser's time implications – and indeed applications in the practical sphere – which Petrarch could certainly not have foreseen. One of these is the concern with legitimate and married love which Spenser pursues in the *Epithalamion* and the *Amoretti*. Another was to be the political aspect, which Sidney would appreciate more keenly perhaps than Spenser. For in the age of Elizabeth it became impossible to separate the cult of the Lady from the cult of the Queen herself. The courtly game, played according to rules which petrachism had developed, became a matter of policy. Thus, whether in projecting marriages or by insisting upon her unique virginity, the Queen made consistent use of the imagery of love poetry:[25] the white and red roses of York and Lancaster meet in her countenance and the moral interest which Petrarch took in the Lady's purity, pity or 'daunger' became matters of political moment.[26] Not that this was new. The court of Elizabeth's father, Henry VIII, had also brought politics and sexuality violently together, and the neo-feudalism of Elizabeth's policies only served to enlist the aesthetic

23. David Summers, *Michaelangelo and the Language of Art*, op.cit., p. 108.
24. See above, p. 96.
25. See Leonard Forster, 'The Political Petrarchism of the Virgin Queen', *The Icy Fire* op.cit., pp. 122–47.
26. Conversely, the Counter-Reformation Church could see the danger of the courtly cult, placing Dante's *Vita nuova* on the Index, see Charles Singleton *Dante's Vita nuova: An Essay on the Vita nuova* (Baltimore, 1977), p. 4. The Church could also see very vividly the political danger in Giordano Bruno's courtly celebration of Elizabeth (see Roche op.cit., p. 118).

surface of petrarchism in the service of this otherwise brutal conjunction.

'The poet who entertains the Queen,' says Puttenham 'must dissemble his conceits as well as his countenance, so that he never speaks as he thinks or thinks as he speaks'.[27] The poet who was a courtier would have learned as much from Castiglione, and would consequently have understood how to use the courtly idiom developed by Petrarch's followers with appropriate *sprezzatura*.

But to those who read Petrarch himself such practices would have led to further problems. Petrarch is profoundly concerned with questions of moral sincerity. Yet this has a particular centrality in his writing because simultaneously he understands that the moral self may be no more than a verbal or social construct: so that where Dante would expect unambiguously to be judged (and seen in his authentic being) by God, Petrarch could, while longing for such authentication, also seek to be judged in regard to the self which his poetry had created by posterity and by those who might bestow on him the laurel crown. Petrarch himself saw the contradictions in his own position. But in the circumstances of a Renaissance court, the issue would become especially acute. On the one hand, the poetic language which the petrarchan employed would be a language of inwardness, resonant with suggestions of spiritual or moral possibility. On the other, this same language would, pragmatically, be a principal means of entry into an arena where eloquence, theatricality of behaviour and the skilful management of courtly convention were the realities of day-to-day life.

In this perspective, the lyric becomes a genre in which the tensions inherent in Renaissance individualism are very fully realised. And two English poets, Wyatt and Sidney, illustrate this particularly well – the one initiating the first sustained period of English petrarchism, the other dealing with the consequences of a later Elizabethan phase. Both Wyatt and Sidney travelled as diplomats to the courts of Italy; both were Protestant in persuasion; both were courtiers, and neither was wholly safe from courtly disappointment, disgrace or peril. In

27. From Puttenham's discussion of the figure of Allegory op.cit., p. 186.

each a self, seeking sovereignty over its own inner nature, enters a social world where self-hood lies in the regard that *others* confer or withhold.

The implications of such a formation are especially clear in Sidney's case. The culture of the Italian courts sharpened his understanding of educational practice, and in England he was the centre of a circle which maintained close links with Italians, including most notably the refugee intellectual Giordano Bruno.[28] Moreover, the myth which grew around him translated into native terms the images of courtliness which had originated in Italy. Yet Sidney was also a Protestant, recommending zealous policies which were not by any means wholly acceptable at Elizabeth's court. He had reason – on the evidence of the *Arcadia* – to interest himself as much in Machiavelli's *realpolitik* as in Castiglione's courtliness. He knew from his experience in presenting *The Lady of May* that the ear of the sovereign could be wilfully obtuse.[29] Even in death the mythic self which had been built around him could be employed for political ends: the ceremonies of his state funeral were timed, it seems, to distract attention from the execution of Mary Queen of Scots.

In Wyatt such contradictions are both more brutal and more subtle. Surrey, writing an epitaph, could celebrate Wyatt's *virtus* in terms which drew both upon classical Rome and upon perceptions of Renaissance sophistication: 'whose courteous talk to virtue did enflame' (l. 18); 'a valiant corps, where force and beauty met' (l. 29) (Jones op.cit., p. 27). Yet the realities of Wyatt's association with Ann Boleyn, both as a member of her protestant party and as a victim of court intrigue, placed him at the centre Henry's sexual politics. And at that centre, he concerns himself in his poetry repeatedly, if confusedly, with 'trouthe', as if poetic making could provide a direction which the agitations of court life had obscured.

28. For Bruno see below, p. 201 and pp. 211–15. Also for Sidney's association with Lodovico Briskett and wider experience of Italy, see John Buxton, *Sir Philip Sidney and the English Renaissance*, 3rd edn. (London, 1987).
29. See discussion in A.C. Hamilton, *Sir Philip Sidney* op.cit.

WYATT, PETRARCH, ALAMANNI AND ARETINO

Wyatt translates or refashions some sixteen of Petrarch's sonnets.[30] His interest in poetic experimentation is well attested; and this interest led him to introduce into English almost twice as many new verse forms as Surrey attempted. Yet for Wyatt, sonnet-writing was itself a highly experimental venture, in regard to theme as well as form. Significantly, the wide diffusion of petrarchism coincided with the revolutionary introduction of printed books; and throughout Europe commentators and critics had begun to recognise the technical and linguistic advances that might be made in poetry through attention to the sonnet.[31] Wyatt, then, would not have needed to adopt any deliberately anti-petrarchan stance to demonstrate his originality (and in any case it would be anachronistic to suppose that a desire for originality were an essential component in his poetic constitution).[32] Of course, on a number of fronts, both technical and thematic, Wyatt does break new ground. He is already aware (as were some Italians) of the absurdity of formulaic petrarchism, as in his parodic treatment of contrary passions of love in the song: 'Of hete and cold when I complain' (Wyatt, CXIII). In a similarly sceptical vein, Wyatt allows no ideal mistress to appear in his poems but rather portrays the day-to-day strains which the lover himself experiences in a highly charged erotic environment: 'it is because I have no other way/To cloak my care but under sport and play'.[33] In technical terms also, Wyatt may be thought to have attempted – knowingly or otherwise – a reconciliation of Italian metrical patterns with the native English tradition. He certainly did develop a form of the sonnet which replaced the usual octet/sestet divisions of the Italian with a structure of three quatrains and a couplet; and this structure, in combination with a diction which has little of the evasiveness of Petrarch's refined style, could lead to emphatic

30. For Wyatt see editions by K. Muir and P. Thompson, *Collected Poems of Sir Thomas Wyatt* (Liverpool, 1969), and R.A. Rebholz, *Sir Thomas Wyatt: The Complete Poems* (New Haven, 1981) quoted here from the Penguin edition of 1978; H.A. Mason, *Humanism and Poetry in the Early Tudor Period* (London, 1959); Patricia Thomson, *Sir Thomas Wyatt and his Background* (Stanford, 1964); John Kerrigan, *Essays and Studies*, n.s.(1981); Daniel Javitch op.cit.; S. Baldi, *La poesia di Sir Thomas Wyatt*, translated as *Sir Thomas Wyatt* by F.T Prince (London, New York, 1959); D.L. Guss, 'Wyatt's Petrarchism', *Huntington Library Quarterly* (xxix), 1965, 1–15.
31. See Roche op.cit., pp. 70–96.
32. Though Petrarch himself does seem to have suffered a certain 'anxiety of influence' in his dealings with Dante, whose works he would not allow to stand on his bookshelf. See *Seniles*, XVII 3 and XVII 4.
33. See the opening poem, l. 14, in the Rebholz ed., p. 76.

effects of closure in the last two lines of his sonnets, as in the example of
XIII which – translating Petrarch's *Rime Sparse*, CCXXIV – also displays
a high degree of resistance to courtly niceties:

> If burning afar off and freezing near
> Are cause that by love myself I destroy
> Yours is the fault and mine the great annoy.[34]

Given that such divergences do exist, it is possible to argue that
Wyatt is at his best when his poems are read as a conscious and often
sympathetic counterpoint against Petrarch's original.[35] Sometimes this
counterpoint reveals violent departure. Yet there is also a case for examining those poems in which Wyatt remains closest, as a translator, to his
source. From an Italian point of view, a number of these translations
reveal considerable inadequacies; and there can be no question of comparing Wyatt and Petrarch in terms of intellectual scope and intensity of
thought. Yet Wyatt himself may be thought to have recognised not
only the value of a close technical attention to Petrarch's text but also a
certain kinship in regard to the thought and ethical field that Petrarch
had opened up.

An example is Wyatt's version of Petrarch's *Rime Sparse*, XIX. Here
Wyatt is generally thought to have made considerable advances in the
handling of the five-foot iambic line. But it is notable that he has also
read closely enough to identify an unusual feature in Petrarch's sonnet,
which allows the eighth line to be a transitional line. Quoting from line
7, one sees that Wyatt accentuates this possibility but also goes on to
engage directly with the thought of the original:

> Ch'i' non son forte ad aspettar la luce
> di questa donna, e non so fare schermi
> di luoghi tenebrosi o d'ore tarde;
> però con gli occhi lagrimosi e 'nfermi
> mio destino a vederla mi conduce,
> e so ben ch'io vo dietro a quel che m'arde.
>
> (*RS*, XIX. 8–14)

(For I am not so strong that I can look upon the light of this lady; and I do
not know how to make screen of shadowy places and late hours. Therefore,
with tearful and feeble eyes, my destiny leads me to see her; and I know well
that I follow that which burns me.)

---

34. References here and throughout are to Rebolz's edition.
35. Cf. A.C. Spearing, *Medieval to Renaissance in English Poetry*, (Cambridge, 1985),
    p. 304, who also allows that Wyatt can at times 'ravish' the Petrarchan text.

Alas, of that sort I may be by right
For to withstand her look I am not able
And yet can I not hide me in no dark place,
Remembrance so followeth me of that face.
So that with teary eyen, swollen and unstable,
My destiny to behold her doth me lead,
Yet do I know I run into the gleed.

(Wyatt, XV. 8–14)

Here more important than the minimal differences between, say, 'm'arde' and 'run into the gleed' is the fact that Wyatt accurately follows Petrarch in representing a profound psychological and moral contradiction: both poets might seek the darkness, in terror at a face which manifests a light which they dare not aspire to, yet neither has any other point of stability than the light which they desire both to see and to hide from.

It is worth asking here, as in many comparable cases, whether the experience being described is in any simple sense an experience of love. Tottel has no doubt that Petrarch and Wyatt are writing love poems, introducing the poems with tags such as 'How the lover perisheth in his delight, as the fly in the fire' or 'Description of the contrarious passions in a lover.' Yet in the lines above, the love language could easily be seen as a metaphorical expression of a religious experience at witnessing God's gaze, or even, for that matter, the gaze of an earthly monarch. It is indeed the polyvalency of the language which is itself at the heart of the experience in both poets: desires and self-contradictions are expressed in a language that allows and suggests in equal measure an erotic, a religious and a political application. The inwardness of the poet is at the mercy of the very terms in which he attempts to chart his own interiority.

It follows that in both Petrarch and Wyatt there is a strangely anonymous egotism, whereby the investigation of the self is always likely to result in the evaporation of any clear understanding of that self. From its origins, the sonnet generated comparable attitudes in its author whose interest was directed inward upon his own psychological condition and often, simultaneously, upon his own artistic prowess, while raising questions and even doubts on both fronts.[36] (Cavalcanti is an extreme

---

36. This can be observed in the earliest Sicilian sonnets as also in poems by Dante's contemporary Guido Cavalcanti which are much concerned with the problems of perception and the relation of the inner image to the outer reality.

example, Dante an exception.) Thus Wyatt is constantly concerned with a 'trouthe' which, unsupported by any systematically philosophical sense, is ambiguously poised between sexual fidelity, political loyalty, honour and penitential humility.[37] Chaucer had thought hard about the implications of the English word, seeking, as we have seen in the Franklin's Tale, a definition which pointed to the integrity of the individual rather than the claims of rational system.[38] But it was Petrarch who – while rarely using any equivalent word – first began to prise 'trouthe' away from its systematic anchorage; and it is he who bequeaths to his followers the ever-shifting language in which at best a new definition of 'trouthe' will be achieved and, at worst, the vacancy of the unsupported self will be revealed anew.

Two of Wyatt's best-known poems, 'I find no peace . . . ' (XVII) and 'My galley charged with forgetfulness . . . ', (XIX) demonstrate the degree to which he followed Petrarch into this same dangerous area of self-contradiction – and how in doing so he was no more content than Petrarch with merely formal contraries in phrase and expression:

Petrarch had written:

Pace no trovo et no ò da far guerra,
e temo e spero, et ardo et son un giacco
et volo sopra 'l cielo giaccio in terra,
et nulla stringe et tutto 'l mondo abbraccio.
Tal m'à in pregion che non m'apre né serra,
né per suo mi ritien né scioglie il laccio,
et non m'ancide Amore et non mi sferra,
né mi vuol vivo né mi trae d'impaccio.e
Veggio senza occhi, et non ò lingua et grido
et bramo di perir et cheggio aita,
et ò in odio me stesso et amo altrui.
Pascomi di dolor, piangendo rido
egualmente mi spiace morte et vita.
In questo stato son, Donna per vui
(*RS*, XVIII)

(I find no peace and have no war to make; I fear and hope and burn and I am ice; and I fly above the heavens and lie on the ground; and I grasp nothing and embrace all the world. A certain one has me in prison who neither opens nor locks, nor keeps me for his own not releases the bonds; and Love does not slay me and does not unchain me and neither wishes me alive nor

37. Compare Spearing, op.cit., p. 292.
38. See above, pp. 62–7.

frees me from entanglement. I see without eyes and I have no tongue and I scream; and I yearn to perish and I ask for help; and I hate myself and I love another. I feed on pain and weeping I laugh; to me death and life are in equal measure distasteful. In this state, Lady I am because of you.)

Wyatt follows closely with:[39]

I find no peace and all my war is done.
I fear and hope, I burn and freeze like ice.
I fly above the wind yet I cannot arise.
And naught I have and all the world I seize on.
That looseth nor locketh, holdeth me in prison
And holdeth me not, yet can I scape no wise;
Nor letteth me live nor die at my device
And yet of death it giveth me occasion.
Withouten eyen I see and without tongue I plain.
I desire to perish and yet I ask health.
I love another and thus I hate myself.
I feed me in sorrow and laugh in all my pain.
Likewise displeaseth me both death and life,
And my delight is causer of this strife.

(Wyatt, XVII)

The most notable feature of Petrarch's poem is its looseness in the syntactical construction of contraries. 'And' is the most important word here, as the list of mutually self-contradictory states is enumerated without direction or logic. Even the 'yet' which Wyatt introduces suggests a degree of authorial calculation and an emphasis upon consequence and contrast, where, in Petrarch, the discontinuous list produces an effect of numb apathy – or *accidia*. It is equally noticeable that Petrarch relies here on an emphatic sequence of verbs and yet does not allow any of these verbs to suggest that actions are purposeful or directed towards goals and predictable objectives. The first quatrain concentrates upon the subject of these actions, the 'io', while the second is devoted to the actions of a force, mysteriously unnamed and indefinite, which now acts upon that erstwhile subject. And this is an effect which Wyatt renders very successfully with his unspecified agent, 'That . . . '. In the sestet Petrarch returns to the 'io', with verbs which are balanced in frustrated poise around a central caesura, an effect which is smudged in Wyatt's poem

---

39. The scanty reference in Muir and Thomson to the 'much used' motif of contraries does no justice to Petrarch's poem, op.cit., p. 286. Greene, *The Light in Troy,* op.cit., p. 255, is particularly good at seeing (following Freccero, *Diacritics*, op.cit.) 'the threat of collapsing reference' in Petrarch, which in Wyatt 'yields to a different semiotic threat, the collapse of traditional principled relationships'.

by a use of 'thus' to establish the consequence which is so painfully missing in Petrarch. Two states are present here, one is a state of desire the other of utter emptiness, so that the verticality of flight which might lead Petrarch 'above the heavens', is simultaneously a horizontal embrace which grasping 'all the world' grasps nothing. The result is a discovery of logical inarticulacy in which the tongue can voice nothing save its own muteness.

If there is a fault in the English version it is that Wyatt has over-constructed his translation. Even in verse-structure he is more rigid than Petrarch. Notably, Petrarch uses here the ABAB quatrain whereas Wyatt has adopted the more demanding and (for Petrarch himself more usual) ABBA. So, too, Wyatt's couplet conclusion is more emphatically defined than is justified by the subtle unresolvedness which Petrarch here produces. Wyatt's 'strife:life' rhyme threatens to become formulaic, and certainly does not capture the complications of praise and blame which Petrarch voices, or the concentration on the verb 'to be', which gives a stark existential edge to Petrarch's conclusion. Yet Wyatt has clearly sought, and found, in Petrarch's poem a text which does voice for him the otherwise unvoiceable depths of contradictions in the self.

A less successful poem (though its reputation among English readers suggests otherwise) is 'My Galley charged with forgetfulness'. The shortcomings here are in part technical, but also arise from an interest in – though failure to grasp – the full implications of Petrarch's moral argument. This failure is compounded by Wyatt's inability to see the connection between this sonnet and the sonnet which immediately follows it in the *Rime Sparse*, 'Una candida cerva . . . ', which Wyatt adapts to quite distinct – if very forceful – effect in 'Whoso list to hunt . . . '.

Passa la nave mia colma d'oblio
per aspro mare a mexzza notte il verno
enfra Scilla et Caribdi, et al governo
siede 'l signore anzi 'l nemico mio;
à ciascun remo un penser pronto et rio
che la tempesta e 'l fin par ch'abbi a scherno;
la vela rompe un vento umido eterno
di sospir, di speranze et di desio;
pioggia di lagrimar, nebbia di sdegni
bagni et rallenta le già stanche sarte
che son d'error con ignoranzia attorto.
Celansi i duo miei dolci usati segni.
morta fra l'onde è la ragion et l'arte

tal ch'incomincio a desperar del porto.

(*RS*, CXC)

(My ship loaded with oblivion passes through a harsh sea, at midnight in
winter, between Scylla and Charybdis, and at the helm sits my lord or rather
my enemy. At every oar is a thought alert and cruel that seems to despise the
storm and the goal; a wet, unchanging wind of sighs, hopes and desires
breaks the sail; a rain of weeping, a mist of disdain dampens and loosens the
wearied sails which are made of error and twisted out of ignorance. My two
accustomed stars are hidden; dead among the waves are reason and skill, so
that I begin to despair of the port.)

My galley charged with forgetfulness
Thorough sharp seas in winter nights doth pass
'Tween rock and rock; and eke mine enemy, alas,
That is my lord, steereth with cruelness;
And every oar a thought in readiness
As though that death were light in such a case.
An endless wind doth tear the sail apace
Of forced sighs and trusty fearfulness.
A rain of tears, a cloud of dark disdain
Hath done the wearied cords great hinderance,
Wreathed with error and eke with ignorance.
The stars be hid that led me to this pain.
Drowned is reason that should me comfort
And I remain despairing of the port.

(Wyatt, XIX)

Internally, the modulations of phonetic pattern which Petrarch achieves
– as in line 1 between 'a' and 'o' – have no counterpart in Wyatt, nor
do the variations which arise in Petrarch's poem from the use of
enjambment and caesura; Wyatt's rhymes are comparatively crass and
repetitive, as is the repeated metric filler 'eke'. Similarly, Wyatt's poem
does not reflect the structural articulation of Petrarch's in regard to the
development of imagery and the resolution of the sonnet: Petrarch
contrives a sinister effect of double-take by reserving until line four the
revelation that the supposed lord – a commanding figure at the helm –
is in fact an *enemy*, with a passenger wholly at his mercy. Wyatt throws
this effect away by inverting the sequence of references and making no
use of the line-ending to create suspense. Finally, Petrarch produces,
once more, an agonisingly open ending, as he emphatically 'begins' to
despair of the port – pointing to a process which will continue into the
silence after the end of the poem – where Wyatt resolves with a

reiteration ('I remain') of the state which he has been exploring.

These technical confusions reflect a very tentative understanding of Petrarch's theme. By replacing '*fin*' – 'goal', 'defining purpose' – with 'death', Wyatt substitutes an obvious emotional flourish for the phrase which, in Petrarch, accurately points to the moral root of his condition of aimlessness: the mind in Petrarch's poem is not simply in the grip of contrarious passions; it is thwarting itself by a perverse refusal to focus upon any distinct goal or 'port'. The tragedy is the tragedy of a mind which is in the grip not of passions but of reckless thought. In this sense, the condition is indeed one of error and ignorance, where the practical skills which would enable the subject to discern its true direction have been lost or even perversely abandoned. But if Wyatt appreciates some of these implications, he still fails to produce the intensely powerful image – 'attorto' – which suggests how the two negative states of intellectual error and of plain ignorance are bound together in rope-like skeins, one against the other.

It would be consistent with such deficiencies in reading 'Passa la nave mia . . . ' that Wyatt should not have recognised how in 'Una candida cerva . . . ', Petrarch envisages a moment which reverses the condition of the previous poem, portraying the direction and satisfaction which the mind may enjoy in contemplating an object of beauty. The sonnet begins:

> Una candida cerva sopra l'erba
> verde m'apparve con duo corna d'oro,
> fra due riviere all'ombra duna alloro
> levandio 'l sole a la stagione acerba.
> (RS, CXC)

(A white doe on the green grass appeared to me, with two golden horns, between two rivers, in the shade of a laurel, when the sun was rising in the unripe season.)

Here, momentarily, a true end or goal is found in the apparition of a 'candida cerva' which communicates not, as allegory might, any definite meaning but rather a plenitude of orderly possibilities, patterned in significant numbers – 'one' and 'two' and quasi-liturgical colours – 'green', 'white' and 'gold'.

So, too, in the conclusion of the sonnet, references occur to the scene of the Resurrection which, without specifying a Christian interpretation, hold out a momentary epiphanic suggestion that images of beauty in this world may be at one with the truths of the God's redemptive order:

'Nessun mi tocchi' al bel collo d'intorno
scritto avea di dimanti e di topazi,
'Libera farmi al mio Cesare parve.'

('Let no one touch me', she bore written with diamonds and topazes around
her lovely neck. 'It has pleased my Cesar to make me free.')

Here, there is every reason to read Wyatt's poem in counterpoint with
the original. For his poem becomes the more painfully evocative of loss
and misdirection the more it distances itself from Petrarch's visionary
moment. Here there are violent effects of power, working unmistakably, in the sexual realm, as a threatening 'Caesar' – sovereign in both
the political and erotic court – stamps the feminine beauty of the doe
with the ornament of scriptural texts. From the first, the atmosphere of
apprehension, fear, instability and untruth, which such a court must
generate in circumstances where such a displacement might occur, run
through the poem from the first:

Whoso list to hunt, I know where is an hind,
But as for me, alas I may no more.
The vain travail hath wearied me so sore,
I am of them that farthest come behind.
Yet may I by no means my wearied mind
Draw from the dear, but as she fleeth afore
Fainting I follow. I leave off therefore
Sithens in a net I seek to hold the wind.
Who list her hunt, I put him out of doubt,
As well as I may spend his time in vain.
And graven with diamonds in letters plain
There is written her fair neck round about:
Noli me tangere for Caesar's I am,
And wild for to hold though I seem tame.
                              (Wyatt, XI)

For Petrarch, the writing of poetry itself seems able at times to fill as
well to reveal the inner space, and even to establish outwardly –
through the fame it may bring to a crowned poet – some alternative to
the disconcerting gaze of an ungraspable truth. Wyatt does not share (as
Sidney will) Petrarch's self-consciousness about the act of writing. He is,
for instance, entirely able to shift away, in an easy and craftsman-like
fashion, from the *gravitas* of Petrarch himself to the courtly wittiness of a
petrarchan such as Serafino.[40] At the same time, in his *Verse Epistles*

40. As for example in XXII based on a *strambotto* by Serafino.

(1536) and in the *Penitential Psalms* (1536–42) – where he draws respectively on the work of Alamanni and of Aretino – Wyatt's appetite for technical innovation seems again to stimulate a seriousness of moral purpose which leads him to seek in literary pursuits a world secure from the dangers of political existence.

In Alamanni, Wyatt found a literary experimentalist who was also concerned, in the satire which Wyatt imitates, to reveal the hypocrisies of court life and defend the integrity of his own intellectual existence. Luigi Alamanni (1495–1556) was a Florentine aristocrat, committed to the ancient if, by his time, outdated ideals of Florentine liberty. He was also a friend of Machiavelli, and in 1522 had joined a conspiracy against the tyranny of the Medici's in the person of Cardinal Giulio (later Pope Clement VII). When the conspiracy failed Alamanni fled to Venice and was later exiled to France (where it is possible that he met Wyatt), dying as an exile in Provençe. To literary history, Alamanni is known for his verse satires, for his concern with the theory of the epic and for his celebration of rural activity in a version of Virgils *Bucolics*, as well as for certain excursions into the prose novella.[41]

Wyatt in his verse epistle 'Mine own John Poyntz . . .' (Wyatt, CXLIX) alludes directly to one of Alamanni's epistolatory satire. In these works, the Italian can be given credit for reviving the hitherto dormant examples of classical satire. But he also returns to the idiom of Dante, adopting the complex *terza rima* form which Dante had used in the *Commedia* (as had Petrarch in the *Trionfi*). Dante himself – in his far-reaching investigation of moral and spiritual corruption – is never concerned merely with the decadence of courtly manners; nor do the solutions which Dante envisages include the idyllic pastoralism which Alamanni cultivates. But he was, like Alamanni, an exile; and Alamanni, in the elevated rhetoric of his own satirical writings, draws upon imagery which Dante had used to express the day-to-day bitterness of the exile in 'climbing another man's stair' (l. 19) (though this line is omitted by Wyatt). Likewise in his use of the *terza rima*, Alamanni can muster something, at least, of vigour and sharpness of cadence which characterises Dante's voice in the *Commedia*.

Wyatt follows Alamanni closely when, in lines 8–10, he speaks – with aristocratic balance and detachment – of how, while neither scorning nor mocking those 'to whom Fortune hath lent/Charge over us', he nevertheless holds such rulers in lower esteem than do the 'common

---

41. For Alamanni see Einstein, op.cit., pp. 351 and 353. See also D.L. Guss, 'Wyatt, Alamanni and Literary Imitation', *Journal of the Rutgers University Library*, XXVI (1962), pp. 6–13.

sort'. Similarly, he follows Alamanni in his attack on flattery and courtly deviousness. It is significant, however, that Wyatt's emphasis here falls more definitely than Alamanni's on the perversion of language which is involved in courtly practices. Wyatt cannot bring himself to excuse courtly arrogance as mere bluntness of manner nor will he excuse the feigning and double-think which represents 'the lecher [as] a lover' or tyranny as 'the right of a prince's reign': 'I cannot, I! No, no it will not be!' (op.cit., 73).

The point at issue here is a contrast between directness and flattery in speech; and Wyatt's line, with its vigorous colloquial insistence upon the integrity of the 'I', dramatises this point in a way which Alamanni's more literary gestures had not. Where Alamanni deliberately cultivates the literary idiom he derives from the classical and vernacular traditions, Wyatt is more casual and direct: the rhymes of his terzine are less emphatic than in Alamanni and his diction more colloquial. Nevertheless, he seems to have discovered in Alamanni a more incisive style than was to be found in Petrarch's tortured refinements of phrase; and this voice is raised – as is Alamanni's own – in passionate defence of his own moral integrity. For Alamanni writing, literature, and even ink and paper themselves, constitute 'a kingdom and treasure house': 'l mio regno, e 'l mio thesoro/Son gli 'nchiostri & le carte' (l. 76). Wyatt asserts a similar sovereignty, through literature, over himself, Fortune and untruth. But, writing after his release from the Tower in 1536, during a period of rustication in Kent, he deliberately roots this sovereignty in a ground where literature, Christianity and Englishness come together:

> But here I am in Kent and Christendom
> Among the Muses where I read and rhyme.
> (op.cit. 100–1)

In writing the Penitential Psalms (1536–40),[42] Wyatt turned to one of the most original and most paradoxical writers of the Italian Cinquecento, Pietro Aretino (1492–1556), who was known to his contemporaries variously as the scourge of princes, yet also as Anti-Christ, and as a bare-faced pornographer who nevertheless could be described as the 'divine'.[43] Aretino earned his living as a professional writer – among

---

42. See here and below on Wyatt's *Penitential Psalms*, the outstanding essay by Stephen Greenblatt in *Renaissance Self-Fashioning from More to Shakespeare* (Chicago, 1980). Also see Lily B. Campbell, *Divine Poetry and Drama in 16th Century England* (Cambridge, 1959) and Don. M Friedman, 'The Thing in Wyatt's Mind', *Essays in Criticism*, xvi, (1966).

43. On Aretino see James Cleugh, *The Divine Aretino* (London, 1965); also Ralph Roeder, *The Man of the Renaissance* (New York, 1958).

the first of his kind; he was able to comment – with a penetration that the traditional humanist could not match, on the events and achievements of the day. But he also reserved the right to parody, for instance, a work as central to Renaissance court culture as Castiglione's *Cortegiano* in a scabrous version of his own entitled *La Cortegiana*, 'The Courtesan'. Yet it is the same man who can write in tones of perfectly practised courtliness to Henry VIII – 'whose deeds are rightly to be comprehended in the depths of silence'.[44]

Throughout, Aretino's writings display a vertiginous combination of licence, directness of speech and libertarianism; and something close to a theory which might explain this combination emerges when Aretino himself boldly identifies 'nature' as the guiding principle of his art: 'Nature, from whose simplicity I take dictation, has dictated what I write; in fact I imitate only myself'.[45]

It is this same vigorous insistence upon the claims of his own outspoken nature which inspires Aretino's resistance to Petrarchan refinements of phrase, and leads him to cultivate not only a capacity for the cutting phrase but also a zestful breadth in the pursuit of recondite and uncanonical vocabulary. On the other hand, in a letter to Vittoria Colonna, Aretino writes that if he did not have to earn his bread 'he would produce nothing but *Miserere*'s';[46] and it is notable that Wyatt, while he must have understood the anti-Petrarchan implications of Aretino's position, turns explicitly to his religious writings.

Among Aretino's religious works – many of which adopted a violently anti-Lutheran stance – was a prose version of the story – found in the *Second Book of Samuel*, 11–12 – which tells of how King David sent his servant Uriah to death in the forefront of battle, so that he might freely enjoy Bathsheba, Uriah's wife. Admonished for his crime by the prophet Nathan, David repents and records his repentance in the Psalms. Aretino had supplied an account of these events in narrative prose; and it is to this narrative frame that Wyatt turns in writing his own metrical version of the *Penitential Psalms*.

It should be said that Aretino is only one of Wyatt's sources (which also include Zwingli, Campensis, Tyndale and Coverdale) and, regardless of Aretino, there is good reason for Wyatt to have been attracted to the *Penitential Psalms*. Theologically, these psalms, with their awareness of how dependent human beings are upon Divine mercy and grace, can

44. See *Lettere*, Book II. 443.
45. To the Cardinal of Ravenna, *Lettere*, V. 319.
46. *Lettere*, II. 443.

bear a distinctly protestant emphasis; and there is some indication that Wyatt was seeking to introduce such an emphasis into Aretino's text. Politically, too, the story of David and Uriah could easily be taken as a reproof to tyrants who misuse their power in pursuit of erotic caprice. On both fronts Wyatt develops a searching examination of his own position in a court where Henry was a scarcely repentant David and Ann Boleyn was at the centre of a Protestant intelligentsia. Engaging so directly here with questions of power and sexuality, Wyatt discloses a moral vista which includes but extends far beyond the confessional inwardness of his Petrarchan lyrics; and it is Aretino's narrative prose which provides him, technically, with the means to achieve this extension.

The prose of Aretino's narrative is marked by an appetite for abundant visual imagery. Notably, Aretino was himself was a close acquaintance of Titian; and the pictorial imagination which he displays in his *Penitential Psalms* can easily be seen to foreshadow the histrionic richness of Baroque spirituality. His retelling makes much of the cave in which David undergoes repentance – of its volumes, depths, silences and *chiaroscuro* lighting effects – as, for instance, where a ray of light is seen glimmering on the moving strings of David's harp (l. 311). And this cave, too, is a potent image in Wyatt's version. It is a space – both pastoral and penitential – in which the conscience seeks simultaneously to hide from and to commune with God. Responding closely to the detail of Aretino's imagery, Wyatt speaks of the statue-like king, contained within this moral and physical frame, striking his theatrical poses yet also shifting his weight uncomfortably from haunch to haunch.

> Right so David, that seemed in that place
> A marble image of singular reverence
> Carved in the rock with eyes and hands on high,
> Made as by craft to plain to sob to sigh.
> His left foot did on the earth erect
> And just thereby remain'th the t'other knee.
> To his left side his weight he doth direct.
>
> (Wyatt, CLIII. 305–11)

So, too, Wyatt exploits the aural drama of a situation in which resonant spaces of the cave are filled with heartfelt cries: to any who positioned himself at the mouth of the cave, it would have seemed – hearing David's sighs – that 'out of the south/A lukewarm wind brought forth a smoky rain' (op.cit., 414).

This strong sense of scene leads in turn to an accumulation of narrative effects and also visual conceits which Petrarch's poetry could never have provided. So, as David's tears fall silently and unnoticed, Wyatt again follows Aretino in comparing these unregarded tears to blood seeping from the veins of a suicide in a hot bath:

> Down from his eyes a storme of tears descends,
> Without feeling, that trickle on the ground,
> As he that bleeds in baine . . .
>
> (op.cit., 405–7)

In other places, Wyatt takes the initiative and expands further upon Aretino's suggestion: at one point David falls silent and Aretino speaks of how 'in that holy silence his silence seemed to discourse' with the cave in which he had hidden himself. But Wyatt goes further:

> This song ended David did stint his voice,
> And in that while about he with eye
> Did seek the Cave with which withouten noise
> His silence seemed to argue and reply
> Upon this peace, this peace that did rejoice
> The soul with mercy, that mercy so did cry,
> And found mercy and mercy's plentiful hand
> Never denied but where it was withstand.
>
> (op.cit., 293–10)

Despite such moments as this, Wyatt – translating prose into verse – for the most part selects, edits and often intensifies the Italian original. Aretino's narrative voice is expansive and sustained to the point of luxuriating in the scenes it depicts and in the long periodic sentences it utters. Wyatt, within the discipline of metre and verse, pursues effects of conciseness in a way which finally underlines the moral force and purpose of his work. As Surrey implies in his prefatory poem, Wyatt himself is here adopting the admonitory stance of a Nathan aghast at the sins of his sovereign, and his urgent emphatic rhythms are consistent with that stance. At the same time, the lessons he enunciates in the vivid imagery of the poem seem also to be directed inward at his own conscience. The psalms here characterise a mind which is profoundly aware of its own sexual responses, and which also seeks to submerge its own transgressions in submission to a superior being – whether God or King:

> Yielding unto the figure and the frame
> That those fair eyes had in his presence glanced,

The form that love had printed in his breast
He honoreth it as thing off things best.
So that forgot the wisdom and forecast
(Which woe to realms when that these kings doth lack
Forgetting eke God's majesty as fast,
Yea and his own . . .

(op.cit., 13–20)

It is notable that the concluding parenthesis (directing this passage at the failings of Kings) has no counterpart in Aretino. But sovereignty in Wyatt's poem is a conception that extends into the moral life of the individual: 'God's majesty and yea his own'. Wyatt must be writing here as much to himself as to Henry, conscious of the sovereignty which all are bound to exert over their passions and turbulent inner natures. Thus the attitude of submission which he depicts, so far from bearing the often sadistic tone of Aretino's extravagantly free prose, reveals a mentality thoroughly attuned to the images of aboslutism, moral as well as political: the courtier who was forced to submit to imprisonment at the hands of Henry is also now seeking a further imprisonment in the jurisidiction of his own conscience or of God's absolute majesty.

SIDNEY AND PETRARCH

Though Wyatt's example remained accessible in editions of Tottel's *Miscellany*, lyric poets in the third quarter of the sixteenth century in large part reinvented petrarchism. Fashion, in the interim, had shifted away from Petrarch towards poets such as Serafino and Tasso. But in the 1580s a new interest arose which was reflected above all in ambitious attempts to emulate Petrarch in writing not only sonnets but also sequences or collections of lyric verse. These attempts seem to have begun with Thomas Watson in his *Hecatompathia* of 1582. But this was also the year in which Sidney probably started upon *Astrophil and Stella*;[47] and he had already been attempting the highly complex verse

---

47. For Sidney's verse see *The Poems of Sir Philip Sidney*, ed. William A. Ringler jr. (Oxford, 1962); for his *The Countess of Pembroke's Arcadia*, see ed. Maurice Evans (London, 1977); on Sidney see A.C. Hamilton, *Sir Philip Sidney*, op.cit.; also ed. Denis Kay, *Sir Philip Sidney: An Anthology of Modern Criticism* (Oxford, 1987). Janet H. MacArthur, *Critical Contexts of Astrophil and Stella and the Amoretti* (Victoria, BC, 1989).

experiments, which he would later intersperse, on the model provided by Sannazaro with the lyrical narrative of the *Arcadia*.

The English sonnet sequence – exemplified by authors as diverse in kind and quality as Lodge, Constable and Daniel – was the expression no doubt of a growing confidence on the part of English literary tradition, ready now to outdo what Daniel called 'the muse of declined Italy'. Nor is it surprising that a strong anti-Petrarchan note should often be audible in this movement. So, in *Astrophil and Stella* Sidney famously, and with apparent good humour, sets himself apart from

> Those that poor Petrarch's long deceased woes
> With new-born sighs and denizened wit do sing.

These protestations could easily corroborated by lines such as the following, where, in spite of the developments of 'witty petrarchism', the originality of Sidney's verse displays itself in effects of dramatic voice, sensuality of phrase and, in this case, a talent for the risqué pun on 'hell':[48]

> O honied sighs, which from that breast do rise,
> Whose pants do make unspilling cream to flow,
> Wing'd with whose breath, so pleasing Zephyrs blow,
> As refresh the hell where my soul fries.
>
> (*AS*, 100. 5–8)

For all that, Sidney's concern in *Astrophil and Stella* is not so much to deride either Petrarch or Petrarchism but rather to contrast fashion and literary conventions of all kinds with the sincerity and directness of utterance which he consistently claims for himself 'when trembling voice brings forth that I do Stella love' (*AS*, 14). But in Petrarch himself he would have found, as Wyatt did, a recurrent concern with the establishment of an inner language: it is Sidney who speaks of 'a want of inward touch', expressing the desire for a private language pitched, in a morally conflictual area, somewhere between sexual reassurance and conscience.

Petrarch in the introductory sonnet of the *Rime Sparse* already envisaged a language which followed experience so closely as to become itself the sound of sighs, 'weeping and discoursing' simultaneously. Petrarch also knew, however, as well any twentieth-century critic, that sincerity is a problematical notion, particularly when viewed in terms of linguistic utterance. And in this regard he anticipates the extreme self-

---

48. On innuendo see Alan Sinfield, 'Sexual Puns in *Astrophil and Stella*', *Essays in Criticism* (1974), pp. 341–55.

consciousness over the act of writing in its logical and ethical implications, which is evidently a major feature of Sidney's work, whether poetic or critical. Thus when Sidney speaks of 'the footsteps of lost liberty' (*AS*, 2 cf. 46) or of 'glory and shame' being simultaneous in his mind (*AS*, 53), he enters an area of ethical debate which Petrarch had opened with his abiding that love might involve the abdication of free will. Moreover, for Petrarch this ethical problem is indistinguishable from a literary question. The glory he pursues is Laura – the laurel crown and woman – and the guilt he feels is that of having possibly wasted time, in an obsessive pursuit of writing itself that might have been spent better in pursuit of some greater freedom. Petrarch realises in advance of Sidney that the act of writing may intrinsically involve a logical insincerity; and both writers look at times upon the verses they compose not only as a channel for sincere self-expression but also, and contradictorily, as the instruments which fuel both shame and deviant desire, or else associates the writer with the dead conventions of an age long-past. This is painfully apparent in, for instance, Canzone 70 of the *Rime Sparse* when Petrarch, compelled to write in pursuit of his own sincere moment, can only produce a sequence of stanzas culminating in quotations from his predecessors in the vernacular tradition such as Dante, Cavalcanti and Arnaut Daniel. Words here become icons of a lost time; and Sidney re-states the problem when, seeking to make utterance so true that his very ink should run in Stella's name, he is simultaneously forced to recognise that 'Cupid's dart an image is, which for ourselves we carve' (*AS*, 5).

In this perspective, both Sidney and Petrarch dare to consider the possibility of abandoning the dangerous ambiguities of literature for a truer alternative. This alternative in Petrarch's case would be the ever-elusive moment of contemplation; in Sidney's case, the abandonment would tend to lead to the heroic life of action. Yet Sidney can envisage the possibility of a truly penitential withdrawal; and in 'Leave me, O Love', he does indeed utter the palinode which is tacitly present in all of Petrarch's poetry:

> Then farewell world, thy uttermost I see
> Eternal Love maintain thy love in me.
> (*Certain Sonnets*, 32. 13–14)

Here it becomes plain that for Sidney, as for any other thinking petrarchan, the terminology of sexual desire is haunted by, and calls to be translated into, the language of religious truth. It is equally clear that, unlike Dante or Chaucer, Sidney and Petrarch are too deeply rooted in the Renaissance cult of the word to imagine a life which is not a literary life. In neither case can there be any simple distinction of, say, sincerity and rhetoric. And this shows itself particularly in the way that each author deals with questions of fame and of naming. For Petrarch, his true self lay in the self that was carried and fashioned through words: the laurel crown would be a public recognition of that self; an answer to his penitential prayers would have been another. But the problematic cycle begins yet again as soon as one realises that Petrarch's meditation on the name 'Laura' was essential to that construction of self-hood.[49] This name, as we have seen, is treated largely as a fiction in which the woman herself frequently disappears from view; yet the name is also a stimulus, revealing possibilities of 'gold', 'dawn', 'spirit' and permanence in the natural world which would otherwise lie hidden. In Sidney, these issues are if anything more acutely realised than they are in Petrarch. The world he inhabited was one in which convention was itself a reality. Thus 'Philisides' may speak in his poetry of the stars he bears on his armour (*AS*, 104). But in the ritual circumstances of courtly life he probably did wear such armour. At the Elizabethan court, metaphor and fiction would be a day-to-day aspect of reality. Psychologically too, names – and even name-play – are an evident part of a lover's reality; and Sidney's infatuated attempts to find meaning in the name 'Rich' or 'Stella' expresses not merely a desire to play upon conventional figures of speech but also an imagination alive to the realities of the person whom he loves: the apparent insincerity of language reveals an expressive sincerity in which the brilliance of the poet's experience would be truly told.

Questions concerning sincerity and the logical adequacy of language are exacerbated, and extended into other areas, when attention turns from the single sonnet to the sonnet sequence. For in this case the poet will be concerned not simply with the compatibility or otherwise of experience and highly formal utterance but also with those questions of time and temporal extension which inevitably arise when a poet undertakes somehow to sustain both the formal virtuosity of the sonnet and a sequence of experiences over an organised span. Sonnet sequences set out to defeat time by creating monuments of sustained poetic intensity but are also always likely to deliver their author into the grip of mere repetition. Even Shakespeare in such circumstances is driven to ask

49. See above, p. 55.

why his verse is 'barren of new pride' – as if writing an ambitious sequence also increased the awareness of his own dependence upon convention. Dante, too, in the *Vita nuova* is constantly concerned to redefine and move away from the tradition in which he wrote his own earliest poetry, so as to discover a language in which he might properly praise those qualities in Beatrice which could not in his view be expressed in any received language.[50]

It is notable that both Dante and Shakespeare have resources available other than the lyric – whether dramatic or narrative – in which to address the problem of Time. But in this perspective the originality of Petrarch is to attempt a purely lyric mode of construction and, in doing so, to create an aesthetic alternative to natural temporality. In writing 365 poems – with an introduction – he creates, numerologically, an alternative to the days of the year; and far from working sequentially, his poems insist upon patterns of cross-reference which, at one point, might reflect the simultaneity of eternal life, at another, the imprisonment of the mind in its own poetic construction. The originality of Sidney, on the other hand, will be to insist in *Astrophil and Stella* upon narrative progress or historical sequence and indeed to devote his most ambitious efforts to the writing of the narrative *Arcadia*. This is not to deny that there may be a scheme of numerological correspondences in *Astrophil and Stella*.[51] Nor, of course, does the *Arcadia* – which on Sannazaro's model is a *prosimetrum,* combining verse and prose – follow a simple model of narrative sequence. Yet, whether it be in the details of his syntax or the progress of psychological motivations, Sidney displays a concern with the analysis of situations and of responses which could not be expressed through the lyric syntheses that Petrarch's sequence exemplified. Even in *Astrophil and Stella*, the height of infatuation is marked – as it is in Troilus – by the lethargy of days that have been created by lover's own imagination:

> suffering the evils both of the day and night
> While no night is more dark than is my day.
>
> (*AS*, 89)

---

50. Dante combines prose and verse in the *Vita nuova*, writing here – as Boethius did in the *Consolation of Philosophy* – a 'prosimetrum', in which the single moments of insight expressed in verse could be developed in a narrative and discursive form which established, as Petrarch never does, an unambiguous understanding of intellectual goals and spiritual purposes. One can discern a similar dialogue between narrative and lyric in Chaucer's *Troilus and Criseyde*.

51. See Roche, op.cit., and Alistair Fowler, *Triumphal Forms: Structural Patterns in Elizabethan Poetry* (Cambridge, 1970).

Against this there is an appetite for action and for results in Sidney which distinguishes him markedly from Petrarch. In Sannazaro, Sidney will find evidence – as in Petrarch – of similarly acute *accidia*. But here, taking a narrative work as his model, he will freely reformulate Sannazaro's narrative mode in a manner which allows him both to experiment with time and to construct a literary field which satisfies his desire to enter a world of political and military action.

SIDNEY, SANNAZARO AND *ARCADIA*

It was natural that the pastoral form should appeal to the Renaisance mentality. As Frances Yates has written:

> the great forward movements of the Renaissance all derive their . . . vigour from looking backwards. The cyclic view of time as a perpetual movement from pristine golden ages of purity and truth through successive brazen and iron ages still held sway, and the search for truth was thus of necessity a search for the early, the ancient, the original gold . . . [52]

Pastoral, then, is the search for an alternative world which is at once an origin and a 'wish-space'.[53] This search might require the scholarly perusal of ancient texts, but could also involve, as Yates shows, alchemical practices or the training of memory; and myth – understood as the repository of ancient or archetypal wisdom – would always be one of the primary instruments employed in the search.[54] At the same time, the myths cultivated in the pastoral could easily be taken as an expression of the 'landscape of the mind'.[55] In this regard, while the pastoral landscape – constructed in myth and imagination – would be the reflection of an inner world, it would also very frequently be charged with satirical implications: the ideal which the author wished to protect or advocate would be tacitly contrasted with the reality from which the poet sought to escape. So Sidney himself in his discussion of the Virgilian pastoral notes that if one lives 'under hard lords or ravening soldiers', it becomes necessary to communicate 'under the pretty tales of wolves and sheep'.[56]

---

52. From *Giordano Bruno and the Hermetic Tradition* (London, 1964), p. 1.
53. See Harry Levin, *The Myth of the Golden World in the Renaissance* (London, 1969).
54. On Giordano Bruno, see below, p. 201 and pp. 211–15.
55. See R. Cody, *The Landscape of the Mind* (Oxford, 1969).
56. See also Annabel Patterson, 'Under . . . Pretty Tales: Intention in Sidney's *Arcadia*', in Kay, *Sir Philip Sidney* op.cit., pp. 265–85 and also her *Courtship and Interpretation: The Conditions of Writing and Reading in Early Modern England* (Madison, Wisconsin, 1984). Also William Empson, *Some Versions of the Pastoral* (London, Hogarth, 1986).

In Chapter 7, we shall see the uses to which the pastoral could be put by English writers, particularly by the dramatists such as Marston and Fletcher. It is Sidney very often who reveals himself as the primary influence in such cases. But the formulae of the genre had already been established in Sannazaro's *Arcadia* of 1504.[57]

From Virgil and from Petrarch, Sannazaro derived a landscape which lay almost entirely beyond historical time, in a region of longings or lyrical desires, and which differed particularly from the landscapes of Petrarch's *Rime Sparse* in being designed to elicit from its fictional inhabitants – and from the reader – an exclusively aesthetic response. When Petrarch sought solitude he abandoned the precise description of the external world which had characterised Dante's poetry; but the vistas he revealed continued to echo with moral tensions and with an irrepressible desire to achieve the freedom of the contemplative moment. The world which Sannazaro portrays is by no means a solitary world. It is, rather, a world inhabited, and devised, by a community of shepherds, bound together in their pursuit of song and in their capacity to turn all that they experience – whether it be the textures of the fleeces of sheep or the penetrating melancholia of the lover – into the subject of the lyrics which are sung at the end of each day.[58] There is an 'evasion' here not only of the demands of the day-to-day world but also of the demands of any definable ethical purpose or argument.

The consequence is that considerations of atmosphere and tone prevail over considerations of narrative direction. The story, such as it is, tells of the arrival of a love-lorn shepherd Sincero in the refuge of Arcadia, and of the consolations which he experiences by exploring, largely through song, the various phases and aspects of his own exile and emotional estrangement. There is certainly a subtext to this narrative. Sincero is the name that Sannazaro himself was given in his academic circle – following

---

57. Sannazaro was born in Naples in 1457 and died there in 1530. Educated as a humanist, he was subsequently active as an academician in close contact with Prince (from 1496, *King*) Frederick of the Spanish Royal House of Aragon which at this time ruled of Naples. In 1501, political negotiations between France and Spain led to an agreement that they should divide the kingdom. Sannazaro followed King Frederick into exile and remained with him in France until he returned in 1504 to Naples on Frederick's death. As well as writing the *Arcadia,* he composed a set of piscatorial eclogues and *De Partu Virginis.*

58. See throughout David Kalstone's excellent account in *Sidney's Poetry* (Cambridge, Mass., 1965). For a translation of, and useful introduction to, the *Arcadia,* see Ralph Nash, *Jacopo Sannazaro: Arcadia and Piscatorial Eclogues* (Detroit, 1966). For the classical pastoral, see Robin Sowerby, *The Classical Legacy in Renaissance Poetry* (London, 1994).

the derivation of the Hebrew 'nazaro' meaning 'pure' and 'sincere'; and some of the experiences described here clearly relate to Sannazaro's view of the world of Naples, from which, for a short time from 1501 to 1504, he suffered voluntary exile. Particularly in *Prosa*, VII, Sannazaro offers a deeply nostalgic account of Neapolitan history, including a reference, which Elizabethans may have found hard to ignore, to the miseries of a court ruled by a queen, as Naples had been in 1414. But such references have a peculiarly literary ring, being consciously imitated from Boccaccio's celebrations of Naples in early works such as the *Teseida*,[59] and are finally incidental to the pursuit of a mysteriously undefined inwardness. The 'sincerity' of Sincero lies – and the paradox is one to which Sidney may have been especially sensitive – in the cultivation of his own artistic persona. Selfhood in the *Arcadia* seems to be located in the poignant melancholia which the writer or singer – like Keats in the *Ode on Melancholy* – 'gluts' and turns to delight through the processes of imagination. Thus when Sincero speaks of his own unhappy love he uses a Dantean vocabulary but replaces Dante's clean rhythms with a lush self-indulgence:

> Elli mi viene una tristezza di mente incurabile, con una compassione grandis-sima di me stesso mossa da le intime medolle, la qual non mi lascia pelo veruno ne la persona che non mi si arricii.
>
> (*Prosa*, VII)

> (There comes upon me a sadness of a mind beyond all remedy, with pertur-bations of feeling deep within myself which arise from the very marrow of my being, so that there is not a hair on my body which does not bristle.)

In place, too, of Petrarch's moral anguish we have here a new mode of feeling which was certainly to harmonise with the sensibility of the Elizabethan age: Shakespeare's Jacques carries something of it with him into the pastoral world of Arden.

Following from this, Sannazaro's plotless and otherwise disconnected narrative follows a rhythm of the emotion and song, exploring never-theless a range of possibilities from elegy to mystery, from ritualistic gravity to nightmare.

Thus in *Prosa*, III, the shepherds are described passing along a silent path lit by a moon as bright as the sun where the only sound is that of the hoarse cry of pheasants; and yet these brittle interruptions are them-selves a source of delight to the travellers. Then again, the shepherd can

---

59. See above, pp. 67–73.

be led into a nightmarish landscape, so dominated by caves and lakes
that the earth seems to have lost all its natural solidity:

> O wonderful artifice of God that the earth which I though to be so firm
> should enclose in its bosom so great a hollowness (concavità).
>
> *(Prosa*, XII)

Here again again the illusory play in the langauge of the *Arcadia* upon
solidity and emptiness is seen as God–given delight.

But the religious world itself in the *Arcadia* is one that is created by
the imagination and needs to be traced, through a sequence of myths
and rituals, to an ever-receding past. So when Sannazaro describes the
origins of the pastoral life he displays an extraordinary talent for the creation of fictional ceremony which, reflecting as it does the interest of
the early Renaissance in myth, also points forward to the ritual drama of
pastoral plays such as Guarini's *Pastor Fido*.[60] Thus in *Prosa*, X,
Sannazaro offers a sustained account of the mysteries of Pan into which
the shepherd is to be initiated: deep in a cave, hidden by a sacred wood
– where once the pines spoke directly to the poet's ear, and where Pan
was worshipped after the unknown gods had departed – there stands a
great idol, leaning upon his stick, which is an entire olive tree; 'his
horns rise straight to the sky and his face has the brightness of a straw-
berry'. The passage proceeds to recount the history of the pastoral form
from classical times onwards and to describe – at the expense of some
three pages – the rites of initiation into the pastoral cult. The neophyte
will be bathed nine times in the sacred waters; a new altar will be built
where the priest

> will take with his left hand a black lamb by the horns, holding a sharp knife
> in the right and, in a loud voice, utter the three hundred names of the
> unknown gods; and then, invoking Night, Darkness, the silent Stars that are
> sharers in the knowledge of secret things and the many-formed Moon . . . he
> will slit the throat of the lamb . . . and pour the blood mixed with oil and
> milk into a trench . . . so that Mother earth may drink it.
>
> *(Prosa*, X)

There is much, then, in Sannazaro that would have encouraged
Sidney to fashion a world which, in its social and religious apparatus,
was the product of his private imaginings, and which corresponded in
emotional tenor to the increasingly tragic cast of Sidney's mind. Yet
there is also much in Sidney's work which differentiates it from

---

60. See below, pp. 255–76.

Sannazaro's. In combining the pastoral with the epic characteristics of the new *Arcadia*, Sidney uses the world of myth and dream for more conspicuously political ends than Sannazaro would allow; and though his narrative, like Sannazaro's, is haunted by effects of stasis and illusion it nevertheless sets itself to deliver coherent and well-plotted conclusions. Even his lyrical prose differs from Sannazaro's; for where the Italian cultivates a richly varied sensuality, Sidney's prose characteristically sees the natural world in a state of continual debate as physical elements war between themselves or else conspire with the fluctuating desires of the protagonists.[61]

Such similarities and differences can also be seen, finally, in Sidney's response to the verse of Sannazaro's *Arcadia*. Among a number of metrical experiments which Sidney performs,[62] the most ambitious is his rendering of 'Ye Goatherd Gods', Sannazaro's fourth Eclogue, cast in the form of a double sestina.

The double sestina represents an extended version of the simple sestina which is a poem in six stanzas, each stanza being six lines long. There are, apparently, no rhymes in he first stanza of a sestina; and reading any one stanza in isolation would produce something of the effect of blank verse. However, with the second stanza, a number of features emerge which reveal how highly patterned this verse form actually is. Thus, the six words which have occupied the final position in each line of the first stanza are now all repeated, and will be repeated in the 'rhyme position' in all subsequent stanzas. But the order in which these words appear changes from stanza to stanza; and these changes follow – broadly – two main rules. The last 'rhyme word' of any one stanza becomes the first rhyme word of the next, so as to yield a linking rhyme across the stanza-break. At the same time, the remaining rhyme words are progressively displaced according to the following rule: The first rhyme word of one stanza now becomes the second rhyme word of the subsequent stanza; the third line, however, ends with the word that occupied fifth place in the previous stanza, the fourth line ends with the word which had previously been placed second, the fifth with the fourth, and the sixth with the third; yielding 6, 1, 5, 2, 4, 3. The arrangement from stanza to stanza rings changes on all possible permutations of the original position. Thus the 'rhymes' in the first three stanzas of a sestina read: ABCDEF/ FAEBDC/

---

61. See John Carey, 'Structure and Rhetoric in Sidney's *Arcadia*', Denis Kay (ed.), op.cit., p. 247.
62. See especially his use of competitive capping forms akin to the *frottola* in the first eclogues. Cf. *Arcadia*, op.cit., p. 852.

CFDABE, and the same formula governs the shifts in subsequent stanzas. In the case of double sestina (twelve stanzas, sometimes concluding with a coda of three lines ABC) the displacements registered in the first half are repeated in the second.

Historically, the sestina has been long associated with conscious displays of virtuosity. From the first, however, it has also been used to reflect processes – often the cyclical processes of time and nature – and to express the melancholic alienation of the lover from the processes which the poem itself portrays.[63] As Sannazaro would have known, even if Sidney did not, the troubadour poet Arnaut Daniel had used the single sestina in this way to express the characteristic alienation of the lover in winter from the good graces of his Lady. And Dante too, pitting himself against Arnaut, had included a sestina among the highly complicated series of poems to the Stony Lady – the *Donna Petrosa* – where again against a background of winter he depicts the emotional and spiritual aridity which arises from his devotion to a Lady who is herself as unresponsive as rock, 'pietra'. Finally, Petrarch includes a double sestina in the *Rime Sparse*, CCCXXXII, and in Petrarch's hands the sestina characteristically turns inward to inspect the processes of the poet's own moral degeneration. Strikingly, the mid-point in Petrarch's poem is used to mark not a development but a final descent on the poet's part into moral passivity, as words prove incapable of winning Laura – Orpheus-like – back from the grasp of Death.

When Sannazaro takes up the form, he introduces as a further complication the antiphonal voices of two singers, thus adding to the possibilities of development through time the opportunity for dramatic interplay. But, on the whole, these opportunities are not taken. William Empson has spoken of the effects of linguistic stasis which he finds in Sidney's 'Ye gote herde gods . . . ', and his interpretation emphasises the way in which by constant repetition the ambiguous associations of the rhyming words are progressively explored.[64] Yet this reading seems far more directly applicable to Sannazaro's version than to Sidney's. Sannazaro, here as elsewhere in his *Arcadia*, allows temporal pattern to revolve, to purely aesthetic effect, in and around itself without narrative movement, whereas Sidney's virtuosity not only creates dramatic voice but also generates a profound and increasing frustration at the limits of virtuosity itself.

63. See R. Durling in the introduction to his translation of the *Rime Sparse*, op.cit., p. 17; and also see (with Ronald L. Martinez) *Time and the Crystal: Studies in Dante's 'Rime Petrose'* (Berkeley and Oxford, 1990).
64. In *Seven Types of Ambiguity* (London, 1930), pp. 45–50.

To illustrate this distinction in full would require quotation to the tune of some 300 lines. Here there is only the opportunity to draw attention in each case to the six rhyme words which the poets have chosen and then to the dynamics of the central turn, as well as, in Sidney's case, the conclusion:

Sannazaro writes:

> Pastori, uccel nè fiera alberga in valle,
>> che non conosca il suon de le mie rime;
>> nè spelunca o caverna è fra gli sassi,
>> che non rimbombe al mio continuo pianto;
>> nè fior nè erbetta nasce in questi campi,
>> ch'io no la calche mille volte il giorno,

(Shepherds there is no bird or beast that dwells in the *valley* that does not know the harmony of my *rhyme*, nor is there any cave or grotto among the *rocks* that does not echo to my unending *lamentation*. There is no flower or bush which grows in these *fields* that I do not trample over a thousand times a *day*.)

> *Elpino*:   (stanza 6 second half)
>>   . . .
>> et una voce udii per mezzo i sassi
>> dirmi: – Elpino, or s'appressa un lieto giorno,
>> che ti farà cantar più dolci rime.

> *Logisto*:   O fortunato, che con altre rime
>> riconsolar potrai la doglia e 'l pianto!
>> ma io lasso pur vo di giorno in giorno
>> noiando il ciel non che le selve e i campi.

(*Elpino*: And I heard a voice in the middle of the rocks, saying: 'Elpino, now a happy *day* approaches, one that will make you sing far sweeter *rhymes*'.

Logisto: O happy one, that with another rhyme can bring new comfort to the pain and *lamentation*. But I alas go on from day to day, troubling the heavens as well as the woods and *fields*.)

Against this Sidney writes:

> *Strephon*:   Ye gote-herde gods, that love the grassy mountains,
>> Ye nymphs that haunt the springs in pleasant valleys,
>> Ye satyrs joy'd with free and quiet forests,
>> Vouchsafe your silent ears to plaining music,
>> Which to my woes gives still an early morning,
>> And draws the dolour on till weary evening.

Claius: O Mercury, foregoer to the evening,
            O heavenly huntress of the savage mountains,
            O lovely star, entitled of the morning,
            While that my voice doth fill these woeful valleys,
            Vouchsafe your silent ears to plaining music
            Which oft hath Echo tired in secret forests.

Strephon: I that was once free-burgess of the forests,
            Where shade from sun, and sport I sought at evening,
            I that was once esteem'd for pleasant music
            Am banish'd now among the monstrous mountains
            Of huge despair, and foul affliction's valleys,
            Am grown a screech-owl to myself each morning.

Claius: I that was once delighted every morning,
            Hunting the wild inhabitants of forests:
            So darken'd am, that all my day is evening;
            Heart-broken so, that molehills seem high mountains,
            And fill the vales with cries instead of music.

Strephon: Long since, alas, my deadly swannish music
            Hath made itself a crier of the morning:
            And hath with wailing strength climb'd highest mountains.
            Long since my thoughts more desert be than forest:
            Long since I see my joys come to their evening,
            And state thrown down to over-trodden valleys.

Claius: Long since the happy dwellers of these valleys
            Have prayed me leave my strange exclaiming music,
            Which troubles their day's work and joys of evening:
            Long since my thoughts chase me like beasts in forests,
            And make me wish myself laid under mountains.

Strephon: Me seems I see the high and stately mountains
            Transform themselves to low dejected valleys:
            Me seems I hear in these ill-changed forests,
            The Nightingale do learn of Owls their music;
            Me seems I feel the comfort of the morning,
            Turn'd to the mortal serene of an evening.

Claius: Me seems I see a filthy cloudy evening,
            As soon as sun begins to climb the mountains:
            Me seems I feel a noisome scent, the morning
            When I do smell the flowers of these valleys:
            Me seems I hear, when I do hear sweet music,
            The dreadful cries of murder'd men in forests.

Strephon: I wish to fire the trees of all these forests;
I give the sun a last farewell each evening;
I curse the fiddling finders out of music:
With envy I do hate the lofty mountains;
And with despite despise the humble valleys:
I do detest night, evening, day and morning.

Claius: Curse to myself my prayer is, the morning
My fire is more than can be made with forests;
My state more base than are the basest valleys;
I wish no evenings more to see, each evening;
Shamed I hate myself in sight of mountains,
And stop mine ears lest I grow mad with music.

Strephon: For she whose parts maintan'd a perfect music,
Whose beauty shin'd more than the blushing morning,
Who much did pass in state the stately mountains,
In straightness pass'd the cedar of the forests,
Hath cast me, wretch, into eternal evening,
By taking her two suns from these dark valleys.

Claius: For she, with whom compar'd, the alps are valleys,
She, whose least word brings from the spheres their music,
At whose approach the sun rose in the evening,
Who, where she went, bare in her forehead morning,
Is gone is gone, from those our spoiled forests,
Turning to deserts our best pastures mountains.

Strephon: These mountains witness shall, so shall these valleys,
These forests eke, made wretched by our music.

Claius: Our morning hymn is this, and song at evening.

First, one finds in Sidney *mountains, valleys, forests, morning, evening, music,* as against Sannazaro's *rime* (rhymes), *pianto* (weeping), *giorno* (day), *campi* (fields), *sassi* (rocks) and *valle* (valley). There is a consistent emphasis in Sidney's poem upon heights and depths, light and dark, and upon process, stressed by the ghost participle ending of '-ing'. And while the two voices of Sidney's poem are similar, this very similarity produces the sense that they are imprisoned in their own music rather than chorically indulging their sadness as Sannazaro's shepherds are. Indeed, the crucial moment occurs at the central turn when, against the endless repetitions of the temporal and artistic cycle, the voices shift to concentrate upon themselves in a shame and guilt which builds up to a violent antagonism against that very art which Sannazaro is concerned to celebrate. So in its middle lines the poem turns from the evocation of a symbolic and mythic landscape to concentrate upon the profoundly alienated 'I' which was once 'free-burgess of the forest' but is now imprisoned in unhappy love, in temporal sequence and in art itself. Melancholia reaches its climax when the song of the Owl is preferred to that of the Nightingale. Yet there is a stage worse than melancholia. For music itself comes to sound like the 'dreadful cries of murdered men in forests'. At first sight, no poem could seem less 'sincere' than this. It arrives, however, finally at a point of self-reflection in which shame itself is dramatised. As in certain troubadours, rhetoric is not artifice but a way of embodying and realising the self which is to take its place in the public world.[65] Here Sidney, like Petrarch, may claim all the prestige of his virtuosity; like Petrarch, he also makes it a central part of that self-proclamation that 'vergogna' – shame – should be the fruit.

65. It was recognised as earlier as the Occitan troubadours that the truest self might be said to reside in the self which is constructed through carefully crafted and publically available words. See Sarah Kay, 'La notion de personalité chez le troubadours: encore la question de la sincerité', *Sonderdruck* (Munich, 1985).

Chapter 4

The Renaissance Epic

INTRODUCTION

Homer in the eighteenth book of the *Iliad* describes the bronze battle-shield of Achilles which had been fashioned by Haephaestus to carry prophetic images of the destiny of Greece. In the *Aeneid*, Book VIII, Virgil imitates this passage; and so does Ariosto in Book XLVI of the *Orlando Furioso*. Yet the object which Ariosto describes, far from being an item of military equipment, is a pavilion – or marquee – erected at a wedding celebration and embroidered long since by the prophetess Cassandra. The images depicted here foretell the future glory of Ariosto's patron Ippolito d'Este and of the audience to whom Ariosto is presenting his own poem: the court is seen to be thronged with poets and philosophers, geographers, musicians and dancing masters (*OF*, XLVI. 92).[1]

The epic has commonly been the form in which poets celebrate the principles and characteristic virtues of the society to which they belong. These may be the military virtues of the Homeric world or the *pietas* of Virgil's Aeneas. Ariosto does not ignore such ancient qualities: his Ippolito will become adept in the strategy of war (*OF*, XLVI. 88). Yet the social order which is depicted in the Pavilion of Time is built upon other and more various principles than war or even public service alone could display. This is the modern and courtly world of Castiglione's *Cortegiano*, rejoicing in a whole spectrum of intellectual and social graces

---

1. Ariosto (1474–1533) served the Ferrarese court under Cardinal Ippolito d'Este and Duke Alfonso I as a diplomat and court poet. His court comedies will be considered below pp. 196, 215–23. For biography, see C.P. Brand, *Ludovico Ariosto: Preface to the Orlando Furioso*, Writers of Italy Series 1 (Edinburgh, 1974); for Ferrara, see W.L. Gundersheimer, *Ferrara: The Style of a Renaissance Despotism* (Princeton, 1973).

and expressing itself, it seems, as much through embroidery as through bronze.

In celebrating the sophistications of the Renaissance world, Ariosto developed a narrative form which was itself markedly different from either the *Iliad* or the *Aeneid*. These two works – whatever the differences between them – each follow a single story-line, leading in the one case to the fall of Troy, in the other, to the arrival of Trojan refugees at their new home in Rome. Yet in the *Orlando Furioso*, Ariosto pursues a multiplicity of narrative strands, and draws attention to this when he declares that the poem is a 'great tapestry' in which his task, as poet, is to draw together all the threads (*OF*, XIII. 80–1). Like Cassandra, he is a weaver, not only of story-lines but also of tones and generic characteristics which constantly shift from the comic to the tragic, from the pastoral to the burlesque, from chivalric heroism to the fantasy world of magic rings and flying Hippogriffs. It remains to be seen whether Ariosto's stories are any more credible than the prophecies of Cassandra. But the irony which allows Ariosto himself to suggest this capricious parallel is the most characteristic note of his poem; and few subsequent writers were prepared to emulate him in this regard. However, in formal terms the unmistakable achievement of the *Orlando Furioso* was to intertwine the strands of classical epic with those of medieval romance. All the writers with whom we shall be concerned here – Tasso, Spenser and Sidney – were to adopt this form. Each would modify it in ways which reflected their own aspirations and the changing climate of the Renaissance. But even Milton who does develop a different sort of poem is prepared to consider among the proper subjects for an epic the possibility of a romance on the theme of Arthur.[2]

Ariosto did not himself invent the epic romance. The *Orlando Furioso* (which was written in three versions appearing in 1516, 1521 and 1532) is cast as a continuation of Boiardo's *Orlando Innamorato* published first in 1483 with the addition of a third part in 1494.[3] Boiardo recognises the epic possibilities of a military theme which had its roots in the battles fought by Charlemagne against the Muslim invasions of Europe. This theme, by the time of Boiardo and Ariosto, had become a source of popular entertainment but had first been treated in the medieval epic,

---

2. See *Epitaphum Damonis,* line 166, and also *Mansus*, lines 80–4, which was written to the Italian patron of the arts Manso after Milton had made his very fruitful visit to Italy and which makes mention of Tasso.
3. Matteo Maria Boiardo (1441–94), Count of Scandiano, was, like Ariosto, a courtier at the Este court of Ferrara.

the *Chanson de Roland* ('Orlando' being an italianised form of 'Roland'). Boiardo had expanded upon the military material by introducing what he himself recognised to be the modern theme of love drawn from the French Romances. In regard both to love and war, Ariosto strengthens and develops Boiardo's treatment. His military writing focusses on an historical event, the assault launched upon the city of Paris by forces of Islam, and produces scenes which, in violence, vie with the fall of Troy in Virgil's *Aeneid*. On the other hand, the *Orlando Furioso* speaks of centrifugal forces which pull both Christian and pagan heroes away from their military duties, usually into the confusing forests of romance literature.[4] For the most part, these forces are aroused by the fleeting figure of the pagan princess Angelica, whose charms attract Christian and pagan alike. But in deciding to extend Boiardo's depiction of an amorous military hero into that of a hero who runs mad for love, Ariosto greatly accentuates the possibilities of romantic confusion.

It has been said that 'in epic, the world closes inexorably, predictably, on the hero, whereas in romance the hero goes in search of the final meaningful encounter that will crown his quest and enable him to know himself'.[5] A combination of epic and romance was bound to hold attractions for a world such as that of the Renaissance which combined a desire for order with a profound dynamism and an equally profound understanding of psychological and philosophical instability. Such an appeal would be as great in England as in Italy, not least since the material of Arthurian romance – on which Boiardo and Ariosto both drew – had been embodied in Malory's *Morte d'Arthur* and was an essential component of Tudor propaganda. But by the time the form arrived in English hands, the characteristics of the epic romance had been greatly complicated: Tasso had produced his own version of the genre in the *Gersualemme Liberata*, where he describes the ultimately successful attempts of the first crusaders to re-take Jerusalem from the Muslims. But there had also been already a good deal of debate, centring on Ariosto's poem and subsequently stimulated by Tasso's *Discorsi dell'arte*

---

4. On Ariosto's themes and procedures, see Graham Hough, *A Preface to The Faerie Queene* (London, 1962); also Marianne Shapiro, *The Poetics of Ariosto* (Detroit, 1988); Albert Russell Ascoli, *Ariosto's Bitter Harmony* (Princeton, 1987); Peter de Sa Wiggins, *Figures in Ariosto's Tapestry: Character and Design in the Orlando Furioso* (Baltimore and London, 1986). A stimulating account of the relations between the Italian epic romance and the English is contained in R. Durling, *The Figure of the Poet in the Renaissance* (Cambridge, Mass., 1965). It is no flippancy to recommend David Lodge, *Small World* (London, 1984) as an excellent introduction to the romance form and to Ariosto.

5. John Stevens, *Medieval Romance* (London, 1973), p. 80.

poetica (ed in particolare sopra il poema eroico), about the appropriate matter and form of the contemporary epic.

THE THEORY OF THE EPIC ROMANCE IN ARIOSTO AND TASSO

The point of departure for theoretical discussion of the epic romance was the question of the relative merits of unity or multiplicity in the action of such a poem. Simultaneous with the appearance of Ariosto's poem, Aristotle's *Poetics* had become prominent in critical debate and – in a way which was to affect conceptions of comedy as well as of epic – had been taken to offer rules for the composition in the vernacular genres.[6] But these rules, which apparently insisted upon unity of action, at first looked to be wholly out of keeping with Ariosto's narrative practice.

Among the most important defenders of Ariosto's technique was the Ferrarese Giraldi Cinthio (1504–73) whose name will appear frequently in subsequent chapters as a critic, a dramatist and short story writer and also as the source for Shakespeare's *Measure for Measure* and *Othello*.[7] Cinthio refuses to allow that theoretical or classical rules should dictate to practising poets.[8] Poets are 'chameleons'; and poetic form must always change to accommodate the products of new understanding. Indeed, if Homer and Virgil had lived in Ariosto's time, they too would have adopted his narrative style, multiplying plots and mixing generic characteristics as he does. In any case, there is, so Cinthio argues, a perceptible unity in Ariosto's poem: it is the unity of growth and of personality: his poem is a 'body' in which all parts are penetrated by the unifying presence of its author.

There is much in Cinthio's defence of Ariosto which anticipates the arguments employed especially by Romantic critics to justify the freedom which Shakespeare displays in his treatment of genre and dramatic unity. Yet this should not lead one to ignore the appeal and stimulus

6. For a discussion of these debates see B. Weinberg, *A History of Literary Criticism in the Italian Renaissance*, 2 vols. (Chicago, 1961). It must be added that Italians such as Gian Giorgio Trissino (1478–1550), in *Italia liberata da' Gotthi* (1547–48), had begun to experiment with regular epic poetry and his use of blank verse is known to have influenced Milton's choice of that medium. See P. and J.C. Bondanella, *Macmillian's Dictionary of Italian Literature* (London, 1979), p. 521.

7. See below, pp. 284–93 and pp. 297–310.

8. For a selection and translation of Cinthio's critical writings, see Allen H. Gilbert, *Literary Criticism: Plato to Dryden* (Detroit, 1970), pp. 242-73.

which writers of the sixteenth century derived from Aristotle. Tasso[9] in particular sets out to compose a regular epic, finding in Aristotle an influence in harmony with at least one strand in his own highly complex personality and no less in tune with the spirit of the age in which he lived.

Here was a man who spent seven years confined by his patron as a lunatic in the hospital of Saint Anna. His disturbed history was to appeal to the Romantic imagination, as is demonstrated by Goethe's play on the subject. But Thomas Kyd seems to have forestalled Goethe in writing a play – now lost – on the subject of Tasso's melancholia, while analogies have been drawn dextrously between Shakespeare's *Hamlet* and Tasso's Aristotelian tragedy on a Scandinavian theme, *Il Re Torrismondo*.[10] But Tasso himself gives clear testimony of his own distractions. His letters speak of possession by demons, but also display a no less paranoid concern over the fate of his own poetry in the hands of irresponsible publishers and of the failing of his own literary powers.[11] Above all, these letters plead for recognition of how orthodox their author is in his adherence both to his patron and to the Catholic faith.[12] Living in the early years of the Counter-Reformation, when the Church itself was seeking to establish a core of orthodoxy in its own doctrine, Tasso at one point positively invites the Inquisition to put his beliefs to scrutiny. But even before his confinement, Tasso had displayed a similar temper in his choice of poetic material and in his theoretical writings. The epic subject he had taken in the *Gerusalemme Liberata* was the victorious First Crusade in which, under the guidance of Godfrey of Bulloigne, Jerusalem had been restored to Christian dominion. Along with its celebration of a Christian triumph, the poem

9. Torquato Tasso (1544–95) lived an agitated life, from his early career as the prodigious author of *Rinaldo*, published when he was 18, through periods of exile in the company of his father – the poet and humanist Bernardo Tasso – to a period of seven years imprisonment for madness between 1579 and 1586. He wrote continually and in a wide variety of forms from epic to pastoral romance and dramatic tragedy in *Il re Torrismondo* – an Aristotelian piece on a Scandinavian theme. See C.P. Brand, *Tasso: A Study of the Poet and his Contribution to English Literature* (Cambridge, 1965).
10. See G. Giampieri, 'Tasso tra Amleto e Segismundo', *Intersezioni*, XII, n.3 (1992). Dekker was paid for alterations to a play entitled *Tasso's Melancholy*, and a play entitled *Jerusalem* was in the repertory of Strange's Men in the 1590s. Kyd's translation of Tasso's prose piece, *Il Padre della famiglia* as *The Householder's Philosophy* (1588), is extant: see A. Freeman, *Thomas Kyd* (Oxford, 1967), pp. 170–4.
11. For example, letters 162, 278, 635, 1190, 1514 in '*Lettere di Torquato Tasso*' a cura di C. Guasti (Florence, 1852–55), Vols I–IV.
12. ibid., 123 and 456.

also aimed at literary orthodoxy in its adherence to Aristotle.

Even so, the *Gerusalemme Liberata* cannot shake off the countervailing influence of Ariosto's work nor can it silence the disruptive tendencies which are always evident in the author's own personality. And the tensions to which this will lead are already apparent in his theoretical work, the *Discorsi dell'arte poetica,* written for the Ferrarese Academy in the 1560s.

Two broad questions dominate the *Discorsi*:[13] the first is whether an epic should follow a single or else a multiple action; the second concerns, broadly, the vexed question of truth and falsehood in poetry which was to exercise all major critics of the sixteenth century, including, of course, Sir Philip Sidney in his *Apology for Poetry*.[14]

For Tasso, as later for Sidney, the purpose of poetry is to encourage in the reader a contemplation of moral truth. The epic in particular will offer great examples of virtue and inspire emotions not – as tragedy would – of pity and terror but rather of admiration in the face of these examples. In this sense, by laying before the reader a model of the perfect 'cavaliere' (*Discorsi*, I. 825), the poet will teach the reader to aspire in delight to the same perfection; and here Tasso's phrasing is all but identical to Spenser's in the *Letter to Raleigh* where, alluding also to Ariosto, Spenser speaks of forming the 'perfect English gentleman'.

In practical terms, it is Aristotle whom Tasso believes can help him to realise these goals. So, as to subject matter, Tasso seeks with Aristotle an historical theme, as a first step towards truthfulness. In the perspective of Ariosto's work – with its many elements of pure fantasy – this is a polemical point to make. Yet at once it leads Tasso into difficulties. For the choice of an historical subject is as much a way to trick ('ingannare') as to edify the reader (I. 822): the historical subject should not be so close in time as to allow living men to comment on the veracity of the treatment (I. 827), for that would deny the poet the freedom of his own imagination, his 'licenzia di fingere' (I. 826). In one respect, this prescription ensures for Tasso, as later for Sidney, that the poet should rise above the mere detail of history which is, for both, a lower intellectual art. At the same time, the 'licenzia di fingere' takes on peculiar weight when

13. Quotations here are translated from the text in *Tasso: Opere*, ed. G. Petrocchi (Turin, 1961). For an English translation see *Discourses on the Heroic Poem*, trans. Mariella Cavalchini and Irene Samuel (Oxford, 1972) and selections in Allan H. Gilbert, op.cit., pp. 466–503. See also Baxter Hathaway, *The Age of Criticism: The Late Renaissance in Italy* (Ithaca NY, 1962), pp. 390–96.

14. On which question see C.S. Lewis, *English Literature in the Sixteenth Century* (Oxford, 1954), pp. 318–19.

Ariosto is considered. A poem must, for Tasso, include 'marvels' or moments of imaginative amazement. Yet these marvels cannot be Ariostan hippogriffs or enchanted castles. They must, Tasso insists, be marvels which reveal the higher truths of Providence (I. 825).

In the second book of the *Discorsi*, Tasso attempts to to argue the case for unity of action. All things (as the Aristotelian Dante would have agreed) must move to their proper end (I. 827); all thinkers, whether poets or philosophers, seek unity (II. 837); and unity is the indispenable principle of all art (I. 825). So, devoted as he is to Ariosto, Tasso attempts to show that in fact the *Orlando Furioso* and Boiardo's *Orlando Innamorato* stand as one poem rather than two incomplete fragments. Likewise, he argues that the Romance form can be made to answer to Aristotelian conceptions of unity: in this case, the demand for variety is legitimate but the poet will display his skill above all in finding variety within a single action (I. 848) in 'una sola azione'.

By 'action' Tasso means, as Aristotle does, a unifying psychological theme. And the liberation of Jerusalem would seem to be precisely such a theme, as indeed it is in the mind of Tasso's single-minded military hero, Goffredo. But at every point within the story Goffredo is challenged and distracted in his task by the tendency of his followers to pursue their own divergent and romantic ends out of love either for errant ladies or for personal glory. Moreover, the very composition of the poem mirrors comparable tensions: in its origins (as the *Rinaldo* which Tasso composed at the age of eighteen), the poem was the work of a youthful prodigy. Tasso re-writes and extends this early work to achieve finally the elevation and unity of the *Gerusalemme Liberata*. Yet this poem is in itself so unstable in Tasso's mind that he is obliged to re-write it as the *Gerusalemme Conquistata*, so as to strengthen its Christian orthodoxy. Subsequently, Tasso also supplies an allegorical explanation of the *Gerusalemme Liberata* itself lest the fabulous or romance qualities of the poem subvert its religious message. It is an indication of how sympathetic such a procedure was to the late sixteenth century that Ariosto's poem, too, was belatedly supplied with an allegorical interpretation by Simone Fornari in 1549.[15]

The Epic Romance, then, had acquired by the time it reached Spenser and Sidney, a highly problematical history. It was now not only a channel for the celebration of public themes but also a genre which demanded virtuosity and even moral endeavour of the authorial voice.

---

15. See Weinberg, 'The Quarrel over Ariosto and Tasso', Vol. II, op.cit., pp. 954–7.

The greatest writers, in particular Spenser and Sidney, were aware of the need to develop their own moral position in relation to the Italian example. But there were also technical advances in regard to language and narrative style which served, as Petrarch's example did in the sphere of the lyric, to encourage comparable developments in English verse. It was, for instance, Drayton who noted the technical skill which had been shown in Ariosto's eight-line verse, 'which holds the tune clean through to the base of the column'.[16] To consider this aspect of the Italian epic more closely, we may begin by examining the response of the earliest translators, Harington and Fairfax, to these works.

ARIOSTO AND HARINGTON

In Canto XXVIII of the *Orlando Furioso*, Ariosto tells the story of two men – reputedly among the most handsome imaginable – who come to realise, first, that their own wives are unsatisfied by such handsomeness and also enjoy the advances of dwarfs and stable-boys, then, secondly, discover that all the women whom, by way of revenge on their wives, they proceed to seduce also have insatiable appetites: even the most faithful of these women contrives to introduce a third lover into bed as the exhausted pair lie sleeping on either side.

According to well-attested legend, it was this same episode that Sir John Harington was translating when Queen Elizabeth discovered him and banished him from court until he had finished all forty-six of Ariosto's cantos.[17]

In substance, the story which Harington had initially chosen is more characteristic of Boccaccio than of Ariosto, and Ariosto himself marks the story off from the rest of his poem. The lady reader is warned not to puruse the canto. Likewise, the teller is supposedly not, for once, the courtly Ariosto himself but rather a taverner in the uncourtly circum-

---

16. In *Preface to the Barron's Warres* (1609), quoted in John Buxton, *Sir Philip Sidney and the English Renaissance* (London, 1954).

17. Sir John Harington (1560–1612), a godson of Queen Elizabeth, produced his *Orlando Furioso in English Heroicall Verse* in 1591. He is renowned for his invention of the flushing lavatory as described in the wittily rhetorical *A New Discourse of a Stale Subject called the Metamorphosis of Ajax* (1596). He was nevertheless a man of some literary pretensions. See his translation of Virgil's *Aeneid*, Book VI, ed. with introduction and notes by Simon Cauchi (Oxford, 1991). For an excellent account of both Harington and Fairfax see Colin Burrow, *Epic Romance* (Oxford, 1993). Also for the text of Harington's translation, Graham Hough (ed.) (London, 1961).

stances of his own tavern. Finally, the fictional audience in Canto XXVII includes Rodomonte who, throughout the *Orlando Furioso*, embodies the negation of courtly virtue and decorous speech; notably, Rodomonte is the descendant of Nimrod (*OF*, XIV. 116–17) who built the tower of Babel; and the last line of Ariosto's poem records the final defeat of this subversive force, as if throughout he had recognised there had been a dark undertow of confusion which the poem had finally to exorcise.

Yet of course such narrative apparatus serves only to confirm Ariosto's control over his own poem as he teases, titillates and colludes with his reader. It is here especially that Ariosto differs from Boccaccio. Where the authorial presence in the *Decameron* is remote and anonymous, Ariosto creates and sustains a narrative voice which draws attention to itself even when it seems to abdicate responsibility; and where Boccaccio tells anecdotes connected only by their inclusion in a day's story-telling, Ariosto interlaces his stories so that – save in Canto XXVIII – there is continual suspense as the climax of one narrative strand is deferred, often over several cantos, to allow for the beginning of another.

When Harington returned to court with his translation complete, it seems that he had come to understand the technical virtuosity of Ariosto's poem and was even prepared to argue for its moral seriousness. As if to assert his own moral reformation, he dutifully includes the allegory which had come to be attached to Ariosto's poem – even though allegorical writing is internally only a small part of Ariosto's work. More significantly, he writes a 'Brief Defence of Poetry' which in its theoretical parts owes much to Sidney, while reserving the right, in defence of Ariosto, to dissent from Sidney's position.[18] Harington is aware of Sidney's suspicion that in epic romance 'Cupido is crept even into the Heroicall Poem' ('Brief Defence', op.cit., p. 209) and also of his doubts about the validity of narrative digression (op.cit., p. 217). Yet he firmly defends the heroical poem even in its romance guise as the genre which makes men 'wiser and honester' (op.cit., p. 210). Likewise, he points out that, in practice, Sidney's *Arcadia* itself makes skilful use of digression, and roundly denies that there can be any fault in a technique which draws the reader 'with a continual thirst toward the end of the book to close up the diverse matters briefly and cleanly' (op.cit., p. 217). Harington also notes astutely (op.cit., p. 217) that Ariosto, unlike

18. Quoted from D. Gregory Smith (ed.), *Elizabethan Critical Essays* (Oxford, 1904).Vol. II, pp. 194–222.

Homer and Virgil, enters into his own poem and decides, pragmatically, that this is an entirely justifiable procedure, since these interventions allow 'an excellent breathing place for the reader'. For the reformed Harington, there is not a word of 'ribaldry or obscenousness in the poem' (op.cit., p. 215); Chaucer has far more 'flat scurillitee' (p. 215). As a comment purely on diction, this is accurate enough, and Harington is right to identify a seriousness of purpose in the *Orlando Furioso*. Indeed, the nature of Ariosto's comedy will probably not be understood until one recognises that – as in Dante – comedy can be an ally of deeply serious intent.

On this score, one should first recall that the *Orlando Furioso* in its three versions was written precisely over the period in which Italy was invaded by foreign armies. Where in Charlemagne's time Europe was threatened by the forces of a foreign religion, Christian Europe is now threatened from within by its own internal dissensions; and there can be no doubt that Ariosto perceives the ironic parallel. In Canto XXXIII, stanza 52, he offers a prophecy which is the reverse of the eulogistic account of the Pavilion of Time, picturing – in terms which range from Dantean venom to an elegiac fatalism characteristic of the original *Chanson de Roland* – the horrors of the profoundly unchivalric wars which were to be fought in the Italian peninsula: at the battle of Pavia, 'the flower of all the chivalry of France lies dead upon the the ground':

> Vedete il meglio de la nobiltade
> di tutta Francia alla campagna estinto.

The plangent rhythm of these verses expresses an unmistakably tragic response to the horrors of modern warfare.

Throughout Ariosto's poem there is an ironic interplay across time between a sophisticated mockery of the ancient aspirations or excesses of the Paladins and, conversely, a realisation that the high values of chivalry have tragically disappeared from the world. Yet the irony itself points to a comic rather than a tragic resolution of the vision, as if the very act of writing poetry in this mode could assert a superior perspective. Notably, as the *Orlando Furioso* progresses from version to version, Ariosto introduces material of a far more sombre cast: there are indeed five extant cantos concerning particularly the treachery of Ganelon (who, in the *Chanson de Roland*, engineers the defeat of Roland at Roncesvalles) which are deliberately omitted from the final version of the *Orlando Furioso* itself. Yet this excision suggests that Ariosto is here consciously pursuing an 'aspro concento', a form in which, as for Dante, bitterness itself becomes part of an ultimately comic perception of harmony.[19]

For T.S. Eliot, writing in the aftermath of the Great War, the romance genre offered a means of seeking out the shattered roots of culture. For Ariosto, the romance serves a similar purpose. On the political level, he affirms the values of a Ferrarese dynasty which did in fact prove resilient in the face of invasion and extended its reign, which had begun in the late thirteenth century, practically to the end of the sixteenth. This is not to say that Ariosto is wholly without scepticism about his patrons or their court: his *Satires* and his avowed dissatisfactions at the appointments he received preclude that interpretation. Yet, as we shall see in his comedies, Ariosto is prepared to fulfill his own role in the ceremonies of courtly entertainment; and it is that role which he idealises in the authorial figure who dominates the *Orlando Furioso* and in his portrayal of the courtly audience. Throughout, he presents himself as if delivering the poem in oral performance to the assembled court; and in the concluding canto he imagines the court itself gathering to reciprocate his praise of them in a celebration of the successful conclusion of the poem. On another level, however, the literary engagement which Ariosto makes with the sources of his own epic, alluding at some point to every major figure in the tradition, from Homer to Dante to Boiardo, is itself an affirmation, in Eliot's phrase, of the relationship between tradition and the individual talent. The culture, however threatened by present events, is shown to be irrepressibly productive.

If *sprezzatura*, on Castiglione's understanding, is the essential virtue of courtly life, then it is *sprezzatura* which Ariosto supremely displays in his dealings with his own court, as his narrative elegantly risks a series of cliff-hangers, false starts and suspended actions only to pull off the appropriate resolution with unfailing ease. But a similar nonchalance extends to Ariosto's treatment of all his literary sources.

Thus in the very conception of the book as a continuation of Boiardo's work, there is an apparent modesty which conceals and reveals Ariosto's confidence in his own power to outdo the original. On the level of style, too, the following lines are enough to indicate how far Ariosto has advanced. Alluding to an episode in the *Orlando Innamorato* where Boiardo has depicted a seascape complete with dolphin and fish of every kind, including tuna, Ariosto exactly parallels the detail of the original. Yet where Boiardo writes:

---

19. See Ascoli's reading in *Ariosto's Bitter Harmony*, op.cit.

Quivi era eran tonni e quivi eran delfini
Lombrine e pesci spade una gran schiera.

(*O lnn*, II. xiii. 57)

(There were tuna here; there were dolphin here and lombrin and sword-fish in a huge shoal.)

Ariosto writes:

Veloci vi correvano i delfini,
vi venia a bocca aperta il grosso tonno.

(*OF*, VI. 36)

(The dolphin here ran swiftly and here came a tuna-fish, huge, with its mouth wide open.)

The brute factuality and crude rhythms of the original have here been transformed into a fluent verse-line which changes pace to contrast the rapidity of the dolphin with lumbering bulk of the tuna. A dextrous shift from Boiardo's plural to the singular 'tonno' along with the graphic phrase 'with gaping mouth' – 'a bocca aperta' – brings the contrast into sharp focus.

On a larger level, too, it is a piece of *sprezzatura* to extend Boiardo's love theme into a madness theme. On the one hand, this extension makes possible a virtuoso display in the depiction of extreme psychological states; on the other, it invites the author to contemplate a realm of illusion in which desires and all kinds of aspiration – erotic or heroic or even literary – can be satirised.[20] And the same theme leads Ariosto into a literary contest with figures far more eminent than Boiardo. His title, for instance, draws directly upon Seneca's *Hercules Furens*.[21] Yet far from producing a Stoical vision of misleading passion, Ariosto seems to recognise that there would be no imaginative spectacle worth considering were it not for the emotional excesses of his hero. As for Petrarch and Dante, the fleeting and illusory figure of Angelica plainly descends from the tradition of the *donna angelicata* which had so far produced both Beatrice and Laura. Yet the woman who, for Dante, provided a point of stable reference and confidence in human nature here throws everything into interesting confusion; and while in describing the scene of such confusions Ariosto constantly employs the idealised language of nature

20. This is particularly evident in the sequence in Canto XXXIV, 68–92, where the English Knight Astolfo travels to the moon to rediscover Orlando's lost wits and witnesses the extent to which 'lunacy' has taken over the life of terrestrial beings.
21. For Ariosto's re-writing of Virgil, see Robert Durling's essay 'The Epic Ideal', in D. Daiches and A. Thorlby (eds.), *Literature and Western Civilization*, 6 vols. (London 1972–6), Vol. II, pp. 105–46.

which Petrarch had developed in the *Rime Sparse*, he refuses to enter the moral debate which Petrarch had so painfully traversed.

An example of how consciously Ariosto readjusts the received idea occurs in Canto XIV, stanza 65, when, marking a moment of narrative suspension, the author declares that his soaring imagination will not permit him to follow one single narrative line:

> Or l'alta fantasia, ch'un sentier solo
> non vuol ch'i' segna ognor, quindi mi guida.

This pause is entirely characteristic of Ariosto's technique. Yet the phrasing alludes directly to the culminating moment of Dante's *Paradiso*, Canto XXXIII, line 141, where Dante – displaying the authorial modesty which Chaucer identified in *The House of Fame* – declares his inability to describe his final vision of God:

> all'alta fantasia qui mancò possa . . .

Now, a confession of religious humility is turned into an affirmation of Ariosto's confidence in the fertility of his own narrative imagination.

The authorial persona which Ariosto creates allows nothing of the problematical inquiry into linguistic and moral questions which one finds in the persona adopted by Dante in the *Commedia* or Chaucer in *Troilus and Criseyde*. There is, however, a continual and usually ironic interplay between the narrator of the *Orlando Furioso* and the characters of the poem. Ariosto regularly represents himself as a sufferer from the same malady of love as Orlando. At the same time, this comparison is, throughout, intended to emphasise that the poem itself, with its cultivation of variety and narrative perspective, offers a means of avoiding the chaotic obsessions which beset the single-minded Orlando. Thus in Canto XXIX, stanza 50, Ariosto declares that 'it would be madness if he ventured to follow each of the mad acts of Orlando one by one':

> Pazzia sarà se le pazzie d'Orlando
> prometto raccontarvi ad una ad una.

Here at a stroke Ariosto asserts that the aesthetic measure and literary decorum which his work displays is a therapeutic resource, to be enjoyed, presumably, by author and audience even where that resource is not available to the fictional hero.

When the author himself is so much the centre of attention one may well be inclined to say that he – as Stanley E. Fish used to say of Milton – is the true hero of his own poem. One might equally well suppose that there was little room here for any attention to the psychological detail of character or situation. Up to a point, this would be an accurate conclusion. Yet it would do no justice to the finely graded spectrum of observations which Ariosto has constructed in his poem. In a way which prepares for the precise anatomy of the heroic mind which Spenser offers in *The Faerie Queene*, Ariosto's characters are so presented as to reveal finely discriminated differences in their response to situations and in the way they conduct their heroic lives. Like Spenser (but unlike Boccaccio), Ariosto sets out to represent the moral and psychological developments – involving the madness and recovery of Orlando and the conversion of the pagan Ruggiero to Christianity – which occur in the course of their questing progress. Notably, however, Spenser is concerned to analyse the inner life of spiritual heroism, whereas Ariosto's concern is above all concerned with a psychology which expresses itself outwardly in acts of loyalty to a principle of social order. Moving, as Castiglione also does, within the sphere of courtly performances, Ariosto himself may be thought to perform a loyal act in the writing of his poem. But the story he has to tell takes as its primary subject the military loyalty of the feudal world; and he proceeds to complicate this theme by displaying the countervailing loyalties to the codes of love and the treacheries and even self-betrayals which arise when the codes of love and codes of military honour clash.

Much of this can be appreciated in translation, and Harington in his translation is sufficiently alive to these thematic implications for a political interpretation of his work to be entirely justified.[22] What he cannot do is to reproduce that extraordinary command of language which expresses, point by point, Ariosto's control over his own material.[23] As an example of both the characteristics of Ariosto's poem and also of the strengths and weaknesses of Harington's translation, one may consider the point in Canto XXIII of the *Orlando Furioso* where Orlando finally descends into madness. In the course of the canto, Orlando has been driven to the point of delirium by the sight of his lady's name written on a rock to declare her love for her new swain, the pagan foot-soldier, Medoro. Initially, Orlando – 'using fraud against himself' (XXIII. 104) – tries to convince himself that 'Medoro' is a pet-name which Angelica has given him. But finally he cannot evade the truth: exhausted, he sinks

22. Cf. Burrow, op.cit.
23. Barbara Reynolds makes some telling observations on the qualities of the text which translation should seek to reproduce in 'The Pleasure Craft', in William Radice and Barbara Reynolds (eds.), *The Translator's Art: Essays in Honour of Betty Radice* (Penguin, 1987), pp. 129–142. Her own translation in 2 vols. (London, 1975) can be confidently recommended.

down on a welcome bed in a peasant's hovel, only to realise instantly that this is the bed on which Angelica and Medoro must first have made love. His mind cracks and, leaving the hovel, he returns to the dark grove which, for Angelica and Medoro, had been a pastoral and amorous retreat and begins to wreak havoc upon the very stones which bear the names of the lovers:

102

I am not I, the man that erst I was,
Orlando he is buried and dead,
His most ungrateful love (ah foolish lasse)
Hath killed Orlando, and cut off his head:
I am his ghost, that up and downe must passe,
In this tormenting hell for ever led,
To be a fearful sample and a just
To all such fools as put in love their trust.

103

Thus wandering still in ways that have no way,
He hapt again to light upon the cave,
Where (in remembrance of their pleasant play)
Medoro did that epigram ingrave.
To see the stones again his woes display
And her ill name and his ill hap deprave,
Did on the sudden all his sense enrage,
With hate with fury, with revenge and rage.

104

Straightways he draweth forth his fatal blade,
And hews the stones, to heav'n the shivers flee,
Accursed was that fountain cave and shade,
The arbor and the flowers and ev'ry tree:
Orlando of all places havoc made,
Where he those names together joyn'd may see,
Yea to the spring he did perpetual hurt,
By filling it with leaves, boughs, stones and dirt.

105

And having done this foolish frantic feat,
He lays him down all weary on the ground,
Distempered in his body with much heat
In minde with pains that no tongue can expound,

But lay with open eyes as in a sound,
The forth with rage and not with reason waked
He rents his clothes and runs around stark naked.

106
His helmet here he flings, his poulderns there;
He casts away his curats and his shield:
His sword he throws away, he cares not where,
He scatters all his armour in the field;
No ragge about his body he doth bear,
As might from cold or might from shame him shield,
And save he left behind his fatal blade,
No doubt he had therewith great havoc made.

107
But his surpassing force did so exceed,
All common men, that neither sword nor bill
Nor any other weapon he did need,
Mere strength suffic'd him to do what he will,
He roots up trees as one would root a weede:
And ev'n as birders laying nets with skill,
Pare slender thorns away with easy strokes,
So did he play with ashes, elmes and oaks.

108
The herdmen and the shepherds that did heare
The hideous noise and unacquainted sound,
With fear and wonder great approached near,
To see and know what was thereof the ground.
But now I must cut off this treatise here,
Lest this my booke do grow beyond his bound:
And if you take some pleasure in this text,
I will go forward with it in the next.

Here Harington seems to have recognised something of the tragedy of
the situation which Ariosto describes. Yet his language is wholly unable
to reproduce either the linguistic elevation or the subtle oscillations of
level which are found in Ariosto's text. Unwitting bathos is never far
away in Harington's translation – as in the phrases 'run about stark
naked'; 'cut off his head', which are dictated more by considerations of
rhyme than of accuracy to the spirit of the original. Ariosto knows what
anti-climax is. But he also knows precisely how to orchestrate his comic
effects, and to control them. So here his poem progresses from a deeper

tragedy than Harington perceives, through shades of compassion, revulsion and horror, to a comic detachment which itself becomes a deeper comedy of measure and harmony as, with the audience of shepherds, the author puts an end to the madness he has depicted here.

Thus, in point of diction, the passage in Ariosto begins: 'Non son, non sono io quel che paio in viso', 'I am not, I am not that which in face I seem to be'. The emphasis upon the negative and the blurring of elisions sound suggests a destruction of identity far greater and more insidious than Harington's heroic declaration. Indeed, the internal echoes eventually reduce the first person pronoun 'io' to the final component in the word 'I seem' - 'paio'. Likewise, where Harington speaks of a 'tormenting Hell', Ariosto has used the reflexive participle – 'tormentandosi': 'tormenting itself' – where the personal pronoun has now changed, in accord with Orlando's loss of identity, from a first- to a third-person form. One may add that Ariosto's diction here is shot through with subliminal allusions to Dante's diction, giving a moral dimension to the scene which Harington cannot match.

Examples of such detail could be multiplied in practically every line, as could examples of shifts in narrative organisation. Ariosto, for instance, has a notable sense of almost filmic editing which leads him in the second stanza to end the sequence with the drawing of Orlando's blade and to begin the next stanza with the verb – 'tagliò': 'he cut' – thus using the stanza break to generate suspense as to what will happen when the raised blade strikes, and to begin the next phase with all the vigour of the violent action itself. Harington confuses this by beginning stanza 104 with the drawing of the blade, having ended stanza 103 with an emotional flourish of hatred and fury. In the process, another suggestive emphasis is lost. For Harington, the blade falls directly on the rock; for Ariosto, it falls upon the *writing* on the rock – 'tagliò lo scritto' – so emphasising the mental object of Orlando's obsessive action and suggesting the futility of a physical act intended to erase an intangibly psychological inscription. So, too, in the transition from stanzas 132 to 133, Harington not only perpetrates the rhyme-bound nonsense of 'run around stark-naked' but fails completely to see the narrative force of the line which opens stanza 133: 'Qui riman l'elmo, e là riman lo scudo'. Here Ariosto's cinematic eye picks out the consequences of Orlando's violent action, focussing point by point on the bits and pieces of Orlando's armour as they lie discarded on the ground. The subject is wholly absent – as indeed, mentally, he is now absent – and the fragmented trappings of his military role are an eloquent expression of Orlando's vacancy and incoherence.

Then finally – since Harington has all along been hard-put to avoid bathos – the effects of comic detachment which Ariosto achieves in the final phases of the action are completely lost. In Ariosto's sequence, the author has begun in close-up, allowing the direct speech of Orlando to dominate the scene. Subsequent stanzas produce descriptive phrases – unparalleled in Harington – which allow close emotional identification between protagonist and reader, as in the opening of stanza 132 (which draws upon the tragic language of Dante's Ugolino episode):[24]

> Afflitto e stanco al fin cade ne l'erba,
> e ficca gli occhi al cielo, e non fa motto.

> (Agonised and exhausted he fall upon the grass; he fixed his eyes on the sky and said not a word.)

But as the catatonic figure rises again after three days of oblivious suffering, he beings to uproot trees with his bare hands 'as if they were herbs and vegetables'. A comic exaggeration, verging in style on that of cartoon animation, sets in, along with a certain judiciousness of moral comment – which Harington, speaking of Orlando's 'foolish and frantic' feats in 105 has adopted all along. In the last stanza, Orlando has become a spectacle, an object of amazement to an audience of unheroic peasants. But the courtly author, too, insists at the last upon distance and control: where Harington brusquely moves forward to the next book, Ariosto ends with a refusal to weary or irritate the sophisticated ear with a prolonged account of such barbarities: 'che v'abbia per lunghezza a fastidire'.

FAIRFAX AND THE *GERUSALEMME LIBERATA*

Though Fairfax (1568–1635) himself did not leave any critical account of his own work comparable to Harington's, a significant debate about the merits of the work took place between Coleridge, Wordsworth, Hazlitt and the Lambs[25] – in which comments on the freedom of Fairfax's translation were interspersed with expressions of admiration for the care which he had taken and the recognition (emphasised by Coleridge) that his style had been influenced as much by Spenser as by Tasso himself.[26]

24. See above, pp. 48–51.
25. Recorded by John Payne Collier in his edition of *Seven Lectures on Shakespeare and Milton* by the late S.T. Coleridge (1856), pp. xxxii–v.
26. Tasso's reputation had grown strong in the course of the eighteenth century and, though new translations appeared, Fairfax's translation was widely read until the middle of that century.

The conversation is evidence of the interest which Tasso's work was to attract as late as the romantic period. As for Fairfax, it would be tempting to say that he was drawn to the work by his known interest in demonology[27] (see D.N.C. Wood, 'Tasso in England' *Spenser Encyclopedia*, op.cit., pp. 679-80). But what is clear is that he has an enthusiasm for the text which often leads to an exaggeration and broadening of Tasso's verbal effects and to the addition of a certain sententiousness, which involves also a loss of much of the concentration and drama through which Tasso himself makes his presence in the poem felt.[28] Fairfax is also scrupulous in including the allegorical explanation which Tasso added to his poem:

> The Army componded of diverse Princes, and of other Christian soldiers, signifieth Man, compounded of soul and body, and of a soul not simple, but divided into many and diverse powers. Godfrey stands for understanding. The two magicians Ismeno and Armida, servants of the devil, which endeavour to remove the Christians from making war are two devilish temptations. Ismeno . . . doth signify that temptation which seeketh to deceive with false belief the virtue (as men call it) Opinative. Armida is that temptation which layeth siege to the power of our desires.
>
> (Lea, op.cit., pp. 89–90)

Throughout the *Gerusalemme Liberata*, the control which Tasso seeks to exert by devices such as allegorical interpretation is frequently (though not invariably) at odds with the imaginative suggestion of the narrative situations he creates and also with the exhuberance of his language. Unlike Ariosto, Tasso follows the classics in avoiding choric or ironic observation. At the same time, despite Tasso's linguistic virtuosity in recasting the classics, *sprezzatura* is largely replaced here by an heroic

27. An edition of Fairfax's translation is available edited by Kathleen M. Lea and T.M. Gang, *Godfrey of Bulloigne: A Critical edition of Edward Fairfax's translation together with Fairfax's original poems* (Oxford, 1981). Also with an introduction by Roberto Weiss (London, 1962). For a modern prose version, see *Jersualem Delivered: Torquato Tasso* trans. and ed. Ralph Nash (Detroit, 1987). An earlier translation of Tasso's poem was written by Richard Carew and published in London in 1594.

28. Lea, op.cit., pp. 22–3, catalogues a series of stylistic features which mark Fairfax's translation: a delight in touching up conceits, a penchant for additional references to classical and biblical material, a taste for moralising additions and above an 'addiction to lists' filling out the line. It should be noted that the textual tradition of the *Gerusalemme Liberata* was extremely complicated. Much to Tasso's own horror, the first edition appeared without his consent; he continued to revise the poem even when he had issued it in an authorised form. Fairfax seems to have worked from an edition published in 1584, though he may have consulted two Venetian editions of 1583 and 1589.

moral conscience which constantly matches its own achievements in moral terms against the pagan original. Tasso's determination to demonstrate his own orthodoxy – both Christian and psychological – has been attested in his letters. Yet these attempts betray the extent of the divergences and transgressions, both literary and moral, which Tasso knows his enterprise will involve.

Effects such as these are immediately apparent in the opening invocation; and it is also apparent that Fairfax, who re-wrote his translation of these stanzas three times, tends to diminish their linguistic and moral complication.

Consider:

> O musa tu che di caduchi allori
> non circondi la fronte in Elicona,
> ma su nel cielo infar i beato cori
> hai di stelle immortali aurea corona,
> tu spira al petto mio celesti ardori,
> tu rischiara il mio canto, e tu perdona
> s'intesso fregi al ver, s'adorno in parte
> d'altri diletti, che de tuoi le carte.

> (*GL*, I. 2)

> O heavenly muse, that not with fading bays
> Deckest thy brow by th' Heliconian spring.
> But sittest crowned with stars immortal rays,
> In heaven where legions of bright Angels sing,
> Inspire life in my wit, my thoughts upraise,
> My verse ennoble, and forgive the thing
> If fictions light I mix with truth divine,
> And fill these lines with others praise then thine.

In Fairfax's translation this passage could be taken as an appeal for inspiration, complicated only by the identification of the Muse as a Heavenly and Christian Divinity. But Tasso allows other strands to enter. The word 'intesso' – 'I weave' – (lost in Fairfax's 'mix') immediately recalls the tapestry metaphor which Ariosto used to describe his own unambiguously secular activity. But even in his invocation of a Christian Muse, Tasso is not at all looking for the spiritual elevation which Fairfax suggests with the words 'upraise' and 'ennoble': rather, the Holy Spirit is being asked, pre-emptively, to forgive the deviations which Tasso, even as he asks forgiveness, knows he is bound to commit. Fairfax's translation distracts attention from the bad faith or guilt of which Tasso knows already he will be guilty. At the same time, Fairfax offers an over-simplified rhythmic balance of 'fictions light' against 'truth divine' which obscures the suspense and tension of Tasso's repeated conditional, 'if I weave . . . ', 'if I adorn . . . '. Nor has the phrase 'fictions light' any of the visual impact or ambiguity of reference that is found in 'fregi' – which is a 'fringe' (often a *woven* fringe) used as a sign of honour but equally, in its etymological history, a sign of dishonour – deriving from the 'Phrygian' embroideries which the Romans took to be luxuriously decadent.

Narratives no less than words can for Tasso be dangerously distracting 'fringes'. Thus, as early as Canto II there is an episode which, even though its immediate intentions seem morally impeccable, nevertheless has to be excised from the *Gerusalemme Conquistata*. The Muslim ruler of Jerusalem – in profoundly Machiavellian manner – has terrorised the Christian members of the population, claiming that a statue of the Virgin Mary which he himself had appropriated has been stolen back by the Christians. Culprits are sought but none are forthcoming until Sofronia, a hitherto chaste and modest girl, decides that she will sacrifice herself to save her community from further persecution. Her confession will be a noble lie – a 'magnanima menzogna' (*GL*, II. 22).[29] But so far the episode is designed to create a piece of moral theatre in which the battle between truth and falsehood is seen to produce unexpected marvels and ironies of a spiritually elevating kind.

Yet as Sofronia pursues her purpose, she is obliged heroically to conquer her own innate modesty and, entering the public arena, walk through the Argus-eyes of the crowd (ibid., 15). Within the crowd is the Christian Olindo who has long admired Sofronia from afar. But as Olindo's eyes fall upon the heroine, so a romantic motif begins to intertwine itself with theme of moral heroism. And the author himself is drawn into this confusion. For Tasso's own phrasing joins with the eye of Olindo to elicit from the situation not only pathos but also a vein of suppressed titillation as Sofronia proceeds 'neither revealing nor exposing her beauties' (ibid., 18) (rather brutally rendered by Fairfax as 'a shop for merchandise/Full of riche stuffe, but none for sale exposed'). And this note becomes ever stronger as the climax of the story approaches: Olindo offers to die in Sofronia's place – thus of course displacing the moral glory which she has painfully deserved; Aladdin, however, decides that both should die; and both are then bound face to

29. Cf. the phrase in Webster, *The Duchess of Malfi*, p. 252.

face to be burned alive on the same pyre. At this point the moral theatre which Tasso had clearly intended becomes an opportunity for a play upon Petrarchan images of binding and the fires of love, voiced entirely through the mouth of Olindo and the complicit male narrator. In the event, the two lovers are saved by the woman-warrior Clorinda who is properly moved by the heroism of each; and a marriage takes place. Yet this happy outcome is clearly not enough, even for Tasso himself, to dispel the subliminal strains of eroticism which he has allowed to resonate in this episode. In a letter to Scipio Gonzaga of 1575, he confesses himself to be troubled that Olindo and Sofronia were bound face to face. Such words do not befit a 'grave, epic poet'; and finding the whole extract aesthetically distracting from the military theme which he needs to establish in the early cantos, he omits it entirely from the *Gerusalemme Conquistata*.

But even if a single episode can be disposed of in this way, there remain comparable difficulties in the most central images of the work, in the psychology of its characters and ultimately in the narrative procedure which Tasso himself adopts.

Thus the besieged city is here much more conspicuously the centre of the action than it is in *Orlando Furioso*. There are woods surrounding Jerusalem and there are journeys which lead through these woods into dangerous areas of romance and even madness. Yet the city provides a constant guarantee of narrative unity and of moral purpose, as if at the intersection of ley-lines, the city attracts to itself both Christian and Pagan, and also – totem-like – stands as a vertical axis, linking heaven to earth and earth to the subterranean forces which the pagans invoke. Even so, the city is an ambiguous image, being graveyard and source of life, a place of suffering as well as of triumph. Goffredo and the Crusaders are seeking to free a tomb (and an empty tomb at that); and though they succeed, their Christian success which also marks the end of heroic and imaginative endeavour is notably anti-climactic: 'and here Goffredo devoutly adores the great Sepulchre, hangs up his arms and fulfils his vow' (GL, XX. 144). It remains for the *Gersualemme Conquistata* to provide a more extended and triumphalist conclusion.

Goffredo's own position in the poem is likewise never free from tension. Though suffering – as Aeneas does – from a reputation for pious tedium, Goffredo undoubtedly reflects Tasso's own profound desire for moral coherence and moral action. His task is to draw together the Christians who initially are seen in overview, frozen like puppets until inspired by a messenger sent from God to advance with renewed zeal on

Jerusalem. Yet that zeal itself, though God-given, proves the source of disruption. Once in motion, the Christians are prone to distraction above all by Armida – the equivalent of both Angelica and Circe – who, acting for the Pagan cause, sows the seeds of animated dissension in the Christian camp and diverts their energies from war to sex. But she, too, in her association with a poetry of desire, is no less an attraction to the author – as Spenser implicitly recognises when, in Book II of *The Faerie Queene*, he sets himself to purify the implications of Tasso's treatment.

For Tasso himself, the appeal of the pagan world extends far further than the sphere of the erotic. For instance, the *Gerusalemme Liberata* displays a great interest in the rituals and magical ceremonies practised by the pagan forces. In Canto IV, Tasso's picture of the formal debate in Hell, evoking the malign force of Demigorgon, exerted an influence over Milton in Book II of *Paradise Lost*, producing in him similar effects of divided attention. But Tasso can also show an almost systematic interest in the workings of the culture and religious thinking of the pagan mind. The Renaissance had come to display considerable attention (as the examples of Pico and of Sannazaro show) to esoteric and cabbalistic practices. Tasso reflects this when he recreates the rites performed, for instance, by the magician Ismene.[30] But he also enters more deeply than Ariosto did into the alien virtues of the pagan mind. Ariosto could attribute dignity to the pagan. But this dignity derived from the same emotions as the Christians experienced and was expressed in a comparably chivalric language. Tasso, particularly in his treatment of Soliman, seems able to imagine a personality which speaks a moral language quite different from that of the Christians themselves. Soliman enters late, bringing his armies as reinforcements to encircle the Christian army. He proves to be the most ferocious of the pagan warriors and, clear-headedly, a rebel against the truths of the Christian God. Yet his position, as Tasso portrays him, is complicated from the first by elements of pathos as well as of terror. At his first appearance he is surrounded by portentous images, and by an heroic aura which Tasso can never generate around Goffredo. As Soliman approaches, witchcraft darkens the sky to conceal his advance. So Fairfax with a fine sense of the macabre speaks of how the clouds become

> Stained with spots of deepest sanguine hew,
> Warm drops of blood on earth's black visage shed,

30. See p. 148.

Supplied the place of pure and precious dew.
The moon and stars for fear of sprites were fled,
The shrieking gobblings each where howling flew,
The furies roar, the ghosts and fairies yell, yell . . .
The earth was filled with devils, and empty Hell.
(*GL*, IX. 14)

Yet this same figure is shown to be a king in exile from his own land, showing, on the one hand, an utter self-reliance – which seems to stand as an alternative to the pious unities which Goffredo offers – and, on the other, a tragic vulnerability to his own feelings and to the destiny imposed upon him by his opposition to the Christian God. In stanza 86, he weeps when his favourite is killed in battle: 'Thou weepest Soliman, thou that beheld/Thy kingdoms lost, and not one tear could'st yield . . . '. Momentarily, Tasso seems to acknowledge that a lonely faith in the heroic self, however ill-founded, can stand as an alternative to the pretensions of Christian belief.

In structural terms, the canto form in *Gerusalemme Liberata* is used not, as in the *Orlando Furioso*, to generate variety but to establish a unity in psychological and imaginative rhythm. Tasso's comparatively short cantos tend to be organised around effects of cross-cutting from one camp or character to another, with an eye to contrast, comparison and interplay. The subtlety with which this technique can be used is illustrated in the battle scene recorded in Canto VI, where, instead of moving mechanically from one army to the other, the warriors of the Christian camp are all identified by a speaker placed on the battlements of Jersualem. But this speaker is Erminia, the most timid and tremulous of a Tasso's heroines, who is in fact hopelessly in love with the Christian hero Tancred. As she names the Christians for reasons, overtly, of military tactics, so, inwardly, the battle becomes for both Erminia and the reader a metaphoric battle of the emotions. Unity here resides in an intense and highly wrought set of contrasts between the literal and the metaphoric, between the military and the erotic, between the inner and the outer. As in a Shakespeare play, unity is to be discerned as much in the patterning of imagery and in the parallelism of situations as in any purely formal balance.

Similar effects appear in an episode from Canto XII – first made famous by Monteverdi's operatic treatment of it – which describes how the Christian Tancredi and the pagan Clorinda meet at night in battle. Tancredi, himself in love with Clorinda, kills her without realising who his opponent has been; Clorinda, with her dying breath asks to be baptised, and Tancredi only recognises her when he raises her visor to perform the last rites. These events – 'worthy', says Tasso, 'of a sun-lit theatre rather than the shades of night' (54) – exemplify the spiritual and psychological 'wonders' with which Tasso sought to replace the fantastic machinery of Ariosto's poem. But the canto in which they occur also pursues with great intensity of image a current of themes, involving darkness, vulnerability and strain, in preparation for the climactic moment.

The episode (translated here by Fairfax) opens with one of Tasso's most subtle and most tragic images of the city:

> Era la notte, e non prendean ristoro
> co'l sonno ancor le faticose genti;
> ma qui vegghiando nel fabril lavoro
> stavano i Franchi a la custodia intenti,
> e la i pagani le difese loro
> già rinforzando tremule e cadenti
> e reintegrandoo le già rotte mura,
> de feriti era commun la cura.
>
> (GL, XII. 1)

> Now in dark night was all the world imbarred;
> But yet the tired armies took no rest,
> The careful French kept heedful watch and ward,
> While their high tower the workmen newly dressed,
> The Pagan crew to reinforce prepared
> The weakened bulwarks, late to earth down cast,
> Their rampires broke and bruised walls to mend,
> Lastly their hurts the wounded knights attend.

Here 'cross-cutting' reveals at once the similarities rather than the differences between pagan and Christian predicament, in the battle-weariness and inherent fragility of each. On one side, there is the great city itself battered by the siege; on the other, the siege-engine which – as an impermanent edifice – needs constantly to be built and rebuilt, with wood which can also serve as a funeral pyre for dead heroes. Then, too, there is the 'common' care of the wounded (which Fairfax fails to register); and, just as at the beginning of Shakespeare's *Hamlet* military preparations disturb the natural order of day and night, so here pagan and Christian alike strain against their own weariness to prepare for the heroic acts to which they have committed themselves.

Such frenetic energies and ultimately the revelation of a similar vulnerability run all through the subsequent episode. Clorinda, zealously impatient for action, wishes to perform a noble and single-handed feat. She is moved by some mysteriously undefined appetite – a '*non so che*': I know not what' (ibid., 5) – which she interprets as love of military glory but which will soon reveal itself to be a prompting of Providence leading her, through death, to Christian redemption. Her old servant, realising that a fatal moment is at hand her, at last relates to her the story of her life: Clorinda is the child of a mother who, being a person of colour, was secretly a Christian and one whose prayers to the Virgin ensured, by auto-suggestion, that her child was born white. It was the wish of Clorinda's mother that her daughter should die as a Christian; and the servant asks that Clorinda now accede to this wish. But Clorinda herself remains resolute in her pagan self-sufficiency, and refuses to contemplate a change in the religion which her faithful servant has himself taught her. She goes out to meet her fate declaring:

> I will not change it for religion new,
> Nor with vain shewes of feare and dread aghast
>   This enterprise forebeare I to pursue.
>   (*GL*, XII. 41)

Clorinda is pursued in the dark by Tancredi and the battle which ensues has profoundly erotic undertones (ibid., 57). As Tancredi struggles with her, so Clorinda seeks to release herself from the binding knots of a fierce enemy not of a lover – 'nodi tenaci . . . nodi di fer nemico e non d'amante'. Nevertheless, she is eventually overcome; and as she dies the promptings of the '*non so che*' return (ibid., 66), counselling her to repentance and finally to conformity with her mother's Christian wishes. Fairfax translates Tasso's undefined '*non so che*' into a 'spirit new' and, prematurely, confirms that this spirit represents a desire for 'faith hope and charity' (ibid., 65). But in Tasso this apparently benign 'spirit' will prove – as part of the 'miracle' that Tasso is attempting to create – to be as destructive as it is redemptive. Tancred, as yet, knows nothing of what he has done but, performing his Christian duty, he fetches water from a stream which is described – in ironically innocent and pastoral terms – as 'murmuring gently' close by. But the moment he begins the redemptive act of baptism, so his own tragedy begins: 'he saw and seeing knew her face and lost therewith his speech and moving quite: O woeful knowledge, ah unhappy sight!'. Smiling, the soul of Clorinda now ascends to Heaven. But the spectacle of Tancredi's madness still

remains to be enacted. He is now at a point comparable to that of
Orlando in discovering the 'infidelity' of Angelica; and, losing all sovereignty over himself (ibid., 72), his growing distraction will lead him in
the course of subsequent cantos into the depths of the enchanted wood,
where every tree which he strikes with his demented sword will scream
at him as if it were the soul of Clorinda.

THE RESPONSE OF SIDNEY AND SPENSER

In Canto XIV, stanza 46, Tasso speaks of how the human mind is a
night-bird in the sun dazzled by the light of primal truth:

> augel notturno al sole
> è nostra mente a i rai del primo Vero.

The same image is found in Sannazaro's *Arcadia*, while Sidney uses it
in both *Astrophil and Stella*, 99 and in his own *Arcadia*, where he speaks
at the end of Chapter 10 of the all-knowing God who sees into the
darkest secrets of the human heart and then proceeds to condemn
Cecropia who 'like a bat, though it have eyes to discern there is a sun,
yet hath so evil eyes that it cannot delight in the sun' (*Arcadia*, op.cit.,
p. 492).

These references – running from the extremes of the Counter-
Reformation to those of the Puritan movement – display a melancholic
understanding of human fallibility and a realisation that, while truth is
providentially assured, the very luminosity of truth may drive the
human mind back into the refuge of darkness and illusion. The irony of
this is as distant as could be from the ironies of the *Orlando Furioso*,
where the author stands as a surrogate for creative providence and sees
the human propensity to illusion as being itself a fertile source of creativity. But Tasso and Sidney have much in common on the plane of
intellectual stance and poetic sensibility. Both authors deny themselves
the exhilarating illusion that poetry is the product of inspiration, and
concentrate upon the responsibilities (and traumas) of technical 'making'. Each in his own way regards literature as a surrogate for action in
the courtly or chivalric life. Where Ariosto concerns himself with loyalty, Tasso and Sidney concern themselves with honour; and each
displays a precise understanding of military and political reality. This
similarity is particularly apparent in the Book III of Sidney's *New
Arcadia*. Technically, Sidney moves away in this book from the

Ariostan *entrelacement* which Harington identified in earlier books and
organises the narrative, as Tasso does, around opposing camps. Siege,
possession and conflicts, intrinsic to the two main characters as they
chafe against their disguises, dominate the mental rhythm here and
generate a violent and erotically charged atmosphere which is directly
analogous to that of the *Gerusalemme Liberata*. But finally, it is the heroic and spiritually elevated apprehension of human vulnerability which
most closely links the two poets. This, in Sidney's work, is realised
most fully in the character of the deeply flawed hero Amphialus; and in
no episode does the frailty of the great warrior show itself more powerfully than when Amphialus – having slain Parthenia's husband, Argalus
– is challenged by the Knight of the Tombs. In this episode, too, the
parallels between Sidney and Tasso become especially apparent. For
only when Amphialus has mortally wounded the Knight of the Tombs,
and is about to decapitate him, does he – like Tasso's Tancredi – realise
that he has slain a woman, Parthenia herself, whose beauty

> all-looked-upon through the spectacles of pity, did even increase the lines of
> her natural fairness, so as Amphialus was astonished with grief compassion
> and shame, detesting his fortune that made him unfortunate in victory.
> ... But Parthenia, who had inward messengers of the desired death's
> approach, looking upon him, and straight turning away her feeble sight as
> from a delightless object drawing out her words which her breath, loth to
> part from so sweet a body, did faintly deliver: Sir, said she, I pray you, if
> prayers have place in enemies, to let my maids take my body untouched by
> you. The only honour I now desire is that I have no honour from you.
>
> (*Arcadia*, op.cit., pp. 528–9)

Here, as in Tasso – even if Sidney had not read the twelfth canto of the
Gerusalemme Liberata – honour, eroticism, and the entanglements of the
chivalric code produce a bleakly tragic perception of the fragilities of the
human mind and body.

Unlike Sidney, Spenser engages directly with his sources in a literary
contest which is often at the same time, a patriotic and moral contest.[31]
In a letter to Gabriel Harvey,[32] Spenser makes it clear that in Book III
of *The Faerie Queene* he intends to 'overgo' Ariosto in the technique of
narrative *entrelacement* (which he had already begun to practise in *The*

---

31. For Ariosto and Spenser see Peter V. Marinelli, 'Ariosto' *The Spenser Encyclopedia*,
    general ed. A.C. Hamilton (Toronto and London, University Press, 1990), pp. 56–7.
    For Spenser and Tasso see David Quint, *Spenser Encyclopedia*, op.cit,. pp. 79–80.
32. See Letter Three in Spenser's *Prose Works*, ed. Ralph Gottfried, variorum edn.
    (Baltimore, 1949), pp. 471–2.

Shepherdes Calendar). This ambition is consistent with his concern to interlace the past and future glories of England through a treatment of the Arthurian myths – so highly favoured by the Tudors – and also by his determination to extend the subject of his poem beyond history into the realms of spiritual and ethical psychology. Ariosto sees in the inter-section of madness and desire a moment of tension in the cultures of love and war which is both challenging and – to the ironical mind – generative. Spenser, however, seeks to rise above the historical moment into a realm of myth where, without irony, the origins and implications of his culture can be observed. *Entrelacement* in Spenser's case combines with allegory to provide an analysis of the origins and ends of desire, as well as of the confusions which arise in the pursuit of moral and political glory.

In constructing his myth, Spenser ranges no less widely than Ariosto over the ancient and modern worlds. And just as in English literature he associates himself with the medieval Malory and Chaucer, so it seems quite probable that in Italian literature Spenser went back beyond Ariosto and Tasso to Dante's *Commedia*. It may be debated whether Spenser's allegorical method is at all comparable to Dante's.[33] But Spenser himself could well have thought it so; and, on that under-standing, he would certainly have found in Dante's work a 'drama of the mind'[34] in which narrative art could produce a parallel to the stages and crises of an ethical education. In both cases, narrative reflects an Aristotelian belief that the virtues can be learned by a progressive acquisition of good habits. Even when Spenser is at his most Ariostan – in apparent digressions and interlacings – his poem, like Dante's, pro-poses, even if it does not finally arrive at, the distinct goals to which journeys move.[35] Discipline is here a matter of recognising and direct-ing the various potentialities that constitute human nature. Both Spenser and Dante, however, as Christian thinkers, recognise possibili-ties which lie beyond the spectrum of Aristotle's understanding, especially in regard to the matter of love. In common with Boiardo, Spenser could see that a modern poem had to be, in some sense, a love poem. He also recognises in the sixth book of *The Faerie Queene* that

33. See R. Kirkpatrick, 'Dante', *Spenser Encyclopedia*, op.cit., pp. 205–8.
34. See the suggestive title of Francis Fergusson's excellent *Dante's Drama of the Mind* (Princeton, 1953).
35. Rosamund Tuve notes how in Spenser we return to characters after digressions who have advanced because of the experiences depicted in those digressions, in *Allegorical Imagery: Some Medieval Books and their Posterity* (Princeton, 1966), p. 363.

courtesy is a supreme expression of love; with Castiglione and the Bembo of the *Cortegiano*, Spenser views courtesy as 'the roote of civill conversation' which 'brancheth forth in brave nobilitie,/And spreads itself through all civilitee' (*FQ*, VI. I. i. and *Proem*, iv); courtesy, as a love of spiritual poise and ultimately of ideal measure' underlies and crowns the political life.[36] But courtesy is also, as in Dante, a virtue in which one moves beyond the sphere of the political to that of an ultimate love for persons, as they might be seen in the court of Heaven by the God who created them. So in Dante the courtly vocabulary which he associates with Beatrice is the language which he finally draws upon in his approach to God, who is said to be supremely courteous;[37] and in that approach he advances immeasurably beyond the language of political justice which Virgil had taught him. Justice – necessary as it is – remains a virtue which fits us for life in public communities; courtesy in the highest sense leads one, rather, into communion, face to face, with other members of a spiritual court. It is a virtue more specific in its aim and more subtle in its expression of particular natures than justice could ever be. In the same way, Spenser moves beyond the justice of his fifth book to a vision, in the sixth book, which demands an attention, cutting across the merely social order, to the 'straunge sight' of a 'jolly Shepheards lasse' and Colin Cloute' as the ultimate, and ultimately particular, embodiment of courtly excellence (*FQ*, VI. x. 16). So, too, Dante in the *Purgatorio* makes it a test of courtesy that one should know and feel free to praise the virtues of particular individuals: the sign that the great age of courtesy is past is that names such as Lizio and Arrigo Manardi can no longer be remembered (*Purgatorio*, XIV. 97–99).

It is frequently observed that English intellectuals tend, very generally, to adopt a moralistic stance towards their original Italian material. Elyot and Tottel are cases in point, and others will emerge in discussion of comedy and the novella. But with the examples of Dante and Aristotle in mind, one need not suppose that Spenser's evident inclination to moralisation is restrictive or reductive. On the contrary, moral concern – allied as in Dante and Aristotle to political and social interests – is here

36. See above, pp. 105–9.
37. See, for instance, Dante's constant insistent upon God's 'larghezza' or generosity which shows itself in the giving of gifts such as 'freedom' (e.g. at *Paradiso* V, lines 18–24). See also *Paradiso* XXIV, line 118, where God's grace is said 'to act the courtly lady' to the human mind, where the verb '*donne*-are' derives from an Occitan term for courtly dalliance.

the stimulus to close inquiry into the possibilities of human nature. So Spenser's ability to create narrative and psychological situations is born of his attention to the details of the examined life – and even Shakespeare will derive a good deal from Spenser in this regard. But Spenser himself locates his own advance upon his Italian exemplars in a comparable ability to examine and find in it a source of imaginative stimulus.

This is particularly noticeable in his treatment of Tasso where, unravelling with considerable analytical power the ambiguities of the original, Spenser gains greatly in clarity of moral vision. He is evidently sensitive both to the undercurrents of eroticism in Tasso's work and also to the tensions that exist there between fact and fiction. It is this which leads him, when dealing with the virtue of Temperance in Book II of *The Faerie Queene*, to engage directly with the figure of Tasso's Armida, who in the *Gerusalemme Liberata* not only stands for the Homeric Circe but is also, like Angelica, the focus of the most distractingly amorous elements of the romance genre.

The extent to which Armida was a problem for Tasso himself is indicated by the revision of her story which he includes in the *Gerusalemme Conquistata*. In the *Gerusalemme Liberata*, Armida had finally been allowed to convert to Christianity. But the militant orthodoxy of the later work forbids any such redemption. And it is evident that Tasso had come to realise the dangerously attractive ambiguity of the figure he had originally created. It is notable that the passages from the *Gerusalemme Liberata* in which Spenser cites the moral ambiguities surrounding Armida are registered with particular intensity in the ambiguities of the author's language and image. Spenser, it seems, has identified a problem which Tasso himself was belatedly to recognise, and has set out in the version he offers in *The Faerie Queene* to provide his own solution.

Thus in Canto XV of the *Gersualemme Liberata*, stanzas 4–5, Tasso imagines a figure who is in every respect shifting and diverse but who, in being so, seems to crystallise and express a range of brilliant possibilities which lie within natural phenomena themselves. Light blazes and sparkles in her face, shining differently in her glances (which are '*cortesi e favorevoli*') and in the curls of her hair. Likewise the colours of her dress change constantly, as colours do in shot silk, from red to blue, so that it seems 'always different from itself'. But this is not merely an effect of art. Nature itself can show the same effects in the variegated plumage of turtle doves or in the way that light enters into the substance of rubies and emeralds. There is, of course, the premonition of deceit in all of this; but there is also, to use Fairfax's translation – which aptly parallels a phrase in Shakespeare's *The Tempest* – something 'rich, pure, faire and strange'.

Spenser's understanding of the confusions here will lead him to distinguish the artifices of the Bower of Blisse from the pure natural images of the Garden of Adonis which offer themselves to single-minded love. But even within the Bower of Blisse, he is capable, while showing how temperance is tested, of suggesting what, in his view, Temperance truly is and what its resources are.

Here he quotes directly from Tasso's Canto XIV, stanzas 62–64; the beguiling words used to entice Guyon in Book II are exactly modelled on those which seduced Rinaldo in the *Gersualemme Liberata*:

> O giovenetti, mentre aprile e maggio
> v'ammantan di fiorite e verdi spoglie,
> di gloria e di virtù fallace raggio
> la tenerella mente ah non v'invoglie!
> Solo chi segue ciò che piace è saggio,
> e in sua stagion de gli anni il frutto coglie.

> Questo grida natura. Or dunque voi
> indurarete l'alma a i detti suoi?
> Folli, perché gettate il caro dono,
> che breve è sìi, di vostra età novella?
> Nome, e senza soggetto idoli sono
> ciò che pregio e valore il mondo appella.
> La fama che invaghisce a un dolce suono
> voi superbi mortali, e par sì bella,
> è un'ecco, un sogno, anzi del sogno un'ombra,
> ch'ad ogni vento si dilegua e sgombra.

> Goda il corpo sicuro, e in lieti oggetti
> l'alma tranquilla appaghi i sensi frali;
> oblii le noie andate, e non affretti
> le sue miserie in aspettando i mali.
> Nulla curi se 'l ciel tuoni o saetti,
> minacci egli a sua voglia e infiammmi strali.
> Questo è saver, questa è felice vita:
> sì l'insegan natura e sì l'addita.

(O young men, while April and May and are bedecking you with green and flourishing array, ah! Let not the deceitful ray of glory and prowess mislead the tender mind! He only is wise who follows that which pleases him and gathers in its due season the fruit of years. Nature cries this aloud. Will you harden your hearts against her words? Fools, why do you cast away the pre-

cious gift of your youth, short as it is. Names and empty images are what the
world calls honour and worth. Fame that enchants you, O prideful mortals
Fame is nothing save a sweet sound; it is an echo, a dream or rather no
dream but a shade. Let your bodies untroubled rejoice; souls rejoice. Let the
tranquil soul feed the frail senses on joyous things. Let it forget past torments,
and let it not hasten misery in expectation of coming ills. Care nothing if
Heaven thunders and strikes with lightening. Let him threaten as he pleases
and let his arrows blaze. This is wisdom; this is the happy life. So Nature
teaches and so she points our way.)

In Tasso's text it is notable and characteristic that, beneath the lyrical
sensuality of these lines, there should be a subtext, and that this should
be Tasso's own dictum from the pastoral play *Aminta* (I. 681) where in
the Golden Age nature is said to have carved the happy law '*S'ei piace, ei
lice*': 'whatever pleases is legitimate'. And nature itself is here enlisted to
support this claim; there is, it seems, a world of truth – and a genre to
embody it – beyond the realm of heroic labour. But not in Spenser.
Here the subtext is Scripture – specifically *St Matthew's Gospel* (6.
25–34) – and heroic conscience is called to realise the blasphemies that
sensuality and literature itself can commit against that text. Hence the
unequivocal violence which Guyon uses to destroy the Bower of Blisse.
But Temperance too is seen as that which derives from a proper reading
of the words that flicker before one: nature has it measure. But this
measure will only reveal itself to those who heroically abdicate their literary and sensuous desires and are prepared to read, in contemplation, a
book that promises peace to those who have faith in it or to those who
through that faith can find find their place in creation alongside the lilies
of the field:

> Behold, O man that toilesome paines doest take,
> The flowres, the fields, and all that pleasant growes,
> How they themselves doe thine ensample make,
> Whiles nothing envious nature them forth throwes
> Out of her fruitful lap; how, no man knowes,
> They spring, they bud, they blossome fresh and faire,
> And deck the worlde with their rich pompous showes;
> Yet no man for them taketh paines or care,
> Yet no man to them can his carefull paines compare.
> The Lilly, Ladie of the flowring field,
> The Flowre-deluce, her lovely Paramoure,
> Bid thee to them thy fruitless labours yield,
> And soon leave off this toylsome wearie stoure;

Loe loe how brave she decks her bounteous boure,
With silken curtens and gold couerlets,
Therein to shroud her sumptuous Belamoure,
Yet neither spinnes nor cardes, ne cares nor frets
But to her mother Nature all her care she lets.
Why then dost thou O man, that of them all
Art Lord, and eke of Nature Soueraine,
Wilfully make thy selfe a wretched thrall,
And wast thy joyous houres in needlesse paine,
Seeking for daunger and adventures vaine?
What bootes it all to have, and nothing use?
Who shall him rew, that swimming in the maine,
Will die for thirst, and water doth refuse?
Refuse such fruitlesse toile, and present plesure chuse.

It is with similar moral aims and similar moral resources that Spenser
enters into intertextual contention with Ariosto. There is little irony in
Spenser, but rather (in the Dantean sense) a comic awareness of the ultimate coherence and harmony of all desires. There is no suggestion in
The Faerie Queene of madness as a power that might, variously, dislocate
and animate a culture. There is, however, an understanding of how an
heroic purpose can encounter and overcome tragically distracting obsta-
cles, and equally an understanding – unaffected by any of Ariosto's
sardonic humour – of glory as that which a Tudor Englishman might
'boast' of in his moral and political life.

At every point, such broad differences of intellectual position are connected to differences in stylistic and formal procedure.

It is striking that Spenser should employ *entrelacement* especially in a
book concerning chastity. In Ariosto, *entrelacement* is a means to stimulate desires – and often erotic desires – in his reader, as one moves from
one unfinished story to story.[38] Yet Spenser's moral purposes are clear:
not only does the method allow distraction to be dramatised, it also
suggests that there is an underlying integrity to be sought. Chastity
throughout Book III is seen as an aspect of the self-possession that the
individual can enjoy when, in love, it recognises its dependence upon
those principles of virtue – whether political or spiritual – which lie
beyond itself. And the displacements of Spenserian *entrelacement* here
can be used effectively to dramatise the perception of ultimate harmony

38. See the notorious incident in *OF*, X. 114–15, where as Ruggiero is about to rape
    Angelica whom he has just saved from certain death, the story breaks of, with
    Ruggiero unable to get his armour off.

as well as to exert, through parallelism and cross-reference, a moral control which the reader, too, is invited to exert on the unfolding narrative.

A central instance of this is the episode of Belphoebe and Timias (*FQ*, III. v) which draws directly upon *Orlando Furioso*, XIX. 22, *et seq.* This is a particularly crucial moment in Ariosto's poem. For here Angelica has taken into her care Medoro, the humble foot-soldier who – in Ariosto's own modification of Virgil's Nisus and Euryalus episode, *Aeneid* IX – has been wounded in a night raid. At last, the hitherto fleeting Angelica begins to display initiative; as she seeks to cure Medoro, so each falls in love with each, and their story will end happily as princess and the foot-soldier disappear from the poem on their way to the Orient. Yet, in spite of this conclusion, the episode is shot through with ironies. The love between these two contradicts all the social and amatory codes that the other heroes of the poem have sought to uphold; the more the wound is healed, the more the wished-for wound of love becomes open, but the closer, too, one comes to the point at which Orlando, discovering evidence of that love in Canto XXIII, will be driven into madness.

For Spenser, too, the episode is a turning-point. Yet in a completely different sense. For, here, as the poem is about to enter the Garden of Adonis, Belphoebe appears as a manifestation of Gloriana or Elizabeth herself. The curing is one which displays her regal pity upon a subject, and which opens the way to an understanding of how the mind, cured of its sensual distractions, can enter through chastity and charity upon an appreciation of the images of a pure nature. To enforce this point, Spenser conducts as conscious a debate with his source, as Ariosto might have done with Boiardo, modifying in the light of his own moral purposes the authorial attitudes, the diction, and also the narrative techniques of his original.

The central conceits of the two situations immediately mark a difference: Medoro, wounded in battle, is cured, while reciprocally Angelica feels the wound of love. Timias – wounded Actaeon-fashion by the chaste ladies of Belphoebe's entourage – continues to be the sufferer, though from a wound of love, while Belphoebe protects her 'rose' of love by a kindly but unsurmountable chastity. In Ariosto the rose of love is plucked by mutual consent in the consummation of the love between them (ibid., 34); Spenser's canto ends with praise of Belphoebe's heroic constancy of mind.

So, linguistically, Ariosto's stanzas traces an erotic process in which sexual implications are delicately framed in a mathematics of rhythmic balance:

> La sua piaga più s'apre e più incrudisce,
> quanto più l'altra si ristringe e salda.
> Il giovine si sana: ella languisce
> di nuova febbre, or agghiacciata, or calda.
> Di giorno in giorno in lui beltà fiorisce:
> la misera si strugge, come falda
> strugger di nieve intempestiva suole,
> ch'in loco aprico abbia scoperta il sole.
>
> (*OF*, XIX. 29)

(Her wound grew the wider and fiercer the more his closed and healed. The youth recovered his health; she languished with new fever, now freezing now warm. From day to day, in him his beauty flourished; wretchedly she melts, as happens with an untimely flake of snow which the sun discovers in a warm place.)

In Spenser there is no process, but rather the attempt to arrest any development and produce a stable moment within it. Thus the image of snow applied in Ariosto to the wasting of Angelica's beauty is reapplied here to Timias:

> Yet still he wasted, as the snow congealed,
> When the brighte sunne his beames theron doth beat;
> Yet never he his hart to her revealed,
> But rather chose to dye for sorrow great,
> Then with dishonourable termes her to entreat.
>
> (*FQ*, III. 49)

Here Timias differs from the melting snow in seeking a coldness of virtue that nature cannot provide. Angelica deliquesces to the point at which, with 'tongue no less daring than her eyes', (ibid., 30) she yields the rose which Ariosto, with some lubricious irony, claims has never been touched before, and allows Medoro into the garden where no one had been so daring as to enter. (ibid., 33). The audience is complicit in this literary seduction; and it is a matter of taste whether one wishes to be so inveigled or not. But Spenser resists, and boldly realises that, to resist most fully, he must take and re-sanctify the ancient image of love as a rose. So the rose (as it might have been for Dante in the final cantos of the *Paradiso*, XXXI) becomes a manifestation of the 'ensample' which 'Eternall God' planted in Paradise:

That dainty Rose, the daughter of her Morne,
  More deare than life she tendered, whose flowre
  The girlond of her honour did adorne;
  Ne suffred she the Middayes scorching powre,
  Ne the sharp Northerne wind thereon to showre,
  But lapped up her silken leaves most chaire,
  When so the froward skye began to lowre:
  But soon was calmed was the Christall aire,
  She did it faire dispred, and let it flourish faire
                    (ibid., 51)

There is enough sensuality in Spenser's language for him not to be accused of prudishness. If anything, he points to a greater sensuality which derives from the richness of an idea and from the pleasure of self-possession. The human body here, while still material, transports itself to a sphere which cannot be touched by the processes of wind or scorching sun.

In authorial attitude, Ariosto orchestrates the responses of his reader by entering the text – before the consummation – to point out how ironical it is that Angelica should fall to a foot-soldier when Orlando and so many Paladins could not win her:

  O conte Orlando, o re di Circassia,
    vostra inclita virtù, dite, che giova?
  (O Count Orlando, O King of Circassia, say, what did
  your splendid virtue avail?)

                    (OF, XIX. 31)

The language shifts into a moral vein, but only to condemn Angelica for the ungratefulness which prevents her from playing her part in the courtly game of love. Virtue here is not the personal virtue which Spenser is trying to defend but rather the 'virtue' of appropriate role-play; and Ariosto, writing from within that code, allows, through the interplay between event and authorial voice, the possibility of an undercutting of that whole code. Spenser, on the other hand, is looking for a way in which to present a true form of pity, whereby chastity might ensure a concern for qualities in the individual other than sexual qualities. And having purified, in his text, the image of the rose, he invites his audience not to ironise or feel the pressures of his narrative but rather to abandon narrative in contemplation of the image he has established. This is in part a political move, and there is some high-minded humour in the allusion here: Ariosto's narrative runs to a rhythm of erotic expectation whereas Spenser concludes in Canto VI with a historical concern – insofar as Belphoebe is Elizabeth – over the fate of the Tudor dynasty. But the chorus which concludes the canto is a chorus rejoicing in moral examples:

> Faire ympes of beautie, whose bright shining beames
> Adorne the world with like to heavenly light
>   And to you wills both royalties and Realmes
> Subdew, through conquest of your goodly girlonds dight,
>   (*FQ*, III. vi)

The only remote irony here is in a morally dangerous rhyme on 'maidenhead' and 'dead' in stanza 54. But by now there can be no doubt of Spenser's intentions. And these extend finally to the management of the canto ending. The art of narrative teasing in Ariosto here gives way to a moral joke. Canto V ends with the processes involved in the pursuit of chastity leading to the perfect point of arrival in Belphoebe's perfection:

> So striving each did other more augment,
> And both encrease the prayse of woman kind,
> And both encrease her beautie excellent;
> So all did make in her a perfect complement.
>   (*FQ*, III. v. 55)

The only transition is to begin again, and to ask the reader's retrospective curiosity at the beginning of Canto VI: contemplating this image, one must consider how Belphoebe lived so perfectly so far from court. In Ariosto the episode ends with Angelica and Medoro speeding across Europe on the way to the East, impeded only – at stanza 42 – on the coast near Barcelona by the sight of a madmen lying like a pig in mud:

> un uom pazzo
> giacer trovaro in su l'estreme arene,
> che come porco, di loto e di guazzo,
> tutto era brutto e volto e petto e schene.

Only ten cantos later do we discover that this madman is Orlando; as yet, since we are still in Canto XIX, the reader knows nothing of the tragic decline described in Canto XXIII.

Chapter 5

Comedy in the Renaissance

INTRODUCTION

Gabriel Harvey, in the fifth letter of his correspondence with Edmund Spenser, speaks of nine comedies which Spenser had himself composed on models provided by Ariosto. These comedies, Harvey declares, may well come closer

> either for the fineness of plausible Elocution or the rareness of Poetical Invention than that the Elvish Queene doth to his *Orlando Furioso*.

Spenser's comedies have either been lost, or – plausibly – were never written. If lost, this at once indicates a problem which always affects the study of the relationships between English and Italian comedy: few scholars doubt the decisive influence of the Italian model on English writing, yet the lines of influence are rarely as direct as those which emerge in considering the lyric and the epic. Comedies, as public entertainment, are by nature, ephemeral and tend to be discarded when the moment of performance is past, or else are progressively displaced by the appearance of newer examples. The study of comedy is therefore often the study of analogy – or of what Louise George Clubb interestingly calls 'theatergrams';[1] and this is as it should be, since comedy seems often to have been inspired as much by reminiscence as by a close imitation of original texts.

---

1. The phrase is used extensively by Clubb in her *Italian Drama in Shakespeare's Time* (New Haven, 1989). Also on the relations between Italian and English comedy see Leo Salingar's excellent *Shakespeare and the Traditions of Comedy* (Cambridge, 1974). English translations of Italian comedy can be found in R. Warwick Bond, *Early Plays from the Italian* (New York, 1911) and in Eric Bentley, *The Genius of the Italian Theater* (New York, 1964).

On the other hand, for many Renaissance authors comedy represented an important aspect of the study of the classical literature and an equally important part of the contribution which a humanist could make to contemporary culture. If Spenser never actually wrote his comedies, then Harvey's reference may well be seen as part of a concerted programme to dignify Spenser's reputation as a master in all literary genres.[2] Spenser's own intentions might have been consistent with the desire which Sidney expresses to see a rectification of comic writing in England. In the *Apology for Poetry*, Sidney declares that 'we have no right comedy', and goes on to distinguish the scurrility which characterises the comic laughter of English audiences from the delight which should be stimulated by true comedy:

> Delight hath a joy in it, either permanent or present. Laughter hath only a scornful tickling . . . We delight in good chances, we laugh at mischances; we delight to hear the happiness of our friends, or country, at which he were worthy to be laughed at that would laugh.[3]

When 'right comedy' does arrive in England – most notably in the work of Ben Jonson with its Sidneian concern over Reason and Nature – as much attention will be given, of course, to classical as to Italian models, even – as in Jonson's *Volpone* or *The Case is Alter'd* – where the setting is Italianate. Nevertheless, Sidney's comments on laughter recall the discussions of humour in Book II of the *Cortegiano*, where, given a degree of intelligence and balance, humour is recognised to be a courtly art. Moreover, Italian authors such as Ariosto were no less concerned with the classical tradition than Jonson was, and were on the whole less likely than Jonson to depart from, or deform, that example.[4] English travellers to Italy such as Sidney would certainly have seen examples of right comedy formed on a classical model – and of other forms of theatrical entertainments – in the courtly circles which they frequented.

The one example of English comedy which I shall consider here is that of George Gascoigne's *Supposes* of 1566, which is modelled directly on Ariosto's *I Suppositi* and which subsequently provided Shakespeare with the sub-plot of *The Taming of the Shrew*.[5] Gascoigne was himself a literary figure of considerable importance in the early Elizabethan period, and is praised by Nashe for having first 'beat the path to that perfection which our best Poets have aspired to . . . by comparing the

2. See M. Bradbrooke, in J.R. Brown and Harris (eds.), *Elizabethan Poetry*, op.cit.
3. Ref. to pp.54–5
4. See Ann Barton, *Ben Jonson Dramatist* (Cambridge, 1984).
5. See below, pp. 279–82.

Italian with the English, as Tullie did *Graeca cum Latinis* ('To the Gentlemen Students of both Universities', in Robert Green's *Menaphon*, p. 12). Moreover, his major work was done in the ambience of the Inns of Court which were at this time beginning to prove their worth as centres for theatrical experimentation, receiving and transmitting the 'theatregrams' – or dramatic motifs and formal developments – which had first been developed in Italy. *Gorboduc* had already been performed when Gascoigne wrote the *Supposes*. And in the same year as this 'fine comedy' appeared, to use Harvey's words, so too did Gascoigne's 'stately tragedy' *Iocasta*, which is a translation (in collaboration with Kinwelmarshe) of Lodovico Dolce's version of the Senecan – and ultimately Euripidean – *Phoenissae*.[6]

But if, with Gascoigne, English writers began to develop the arts of formulation and reformulation on which comedy thrives, Italy itself by this time had advanced considerably in technical experiment. It is to Italy that one must look first for a brief history of the comic form and its possibilities. And as one turns to Italy one also becomes aware of how central a feature of Renaissance culture the comic form could be. First, as a form of entertainment, comedy directly reflects the habits and tastes of the period in which it was written. Similarly, in their engagement with the classical past, comic authors were able to display not only learning but also considerable originality or virtuosity in the imitation and redirection of their models. Then, finally, in the hands of, say, Machiavelli and Giordano Bruno, the comic form itself becomes a medium for philosophical or political expression, as authors reflect upon the underlying principles of the socials world which their comedies depict.

THE DEVELOPMENT OF ITALIAN COMEDY

Towards the end of the fifteenth century, a form of stage comedy, known as *commedia erudita*, came to be developed by humanists which was 'erudite' in being constructed according to rules drawn from Latin models.[7]

6. For Gascoigne, see especialy C.T. Prouty, *George Gascoigne: Elizabethan Courtier Soldier and Poet* (New York, 1942). For the text of Gascoigne's works, see *The Complete Works of George Gascoigne*, 2 vols, ed. J.W. Cunliffe (Cambridge, 1907–10). See also above, p. 224.
7. For the development of Italian comedy, see especially Douglas Radcliffe-Umstead, *The Birth of Modern Comedy in Renaissance Italy* (Chicago and London, 1969); M. Herrick, *Italian Comedy in the Renaissance* (Urbana, 1966); M. Baratto, *La Commedia del Cinquecento* (Vicenza, 1975) and, more recently, Richard Andrews, *Scripts and Scenarios: The Performance of Comedy in Renaissance Italy* (Cambridge, 1993).

In Italy as in England, there had been a long tradition of Latin plays often written for educational purposes. Petrarch himself had written at least one such comedy the *Philologia*, modelled roughly on Terence's work,[8] and teachers such as Vergerio quickly followed suit.

In English educational circles similar intellectual interests were to produce plays such as *Ralph Roister Doister* Udall and 'Mr S. Master of Arts' *Gammer Gurton's Needle*. But in Italy the movement towards a vernacular treatment of comic themes was, from the first, associated not only with teaching but also with the original research of humanist scholars and with the most sophisticated levels of court entertainment (in which pedants quickly became stock characters). In 1448, the scholar and philosopher Nicholas Cusanus discovered the manuscript of twelve hitherto unknown comedies by Plautus. Previously the only classical model available was Terence, whose work was considered so instructive, in a moral sense, that it could be studied by nuns in the Middle Ages. But now a rage began for the bawdier style of Plautine comedy – as did competition for the possession of this prestigious manuscript.[9] A hundred years later a renewed stimulus was given by the re-discovery of Aristotle's *Poetics*: the model of Sophocles' *Oedipus,* in regard to the unities of time, space and action and also to dramatic recognition, was to influence not only tragic but also comic writing, and would also contribute – as will be seen in Chapter Seven – to the development of tragi-comic forms.[10]

It was Ariosto, however, building on Roman comedy and writing for the court of Ferrara, who provided the earliest practical models, and who first developed the art of *contaminatio*, which is the interweaving of received material with new plots and new emphases. So in the prologues to *La Cassaria* (1508) and *La Lena* (1528), Ariosto presents himself (as he does in the *Orlando Furioso*) as the modest servant of the court of Ferrara – which, he acknowledges, would rather be involved in dancing that in watching a comedy.[11] Less modestly, however, he declares that even the best of the classical writers never invented much of their own material and consequently claims the right to present a new comedy, 'which had never been played in the Greek or Latin tongues'.

Here the linguistic *contaminatio* which Ariosto defends is compatible with a profound interest in the vernacular – at a time when Latin was in

8. See Petrarch's letter to Giovanni Colonna di San Vito. For summaries of these Latin works see Radcliffe-Umstead, op.cit.
9. Radcliffe-Umstead, op.cit, pp. 59–60.
10. Northrope Frye stresses that Sophoclean structure came to be applied to comedy as well as to tragedy, *The Anatomy of Criticism* (Princeton, 1957).
11. Compare his authorial stance in the epic above, p. 156 and p. 165.

the ascendancy – and this same interest resonated throughout Italy, liberating the vernacular speech of authors such as the Paduan Ruzzante and the Neapolitan Giordano Bruno. At the same time, *contaminatio* quickly extended to the adoption of plots from vernacular sources, in particular from the comic writings of Boccaccio. Like Roman comedy, erudite comedy was almost invariably urban – depicting the the middle and lower classes of the city – and concerned to generate a general atmosphere delusion in tracing the comic misapprehensions that might arise within the labyrinth of a city. But with Boccaccio in mind, attention could be paid to contemporary situations and to activities characteristic of the new urban centres, while similarly the range of characters could also be extended so that, alongside the traditional soldiers, masters and servants, lovers began to appear and with lovers, women. Ariosto's *La Lena* pictures a particularly enterprising woman of Boccaccian temperament.

Erudite comedy was for the most part performed by amateurs.[12] Indeed, as the vogue developed, so did half-serious 'academies' in which leading citizens would gather to compose and perform comic plays – often giving themselves silly names, as in the Sienese academy of the *Intronati* or 'Thunderstruck'. But in Ariosto's Ferrara, as elsewhere, it was the court – with its financial resources and an available supply of amateur actors in the form of attendant intellectuals and pages – where the genre developed most fully. (Shakespeare in *Love's Labours Lost* characteristically creates a combination of courtly and academic comedy in the play of the Nine Worthies.) In these circumstances, comedy became the occasion for often prodigiously luxurious entertainment, displaying to visiting ambassadors, or in celebration of dynastic marriages, all the talents that the court could command, literary and otherwise.

The effect of one such occasion is graphically registered in the words of Castiglione describing the performance in 1513 of a play (which will be considered in more detail later) by no less a figure than Cardinal Bibbiena, the scholar and protégé of Pope Leo X:

> To the ceiling of the [auditorium] were attached great baskets of greenery, so that the vault was almost entirely concealed from view. From the rose decorations on the ceiling wires were hanging. These held candelbra, draped from one side of the hall to the other, forming the letters of the alphabet which 'spell delights to the people'.
>
> *Il Calandro* went very well.

12. The *commedia dell'arte* – where 'arte' signifies 'professional' – developed later than erudite comedy and, though its influence was to be enormous, it drew the the basic situations from those developed in learned works. See R. Andrews, *Scripts and Scenarios*, op.cit. and Louise G. Clubb, *Italian Drama in Shakespeare's Time*, op.cit.

But what of the *intermezzi?* The first was a Moorish dance, involving Jason who appeared on stage armed in antique fashion, with sword and magnificent shield: on the other side were seen two bulls so life-like that one would have thought they were real, both breathing fire. The good Jason came up to them, and set them to plough . . . and then he set to sowing dragon's teeth, until armed men began to grow out of the stage floor.

Here a single, very casual, line is devoted to the Bibbiena's play, as Castiglione luxuriates in details of decor and the mechanisms of the interludes. Yet this is only to be expected. Court-life itself was for Castiglione a form of theatre; and with a characteristic undertone of calculation Castiglione speaks in Book II of *The Courtier* of the disguises which courtiers at such a performance might adopt to best advantage. Now he describes an opportunity for, as it were, communal *sprezzatura.* The comic author will of course make his contribution. But so too do the interior decorators, dancing masters, musicians and stage designers. Even (or especially) the patron or autocratic ruler would have his part to play. For the whole edifice might be dismantled with as effortless a *sprezzatura* as it was assembled in the first place. Thus in 1561 Leone di Somi writes of the 'magnanimity' of the Duke Guglielmo Gonzaga in spending 'many thousands of ducats on [a] marvellous set and then destroying it when it had served its immediate purpose'.[13] If the author was to play upon themes of illusion and ephemerality, then so, too, was the Duke.

Even, then, before the play had begun, the audience would have been presented with a script of social, political or economic emblems which, as it were, they themselves had to read and enact as part of their own script. But in the same way, the space in which the actors performed would be dominated by an extremely potent visual image; for the action in Renaissance comedy invariably took place against an unchanging backdrop representing a city or townscape. This was no casual device. Artists as eminent as Raphael could be commissioned to create this scenic prop; and such artists would bring with them as much learning and expertise in their own field as the author did in his. Vitruvius's architectural studies for the theatre had, for instance, been rediscovered in 1414 and published in

---

13. See L. Salingar, *Shakespeare and the Traditions of Comedy* (Cambridge, 1974). Also Sidney Anglo, 'Humanism and the Court Arts', in Antony Goodman and Angus Mackay (eds.), *The Impact of Humanism on Western Europe* (London and New York, 1990), p. 85. Anglo speaks of similar instances of conspicuous consumption in England. See also Werner L. Gundersheimer, 'Popular Spectacle and the Theatre in Renaissance Ferrara', and Charles M. Rosenberg, 'The Use of Celebration in Public and Semi-Public Affairs in Fifteenth Century Ferrara', both in *Il teatro italiano del Rinascimento* a cura di Maristella de Panizza Lorch (Milan, 1980).

1486,[14] giving classical prestige to the the art of theatre design. And visual *contaminatio* was possible when scholarly material of this sort came into combination with the native advances which Renaissance artists had made in their use of perspectival illusion to exert a grip upon the 'real' world. Art here conspicuously allies itself with power: the city was ruled by the aristocratic audience which witnessed the play and, through the illusions created by dramatists and stage-designers, the same city was symbolically offered for those who ruled it to enjoy afresh.

Illustrations of model sets are to be found in Book Two of Sebastiano Serlio's architectural theory,[15] as, for instance, in the figure below which is taken significantly enough from the conclusion of a lengthy study of perspective:

14. The works of the first-century Roman architect M. Virtuvius Pollio are the only examples of architectural theory to survive from the classical antiquity. Though the work was known throughout the Middle Ages, the discovery of a superior manuscript and its printed publication in 1486 led to considerable advances.

15. Sebastiano Serlio (born Bologna 1475, died Lyons 1554) published his five-volume study of architectural theory in 1547. An English translation (from the Dutch) appeared in 1611 and can now be read in Dover Books (New York and London, 1982).

One notes here the command of space and of architectural detail, made possible through the accurate orthogonals of the chequer-board floor. Nor can one mistake – as a component in the humour of the comedy – the delight which is revealed by Serlio's subsequent comments on the *sprezzatura* of this illusory reality:

> Among all the things that may be made by men's hands, thereby to yield admiration and pleasure to the sight, and to content the fantasies of men, I think it is the placing of a scene as it is shewed to your sight, where a man in a small space may see built by Carpenters or Masons skilful in Perspective worke, great palaces, large Temples . . . abounding with innumerable lights.

As the last phrase indicates, the aesthetic effects of the comedy had by Serlio's time come to include lighting; Serlio himself gives specifications for producing – chemically – flames of different colours. But the political undertone of such technical refinement is audible even in the technical prescriptions which Serlio offers when he stresses that comic plays – as contrasted with tragedies – must be set in a bourgeois rather than aristocratic ambience, and also when he carefully includes in the ideal scene the 'bawdy house and the great inn'. The activities of the middle and lower classes were to be displayed in some detail for the pleasure of an aristocratic audience.

The implications of such a setting were not lost on contemporary theorists. Thus the critic Castelvetro (1505–71) strikingly insists that tragedy can only appear in a democracy whereas comedy is a form appropriate to despotisms. Tragic characters are a law unto themselves and meet their fate with extreme and disruptive responses. Comic situations tend to be resolved by the revelation of an underlying order or rule which, although benevolent, lies beyond the immediate control of the actors in the drama. So Castelvetro declares:

> The persons of Comedy are of poor spirit and inclined to obey the magistrates and live under the law. They do not, unlike the tragic hero, make a law unto themselves. And where the tragic hero has to seek happiness through a rise and fall, in comedy because the figures are in poor and humble state – their happiness can increase through many steps and through moderate happenings such as a wedding that is desired.[16]

16. Quoted from p. 330 of A.H. Gilbert, *Literary Criticism: Plato to Dryden* (Detroit, 1970). This collection offers a valuable introduction to the literary theorists of the the Italian fifteenth century. See also on L. Castelvetro, *On the Art of Poetry*, an abridged translation of *Poetica d'Aristotele*, by Andrew Bongiorno, Medieval and Renaissance Texts and Studies 29 (Binghampton, NY, 1984).

Order, then, becomes an implicit theme in comedy. And if the Renaissance inherited from Roman comedy an interest in comic misapprehension, it also developed an interest in the political and artistic resolution of order which Rome may not explicitly have recognised. Now, actors – in situations provoked by a human capacity for error and sexual confusion – move across a chequer-board which assures the audience at least of the law and permanence which the artists have put in place on the command, ultimately, of a princely patron. There is much here of the spirit of Carnival where a period of licensed confusion may be enjoyed; and at a deeper level still there may have been elements of repressed defensive anxiety of the kind which explicitly finds its way into tragedies of the period. But the humour would also be that of delighted superiority as an audience, adept at enjoying effects of illusion in the work of their artists, saw enacted before them the errors of those who could not benefit from that overview. One may add that with every elegant interlude between the acts such an audience would also be able to lift its eyes from these illusory realities to the higher illusion of the mythological guessing game.

In the examples which are now to be considered, Bibbiena and, later, Ariosto – in the play which Gascoigne translates – will dextrously explore the possibilities embodied in the form as it has so far been described and show much artistic sensitivity to the play of order and disorder. In the work of Machiavelli and Giordano Bruno, however, these same forms will reveal more subversive possibilities, looking forward – whether directly or not – to opportunities which would be developed by the English comic writer of the later Elizabethan period.

BIBBIENA'S *LA CALANDRIA*

Bibbiena's *La Calandria* is a classic instance of *contaminatio*, in which motifs from Plautus are combined with sustained reference to Boccaccio; and much of the pleasure which the original audience derived from the play must have been due to an understanding – akin to that which they would have received from Ariosto's *Orlando Furioso* – of the skill with which the author had commanded and redirected his literary sources.[17] Comparably, an appreciation of authorial *sprezzatura* would have been stimulated by the play of complication and resolution within the plot itself.

17. A translation of Bibbiena's *La Calandria* is contained in E. Bentley, *The Genius of The Italian Theatre* (New York, 1964), op.cit.

La Calandria begins with an authorial prologue in which the scarcely competent author, waking from a lubricious dream, presents an apology for the coming play. This opening scene, with its hints of sexual licence and of play-within-play, contains many of the possibilities which writers such as Bruno or Shakespeare would later develop in an inherently disruptive fashion. But Bibbiena's prologue is a piece of controlled mock-modesty, preparing for the *sprezzatura* of the subsequent treatment. From the first, for instance, one is made aware of the theatrical illusion which allows that the greatness of Rome – where the play is set – should be reduced and transported to Urbino – where the play is being performed.

In the comedy itself, Bibbiena (following Plautus as Shakespeare was also to do in *The Comedy of Errors* and in *Twelfth Night*) tells of Greek twins who have been separated at an early age in the course of a Turkish raid on their native city and who have then, unknown to each other, found their way to Rome under the protection of their servants. Bibbiena, however, departs at once from Plautus in giving different sexes to his twins. As a further exhilarating complication – which also prepares for a good deal of sexual innuendo – he also makes each twin a transvestite. To safeguard her honour, Santilla has dressed as a boy, calling herself by her brother's name, Lidio. Now, however, her benign protector in Rome wishes – in ignorance of her sex – to marry her to his only daughter. The male Lidio, meanwhile, has arrived in Rome; and the play opens with an account of the affair which he is pursuing with the wife of Calandro, astutely (as it seems) disguised as a woman to gain unsuspected access. The only drawback to this scheme is that Calandro is enchanted by Lidio's cross-dressed charms and seeks to seduce him.

Complications such as these already lead to the expression of Boccaccian sentiment in regard particularly to Fortune, witnessed in the history of past calamities, to Nature in the urges of lovers, and to Wit in the astuteness of both the lovers themselves and of their servants. Appropriately, these themes are generally voiced by a knowing servant, Fessenio, whose vivacity of mind makes him the temporary equal of his master, and who needs to keep his wits about him 'if by serving three masters the whole ruin is not to fall on [his own] head'.

The action in Bibbiena's play does not in fact allow as much scope to the initiative of the servant as Boccaccio's stories might. Nevertheless, the comic action is dominated by two highly Boccaccian figures, the dim-witted Calandro and his insatiably passionate wife, Fulvia. Fulvia, to make sure that Lidio never leaves her, employs a highly incompetent magician to enchant him. Unfortunately, the only 'Lidio' known to the magician is the ward of the merchant Perillo, in other words the cross-dressed Santilla. When Santilla is approached in the street she denies all knowledge of Fulvia, who is further distressed when Fessenio informs her that Lidio is about to leave Rome in search of his sister. It seems that the magician's charms have acted in exactly the opposite way from that which was intended.

Fulvia's obsessions already occupy a central place in the action. And they are soon joined as a point of interest by the idiocies of the Boccaccian Calandro, who now falls victim to the wiles of servants, prostitutes and customs men. Fessenio persuades Calandro that Lidio — in the guise of Santilla — is ready to yield to his advances. Calandro agrees to be enclosed in a chest so that he can be carried to his mistress, who will in fact prove to be a prostitute hired to impersonate the supposed Santilla. The chest carrying Calandro is apprehended by custom officers, speaking in Venetian dialect, who are told that this is the corpse of a plague victim about to be thrown into the river. (The motif will of course recur in Shakespeare's *The Merry Wives of Windsor*.)[18] Calandro starts up in terror, and his screams — as of the living dead — frighten off the officers. Calandro is made to carry the chest to Lidio's house.

Fulvia, meanwhile — now dressed as a man — has gone in search of Lidio. And it is here that the perspectival set begins to come into its own; for while all scenes are played in the open, there now begins a vertiginous cross-cutting of events from one house to another which draws attention to the patterns of urban transactions. The true Santilla, seeking to escape impending marriage, has arrived at Calandro's house. Fulvia, returning home to find, as she thinks, Lidio, is horrified when her embraces discover a woman in Lidio's place: she accuses the magician of having transformed the sex of her lover. The denouement is now close at hand. The servant Samia, wandering around the town, meets both Lidio and Santilla and begins to realise that there are twins abroad; and when, shortly after, Fessenio meets Santilla and discovers her name and sex, he puts two and two together. Chance is beginning to yield to the orderly influence of the townscape, so that when the real Lidio comes on stage he is able to be reunited with the real Santilla. Lidio can now return to Fulvia but is discovered in the act by Calandro.

18. Which, according to Leo Salingar, is Shakespeare's most Italianate play, *Shakespeare and the Traditions of Comedy*, op.cit. p. 273.

To avert disaster, Santilla switches places with Lidio; and Calandro is persuaded to believe that Fulvia's companion has all along been a woman. Now that these complications have been resolved, there is a husband available for the merchant's daughter Virginia — Lidio himself. Fulvia, however, helps to complete the pattern. She has a son who wishes to marry Santilla. So (as Castelvetro would have led one to expect) two weddings — two 'small and gradually developed events' — conclude the comedy. These are, of course, marriages purely of social convenience: the affair between Lidio and Fulvia presumably can still go on. But the satisfactions of an artistically neat and socially conservative solution displace the need for an emotional resolution. The sentiment that 'it is better to be an Italian than a Greek' triumphantly concludes the play, as the Greek twins set up households in their adopted country.

Throughout, the effect of *La Calandria* depends upon the control which the author exerts over thematic patternings and ironies of situation. There is a degree of social observation here, for instance in the use of Venetian dialect for customs officers and also in the approximation to Greek syntax in the language of the twins. But the audience is never likely to be challenged by anything approaching realism, nor will it need to reconsider the essential principles of the social order. And it is here that the difference arises between this play and Boccaccio's *novellas*, where in spite of the aristocratic cornice, the stories are designed to encourage rather than to suppress ambiguities of social and psychological response.

Consider, for instance, the figure of the wife Fulvia, in whom there are discernible references to at least three Boccaccio stories.[19] Psychologically, Fulvia is the strongest figure in the play and voices the only challenge that the play contemplates to the settled order of social and domestic constraints of marriage, as when she speaks in soliloquy (*Cal*. III. vii.) of how love has made her bold enough to leave the confines of her room. Such challenges are, of course, familiar enough in Boccaccio; and Bibbiena draws directly on the *Decameron* when Fulvia needs to speak in outrage at her husband's dalliance with the disguised Lidio:

> What a marvellous husband you are! You were going to the farm, were you? Don't you have enough to do at home? You've got to go wandering off like this? And to think that this is the man I have loved and served faithfully all these years. Now I know why you have been keeping away from me the last few nights. You've been conserving your energies. I don't know how I keep myself from tearing your eyes out. Did you think you could fool me so easi-

19. See also *Dec* V. 10 and VII. 4.

ly? I heard about it before this, and that's why I'm all dressed up like this – to discover whether it was true . . . Do you suppose that if I were like you and didn't care what I did, I couldn't have a good time, too? I'm not so old or so ugly as that. It's just that I respect myself. Otherwise I'd certainly have revenged myself on that woman I found you with.

(*Cal.*, III. xii.)

Now the ironies of this barefaced piece of aggressive defence will be immediately apparent to an audience. Yet the situation is quite other-wise in Boccaccio, where a similar speech derives unresolvable tensions from a context which is full of violence and darkly erotic practices. Here, in *Decameron*, III. vi, the wife, Catella, is simultaneously jealous and chaste, and yet still falls victim to the trickery of an unwanted lover. Led to suppose by this lover that her husband is having an affair, she is deluded into a bed-trick whereby she thinks she can sleep with her own husband in the darkened room of the brothel he is supposed to frequent, only to discover that the man she has slept with is the lover. Though she learns apparently to enjoy the caresses of this lover, this does not alter the venom of offended chastity which she expresses in the speech which Bibbiena draws upon; and the resonances of victimisation contin-ue into the silence which Boccaccio's audience maintains at the end of this story.

There are, then, areas of suggestion which Bibbiena seems deliberate-ly to leave out of his play. And this is true also of his treatment of Calandro. In Boccaccio, the character of Calandrino – taken from his-torical anecdote – is a working-man, a painter who is the constant butt of his more intelligent companions:

a simple soul, of uncouth manners, that spent most of his time with two other painters, Bruno and Buffalmaco by name, pleasant enough fellows, but not without their full share of sound and shrewd sense.

(*Decameron*, VIII. iii)

Boccaccio's Calandrino is not a sympathetic figure. He is crass, ambi-tious and sexually appetitive. Moreover, in his stupidity he shows no understanding of the arts of illusion, even though he is a painter of fres-cos. And in this incongruity lies the essence of Boccaccio's humour. Once set upon an absurd or delusive course, Calandrino carries the plot to a literal and logical end quite beyond what is expected.[20] Thus in the *Decameron*, VIII. iii, Calandrino is convinced that if he can only discover the heliotrope stone, he will become invisible and thus be able to pursue

20. An excellent analysis of the Calandrino stories is contained in David Wallace, *The Decameron* (Landmarks of World Literature Cambridge, 1991), pp. 91–8.

his deepest and most nefarious desires. Collecting as many stones as he can carry in the heat of the day, he is convinced that he has found what he desires when his friends pelt him with stones pretending that they are aiming at the empty air. Bruised, over-laden but rejoicing, he returns home, presenting an image which plays with deeply poetic effect on aspirations to invisibility and the realities of gross matter.

It has been said that Boccaccio's Calandrino represents an enduring 'other' in Florentine culture which needs to be 'policed' and kept in check by the laughter of his more sophisticated compatriots: his gross-ness is a challenge as well as a source of festivity. Such an interpretation, however, would be impossible in the case of Bibbiena's Calandro. In the first place, Calandro has been transported by Bibbiena from the mar-gins of social acceptability to the centre; here he is a well-to-do bourgeois, eligible enough to marry the rich and noble Fulvia – a fitting stooge, within the aristocratic scheme of things. And this same view runs through the three scenes in the central phases of the comic action. In outline, these all are built upon japes akin to those which Boccaccio devised in the heliotrope story: the essential stratagem is that Calandro should be put in a chest and play dead – and end up with the threat of being thrown in a river. These scenes have their comic force and are paced with great dramatic skill. Yet, throughout, the moving force in the action is the servant Fessenio who acts as stage manager and direc-tor, as for instance when he graphically shows Calandro how to play the part of a corpse (*Cal.*, II. ix). Significantly, it is Fessenio who develops the situation to the full, replying to Calandro's own objection that he will not fit into the chest by saying that he must therefore consent to being cut into convenient parcels; but what then about the moment of arrival?

Fess: If you had ever sailed on a ship you would know (*how people are reassembled*): when there are hundreds of people that have to be fitted into a boat, the only way it can be done is to take a leg from one, an arm from another, and so on on until they are all neatly stowed like any other cargo.

Calandro: But what happens after that?

Fess: When they get into port each person claims the part of him that has been taken away, and sometimes through carelessness or mal-ice, a man will take a limb that belongs to someone else . . . and because its either too big or too small, they look crippled or lop-sided.

(ibid., III. vi)

In reply to this, Calandro, who is on his way to a tryst, can only muster a determination that he will make sure his 'member' is not exchanged for someone else's.

At the conclusion of the sequence, the joke is that Calandro, in spite of his class, is forced to act the servant:

Fess: You'll have to be the porter yourself . . . you've already taken off most of your clothes, and since you've been dead for a short time, your face has changed somewhat. I'll pretend to be the carpenter who made the trunk.

(ibid., III. iii)

The humour here, as throughout, derives from a recognition of how absurd it is that the social order should even momentarily be disrupted. This is the spirit of misrule and carnival. But it depends upon a prevailing understanding that in the end even the servant Fessenio will return to his allotted place in the social hierarchy.

MACHIAVELLI'S *MANDRAGOLA* AND GIORDANO BRUNO'S *CANDELAIO*

Where Bibbiena, like Ariosto, composed for court occasions, Machiavelli wrote the *Mandragola* (c.1518) originally for a circle of amateur actors, offering, in effect, a city comedy to an audience of citizens: the chief actor in a production of 1520 was the municipal herald. It is also plain that the political philosopher of the *Principe* and the *Discorsi* took the play as an opportunity to extend his study of corruption in the public sphere into the private realm of sexual intrigue.

There can be no doubt that Machiavelli brought to the work a good deal of purely literary interest and skill. The *Mandragola* is only one of several comedies that Machiavelli wrote,[21] and his ability as a writer of comic narrative is attested in the comic novella, *Belfagor*. In this respect, Machiavelli can be as dextrous as Bibbiena in combining elements of classical learning with material drawn from Boccaccio. Nevertheless, in his case, this *contaminatio* leads to a searching account of the relations between ancient and modern culture. On the one hand it is clear that in this work Machiavelli owes much to the Boccaccian opposition of Fortune and pragmatic *virtù*. Yet this opposition becomes tantalisingly complicated

---

21. Others include the *Andria* and the *Clizia,* while Machiavelli's fictional writings include the novella *Belfagor* and the verse narrative in *terza rima Dell'Asino d'Oro*.

when one realises that Machiavelli is also referring in the *Mandragola* to the tragic violation of Roman virtue which is described in Livy's account of the rape of Lucrece. With a daring that anticipates Shakespeare's *contaminatio* of medieval and classical sources in *Troilus and Cressida*, Machiavelli transfers the story of Lucrece to a Florentine setting in which, as he says in his prologue, ancient virtue has been entirely lost.[22]

Just as in Livy, Tarquin hears of the beauty of Lucretia from a distant camp, so in the *Madragola* Callimacho hears of the Florentine Lucrezia's beauty while away in France. Impelled by a Machiavellian version of love from afar, he decides to risk returning from the safety of Paris to the corrupt and embattled Florence to win her. From this point on the story is a calculated reversal of the story told in Livy. Here, the husband of Lucretia actually conspires in her violation; and there is arguably a certain sympathy shown for the daring of the would-be rapist Callimacho, along with similar admiration for his ultimately compliant victim. In any case, the impediment to Callimacho's success is no public standard of honour or *pietas* but the private jealousy of Lucrezia's husband, Nicia. Nicia is a doctor of law, and thus in part fills the conventional role of pedant. And yet while Machiavelli may satirise Nicia's learned stupidity, he also goes beyond type, to criticise on psychological grounds the obsessiveness of this character. In the end Nicia's weakness proves to be, ironically enough, the most natural and most sympathetic feature of his character, his desire for a child. For the stratagem which Callimacho develops – on the advice of the parasite Ligurio – involves implicating Nicia in the adulterous begetting of the child which hitherto he has been unable to father. At Ligurio's prompting, Callimacho disguises himself as a physician and persuades Nicia that the one sure remedy against infertility is that his wife should eat a Mandrake root – the 'mandragola'. Unfortunately, there is the likelihood that the first person to sleep with the woman after this remedy will die. To avoid, this, a tramp – who will be Callimacho in disguise – must be allowed to sleep with the woman and draw the venom to himself. Nicia, caught on the psychological raw, nevertheless consents to this ruthless plan when told that the King of France himself once agreed to a similar proposition.

Attention now turns to the character of Lucrezia. For she, like her Roman namesake, is a woman of undoubted, even fanatical, integrity. Indeed, the only way in which she can be turned into a Boccaccian pur-

---

22. See Anne Paolucci, 'Livy's Lucretia, Shakespeare's 'Lucrece' and Machiavelli's *Mandragola*' in Lorch (ed.), *Il teatro Italiano del Rinascimento*, op.cit.

suer of her own passions is by the intercession of a priest who will persuade her that her action is indeed honourable. Under the influence of the Fra Timoteo and also of her own mother, who shares with Nicia an appetite for descendants, Lucrezia yields. Indeed, she becomes as passionate in response to the attentions of Callimacho as she had hitherto been in her pursuit of moral virtue. The Boccaccian turn has been accomplished, and the work draws to its conclusion with the grandparent and elderly father enjoying the sentimental prospect of the child who was duly conceived when Callimacho slept with Lucrezia. Their affair, presumably, now enters a new phase; and, to celebrate the happy conclusion, Fra Timoteo invites one and all to his Church.

On one interpretation, there is an element of carnival in this conclusion. And certainly, from the point of view of Machiavellian and Boccaccian *virtù*, there is much to celebrate here: a vigorous and anarchic energy is released as the old virtue falls into ruin. Yet the story has a mythic power which gives many implications beyond such a solution. Suggestions, which Bibbiena would have kept firmly at bay, concerning death, sexuality and even the role of religion all have their place. Equally, the conclusion of the play could well be seen as moral rather than simply ludic position in picturing accurately the disaster that befalls a state where there are no principles of *pietas* and where even the Church fails to stand as the repository of moral value.

But caught between such interpretations, there is no possibility that Machiavelli's reader should return to the clarity of Livy's moral position. Rather, the play is formulated so as to demand that the audience should display a *virtù* of its own, in responding with a Machiavellian realism to the situation presented by the play, and in avoiding the traps of sentiment or and stupidity which an over-simplified interpretation would represent.

One expression of such a demand is to be found in the prologues and the *intermezzi* which here replace the formal choreography of plays by Ariosto and Bibbiena. In the *Mandragola* there are no deferential authors or mythological tableaux. Machiavelli opens the play with a parodically ingratiating song by nymphs and shepherds, only to subvert this with the crabbed and world-weary voice of the authorial chorus, who cynically expects as his reward that the audience which will stand and sneer on the sidelines, speaking ill of what it sees. The tone is continued in subsequent *interactes* where Dantean and Petrarchan sentiments about love are enlisted in sardonic celebration of the obscene action.

The subversive voice of the prologue is carried into the centre of the play by the figure of Fra Timoteo, who, through his soliloquies, exerts a choric and yet highly ambiguous influence. On the one hand, he is the offspring of Boccaccio's satire against the clergy and also embodies Machiavelli's own understanding of the illusory nature of religion. In this light, he exemplifies the decay of public standards into a very un-Roman morass of lust and greed. On the other hand, Timoteo displays an exhilarating skill akin to that of Boccaccio's Ceparello[23] in the contribution he makes to Callimacho's plot. His language, particularly in persuading Lucrezia that to sleep with Callimacho would be an honourable action, reflects a terrible brilliance in argumentation which could only have come from Machiavelli himself. In soliloquy he declares:

> It's certainly true that I expect there to be difficulties: Lucrezia is a woman of great goodness and wisdom. But I shall take advantage of her goodness; after all, women have very little intelligence.
>
> (*Mand.*, III. ix)

And then in the confessional scene he proceeds:

> I want to return to what I was saying before. You have really to get a grip on this general principle that where there is a good which is certain and an evil which is uncertain one must never lose the good out of fear of the evil. In this case there certainly is a good, that you become pregnant and produce a new soul for Our Lord God; the evil here is that he who lies with you might. And because there is an uncertainty here, it is better that Nicia should not run that risk. As to whether the act itself is a sin that is a nonsense; for it is the will and not the body which sins; and the sin in this case would be a husband's displeasure, whereas you intend to please him. What is more, the goal has to be considered in all things. And your goal here is to fill a seat in Heaven and to pleasure your husband
>
> (*Mand.*, III. xi)

The disconcerting energies of this speech are reflected to some degree in the other tricksters of the play, Callimacho and Ligurio, and are in clear contrast to the inflated nothings uttered by Nicia. The aim is not perhaps to characterise inwardly in the way that a modern audience would expect but rather through words to generate a moment of public action. Yet speech characteristics are here specific enough to escape from type. This is particularly true of Ligurio who, though conventionally a parasite, scarcely mentions food in his frenzied delight over the success of his own trickery. Such innovation may account for complaints that were voiced in Machiavelli's own time that the fourth act lacked sufficient plot

23. See above, pp. 37–8.

interest. Machiavelli here shifts his attention from the formal complications which Bibbiena had laid before his audience so as to dwell upon the motivations and appetites of the characters themselves, the ardent expectations of Callimacho, the enthusiastic stage management of Ligurio – 'change your face like this: don't stand on ceremony' – the emotional confusions of Nicia, and Fra Timoteo's desire neither to be outdone in trickery nor to risk exposure. It is the plotters themselves rather than some ever-present author who seem to provide the complications here.

If comedy is in a matter of pace and timing, then the fourth act of the *Mandragola* succeeds in generating a brilliant urgency which can easily leave the audience lagging. The audience is not allowed the superior pleasure of contemplating a well-laid plan: the ingenuity of the characters and a dramatic style which uses, for instance, scene endings to create surprise or suspense subvert the social or literary complacency of the audience, appealing, like *The Prince* itself, directly to *virtù* in the immediacy of the response it requires.

Of all Renaissance comedies, however, the most thoroughly subversive is Bruno's *Il Candelaio*.[24] The play was never performed in the author's lifetime, and rarely has been since. But it is an early and characteristic product of a man whose turbulent intellectual life ran in parallel, probably, with a career as a spy, and whose philosophy – which included in its many facets a defence of Copernicus – was so offensive to the Church that eventually he was burned at the stake for defending it.[25] Exile and, probably, espionage brought Bruno to England, where he lectured – contentiously – at Oxford, and became closely associated with Sir Philip Sidney, with whom, it seems, he discussed the notion of 'heroic love' and to whom he dedicated his *Cena dei Ceneri*. It has been argued that Berowne in Shakespeare's *Love's Labours Lost* is a portrait of Bruno – and that Shakespeare intended his work as a satire on both the new and the old styles of Renaissance intellectual.

Whatever Shakespeare's satirical intentions, Bruno himself uses *Il Candelaio* simultaneously to reflect some of the essential principles of his

24. On Bruno see Frances A. Yates, *Giordano Bruno and the Hermetic Tradition* (London, 1964); *The Art of Memory* (1966); also *A Study of Love's Labour's Lost* (Cambridge, 1936); John Buxton, *Sir Philip Sidney and the English Renaissance* (London, 1954); D.W. Singer *Giordano Bruno: His Life and Thought* (New York, 1950); also John Bossy, *Giordano Bruno and the Embassy Affair* (New Haven and London, 1991). For the text see Giordano Bruno, *Il Candelaio*, introduzione e note Isa Guerrini Angrisani (Milan, 1976). For a translation by J.R. Hale see Bentley, op.cit.

25. Thomas P. Roche jr., *Petrarch and The English Sonnet Sequence*, (New York, 1989) is good on Bruno's intellectual position, pp. 123–53.

own thinking and to reveal, satirically, the limitations of the learning and culture from which his own comedy sprang. Thus, at the opening of the play he insists that those who understand the action of the play in the spirit of Heraclitus and Democritus (*Proprologo*) will find much to divert them. He has already declared that the world he depicts is one in which 'all things change; nothing is turned to nothing' (*Dedication*). But this declaration immediately establishes a philosophical framework which emphasises flux and has little in common with the ideas of change embodied in the traditional comic notions of Fortune. More profoundly, Bruno, here as elsewhere, resists the Aristotelian conception of a world in which all things move through desire to an orderly end. Bruno's philosophy is atomist; yet – in a way which foreshadows Spinzoa and Schelling – Bruno also envisaged a universe in which, beyond the flux of illusion, lay an ultimate principle of stability and per-manence.[26] Identifying the universe with the substance that comprises both form and matter, Bruno states that

> the universe is one and infinite; it is being, true and one, whereas all particu-lar things are mere accidents and subject to destruction. There is no plurality of substances in the world, but merely a plurality of manifestations of a single substance. The plurality of things is only apparent and belongs to the surface grasped by the senses, whereas our minds grasp beyond this surface, the one substance in which all apparent contrasts coincide.[27]

Associated with this view is Bruno's conception of memory and, indeed, of theatre. It is in memory that the mind may comprehend how, beneath the perennial mutability of things, there persists an origi-nal and ideal structure, an immutable principle of reality. This leads Bruno to develop his art of memory; for it was through memory that one could unlock the way to the correspondences which lay beyond the flux of particulars. But the theatre itself had long provided imagery essential to the arts of memory. Indeed, it has been suggested that the purpose of calling a theatre the Globe was to express an understanding of how a mystic totality could be attained within its walls.[28] So already in presenting his comedy, Bruno anticipates the ways in which an audi-ence – relying now on memory rather than on the perspectival constructions of artists – should be able to penetrate the illusory nature

26. See Charles Taylor, The *Sources of the Self* (Cambridge, 1989), p. 416.
27. *Dialoghi metafisici*, ed. G. Gentile (Bari, 1925), p. 176; trans. S. Greenberg in *The Infinite in Giordano Bruno* (New York, 1950), pp. 247–56. See also P.O. Kristeller, *Eight Philosophers of the Renaissance* (Stanford, 1964), p. 134.
28. See Frances Yates, *The Art of Memory* (London, 1966), pp. 330–54.

of the action it is to witness and to exercise its command over worldly vanities.

The story itself tells of the duping and cruel disappointments of a Lover, a Miser and a Pedant who all, in their own interconnected ways, set their minds upon particular objects and demonstrate by the insatiability of their desires, how fallacious and empty such objects must be. But even before the story begins, the comedy has disrupted any expectations of stability which the reader or audience may have brought to it by a sequence of no less than six prologues, in which the language and conventions of traditional comedy are point by point dismantled and ridiculed, as for instance when Petrarchan conceptions of an elevated earthly love are brutally associated with the 'rutting time' of Spring.

Within this already shifting frame, the play – set in Naples and written in Neapolitan dialect – offers for comparison and contrast the three dupes, Bonifacio the lover, Bartolomeo the miser, and Manfurio the pedant. Against these, the one figure who shows any competence or control is Giovanni Bernardo, usually taken as the mouth-piece for Giordano Bruno himself. And he, significantly, is a painter, a master of illusion, who in the course of the play manipulates dress and disguise so as to find his way into the favours of the wife of Bonifacio. But in contrast to Bibbiena's work, where rapidity and complication of action are the dominant features, *Il Candelaio* is structured around the representation of persons and attitudes of mind, so as to reveal – often through soliloquy – the psychological common denominators in the folly of the three main characters.

Boniface – the forty-something husband of the highly desirable wife whom Bernardo eventually beds – has, it seems, until now, been a covert homosexual but changes his tune out of love for the courtesan Vittoria:

It is my luck not to be able to make this traitress love me or even pretend to. Well, who knows perhaps what my words my love my frenzy can't move can be shifted by this occult philosophy. They say that magic hath such force it can turn rivers in their courses back against nature, halt the tides, make the mountains bellow, the abyss cry out, can blot out the sun, veil the moon, pluck out the stars, turn day into night. As the Academician sans academy wrote in that lost poem with the impossible title:

Earth air fire water it confounds together
And blows about man's purpose like a
            feather.

Everything is open to doubt; and as far as love is concerned we see the proof of that last remark every day.

(*Cand.*, I. ii)

When the direct approach to Vittoria fails, Bonifacio turns, idiotically, to magic. But it is this which links him to the miser Bartolomeo whose love of money leads him to place his trust in alchemy as the controlling principle of the universe:

> Metals like gold and silver are the source of everything: these are the causes of words, plants, and stones; flax, wood, silk, fruit, corn, wine oil, everything desirable on earth depends on them. I give them this importance because without them you can have none of the others.
>
> This is why gold is called the substance of the sun, and silver of the moon. Take these two planets from the sky and what happens to your generative powers, where is the light of the universe. Take gold and silver from the earth, how does life begin, grow, flourish . . . Plants, words and stones are quintessentials to crazed and feckless philosophers, hated by God nature and fortune, who drag out their lives without a penny piece in their pockets and die of starvation, all the time assuaging their envy, by cursing gold and silver and those who possess them . . . I'll only value the one thing that gives value to all else. Money subsumes the very elements; he who lacks money not only lacks stones, plants and words but air, earth, water, fire and life itself. This is the whole of life, temporal and eternal, knowing how to use it and being charitable in which one must be moderate and not let your purse lose its soul by losing count of what is in its: as the saying has it, *Si bene feceris, vide cui. But there is no profit in this*. I've heard that there is to be an order lowering the exchange value of the guinea, and before its promulgated, I want to change mine into francs.

(*Cand.*, III. i)

In his turn the pedant Manfurio shows himself to be at the mercy of those words which Bartolomeo derides as merely secondary things; and, on the whole, the comedy in his case depends too much upon rhetorical pretension and the distortion of Latin jargon to benefit from translation and quotation. However, it is on the pedant Manufurio in particular that the cruel resolution of the action falls most severely. Throughout the play, fool has mocked fool, or else has revealed his folly directly to the audience in soliloquy. There is no need here for any appeal to superior – or hitherto silent – authority. All has been clear throughout and in any case, no superior authority, other than that of intelligent analysis, is conceivable in Bruno's world. Nor does the author step forward to take control. Instead, through the trickery of Bernardo, Manfurio finds himself in the clutches of a band of loutish policemen, whose authority itself is manifestly ill-founded. Like a school-boy, Manufurio is beaten on both hands and buttocks. He approaches the audience wincing with pain, and terrified lest the 'players' should return to continue the beating – fearing, it seems, the actors themselves as much as the characters they portray. Facing out to what might, to the enlightened eye, be the 'theatre' of transcendent memory, he seeks only to hasten the play to an end with an appeal for applause.

Learning here, in its degenerate guise, is as ineffective as law. The audience is faced finally with the 'web' of stupidity that Bruno spoke of in his prologue – in which the intersections of folly rather than those of providence or benignly despotic power have been revealed to view. Humour here must lead its audience beyond that web to the higher understanding which Bruno himself philosophically enjoys.

GEORGE GASCOIGNE'S *SUPPOSES* AND ARIOSTO'S *I SUPPOSITI*

George Gascoigne, in choosing to translate Ariosto's *I Suppositi* of 1509, identified a comedy which was among the most perfectly formed in the vernacular tradition but also more conservative than comedy would become in the hands of Aretino, Machiavelli and Bruno. Though Ariosto was capable, in his satires and in the ironies of the *Orlando Furioso*, of revealing the shortcomings of life at court, his comedies offer themselves as courtly entertainment and mirror the implicit ideologies of courtly life. The humour they provide lies in the confidence they promote and the skill they display in doing so.

I suppositi, in particular, demonstrates the process of *contaminatio* not only in reconciling classical motifs with strongly Boccaccian themes but also in providing material which Shakespeare, through Gascoigne, was subsequently to use in the sub-plot of *The Taming of the Shrew* and also in *The Comedy of Errors*. The name 'Petruchio' is derived no doubt from that of a servant in Gascoigne's play.[29] The story itself is familiar from Shakespeare's version, and relates a day of crisis and ultimate resolution in the complicated life of a young lover. For two years, the Sicilian

---

29. For Ariosto see *Le Commedie a cura di Michele Catalano*, 2 vols, (Bologna, 1940). A modern translation is to be found in *The Comedies of Ariosto*, ed. Edmond M. Beame and Leonard G. Sbrocchi (Chicago and London, 1975).

Erostrato has been able to enjoy the utmost intimacy with Polinesta, disguising himself as her servant, while his own servant Dulipo takes his master's place as a student at the University of Ferrara. The trouble begins when Polinesta's father seems finally to have been persuaded that his daughter should marry the ageing but wealthy lawyer, Cleandro. To counter Cleandro's claim, the servant Dulipo bamboozles an elderly foreigner into taking the part of Erostrato's father and into offering, while so disguised, a greater settlement than Cleandro. Erostrato's affair is at this point discovered by Polinesta's father. To complicate matters his own father arrives in search of him from Sicily. In the denouement, it proves that the lawyer Cleandro who had himself been driven from Sicily by the Turks, losing his son as he fled, is in fact the father of the servant Dulipo. This reconciliation of father and son leads to a second such reconciliation as Erostrato, by now imprisoned, is restored to his father. The play ends with father and son reunited and the prospect of marriage between Erostrato and Polinesta.

In the prologue to *I Suppositi*, Ariosto declares that, unlike the play he had written a year earlier – *La Cassaria* – this play will faithfully adhere to a Ferrarese location (as will his later play, *La Lena*). It is this determination which prepares for the subtle eulogy which occurs when the distraught father of Erostrato, faced with protestations that Erostrato already has a father, demands to know whether there is any justice or magistrate in the city to whom he might appeal and is roundly assured by a passing Ferrarese citizen that Ferrara indeed boasts magistrates and above all one prince of highest justice (*Sup.*, IV. viii). In this play confusions of identity will not run so deep that Ferrara cannot solve them. Philogeno may exclaim: 'O unfortunate old man! Is there no judge or captain or magistrate or other person of authority in this land to whom I can appeal?' (ibid.). But eventually, of course, it proves that there is such an authority and that the city can be trusted to produce a just solution.

Notably, Gascoigne makes no attempt to transfer the scene to an English city. Indeed, in retaining most of Ariosto's references to Ferrara, he also intensifies the conservatism of the piece, introducing a pious 'O eternal God' into the reply offered above by the Ferrarese citizen. This is predictable, in view of Gascoigne's own circumstances and his prevailing social and moral stance. For he is both a courtier – though not a wholly successful one – and also, increasingly, a moralist who saw that drama could fulfil a moral function. He knew what it was to work, as an amateur, within a court setting. He had contributed to 'shewes' for royal entertainments at Kenilworth and had written a masque to gain patronage from the Viscount Montacute (associating the English Montacutes with the Italian Montecchi). At the same time, the reference he makes to Petrarch in his *Elegies* displays a serious moral intent,[30] and this was carried over into his final play *The Glasse of Government* which treats a Dutch theme of the prodigal son with what has been described as 'calvinistic' severity.[31]

Whether in the public or private spheres, Gascoigne was a writer of considerable versatility; and, in writing for the Inns of Court, he seems to have understood what might catch the eye of the literary connoisseur. He had himself shown a receptiveness to the tones of irony in Ariosto's *Orlando Furioso* when, in a narrative poem of his own, he refers to Alcina's seduction of Ruggiero in 'The Adventures of Master F.J' (*Works*, I. p. 413), and is also responsive to the darker aspects of Ariosto's work as represented by the *Cinque Canti* – to which he alludes in 'Certeyn notes of instruction'.[32] His understanding of tonal variation points to some of the virtues of his translation of *I Suppositi*. Likewise, he shows a marked attention – as Ariosto would have required – to the surprises or subtleties of narrative and dramatic structure. His prologue to the *Supposes* is an intimate and playful appeal to the audience, alerting them to complexities of 'supposing' in the work they are about to see. This appeal is strengthened in the printed version of the play by a chorus of marginalia, in which at every point Gascoigne is concerned to underline the 'suppose' or misapprehension that he has contrived to introduce into the plot, commenting on the nature of the suppose, be it 'shrewde', 'doltish', or simply 'another'. Author and audience are to be aware at all times of the structural irony; and Gascoigne is particularly aware of the way in which – working within the unified action of a single day – long-standing 'supposes' are finally and dextrously to be resolved. On this score, he is more emphatic than Ariosto himself. Thus Ariosto speaks of how the lover's stratagem has now lasted for two years and now on this 'dreadful day' ('*scelerato giorno*') is about to be resolved. But Gascoigne expands this, developing a piquant sense of incipient

---

30. In *The Griefe of Joye*, Gascoigne claims to have based his meditations on the ubiquity of death upon a reading of Petrarch: 'Touching the *Methode* and *Invention*, even as Petrark in his workes *De Remediis* I do recount the uncerteine Joyes of men in severall dialogues, so have I in these Elegies distributed the same into sundrie songs.' (*Works*, II. op.cit., pp. 514).

31. F.T. Boas, 'Early English Comedy', in *The Cambridge History of English Literature*, Vol. V.

32. *Works*, I. p. 466.

tragedy through emphatic images and a strong pattern of alliterative phrases:

> *Dulipo*:   But alas, thou hast brought him even in the very worst of time, to plunge us all in the pit of perdition. Neither art content to entangle me alone in thy ruinous ropes, but thou must also catch the right Erostrato in thy crooked clawes, to reward us both with open shame and rebuke. Two years hast thou kept secret our subtle Supposes, even this day to decipher them with a sorrowful success.
>
> (*Supposes*, V. iii)

Though Gascoigne is a very faithful translator, his close attention is critical rather than slavish. He seems in fact to have consulted both the prose original of Ariosto's play and a later version in verse; and – apparently having both versions by him as he translated – he makes minute adjustments and selections on grounds which are as often dramatic as they are scholarly. Nor can there be any doubt that this critical process led him to develop a style of dramatic prose which responded to the English ear and laid the foundations for much that was to come in the later Elizabethan period.

Given the attention to detail which Gascoigne paid to it, Ariosto's own text reveal an inherent vitality of thought, prose style and dramatic structure. In the prose itself, Ariosto is capable of a sober realism and also a responsiveness to sentiment, which encourages serious moral reflection, as for instance in his treatment of the theme of Fortune (where Gascoigne's translation can be trusted to give much of the appropriate effect):

> This amorous cause that hangeth in controversy between Domine doctor and me may be compared to them that play at primero. Of whom someone peradventure shall lose a great sum of money before he win one stake, and at last, half in anger, shall set up his rest; win it ... Thus have I been tossed now over, now under, even as fortune list to whirl the wheel, neither sure to win nor certain to lose the wager. And this practice that now my servant hath devised, although hitherto it hath not succeeded amiss, yet can I not count myself assured of it; for I fear that one mischance or another will come and turn it topsy turvy.
>
> (*Supposes*, III. ii)

This passage is Boccacian in the connections it draws of chance, love and money, and astuteness. Yet there is nothing here of Boccaccio's abrasiveness and daring. On the contrary, the presumption is that an

audience will enjoy overseeing the 'supposes' that Fortune produces.
The eye of the audience is constantly directed away from the intense
ambiguities of the Boccaccian situation towards a perspective of poetical
justice. When that justice finally reveals itself, the agency is neither a
transcendent power nor human ingenuity or character but authorial skill
revealed in the disentanglement of the 'supposes' which the author had
himself first created.

There are comparable modifications to the theme of romantic love.
At many points Ariosto draws upon Petrarchan turns of phrase and
Gascoigne is qualified by his own reading of Petrarch to follow suit. But
again attention is subtly deflected from the complexities of Petrarchan
love – or, for that matter, Boccaccian sex – so that it can fall upon the
formal dexterity of the author's own constructions. The opening scene
of the play – between Polinesta and her nurse – reveals unembarrassedly
how strong love may be, even in a woman; and the scene may have
been remembered by Shakespeare in writing for the nurse in *Romeo and
Juliet*. Yet after this scene, Polinesta plays no further part in the action.
The way is clear for a play upon conceits and witty parallels rather than
upon passion. So, Ariosto provides a parasite whose love of food can be
compared (in a motif which goes back to Dante) to high-principled love
of a true spiritual object. And Gascoigne, picking up this parallel
emphasises the contradictions in a series of Petrarchan oxymorons which
are even more strongly drawn than in Ariosto:

> thinking that a shivering cold by glowing fire, thirst by drink, hunger by
> pleasant repasts and a thousand such like passions finde remedy by their con-
> traries, so my restless desire might have found quiet only by continual
> contemplation. But, alas, I find that only love is unsatiable.

Then further elements are introduced to strengthen this theme:

> as the fly playeth with the flame till at last she is cause of her owne decay, so
> the lover that thinketh with kissing and colling to content his unbridled
> appetite is commonly seen the only cause of his own consumption.
>
> (*Supposes*, I. iii)

It is striking that, as the play continues, the theme of young love is
displaced by the theme of paternal love, which is frequently viewed
here as the superior form of affection. This shift indeed is expressed in
the very structure of the play, for the resolution of the action depends
ultimately not upon the lovers themselves, nor for that matter upon
their servants, but rather upon the negotiations of the fathers in the case,
which brings them from what appeared the sub-plot of the play into its

main action. The initially foolish Cleandro – the wealthy but ill-quali-
fied lover of Polinesta – is particularly important in this regard. For it is
when he, in being reconciled with his long lost-son Dulippo, emerges
from the sub-plot that the play begins to move towards its happy ending. One realises suddenly that, throughout, his motive in wooing
Polinesta has not been romantic love but a passion, far from negligible
either to Ariosto or Gascoigne, for breeding and a repressed desire to
replace the son he thinks he has lost many years before. And this crucial
shift in both sentiment and action is underlined by the pathos with
which Cleandro repeatedly utters the name of his long-lost son. Here at
least character does seem to be a significant factor for both Ariosto and
for Gascoigne.

Accurate and faithful as Gascoigne's translation is, he has, in at least
two respects, modified Ariosto's original or introduced his own
emphases: first, in the process of developing his own English prose, he
also develops a lively sense of dramatic repartee; secondly, he tends to
strengthen the moral sententiousness of the original most notably in his
expression of those patriarchal emotions which centre upon the fathers
of Erostrato and Dulippo.

As to repartee, one finds in Act I. ii., after the parasite, Pasiphilo, has
comically misquoted the Bible, that Ariosto in a rather pedestrian way
has (on a literal translation):

You are not very well learned when it comes to the Bible.

I am very learned indeed when it comes to the contents of barrels.

Gascoigne, however, responds immediately to the chance of a pun on
'bible' and 'bibulousness':

I perceive you are no very good Bibler,

Pasiphilo: Yes sir an excellent good Bibbeler, specially in a bottle.

Equally, Gascoigne can resort to alliterative patterning – a regular source
of emphasis in his style – to give life to a reply. Ariosto writes:

he plays the grandee in this country. Yes, and no one will deny that. But let
him do what he likes. Your qualities are worth the whole of Sicily.

Gascoigne has:

Yea, he taketh it upon him bravely in this country. Yea, where no man
knoweth the contrary: but let him brave it, boast his birth, and do what he
can; the virtue and knowledge that is within this body of yours, is worth
more than all the country he came from.

In a similar way, Gascoigne has a shrewd eye for stage business. When the Cook and his skivvy Crapino appear in Ariosto, the cook complains loud and long at how Crapino dawdles, and through the words of the cook the audience receives a good enough picture of what has been happening off-stage: Crapino chases dogs, gawps at bears and cannot resist taunting any Jew or porter that he sees. But Gascoigne speaks of the stick that Crapino carries, emphasising not simply the tardiness of the servant in gazing at passing distractions but also the positive energy which leads him to wield his stick. Simultaneously, Gascoigne develops to a very considerable extent the possibility of physical stage business in the scene which the audience is witnessing:

> By the time we come to the house, I trust that of these twenty eggs in the basket we shall find very few whole. But it is folly to talk to him. What the devil, will thou never lay that stick out of thy hand? He fighteth with the dogges, beateth the beares, at everything in the street he findeth occasion to tarry: if he spy a slipstring by the way such another as himself, a Page, a Lackie or a dwarf, the devil of hell cannot hold him in chains, but he will be doing with him [i.e. go off with the devil]. I cannot go two steps but I must look backe for my yonker.
>
> (*Supposes*, III. i)

Then, finally, on the level of theme, there is an extensive addition to Ariosto's text which clearly declares Gascoigne's commitment to the order which resides in the settled emotions of fatherhood and the value of lawful conduct. In the *Supposes* as in *I Suppositi*, the father of Polinesta laments that his own law-abidingness will not allow him to take due revenge upon the lover who has has penetrated his household. But Gascoigne extends the lamentations of the offended householder and, while leaving out certain salacious phrases from the Italian, generates considerable pathos and complexity of emotional response. In particular, the father here is wracked by the sense that, in failing to keep a check upon his daughter, he has also failed in his duty to his dead wife; outrage mingles with feelings of shame and self-recrimination. If Ariosto had provided the structural shift from lovers to fathers, Gascoigne responds in kind and, with evident enthusiasm, greatly expands upon the original in the following speech, which shows – at times with potentially tragic force – the power which Gascoigne's native English could summon up:

> Alas, alas, I myself have been the cause of all these cares, and have deserved to bear the punishment of all these mishaps. Alas, I should not have committed my dearest darling in custody to so careless a creature as this old Nurse.

For we see by common proof, that these old women be either peevish, or pitiful: either easily inclined to evil or quickly corrupted with bribes and rewards. O my wife, my good wife (that now liest cold in the grave) now may I bemoan that I miss thee: if thou had lived (such was thy government of the least things) that thou wouldest prudently have provided for the preservation of this pearl. A costly jewel may I well accompt her and price for the Prince . . . she that hath been my chief comfort in youth and is now become the corrosive of mine age . . . For of all the duties that are requisite in humane life, only obedience is by the parents to be required of the child: where on the other side the parents are bound first, to beget them, then to bring them forth, after to nourish them, to preserve them from bodily perils in the cradle, from daunger of soul by godly education, to match them in consort inclined to vertue, to banish them all wild and wanton company, to allow them sufficient for their sustentation, to cut off excess, the open gate of sin, seldom or never to smile on them unless it be to their encouragement in virtue, and finally to provide them in marriages in time convenient lest (neglected of us) they learn to set either too much or too little by themselves. Five years are past since I might have married her, when by continual excuses I have prolonged it to my own perdition. Alas, I should have considered she is a collop of my own flesh: what should I think to make her a princess? Alas, alas, a poor kingdom have I now caught to endow her with. It is too true that of all sorrows this is the head source and chief fountain of all fires: the goods of the world are uncertain, the gains little to be rejoiced at, and the loss not greatly to be lamented: only the children cast away, cutteth the parents throat with the knife of inward care, which knife will kill me surely, I make none other accompt.

(*Supposes*, III. iii)

For a more subversive treatment of the patriarchal theme, one must wait for Shakespeare's *The Taming of the Shrew*,[33] where, along with the challenges that both Katherine and Bianca pose to the sentiments which are expressed in this speech, there are also to be found elements of dreams and of metatheatre which themselves throw into doubt the frame of the established order.[34] Or else one would need to go to Jonson who in his treatment of Aretino's *Il Marescalco* in *Epicoene* is able to combine a strict sense of a moral order with the carnivalesque properties of the skimmington ride. As for Gascoigne, he has introduced the essential formulae of Ariostan comedy into the blood-stream of English theatre; and, on his own account, he has shown a profound attachment to values of order which, if questionable, still need to be voiced before

33. See below, pp. 279–82.
34. See below, pp. 279–82.

any subsequent assault can be launched. One notes, finally, that while in the essentially comic tension between order and disorder, Gascoigne firmly commits himself to a defence of the existing scheme, he nevertheless ends the play – through his own obsession with 'supposing' – with a stroke of carnivalesque banter more daring than any in Ariosto: the shackles which had been prepared for Erostrato (by the strong arm of the otherwise celebrated law) may now be seen as mere 'suppositories' (with which one knows what to do):

> To make a right end of our supposes, lay one of these bolts in the fire, and make thee a suppository as long as mine arm.

Chapter 6

The Novella in Italy and England

INTRODUCTION

In 'The Adventures of Master F.J' (1573, 1575) – a composition which has been described as 'the first *original* novel in English', George Gascoigne prefers to present his work as a translation from 'the Italian riding tales of Bartello' (*Works*, I. 383) rather than to advertise the inventiveness which he seems to have exercised.[1] His purpose may have been to claim the same reflected glory that he acquires in translating Ariosto's *I Suppositi*. More likely, he wished to conceal, under this attribution to a fictitious 'Bartello', the confessedly wanton and possibly libellous speech of a work which may well have referred to contemporary court scandals in England (*Works*, I. 3). In either case, Gascoigne's tactics point to features both of the Italian novella itself and of the use to which it was put in England initially by translators such as Painter, Whetstone and Fenton and later by the dramatists of the period.

Vice and luxury were characteristics which English authors of the Elizabethan period proved quick to associate with contemporary Italy. Couched in often lurid terms, a myth developed which was to be as influential in forming the English literary imagination as were the direct examples of genre or style. The English were skilful in putting the myth to a wide range of patriotic or satirical purposes, especially in expressing the divisions between Protestant and Catholic causes; and, as we shall see, Shakespeare and his contemporaries found in sixteenth-century Italy a ready source of material in their investigations of moral decadence and degenerate power. Such perceptions of Italy were, of course, consistent

---

1. L. Bradner, 'The First English Novel, A Study of George Gascoigne's "Adventures of Master F.J" ', *PMLA*, XLV (1930) 543–52. See also C.T. Prouty, *George Gascoigne: Elizabethan Courtier Soldier and Poet* (New York, 1942), pp. 189–212.

with an emphasis on the more sinister aspects of Machiavellianism.[2] But it was from the novella that the details and quasi-historical validity of this view were primarily derived.

The Italians themselves seem to have done little to discourage this violent misinterpretation of their history. On the contrary, authors such as Bandello and Cinthio deliberately pursued an interest in situations which might depict the 'quick gush of blood, the sound of chattering teeth, the odour of carrion and sudden attack of nausea',[3] exploring at all times the narrative possibilities offered by extreme states of passion and perversity. This was in part a technical exercise. But in many cases, with a candour or daring that Gascoigne apparently could not emulate, the Italian novella writers represented their work as a true account of events in the Italy of their own day.

An unmistakable feature of the Italian novella is an 'ethical ambiguity' whereby scandal frequently appears the more piquant in that it is accompanied by pretensions to moral rectitude.[4] Yet it needs to be emphasised that such ambiguity reflects a real uncertainty which had lodged itself in the sensibility of the Italian Cinquecento. The French and Spanish invasions that dominated the first quarter of the century changed the political character of the peninsula; and the ancient aristocratic courts which became a favoured setting for the *novelle* were often distant now from the centres of power, and were inclined to express their traditions, sophisticated interests and cultivated tastes in the way which decaying societies invariably do, through a subtle deformation of their earlier codes and standards.

It should also be noted that communications across the international scene were improving at this time, particularly through the introduction of printing. The novella, answering in part to a taste both for journalism and gossip, was perhaps the first form to be conceived with this resource in mind. The printed text was a channel through which fifteenth-century society could diffuse the enjoyment it took in the contemplation of its own decay, as sophisticated entertainment, from one corner of Europe to the other. (Many of Bandello's stories, though published in Italy, were written while the author was in France.) In this aspect, books

2. See especially G.K. Hunter 'English Folly and Italian Vice' contained in *Jacobean Theatre*, ed. J.R. Brown and B. Harris (London, Stratford-upon-Avon Studies, 1960).
3. Yvonne Rodax, *The Real and the Ideal in the Novella,* (Chapel Hill, 1968), p. 83, and William Nelson, *Fact or Fiction: The Dilemma of the Renaissance Story-Teller* (Cambridge, Mass., 1973); D.P. Rotonda, *Motif Index of the Italian Novella in Prose* (Bloomington, 1942).
4. Janet Smarr, *Italian Renaissance Tales* (Rochester, Michigan, 1983), p. xvi.

were becoming consumer goods; and descriptions can be found in which metaphors are pursued emphasising the 'savour' and 'relish' of reading.[5]

There is, nevertheless, more than exquisite decadence in all this. It was in this same period that the Counter-Reformation began to form and to impose a new moral language. Imaginative purpose was often, as in the case of Tasso,[6] voiced through the distorting veils of censorship or self-censorship. But on certain matters, some of the novella writers appear to have been anxiously sympathetic to emphases which were increasingly apparent in the morality of the period. In particular, marriage begins to be seen, not only as a matter of social convenience but also as one of personal virtue and sentiment. Simultaneously, religious thinking begins to concern itself with the mysteries of Divine Providence, and increasingly stresses the importance of obedience, in the heart, to higher and hidden authority. Marriage and Providence are recurrent themes in the *novelle*, as they will also be in the tragi-comic genres of the period.[7] And English writers – despite an increasing difference of religious posture – came readily to share an interest in these themes.

In Italy and also in England, as Gascoigne's self-censorship shows, the novella reveals the tensions that arise when a concern with the fundamentals of Christianity – whether Puritan or Counter-Reformatory – conflict with or seek expression through a highly developed literary imagination. Like the comedy, the novella owed much in its origins to Boccaccio. In the *brigata* of the *Decameron,* Boccaccio had pictured a prophetic dream of the courtly society which, after the flowering which Castiglione celebrates in the *Cortegiano,* was now falling into decline. Story-telling in that dream had seemed to be an important resource in the development of a free and intelligent social order. In a similar way, Boccaccio had come to be a model for the writing of literary prose, as important in that respect as Petrarch was in the writing of verse.[8] At the same time, in the Counter-Reformation his works were now formally put on the Index in this period and re-written, to exclude all offensive references to nuns, friars and priests, by Borgini for the Giunti edition of 1573.[9]

---

5. See the contemporary letter by Andrea Calmo cited by M. Ciccuto, *Novelle Italiane: Il Cinquecento* (Milan, 1982), pp. xii–xii.
6. See above, p. 159.
7. See below, p. 267.
8. See above, Chapter 3 *passim*.
9. See Flora, op.cit., p. 156.

The consequence in regard to the history of story-telling was a version of Boccaccio's project which differed markedly from the original. In some cases, the *novelle* of the sixteenth century retreat into triviality and light entertainment. Where Boccaccio's work had claimed the right to experiment freely with notions of power, gender and social organisation, some at least of his successors envisage story-telling as one of the many forms of party-game which the period developed. Where Boccaccio could see wit as a resource which cut across social boundaries, an audience of courtly readers could now be asked to ponder, for instance, which admirer a lady ought to throw overboard if there happened to be one too many in a sinking boat.[10] On the other hand, certain of the *novelle* – particularly those which came to be favoured in translation – tend to give emphasis to the tragic components of the *Decameron*. The age was a horrific enough in its historical circumstance; and the real horrors of the period combined with a growing literary taste for tragedy in a Senecan style, particularly in the works of Cinthio and in Bandello, who had translated Euripides' *Hecuba*. This is not to deny the variety of tone that the novella could command; and tonal variety was also encouraged by the fact that the authors of *novelle* came increasingly from regions other than Boccaccio's Tuscany. So, as foreign authors began to adapt the novella to their own tongue, they found a form which was capable of elevation but which was also flexible in regard to genre and stylistic level. In this respect, it was comparable to the theatrical tragi-comedy which will be considered in the following chapter. Certainly, Shakespeare recognises this when he draws upon the novella tradition in *All's Well* and *Measure for Measure*. Webster, likewise, when writing *The Duchess of Malfi* found in the novella tradition situations where Senecan interests could be translated onto the level of contemporary reference.

Both morally and artistically, the characteristics of the sixteenth-century novella – and the differences between this form and Boccaccio's – are exemplified in the framing devices which authors proceeded to develop. Boccaccio had created a frame which admitted, simultaneously, a tragic and a comic view: his courtly *brigata* might adopt a prevailingly festive or ludic stance but behind that there lay the plague which Boccaccio had described so vividly in his prologue. Now, writers tend to establish either a purely festive or a purely tragic frame for their stories, as when one author, Il Lasca, pictures his *brigata* engaged in a

10. See Griffiths, op.cit., p. 82.

snow-ball fight or when Cinthio sets his tales against the background of the Sack of Rome.[11] It was in the construction of a frame that an author's critical understanding of his own purposes was likely to display itself most clearly. But where the *Decameron* favours an ambiguity which at best could express a liberation from old certainties, it was also in the frame-narrative that the new certainties of the novella writers – in England as well as in Italy – began to be revealed.

If developments occurred within the Italian tradition itself, then such developments were accelerated as the tradition came to be diffused throughout Europe. Just as Boccaccio's works had travelled widely and rapidly, so too did those particularly of Bandello. It was still possible for writers to return directly to the Boccaccian original, particularly as a model of narrative prose. In England, William Painter is one such; and though England had its own narrative prose tradition, it could still respond with unacknowledged enthusiasm to the example of Italian: Lyly's style has been described as a degenerate form of Italian prose,[12] while the progenitor of euphuism is regularly identified as George Pettie (1548–89), author of a novella collection entitled – euphuistically – *A petite pallace of Pettie his pleasures* (1576).[13] Nevertheless, in many cases the Italian texts seem to have arrived in English hands through French intermediaries; and while critics have perhaps exaggerated the influence of these French translations and underplayed the competence in Italian of Elizabethan English writers, the French texts often did interpose a degree of verbosity and didacticism which shielded the English from the rawer edges of the Italian original or else encouraged a detachedly moralising posture.[14] Whatever the influence of the French translators such as Belleforest and Boiastuau might have been, English writers were clearly impelled towards the Italian text by a range of independent interests which took particular and sometimes invidious pleasure in the sight of a great culture dramatically attempting to redeem itself from contemporary danger.

---

11. Il Lasca is the alias of the Florentine Anton Francesco Grazzini (1503–1582) who was notable for his championship of popular literary forms and who was significantly critical of the expurgated version of Boccaccio's *Decameron* which appeared in 1573.
12. See G.K. Hunter, *John Lyly: The Humanist as Courtier* (London, 1962).
13. See edition by I. Gollancz (London, 1908).
14. See René Pruvost, *Matteo Bandello and Elizabethan Fiction* (Paris, 1937).

CINTHIO AND BANDELLO

The gravity of the issues which the novella could set itself to tackle can be best be seen in the work of Giovambattista Giraldi, henceforth referred to by his adopted name Cinthio. Cinthio has already appeared as an excellent critic of Ariosto and will contribute a good deal to discussion in the concluding chapters of this book:[15] not only was he the author of stories that Shakespeare drew upon in *Measure for Measure* and *Othello*, but his theories, as expounded in works such as the *Discorsi intorno al comporre de i Romanzi, delle Commedie e delle Tragedie* (Venice, 1554) also did much to encourage experimentation in mixed genres.[16] He himself wrote tragedies in a violently Senecan vein and showed in a number of cases, including the original for *Measure for Measure*, how the stories of the Boccaccian novella could be used also for dramatic and even tragic purposes.[17]

In all his theoretical works, Cinthio is seriously concerned with questions concerning the representation of violence in artistic form. His tastes led him to challenge the precepts of Aristotelian theory and produce manifestations of violence on stage in his tragedies. But he was also concerned, as tragi-comedy will prove to be, with situations in which the possibility of death and horror could be contemplated while the reality – by virtue of some unexpected turn of events – was ultimately avoided. Often the appeal in such cases is to Providential action, supported by a stoical turn of mind derived from Seneca; and similar considerations dominate the moral as well as the literary characteristics of the frame which he provides for his novella collection, the *Hecatomitthi* of 1565.

The prologue to the tales describes the devastation of Rome in 1527 by invading Imperial forces. In choosing, as the occasion for story-telling, a disaster which made as great an impact on the sixteenth-century Italians as the plague did on the fourteenth, Cinthio follows Boccaccio (though departing from him in other respects), and firmly pursues a tragic rather than a festive model. Indeed, Cinthio claims, remarkably enough, that the very purpose of our possessing the power of speech is to enable us to recount disaster. Though he admits, as Boccaccio would, that story-telling is therapeutic, he nevertheless adopts from the first the position of

---

15. See above, pp. 158–9 and below, pp. 288–9.
16. See below, pp. 259–61.
17. In particular in *Orbecche*, Cinthio seems to draw upon the horrors of *Decameron*, IV. i discussed below, pp. 243–6.

an eye witness, recording tales of moral horror for the benefit of posterity: nature gives us the capacity to speak and to write so that, as well as being useful or consoling to those who were present at ghastly events, we should be able to give a 'perpetual image' of the strokes of misfortune to those who are 'distant' from them. More like Tasso than Boccaccio, Cinthio is concerned to base the veracity of the marvels he will relate in historical reality; and he is comparable to Tasso also in seeking to oppose an orthodox moral position against his own indulgence in the lurid possibilities of his fiction. So while alluding to Dante's *selva oscura* as an image of the corrupt age in which he lives, he also evokes the Dantean principle of free will as the means which will allow us to escape from the 'labyrinth' of disaster (and presumably of fiction) in which we are lost ('*smarriamo*').[18]

Against this background, Cinthio strongly emphasises the impiety which was displayed by the marauding forces in their attack on Rome, recalling continually that these troops were Lutherans who defiled the sacred places of the Mother Church. He also emphasises that the Romans themselves responded to this attack on the great city with the *virtù* of their classical forebears. 'Stained with the pestilential heresy of Lutheranism', the mercenaries are seen to visit 'harsh horrors' ('*aspri orrori*') on the sacred places:

> no mercy was shown to sex or to person, neither to years or to age, nor to the sacraments of the religion of our Lord and Redeemer . . . Here greatness of rank was useless, and nobility of birth. Nor were the tears of mothers of any avail; for their ears were everywhere closed against pity and rectitude (*pietà*). Children were seen running to the breast of their desolate mothers, who – dishevelled as they were – twined their own hands in the beards of their assailants, seeking to prevent their daughters from the brutality of these cruel men. This served no purpose save to increase their evil appetite. For these villains plucked up the mothers and, flinging them to the earth (O dreadful spectacle) raped their own virgin daughters on top of them. And when they had satisfied their lust many times over, they slaughtered both mother and daughter before the eyes of their fathers and husbands, who were their prisoners . . . The fathers stood mute like statues, while the mothers, seeing such abominable offences against their daughters, in many cases clawed out their eyes with their own fingers.[19]

There can be no doubt that literary influences, from Sophocles to Lucan, play their part in this passage. Equally, there is no mistaking the

18. Dante is lost – 'smarrito' – in the dark wood of *Inferno*, I. 3.
19. Translated from the Venice edition of 1608, held in Cambridge University Library.

vivid sense of an actual event (expressed as in Tasso by authorial excla-
mations) here afflicting Catholic sensibilities with the violence that
Marlowe, say, was to summon up when he spoke out with Protestant
indignation against the massacre of Paris. (In his translation of the
Pharsalia, Marlowe, one might add, also shares with Cinthio an understanding of what, stylistically, Lucan can contribute to the evocation of
tragic violence.)

Yet Cinthio is concerned not only with a vision of disaster but also
with moral solutions. One such solution will lie in the lap of
Providence: famine and pestilence follows war, 'men become like shad-
ows' (ibid., p. 18), but the pestilence falls providentially on the victors as
well as on the victims. Human ingenuity too has its place here; so, as
Cinthio pictures it, a group of survivors gathers, as in the *Decameron*, to
discuss a strategy for escape. Eventually this group will leave Rome by
ship for the safety of Marseilles, and their leisure-time on the voyage
will be occupied by story-telling. But here marked differences begin to
show between Boccaccio's position and Cinthio's .

As Cinthio represents it, the decision to leave Rome closely follows
the argument of the *brigata* in the Decameron, that it would be useless
to remain in a doomed city. But notably, where in Boccaccio women
are in the majority among the *brigata* – and demonstrate a degree of wit
in contemplating the unthinkable escape from Florence – in the
Hecatommithi men are in the ascendancy, and men who are endowed
both with rank and the *gravitas* of age. The guiding presence here is not
the witty Pampinea, nor for that matter a young and anarchic Dioneo.
The women of the *brigata* are widows, white-haired severe; and, among
the men, the lead is taken by the grave figure of Fabio. Fabio understands the value of entertainment and diversion. Yet in person and in
the words he speaks, Fabio expresses the standards which have been
offended by the Sack of Rome. His words likewise insist upon hierarchical and moral sentiments of the most orthodox kind. Thus he admits
that love should be a topic of debate. Yet, contrary to the spirit not only
of Boccaccio but also of Castiglione, Cinthio puts into Fabio's mouth a
homily – several pages in length – the burden of which is that sexual
appetite can only be expressed legitimately in the begetting of children:

> And therefore in conclusion I say that only that form of love proceeds from
> reason, having matrimony for its end. It is this which for true and wise lovers
> is a source of peace, coupled as it is – for the refreshment *(refrigerio)* of lover's
> flames with wise discourse and legitimate union.

In large part, then, Cinthio's cornice alerts one to the extreme realities of contemporary circumstance, while providing a correspondingly extreme moral frame in which to view them. It would not, however, be surprising if in practice the moral frame served not to control but rather to underline and enhance the appreciation of transgression; and this is certainly in keeping with the view of the novella which emerges from one of the few works of theory which accompanies the relatively untheorised novella form. Thus Francesco Boncioni in his *Lezioni sopra il comporre delle novelle* (read to the Accademmia degli Alterati in 1574)[20] argues that

> the most 'marvellous' or extraordinary thing in the Universe – and therefore the most suitable subject for a novella – is the extremes produced by the human mind. We accept the orderliness and stability of God's universe and are not astonished by it; we see the changes of fortune in the contingent world but would only be amazed if the skies rained stones and blood. But much more amazing is the human intellect especially in its moments of perversity: love can lead us to destroy the object of love, as Deianira destroyed Hercules: in Oedipus we can see a trust in reason lead to its own overthrow: amazingly, it is as if in the human intellect there were a living force that destroyed the rationality of that intellect and the arguments that rationality might employ so as not to fall into such error.

Here Boncioni not only lays aside the divine order of Dante's world and the stimulating vicissitudes of Boccaccio's, but also provides a reverse-image of much that one associates with the myth of the Renaissance: while attributing enormous powers of will and intellect to human beings, it is our destructive rather than constructive capacities which are of interest to the novella writer.

In its pursuit of the extraordinary, the Italian novella is necessarily distinguished from the modern novel with its fundamentally realistic cast.[21] But if, recently, one has come to speak of magical realism in the modern novel, so, in regard to the novella, one might speak of 'marvellous' realism. For while the novella writers may seek out, as Boccaccio did, the most spectacular manifestations of human behaviour, they also frequently claimed for themselves in doing so the role of journalistic eye witness, developing forms of prose and of narrative which, while always alert to the spectacular dimension, equally claim to be sanctioned by an attention to everyday circumstance. At its best, the novella manages to

---

20. Translated here from Ciccuto, op.cit., p. x.
21. Cf. Rodax, op.cit., p. 5, on the magical realism of Bandello.

investigate the real world as precisely as, say, Leonardo does in his draw-
ings of grotesques or of mushroom-growths; and though the usual area
for investigation is the courtly ambience which Castiglione described,
the mentality which underlies such investigation is as likely to be that of
a covert Machiavelli, seeking no underlying principle but prepared to
tolerate as fact whatever it lights upon.

This is particularly well exemplified in the work of Matteo Bandello
(1485–1561). Bandello, whose works antedate those of Cinthio, was a
Domenican friar of noble family and worldly leanings. He saw at first
hand the horrors of the early sixteenth century in Italy, displayed in the
invasion of Milan in 1525, where he had made his home and which at
this time was a more flourishing city than London or Paris. After a long
period of wandering in the service of many courtly patrons, he found
himself rewarded by becoming Bishop of Agen. Bandello was an
accomplished humanist, turning his hand to both poetry and drama.[22]
But his experiences and achievements are most fully reflected in his
massive collection of stories published at Lucca in 1554 in three volumes
amounting to 186 stories. The originality of these stories in part lies in
the break which their author makes with his own humanist formation.
Bandello is always ready to confess – and thus to emphasise – the simplicity and even roughness of his own prose style in comparison with
the elevations of Boccaccio; he is well aware of the contemporary
debates concerning the appropriate forms of literary Italian,[23] but choosing to write in his native Lombard, he deliberately adopts a neutral or
even or, so he says, 'non-existent' style.[24]

Bandello consistently describes his stories as 'ciance' – 'prattle' or
'gossip' – as he does , for example, in a letter to Castiglione (Vol. I. 44).
No doubt there is a degree of *sprezzatura* in this. Yet these unassuming
views point to a programme and even to a theory of some considerable
interest. Certainly in practice, the simple style which Bandello assumes
proves flexible enough to cope with a wide variety of tones and social
situations. So, telling a tale of Calandro-like idiocies among the ranks of
the merchant classes, Bandello introduces the protagonists with the
casually ironic understatement that 'the husband wasn't the most handsome man in the world while his wife would certainly not have

22. For the Italian text of Bandello's work, see *Tutte Le Opere di Matteo Bandello a cura di
    Francesco Flora*, 4 vols (Milan, 1934). See also Gwynfor Griffith, *Bandello's Fiction*
    (Oxford, 1955) and K. Bartley, *Bandello and the Heptameron* (Melbourne, 1960).
23. See above, p. 118.
24. Griffiths, op.cit., p. 41, quoting Bandello's Preface to Part I of the *Novelle*.

deprived the sky of beauty'. But the appeal, as in erudite comedy, is still to a courtly rather than a bourgeois or popular audience; and while maintaining a level of elegant chatter and badinage – and hence an affiliation with oral culture – the *novelle* are still clearly intended for publication in printed form.

The frame which Bandello adopts, and the theoretical considerations embodied in that frame, are consistent with the characteristics of his prose. In fact, Bandello abandons any semblance of the Boccaccian *cornice* – which Cinthio was to re-introduce – in favour of a series of epistles, the purpose of which is not, ostensibly, to set up an authenticating *fiction* but to establish the *facts* of how the author himself came to hear each of the stories, and thus to present an historical lineage of eye-witness accounts. These epistles, to friends and to dignitaries alike, no doubt reflect Bandello's tuft-hunting days as a freelance courtier. But it is perfectly possible that the histories of reception which they offer are themselves largely invented, and therefore part of a new programme of authorial procedure. Thus, in rejecting the Boccaccian frame, Bandello proposes a view – which itself must be considered a theoretical advance – of real events as random occurrences, more amenable to opinion than to principled analysis. 'My stories,' he says, 'do not deal with connected history but are rather a miscellany of diverse happenings.' Likewise, he is prepared to defend the value of opinion as form of thought against the claims of rational argument and the iron necessities of principle: rationally organised discourse may, it seems, prove to be a distortion of the realities which opinion – or even perhaps gossip – accurately reflects. For similar reasons, the imagination must be free to countenance situations which are not at first rationally plausible. In Vol. III. i, Bandello asserts that 'when a proposition is possible it must be accepted': Bandello will overtly pursue verisimilitude, but this will not inhibit his interest in extreme situations.

It follows that Bandello adopts a far less definite moral stance than Cinthio does; and Bandello's translators, particularly in French, are much concerned to reintroduce the moral certainties which Bandello himself avoids. Bandello's own concern is to find a form in which to record the realities of the age in which he lives. So in the Introduction to Vol. III. 62 he declares: 'I believe that the age in which we live is one which above all others displays things which inspire amazement, compassion and blame.' He also recognises that the age is one of profound moral turmoil and continues in the same place – like Cinthio – to contemplate the confusions that have arisen in Europe through the impact of

Lutheranism, which has 'led many to desert the ways of their forebears and the great teachers of the past' and has even allowed the civilisation of Europe to be threatened by the incursions of the Ottoman Empire. Yet, strikingly, this prologue does not produce any large moral or religious programme. It remains a letter, intended at best to cement the bonds of personal friendship between himself and his correspondent through a literary exchange. And while it is notable that the story which this letter introduces tells of Henry VIII of England, it quickly moves from the level of religious and political polemic to that of domestic curiosity. Initially, Henry appears as a dire example of what may happen when a sovereign deserts the Catholic Church. But the narrative interest wholly derives from the intrigues of a High Renaissance court and the lurid details of Henry's six marriages. So Bandello, improving in sensationalism on his sources, ends this tale of Henry 'in regard to women and the Christian religion' with the neatly erroneous conclusions that, after his marriage to his last wife, the King still continued to visit Anne of Cleves.

Attempting to record for posterity the 'marvels' of his age, Bandello, in the narrative and linguistic forms which he adopts, demonstrates a fluidity of moral and intellectual principle which is itself an accurate reflection of the age in which he lives. The 'ethical ambiguity' which self-evidently is a characteristic of his work is itself deliberately cultivated as a part of his literary programme. 'Marvels' for Bandello are neither the fantastic flights of imagination which Ariosto creates nor the miracles of faith which Tasso seeks to portray. Here one may move from tales which tell of how a girl came to eat the testicles of a castrated priest (III. 30), to stories in which a wild Petrarchan gallantry leads a lover to jump, horse and all, into a raging torrent to prove the literal ardour of his fiery passions. Equally 'marvellous' is the story – with Oedipal subtext – of the marriage between a man and a woman who was already his own sister and daughter (II. 35), or else the story of Romeo and Juliet (II. 9), told with a constant attention to effects of pathos and sentiment. In each case, Bandello maintains the historical veracity of the marvel while heightening its imaginative appeal by any fictional means available. Throughout, his stories mirror a cultural situation in which there is no stable viewpoint. The codes of behaviour and of intellectual procedure which the Renaissance had developed are still fully understood but they have been dislodged from their point of attachment. Gossip, opinion and manipulation are the channels through which these principles now run; and the consequences of such instability can prove to be as tragic as they are marvellous. This is shown in the fifth novella of Part IV.

This story tells of secret marriages and illicit passions at the court of Burgundy in which a faithful counsellor is destroyed by a wicked Duchess when he refuses to accede to her amorous advances. The story itself is not contemporary in setting; there are allusions here both to Boccaccio and to Marguerite of Navarre. Nevertheless, Bandello claims to have heard the story during a lull in a wedding feast which he happened to be attending, and to have written it down at the time, thus producing not only a claim to authenticity but also a set of tacit parallels between the courtly wedding at which he himself was present and the degenerate marriage which his story depicts. Within the story, the chain of gossip to which Bandello attaches himself exerts its grip in an unremitting concern with rumour, scandal and secrecy as the realities of court life.[25]

A young man, noble but poor, has been brought up by the generous Duke of Burgundy and has served him faithfully throughout his adult life. The relationship of trust between the two men remains constant throughout the story. But confusion begins to threaten when the second wife of the Duke casts her eye upon the servant. He resists; and the first phase of the story comes to a climax with the portrayal of an attempted seduction, in which both players – with opposite goals in view – prove expert in their manipulation of the codes of love and loyal service. The queen approaches the young man in the spirit of courtly game. Everyone at court plays the '*servitore de le dame*' – 'the servant of courtly ladies' (p. 218) – so why, asks the Duchess, does not the young man himself choose to participate like a true courtier. The story has not yet revealed that the young man is in fact secretly married. Nor does he himself mention it now. Instead, playing upon a modesty-*topos*, he maintains that he is unworthy to enter the game. Self-knowledge, he asserts disingenuously, warns him to avoid the perilous labyrinth of love (p. 220). Already, two kinds of moral language are being used – the one drawn from social practice, the other from the ethics of personal integrity – and each is employed quite knowingly in the furtherance of ends for which they were not initially designed. The queen thinks she must put aside the mask (p. 220), declaring her own feelings, with '*sincerity*', so as to strengthen the young man's confidence. Now in perilous straits, he for his part *feigns*, summoning the diplomatic skill of a Castiglione to deliver, obliquely, a moral reprimand to the Duchess through an insistence upon his own humble loyalty to his Lord. The Duchess reads these coded words accurately; and, though her body language betrays

25. References here are to the pagination of Flora's edition, op.cit., from which passages are translated.

her true feelings of sexual excitement and indignation (p. 221), she is quick to resort to the lie direct. Accusing the servant of that very arrogance which he has just disclaimed, she denounces him to the King as if he had attempted to seduce her.

The codes which now begin to operate are those of the language of domestic nagging, whereby the Duchess attempts to persuade her husband to exact vengeance. The Duke is unwilling to mistrust his servant and is never convinced by his wife's protestations. But then comes the truly Bandellian touch. The Duke has a fatal flaw which is precisely his curiosity and love of gossip. Suddenly, the high moral tone of his own lordly fidelity to a trusted servant vanishes, and is replaced by an everyday itch for tittle-tattle. The Duke himself in his young day had been a philanderer. Now he suspects that there must be some hidden reason for the servant's behaviour (p. 233). He tests his servant and has no doubt about his good faith. But the Duchess now turns her knowledge of her husband's character against him; to the Duke himself, it begins to seem suspicious that his servant will neither show any sign of being – conventionally – what a young man should be nor satisfy his master's curiosity about the reasons for his behaviour. Under an oath of absolute secrecy, the Duke finally extracts from the young man the story that he has wanted to hear – which tells of a long-standing but secret marriage to a kinswoman of the Duke himself. There is no hint of offended family pride in the Duke's response, rather a delight which is sharpened when he is told the full story (or, indeed, novella-within-a-novella) of how the clandestine affair has been conducted.

The story now shifts so far from high heroics as to take the secret wife's pet puppy as its main character: in a Watteau-like scene, the Duke is shown how the secret wife lets loose her dog into a moonlit garden; the barking of the dog will then signal to her husband that he can safely come to her chamber.

But, against the delicate sentimentality of this scene, the tone of the story now darkens progressively towards tragedy. The Duchess – who at this stage is firmly identified as a 'serpent' by the authorial voice – again resorts to nagging; and the Duke, who remains 'loyal' to her even though he fully recognises her perfidious nature, cannot eventually resist the temptation to break his oath and share the story with her. The Queen herself is now consumed with curiosity as to the name of the wife. Ironically enough, she plays the card of matrimonial convention in a move which will destroy the marriage of the secret pair: husband and wife, she argues, are one flesh, so it is only right that her own husband should divulge the name of the other man's wife. The Duke eventually does. And the Duchess makes use of her knowledge, in the drawing-room setting of a palace reception, to intimate to the wife that she knows her secret. At first the response she receives is one of skilfully barbed wit. The wife, hearing the Duchess refer to the little dog as an authenticating detail, replies cuttingly that she herself does not understand the language of beasts. But, having thrust this reproach at the Duchess, she makes for the privacy of a bed-chamber and there breaks down. The Duke is alerted by an eavesdropping maid, and cannot stop himself from peeping, too. By now the wife is as cold as a marble monument, her heart breaking at the offence to good faith which she has suffered. Her husband is called, and enters to receive one last baleful glance from his stricken wife. Accusing himself bitterly of having broken his oath and of having become a prattler, he stabs himself. The Duke has witnessed the whole scene from a hidden position; and – realising belatedly that oaths are sacred – now snatches up the suicide's knife, dashes back to the reception and, in full view of the court, murders his wife as she dances before him. He orders a monument to be set up to the memory of the two lovers, and retires into religious seclusion.

Bandello began this novella with a series of moral injunctions: one should be wary of the snares of love; one should love with temperance and never divulge what one does not wish to be known to any person at all. But these sentiments are scarcely reflected in the story itself, and Bandello's interest in the shifting tones and registers of the tale prevent it from standing as an illustration of any such moral. In any case, language itself, on the view offered by this novella, is incapable of carrying moral purposes to their conclusion: social pressures and an insuppressibly natural appetite for chatter render oaths and vows entirely empty. And this is a situation in which moralists more severe than Bandello will quickly come to interest themselves. Spenser will recognise that gossip is a danger intrinsic to courtly culture when he makes the Blatant – or 'blathering' – Beast the enemy of true courtesy.[26] The issue will also prove central in Shakespeare's *Othello* where the gossip of Iago also threatens to dissolve the vows made between two lovers.[27] In both of these cases, the authors provide alternatives to the linguistic uncertainties which Bandello, in this story as in so many others, seems to make the central feature of his narrative procedure. But neither Spenser nor Shakespeare would have have been able to provide their

26. See above, p. 184.
27. See below, p. 301.

answers if the novella – particularly in the hands of Bandello – had not first raised the question.

THE ENGLISH NOVELLA COLLECTIONS: FENTON, WHETSTONE AND PAINTER

The general characteristic of the English novella writers is that, while tending to concentrate on tragic tales from the Italian, they also maintain a moral and didactic purpose which dissipates the tragic complexities of the original text. This is particularly evident in cases such as that of Geoffrey Fenton where overtly moral concerns are combined with patriotic interests and a notable violence of rhetorical manner.[28]

Fenton – in the course of a life which led him to participate with considerable brutality in the colonial pacification of Ireland – found time to translate (from a French version) Guicciardini's *History of Italy*, which he dedicated to Queen Elizabeth and also thirteen stories from Bandello (again with help from the French) which he entitled *Certain Tragical Discourses* and dedicated in 1567 to Sir Philip Sidney's sister, Mary.[29]

This collection offers itself as a way to teach the value of 'policy in worldly things' *(Dedication,* p. 4): the Scriptures rightly teach 'faith and fear in God'. But policy must be learned from 'histories, who are the only and true tables whereon are drawn in perfect colours the virtues and vices of every condition of man'. Ostensibly, the reader is to find in the *Discourses* 'good and wholesome lessons' in regard to private conduct and for the benefit or 'commodity' of the nation.

There follows a series of stories in which, where Bandello had maintained a level of undecorated prose, Fenton takes every opportunity for rhetorical display and at every point aims his rhetoric at some obviously moral target.[30] It would be easy to discern here, as in Tasso, a degree of

---

28. See Pruvost, op.cit. Fenton (*c.* 1539–1608) was a ferocious Protestant, always ready to advise the use of the 'rack against Rome'. His interest in Italy nevertheless won him the disapproval of Ascham.

29. See *Certain tragical discourses of Bandello,* trans. into English by Geffraie Fenton *anno* 1567, quoted here from the edition with introduction by R.L. Douglas (London, 1898) 2 vols.

30. On prose style in Fenton and generally in the English novella, see W.G. Crane, *Wit and Rhetoric in the Renaissance: The Formal Basis of Elizabethan Prose Style* (New York, Morningside Heights, 1937).

overcompensation for the imaginative relish which the narrative provides.[31] But Fenton rarely relaxes his guard and is always ready, as in his
translation of Guicciardini, to reinforce his moral position with a patriotic horror at the depravity of the Italian world. So when Bandello tells
the oft-told story of the Lady of Celant,[32] who was finally beheaded
after a series of ruthlessly lustful escapades, the Italian author does not
scruple to say how he himself was acquainted with the infamous
nymphomaniac; nor does he hesitate to point out that one may still see
her face – if one has a sufficiently ghoulish tastes – in a certain portrait
of St Catherine since, after her execution in 1526, the decapitated head
of the Lady of Celant was used as a model for that of the decapitated
saint. In telling the same tale, however, Fenton, from the first, openly
lays out his moral and xenophobic position. The Duchess was damned
from birth: her mother was Greek and the daughter herself – apparently
as a consequence – was 'more fair than virtuous, less honest than was
necessary and worse disposed than well given anyway' (ibid., p. 15).
Nor is it much to her credit in Fenton's eyes that, during her youth, the
'chief and common exercise' of the Lady of Celant' was to force 'a
frizilation of her hair with the bodkin, converting the natural colour
into a glistering glee, suborned by art to abuse God and nature' (op.cit.,
p. 17). None of this, however, will prevent Fenton himself from displaying a covert eroticism which draws at times upon Aretino in its
mixing of amorous and military metaphors. A sympathetic view might
speak of the psychological insecurity which is betrayed by Fenton's
venom; the alternative is to emphasise the incoherence of his moral
imagination and to regard it as symptomatic of the era in which he
wrote.

Not all the English novella writers, however, are as vehement as
Fenton. George Whetstone – whose play *Promos and Cassandra* was a
source for Shakespeare's *Measure for Measure* –[33] is no less concerned than
Fenton is with the educative value of the short story, but proves much
more sympathetic to the Italian example, finding particular merit in
Castiglione and Stefano Guazzo. Following these authors, Whetstone's
purpose in his *Heptameron of Civill Discourses* (1581) is to introduce some-

---

31. See above, pp. 176–81, for Tasso's extended use of similar conceits.

32. ibid., *Discourse*, VII. II. 1–56. This story was also told by Whetstone and by John
Marston in *The Insatiate Countess* (1609–11?).

33. George Whetstone (1544?–1587) was a close associate of George Gascoigne (see
above, pp. 215–23 and p. 224) and, like Gascoigne, lived a life between military,
courtly and literary activities. On Whetstone, see Thomas C. Izard, *George Whetstone:
Mid-Elizabethan Gentleman of Letters* (New York, 1942).

thing of the Italian delicacy of social manner into England; and characteristically, he wishes to translate good manners (as Elyot might have done) from the courtly to the domestic sphere. His overriding concern, however, throughout the seven days of narrative 'exercise' is to emphasise the virtues of married life, dealing variously with the differences between the married and single states, with 'the inconveniencies of forced marriages' or of 'rash marriages' and above all with the 'excellency of marriage, with many sound laws and laudable directions to continue love between the married', 'all of which principles', he declares in setting up his themes for the first day of story-telling 'are intercoursed with other moral conclusions of necessary regard' (*Themes for the First Day*). Occasionally, Whetstone shows an understanding of how, for any Elizabethan, marriage must be a political matter as well as a private matter.[34] But for the most part his stories focus upon companionate marriage; and when he speaks of love, it is clear that anything other than married love must be regarded as a playful topic, producing at most the occasion for urbane badinage. Guazzo's approach to etiquette as a matter of social decorum is more important here than the searching investigations of a Castiglione. This does not, however, prevent Whetstone from producing a good deal of light and lively prose.

Some of Whetstone's liveliest writing is to be found in the frame which he constructs for the *Heptameron*. This frame is distinctly festive in character and – for an English author – exceptionally well developed.[35] Thus Whetstone, claiming some of Bandello's authority as an eye witness, sets out to describe the hospitality he enjoyed over the Christmas festival at a the country palace near Ravenna. Here, already, he begins to claim, as Bandello did, the authority of an eye witness and social initiate. When he tabulates the rules of conduct which were to be followed at these proceedings, it is evident that, while his stories draw substantially upon Cinthio's *novelle*, he nevertheless has moved some distance from the predominantly tragic original in his tone and intention, entering a world of party games and well-regulated flirtations:

> Item: Every gentleman was bound to serve some one mistress . . . upon pain to be turned into the great hall among the country thralls the whole Christmas.
>
> Item: Every gentleman was bound to court his mistress with civil speeches, upon pain to be forbidden to talk of love for three days. For he was account-

34. Izard, op.cit., pp. 122–3.
35. George Pettie translates Guazzo's books on etiquette (1581). See T. McAlinden, *Shakespeare and Decorum* (London, 1973).

ed base mannered or very gross witted that could not pleasantly entertain time with civil discourse.[36]

The most ambitious of all the novella collections in English is also the earliest – William Painter's *The Palace of Pleasure*, originally entitled *The City of Civility*, which appeared in three volumes between 1566 and 1575.[37] Painter's work attracted censure on moral grounds from Stephen Gosson in his *Theatre Playes Confuted in Five Actions* (London, 1582), and certainly the collection offers a wider variety of comic and tragic elements than either Fenton or Whetstone. But as well as the (by now) predictable moral purpose, there is a clear artistic ambition in Painter's work. He writes, as he says in his dedication to the Earl of Warwick, of the 'Theatre of the world, given to one who has been an actor in the same' (p. 6), and though his initial intention seems to have been to use only classical material, his critical interests led him to broaden the range of selection very considerably to provide a comprehensive survey of narrative fiction in both classical and vernacular form. Most notably, in dealing with Italian literature, he is insistent upon the value of returning to the original text of stories by Boccaccio. In refering to Bandello it is enough, it seems, to use French intermediaries. But the example of Boccaccio's prose style demands direct translation from the Italian: the works of Boccaccio for his style, order of writing, gravity and sententious discourse . . . are worthy of entire promulgation' (op.cit., p. 11). As for Bandello, he 'is no trim Tuscan' and can therefore be satisfactorily approached through French. It is perhaps a product of Painter's attention to Boccaccio's elevated but restrained example that his style remains remarkably free from euphuistic tendencies. It is also noticeable that Painter is most inclined to moralisation when he draws most heavily upon French translations, as in the last phases of the Romeo and Juliet story where Juliet has time and energy to expend on a great deal of tragic complaint.

Of the one hundred stories in *The Palace of Pleasure*, twenty-four are taken from the Italian; and of these, two are from Cinthio, six are from Bandello (including the story of the Duchess of Malfi), and no less than eight from Boccaccio, while others are drawn from other figures in the

36. Compare Izard, op.cit., pp. 82–3.
37. William Painter (*c.* 1525–1594) was educated at St John's College Cambridge and served for some years as headmaster of Sevenoaks School in his native Kent. He was appointed in 1561 as Clerk of the Ordnance in the Tower of London under the Earl of Warwick and, despite evidence of embezzlement, remained in post until his death, under the protection of Warwick. *The Palace of Pleasure* is now available in Dover Books, New York, 1966.

novella tradition such as Giovanni Fiorento, Masuccio Salernitano and Il Pecorone.[38] Even this Italian contingent suggests that, in terms of broad construction, Painter well understood the need for variety. But his versions also deserve to be examined for the qualities of their prose and for the close attention they encourage to Boccaccio's text.

An example which, had it not been for the subsequent fame of *Romeo and Juliet*, might have become a familiar example of the tragic novella is the story of Tancredi and Ghismonda, which originally was the first story in the Fourth Day of the *Decameron* and is retold by Painter as the tenth story of Book X.[39]

A widowed Princess, Ghismonda, realising that her father will never allow her to remarry, chooses a virtuous but poor member of her father's entourage as a lover. Her father discovers the affair, has the lover secretly executed and presents his heart in a golden chalice to his daughter. She fills the chalice with poison, drinks it and dies.

Through the figure of Ghismonda, Boccaccio voices a powerful defence of the rights of women to freedom of choice and to sexual satisfaction. These are seen as natural rights, and in defending them Ghismonda also – if largely by implication – calls into question her father's obsession with the conventions of rank which disallow her choice of consort. In Ghismonda's elevated and tragic speeches of defiance, Painter would undoubtedly have found the qualities of formal prose which drew him to Boccaccio's original text; and though there is a degree of clumsiness in his rendering, this tends to arise through an apparent desire to give full weight to the conceptual complexities of Boccaccio's text. Thus in Boccaccio questions of style and register are here closely related to questions of psychological stance: Ghismonda speaks to her father with the utmost self-possession – in a style in which logical emphasis and connection are fully observed – even though the burden of her argument is that she was overcome by irresistible forces in her own nature and circumstance. Her words are not offered as an excuse but as a demonstration of what, constitutionally, a human being can be, in the interaction and mutual reciprocation of its rational and sexual nature. The picture which emerges is not of reason overthrown by passion but of reason consciously choosing to submit to forces which it recognises as natural in itself.

Painter is clearly alert to such features and – even at the risk of substi-

38. See the excellent cross-section offered in Smarr, op.cit.
39. A play on the theme, *Tancred and Ghismonda*, was produced in 1568, and Dryden, for instance, saw the tragic potential of this tale in his narrative adaptation of Boccaccio's story, *Sigismonda and Guiscardo*.

tuting a repetition of phrase for Boccaccian variations – he strongly underscores the play of 'forces' and faculties at work in Ghismonda's speech:

> I am then as you be, begotten of flesh, and my years so few, as yet but young, and therby full of lust and delight. Wherunto the knowledge which I have had already in marriage, *forceth* me to accomplish that desire; and to the same be added marvellous *forces*, against which it is impossible for me to resist, but rather to follow, wherunto they draw me. I am become amorous like a young woman, and like a woman as I am, and certainly I would have employed my whole *force* that way, so far as I could not to commit any shame to you or to my self in that, whereunto my natural offence hath *forced* me. [*my italics*]

There is, however, another aspect of the story to which Painter is not so sensitive and which indeed he tends to obscure, namely the aura of ambiguity that, in Boccaccio's version, surrounds the motivations of Tancred the King.[40] Here, Boccaccio traces a psychological tragedy in which a King who once was humane and well-intentioned in all his actions is led by the very intensity of his feelings for his daughter to an ever-more perverse expression of those feelings and, eventually, to an act of murder. The King is portrayed finding his way for filial consolation to his Ghismonda's bedroom, falling asleep and then waking only to eavesdrop and peep in on his daughter's love-making. Through all this, there is an increasing sense that his affection (or as Boccaccio repeatedly puts it his 'tenderness of heart') as well as his protectiveness reveal an incestuous undercurrent: it is thus possible, for instance, to read the fashioning of a gold receptacle for the lover's heart not as a piece of sadism but as a confused attempt to placate, or indeed to regale, his errant daughter. Moreover, there is a clear reversal of traditonal gender roles here; for while Ghismonda acts with enterprise and speaks 'not like a weeping woman, but with a dry and bold countenance', so her father is shown constantly to be on the verge of tears. If Ghismonda is one victim of the patriarchal system, her father becomes yet another. His rank, and the expectation that he will act in keeping with his kingly role, put him in a position to destroy not only his daughter but also his own better nature and inclination.

Though many of these suggestions must have remained implicit even for Boccaccio, it is nevertheless striking that Painter either stumbles – or deliberately alters the text – in dealing with those moments where implications of this sort arise. At the outset, Boccacio speaks of the con-

40. Compare G. Almansi, *The Writer As Liar* (London, 1975).

tradiction which leads the benign King Tancred to befoul his hands with blood in his latter days. Painter speaks of Tancred imbruing his hands 'with the blood of his own daughter'. This phrase, which is not strictly true, distracts attention away from Tancred towards the pathos of his daughter's death, and obscures the fact that the daughter herself, emphatically and heroically, chooses to die by her own hand.

It is also significant that in Boccaccio's version Ghismonda consistently addresses her father by his given name as 'Tancredi', whereas Painter inserts 'father' or 'dear father' as a denotation of role and relationship. The equality which Ghismonda claims – and her father may himself subconsciously wish for – are expressed in Boccaccio's preference for the personal name; Painter seems reluctant to depart from formalities and predictable social postures.[41]

This tendency is particularly noticeable at two points. When Tancred first confronts Ghismonda with his knowledge of her liaison, his concern is that she should have time to prepare a defence for herself. And here Painter introduces a fatherly kiss which may indeed be a sign of tenderness but also suggests Tancredi's continuing attempt to maintain his paternal role: 'When he had spoken those wordes, he kissed her face, weeping very bitterly like a child that had been beaten'. Boccaccio makes no reference to a kiss; instead, Tancredi moves immediately and incongruously from his regal and fatherly position into child-like sobs and lowered countenance.

In a similar way, Painter cannot quite allow Ghismonda the fortitude which Boccaccio insists upon in her reversal of role. So without responding at all to her father's pitiable behaviour, Boccaccio's Ghismonda at once realises that her lover has been arrested; and though she comes close to making a great display of her grief, 'as for the most part women do', she precisely does not give way to this impulse but steels herself into a fatalistic but dignified stance by assuming, as far she is concerned, that her lover is already dead:

> dolore inestimabile sentì, e a mostrarlo con romore e con lagrime come il più le femine fanno, fu assai volte vicina, ma pur questa viltà vincendo il suo animo altiero, il viso suo con meravigliosa forza fermò.

> (She felt immeasurable grief, and she was very close to expressing that grief – as for the most part women do – in tears and clamour, but overcoming this ignoble weakness, her proud mind remained unchanging, with remarkable firmness.)

41. Dryden in his conclusion, departs even further from the ambiguities which Boccaccio created, insisting that all three parties – including the lover – are guilty.

In Painter, Ghismonda's cries are uttered 'many times' before courage takes control. Even then the death of Guiscardo, is here presented as, lamentably, an actual fact, whereas in Boccaccio the murder has not yet occurred and Ghismonda must assume that it has in order to brace herself for the rhetorical task ahead:

> Ghismonda, hearing her father, and knowing that not only her secret love was discovered, but also her lover Guiscardo to be in prison, conceived an inestimable sorrow, uttering the same many times, howbeit her great courage surpassed her weaknesse and did set a bold face on the matter, with marvellous stoutness, determining, before she made any suit for herself, no longer to live, seeing that her friend Guiscardo was already dead.

Such minutiae do not discredit the perceptiveness of Painter's translation. They do, however, suggest how deeply part of the language and stance of the translator were the moral resistances and social preconceptions which would be voiced by subsequent English novella writers.

WEBSTER AND THE IDIOM OF THE NOVELLA

Apart from Shakespeare, who is the subject of Chapter 8, no English writer makes fuller use of the novella tradition than Webster; and, though his work falls strictly beyond the compass of the present volume, it deserves attention here, not least because it serves to identify issues which had proved to be particularly important to dramatists in their response to Italy during the first years of the seventeenth century. The moral situations which Webster investigates are akin to those described in many sixteenth-century *novelles*; and like the *novellieri*, his concern is to observe the workings of a plausible historical present, displaying not so much the heroic activity of the individual as the extreme consequences that flow from the degeneracies of the contemporary social order. In this regard, his theatre frequently combines effects of tragic violence with effects of comedy in a way which reflects not only the fluidity of tone which Bandello, say, commands but also developments in tragi-comic dramaturgy which – as will be seen in the next chapter – were encouraged by Cinthio and ran in parallel with the development of the novella.[42]

At the same time, the myth of Italy, which by Webster's time had

---

42. See especially J. Pearson, *Tragedy and Tragicomedy in the Plays of John Webster* (Manchester, London, 1980).

come to represent a 'mode of human experience',[43] is central to
Webster's theatre; and in returning to the revenge-play idiom, Webster
concerns himself less with the great issues of justice and personal
courage which had lain at the heart of earlier revenge plays than with an
investigation of this particular mode of experience. 'Italy' here is indeed
represented pre-eminently as a realm of ethical ambiguity. Yet Webster,
in responding to this, does not simply reproduce the ambiguity. His language, for one thing, has qualities which generate a violence and
immediacy, in the apprehension of moral dangers, which would be
unthinkable in Italian. Yet against this, his stagecraft and his understanding of dramatic situation also demands of his audience an ethical
sensitivity which, again, neither the novella nor the tragi-comic theatre
of Italy could have achieved.

The Devil's Law Case (1623), as one of Webster's later plays, shows
particularly clearly how Webster understood and used the resources of
Italy. Here he tells of how the merchant Romelio, displeased by his sister's choice of husband, pits his wits and his murderous energies against
the match, but finds himself opposed not only by fortune – which
ensures that his argosies fail – but also by his own mother, Leonora. She
is in love with the suitor to her own daughter, a man whom her son not
only despises but attempts to kill. Leonora herself, learning of the
attempted murder, is prepared to accept humiliation in open court so as
to defame and disinherit her son Romelio, declaring him (falsely) to be
a bastard. Her designs are discovered by an upright judge, who dispenses
equitable justice to all in the final scene.

This play – which seems to be entirely Webster's invention – runs the
whole gamut of Italian possibilities from Boccaccio to Machiavelli to
Ariosto (whose name is appropriated to that of the judge and whose
Orlando Furioso is also mentioned – in reference to madness in the
closing lines of the play). In Romelio, Webster shows an exact under-
standing of the connection between the commercial rapacity of the
Italian mercantile ethic and the power politics that Machiavelli develops.
No doubt there is much here that reflects Shakespeare's *The Merchant of
Venice*, too. Romelio could be seen as an extraordinary combination of
Shylock and Antonio, schemer, loser, manipulator all in one. Yet the
man who – as Ariosto notes – can call his ships 'The Storm's Defiance'

---

43. See G.K. and S.K. Hunter, *John Webster* (London, 1970). Also Ralph Berry, *The Art
of John Webster* (Toronto, 1972); Gunnar Boklund, *The Sources of the White Devil*
(Uppsala, 1957) and his *The Duchess of Malfi: Sources, Themes Characters* (Cambridge
Mass., 1962); J.W. Lever, *The Tragedy of State* (London, 1971).

and 'The Scourge of the Sea' (III. iii. 53), is better entitled than most to be described as a Boccaccian merchant-hero, and also as a Machiavellian, fighting against Fortune. It is indeed pure luck which undoes him – and leads eventually to the happy ending of the tragi-comedy – when the needle-like knife, with which he hopes to murder the unwelcome suitor of his sister, lands exactly at a spot that discharges an otherwise lethal sac of poison. In revealing the appetite for power in the merchant, Webster also calls into question the claims of aristocracy of birth, while in his treatment of Leonora he countenances – in the way that the novella form had always been prepared to do – a mixture of extreme sensations and sentiments, involving the covert relationship of mother and son-in-law, where Oedipus and suburban passion join hands. Yet the answer to the questions which are raised here does not involve a disparagement of inbred nobility, nor for that matter of excit-ed sexuality. Courtesy, of a kind which Castiglione would have recognised, is shown to have its value alongside the imaginative appeal of Machiavellian energy, when rival suitors display their delicately ago-nised concern as much for each other as for their own honour. Nor does the delicacy of these lovers discredit the tremendous sexual urge which leads a mother – out of an obsession for a younger man – to seek to defame and disinherit her own villainous son. Power, nobility and disruptive sexual energy are all allowed to have their place as they might in either a Boccaccian or a Bandellian novella. But the comedy is that these forces can be reconciled under the auspices of a just judge. And Ariosto – acting with much of the perspective of the historical Ariosto, and a good deal more insight than the Duke in Shakespeare's *Measure for Measure* – is able to arrive at a conclusion which discovers a socially use-ful punishment for all the miscreants in the case. This is a solution which, despite the energies unleashed in the course of the play, would not have disgraced the conclusions of the prime author of mixed genres, Ariosto himself.

In the tragedies proper, *The White Devil* and *The Duchess of Malfi*, Webster displays a similarly analytical awareness of the Italian ethos. It has been said that the 'white devil', in a play which draws upon histori-cal events contemporary with Webster himself, is not Vittoria Corombona, the Venetian courtesan, but rather European culture itself.[44] Webster here looks critically at an Italy which is the prototype

44. Lever, op.cit., p. 87.

for a courtly and political Europe extending as far Whitehall.[45] It is clear from this play that Webster's interest, in line with the journalistic concerns of the novella writers, is in the way in which power and sexuality intermingle in the distortion of individual psychologies. Likewise, the style he adopts, far from suggesting an authorial confidence of position, is one which has its counterpart in the novella, avoiding any consistent viewpoint in favour of a continual series of discontinuities in presentation and in character. The audience has here almost a duty to discover a viewpoint of its own.

Such effects in *The White Devil* are developed to a higher degree in *The Duchess of Malfi* which derives, via Painter and Belleforest, from the twenty-sixth story in the first volume of Bandello's work. But where Bandello proves in moral terms to be surprisingly sensitive, the French intermediary has produced in Painter a moralising stance of particular virulence.

In his dedicatory letter, Bandello speaks of the tale as an example of the injustice of male rule: men, out of jealousy and possessiveness, commit all manner of cruelty, with poisonings and strangulation, against women. It would be better if women, who are moved by humanity and pity, themselves 'turned the wheels' of the world. Nor is it logical that men should place their honour only upon the chastity of their women-folk, when they themselves can destroy the honour of a family through advantageous marriages to socially inferior wives. It should be said that the tone of this passage is one of observation rather than moral fervour. Moreover, it is typical of Bandello that, without apparent compunction, he should dedicate his thirty-second story to the same Cardinal of Aragon who in story twenty-six had arranged for his sister's murder, and that he should declare himself much beholden to the Cardinal for past favours. Within the twenty-sixth story itself Bandello is notably as vague as Webster is specific in attributing the Duchess's death to her brothers: in Bandello, the duchess and two of her sons are simply 'found dead'. For all that, in the novella the Duchess is given many of the heroic qualities of Boccaccio's Ghismonda, choosing as a husband a man of great worth and openly justifying her choice with an emphasis (which is absent from Boccaccio) not simply on natural impulse but on the sanctity of marriage.

---

45. Parallels can be drawn between the situation described in *The White Devil* and that of Arabella Stuart, a possible claimant to the throne who, after a clandestine marriage, was imprisoned for life on a charge of conspiracy against James I. See J.R. Brown, ed. of the play, *The Revels Plays* (London, 1964), p. xxxix.

Yet Painter, in spite of his responsiveness to the figure of Ghismonda, is led, under the influence of Belleforest, into a position which takes as its starting point a powerful emphasis on the importance of male rule and a recommendation that 'above all modesty ought to be kept by women'. The authorial voice is strongly marked in Painter's story, entering to divide the tragedy into its various acts: 'Beholde the first act of this tragedy.' But it is also a voice which is remarkably confused in its moral positioning. Throughout, there is a notable fear of the fantasies and false imaginings of love:

> as ordinarily you see that lovers conceive all things for their advantage, and fantasy dreams agreeable to their most desire, resembling the mad and Bedlem persons which have before their eyes, the figured fancies which cause the conceit of their fury.

Here, as also in Painter's references to the Oedipus legend, there is a clear but horrified understanding of the complications that lie hidden in the human psyche; and for the most part, his tale seems to be written, in constant apprehension lest they erupt, as a warning against 'the thousand thousand slippery sleights of love's gallantise'. For all that, compassion is allowed, especially for the murdered children of the Duchess, and Christian forgiveness is also invoked to demonstrate how far the vengeance of the Cardinal of Aragon had led him away from the example of the apostles who never 'hired ruffians and murderers to cut the throats of them which did them hurt'.

It is curious, when Painter's moral stance is both so extreme and so uncertain, that Webster's own work should ever have been considered, by contrast, amoral or centreless.[46] Certainly, Webster abandons the simple moral refuge which Painter had erected for himself in the margins of Bandello's story. But in doing so he prepares for a subtler ethical vision than can be expressed through the language of authority and misogynism. Indeed, there are two features of his version which suggest that he has understood how such a language may itself be profoundly immoral. Thus in Webster's Frederick, it is an indication both of his dawning madness and of his appropriation of moral principle that he, of all people, should express outrage that the Duchess's children may not have been baptised (III. iii. 64). More striking still, Webster takes words which Painter had uttered in his own authorial voice, to condemn the trivialisation of religion, and puts this authorial scruple in the mouth of the Duchess's maid:

---

46. Most notably T.S. Eliot in 'Four Elizabethan Dramatists', *Selected Essays* (London, 1951), p. 117.

it is Cariola in Webster's version story who considers the device of a pilgrimage to be a 'jesting with religion' (p. 231). There are scruples here which are not, however, embodied in the public language of morality but lie half-hidden in the responses of particular persons. Thus even the Duchess in Webster's version can speak to Antonio of how 'in the eternal Church, sir, I do hope we shall not part thus' (III. v. 68–9).

Webster uses his theatre as a means of alerting the audience to the continuing half-life of moral value. Yet, clearly, he analyses a condition in which the familiar instruments of moral perception have been disoriented and perverted. The opening speech of the play contrasts the confusions of Italy with the firm principles of a nation-state such as France where,

> In seeking to reduce both State and people
> To a fixed order, their judicious King
> Begins at home.

In the perverted court of Italy not only do the practices of Castiglione become instruments of corrupt policy but the play of Machiavellian power is now used in pursuit of entirely private and personal ends. Virtue itself becomes vice. Thus in France (I. ii. 65): 'out of brave horsemanship, arises the first sparks of growing resolution that raises the mind to noble action'. But in Italy as Bosola declares:

> to avoid ingratitude
> For the good deed you have done me, I must do
> All the ill men can invent.
>
> (I. ii. 197–9)

And it is this process which erodes the centre of the personality that Webster sets himself to trace, particularly in the parallel figures of Bosola and the Duchess herself.

Bosola, who appears in the sources merely as a hired assassin, is Webster's principal invention, and the core of his nature is an exceptional, if deranged, sensitivity to persons and situations, and even to physical sensations:

> Sure I did hear a woman shriek: list ha?
> . . . . there's some stratagem
> In the confining of all our courtiers
> To their several wards. I must have part of it,
> My intelligence will freeze else.
>
> (II. iii. 1–6)

But this 'speculative man' (III. iii. 46) – containing within himself the talents and most brutal experiences of courtly politics – serves in the course of the play to emphasise the position of the Duchess herself. She, like Bosola, is the victim of a corrupt courtly order and also a skilful practitioner within it, knowing that we are 'forc'd to express our violent passions/in riddles and in dreams'. But in her case the overwrought sensitivity which she shares with Bosola – 'what would it pleasure me to have my throat cut/With diamonds' – points towards a moral resolution which none of Webster's immediate sources could have countenanced. For where Bosola's mind works constantly on images of physical degeneration, the Duchess displays a pica (literally so in the 'apricot' scene), an acute responsiveness to the touch and texture of things, above all of the human thing. And from this itself derives an inarticulate but primitive sense of human value. When at her death she asks that

> thou giv'st my little boy
> Some syrup for his cold and let the girl
> Say her prayers ere she sleep.

there can be no breath of sentimentality. Her concern for the simplest needs of the human being stands in direct and considered contrast to Bosola's dismissal of the human being as 'a box of worm seed', or his disparagement of pregnancy as 'a waning of the cheek and waxing fat of the flank' (II. i. 70). It was a similar immediacy of concern that was expressed earlier in the domestic lightness of touch which Antonio and the Duchess were shown to display – and have apparently maintained – even in the unnatural confines of a long-standing clandestine marriage (III. ii.). Principles of hierarchical order and distorted conceptions of marriage are themselves the forces of immorality which threaten this essential, if fragile, conception of value.

At one point the Duchess explicitly quotes Tasso when, in pursuit of a desperate stratagem, she asks Antonio to consent to a 'magnanima menzogna'.[47] This is only a slight misapplication of Tasso's original sense, where, in desperate and oppressive circumstances, morality needs to learn something from Machiavelli. Yet there comes a point in *The Duchess of Malfi* where the illusions and deceits which a decadent society precipitates in the mind of its victims is seen to meet resistance. Strikingly, where Painter's tale is obsessed with the dangerous inner fantasies of lovers, these fantasies become externalised in Webster's play in

47. See above, p. 175.

the form of madmen and wax figures (or else are shown to be the characteristic of the Duchess's incestuously inclined twin, Ferdinand): the Duchess is plagued with art (IV. i. 110) created by Vincentio Laureola who is credited with a special skill in the management of sculptural illusion. Yet the illusions of Webster's own theatre release a pathos which carries with it its own moral standard. Bandello had claimed that pity would be the appropriate response to the story of the Duchess of Malfi; and it is notable that, though this play has no moral chorus, the figure of Delio provides some point of reference. He is neither heroic nor clearcut in his moral position. In fact he seems almost to be a representation of Bandello himself or of the chain of eye-witness accounts which for Bandello are the seed-bed of the novella. But, for once, the attention which Bandello historically encourages in his *novelle* to detail and to the surprisingness of human existence here rises above gossip to provide an alternative to any dangerously heroic moral pretension. The figure to whom Webster's play finally draws attention is the son whom the Duchess herself was concerned to save.

Chapter 7

Pastoral Experiment in the Plays of Guarini, Marston and Fletcher

INTRODUCTION

Towards the end of the sixteenth century, Italian theatre began to develop an interest, which in part had been anticipated by the epic and by the novella, in the mixing of generic forms. For instance, 'serious'[1] comedies began to be written, such as Della Porta's *I Fratelli Rivali*;[1] and so, too, with a greater degree of critical acknowledgement, did tragi-comedies, tragedies with happy endings, and pastoral plays with an admixture of both tragic and comic tonalities. In large part, developments in the area of tragi-comedy were a result of theoretical reflections on drama deriving from a study of Aristotle which, as was seen in considering both erudite comedy and the epic, became particularly intense in the middle of the century.[2] The shifting sensibilities of the Counter-Reformation had a part to play in these developments, as – in a different way – did the success of Tasso's pastoral *Aminta* which appeared on stage in 1573.[3]

There seems little doubt that both the theory of mixed genres and the dramatic practices associated with that theory made an impression on contemporary English theatre. In the 1620s, Webster could arguably divert tragi-comic features to his own ends both in *The Devil's Law Case* and also in *The Duchess of Malfi*.[4] But there is evidence of this influence

---

1. See Louise George Clubb, *Italian Drama in Shakespeare's Time* (New Haven, 1989), who argues that this play has a direct influence on Shakespeare's *Much Ado about Nothing*.
2. See, p. 196 above.
3. Earlier instances are Cinthio's *Egle* (1545) and Agostino de' Beccari's *Sacrificio* of 1554.
4. See J. Pearson, *Tragedy and Tragi Comedy in the Plays of John Webster* (Manchester, 1980).

as early as 1600;[5] and by 1608, John Fletcher's *The Faithful Shepherdess* had been performed at Blackfriars.[6]

The Faithful Shepherdess is one of the best documented disasters in the theatrical history of the period. The failure, however, seems to have rankled sufficiently to stir Fletcher to critical activity. On publication, the text of the play comes accompanied by no less than four testimonials, from Ben Jonson, Beaumont, Chapman and Field. Fletcher himself makes a pre-emptive bid at this point for the sympathy of the reader, providing a vivid account of how the play had originally been received:

> It is a pastoral Tragi-comedy, which the people seeing when it was played, having ever a singular gift in defining, concluded to be a play of country hired Shepherds, in gray cloaks, with curtailed dogs in strings, sometimes laughing together, and sometimes killing one another. And missing Whitsun ales, cream, wassel and morris dances, began to be angry.

Clearly, the original audience was not ready for the refinements which Fletcher had laid before them. And a similar lack of sophistication may be thought to account for the failure of earlier attempts at 'pastoral tragi-comedy', notably Marston's *Antonio and Mellida* of 1601. Certainly in Fletcher's view, his work needed to be seen as an attempt to break new theatrical ground by the adoption of an Italian genre. Thus in his title Fletcher alludes, with a significant alteration of gender, to Guarini's *Il Pastor Fido – The Faithful Shepherd*. Around 1600, Guarini's play was distinctly in the European avant garde; and for this reason as well as for the impact it must have made upon Fletcher, it deserves close attention.[7]

5. On this change of taste, see particularly G.K. Hunter, 'Italian Tragicomedy and the English Stage', *Renaissance Drama*, n.s. VI (1973), pp. 123–48, and his 'The Beginnings of Elizabethan Drama: Revolution and Continuity', *Renaissance Drama* XVI (1986), pp. 29–52. See also Hunter, *Dramatic Identities and Cultural Tradition* (Liverpool, 1978).
6. On Fletcher see Clifford Leech, *The John Fletcher Plays* (London, 1966). For *The Faithful Shepherdess*, see ed. Cyrus Hoy in *The Dramatic Works in the Beaumont and Fletcher Canon*, general ed. Fredson Bowers (Cambridge, 1976), Vol. III.
7. Battista Guarini (1538–1612) was a Ferrarese diplomat and teacher of rhetoric who came to replace Tasso as the court poet of Ferrara when the latter fell into disgrace. He wrote little save *Il Pastor Fido* and the critical writings associated with it. These writings are cast in the form of marginal notes to *Il Pastor Fido*. Two initially pseudonymous pieces defending the play from the attacks of the critic Giason Denores, *Il Verrato* (1588) and *Il Verrato secondo* (c. 1593), were later published as one in the *Compendio della Poesia Tragicomica*. (Venice, 1602). On Guarini, see Eric Cochrane, *Italy 1530–1630*, ed. Julius Kirshner (London, 1988), pp. 69–105. There was a translation of Guarini's play – probably by Sir John Dymock – in 1602 and another in 1647 by Sir Richard Fanshawe, now published in parallel with the Italian text (and with an excellent introduction) in an edition by J.H. Whitfield (Edinburgh, Edinburgh Bilingual Library 11, 1976). For Fanshawe see also the edition of his translation by Walter F.

Guarini, it seems, had taken four, or even as long as ten years, to write the piece. It had already begun to circulate in manuscript in the 1580s and was finally published in Italy in 1589. In Italy, the play was an immediate, if controversial, success. Guarini himself was quick to stir the controversy, and to reveal the highly ambitious theory that lay beneath the work. Guarini had strong academic affiliations, descended from the line of humanist and educators which had been founded by Guarino in the fourteenth century.[8] His text comes surrounded by an apparatus of (largely self-approbatory) annotations while, anonymously, the author composed a defence of the form in which he wrote – *Il Verrato* – far exceeding in length any comparable English apology.[9] Such theoretical zeal did not inhibit the popularity of the work. Within forty years of publication, there were translations of *Il Pastor Fido* in Spanish, German, Portuguese and Dutch, while in France its fame lasted long enough for the work to be mentioned favourably by Rousseau. In England, the Italian text was itself published by John Woolfe no more than a year after its first appearance. A translation – attributed to Sir John Dymock – appeared in 1602, to be followed by Fanshawe's version in 1647. By 1605, Ben Jonson, writing in *Volpone*, could declare:

> All our English writers,
> I mean such as are happy in the Italian,
> Will deign to steal out of this author, mainly:
> Almost as much as from Montaignié:
> He has so modern and facile a vein.
> Fitting the time and catching the court-ear!
> (III. iv. 87–92)[10]

It is generally agreed that during this same period a notable shift in taste and stylistic direction had begun to take place in the English theatre, which involved a progressive retreat from the heroic and

---

Simeone (Oxford, 1964). For the pastoral in general see Helen Cooper, *Pastoral* (Ipswich, Brewer, 1977). See also R. Sowerby, *The Classical Legacy in Renaissance Poetry* (London, 1994) on the classical origins of pastoral.

8. See above, pp. 89–90.

9. For translations of Guarini's criticism and theory see Allen. H. Gilbert, *Literary Criticism: Plato to Dryden* (Detroit, 1970) and Bernard Weinberg, *A History of Literary Criticism in the Italian Renaissance*, 2 vols (Chicago, 1961), especially part II, cap. 21; see also Paul Grendler, *Critics of the Italian World* (Madison, Wis., 1969). On the tragicomic form see M.T. Herrick, *Tragicomedy* (Urbana, 1955); see also Madeleine Doran, *Endeavours of Art: a study of form, Elizabethan Drama* (Madison, 1954).

10. Compare Shakespeare's reference in *As You Like it* V. ii. 76: 'You are followed by a faithful shepherd'.

sometimes violent idiom adopted, typically, in the early tragedies of revenge.[11] The influence of Guarini's writings cannot explain all aspects of that change. A full account would need to admit, if nothing else, the influence which Shakespeare's success might have had on his own contemporaries; after all, the developments in question begin with – or even, perhaps, follow from – the public appearance of *Hamlet*. Likewise a later phase of interest in the pastoral tragi-comedy begins with – or, again, perhaps follows from – *Pericles*. Nevertheless, Guarini's work was available at this time; and, along with his critical writings, it provides at the very least a means of charting the currents of theatrical experiment which in this period seem to have affected even Shakespeare himself.

These experiments were three-fold in character. First, and most obviously, there is experimentation with genre itself. The burden of Fletcher's complaint is that his original audience – with its 'singular gift in defining' – was disconcerted when *The Faithful Shepherdess* failed to fit the expectations that simple comedy or simple pastoral arouses. Conversely, Fletcher's appeal to subsequent audiences is founded upon an extension of genre boundaries, whereby we are asked to approach his work not merely as a pastoral but rather as a pastoral in tragi-comic mode. Such niceties might now recall Polonius's discussion of the matter; but Fletcher plainly had Guarini in mind, and comes close to suggesting that no one will properly understand his play who does not understand Guarini's theory.

Experimentation in genre leads, inevitably perhaps, to experimentation in dramaturgy or in stagecraft. On Jonson's account, Guarini seems to have uncovered a 'modern' and also a 'facile vein', and to have encouraged a desire for greater refinement in both comic and tragic presentation than had hitherto been available. (Sannazaro's pastoral *Arcadia* had, as we have seen, already stimulated similar interests in regard to verse-form and prose narrative.)[12] But formal experimentation in turn suggests a third area of development, in which, as presentation changed, so too did moral stance and ethical perception. Thus Jonson in his defence of Fletcher reveals that it was the ethical as much as the formal novelty of Fletcher's play which so infuriated its original audience, who

> . . . before
> They saw it halfe, damned the whole play, and more,

11. Clifford Leech, op.cit., p. 27.
12. See above, pp. 146–54.

> Their motives were, since it had not to do
> With vices, which they look'd for, and came to.

As for himself, Jonson adds:

> I, that am glad thy innocence was thy guilt,
> And wish that all the muses blood were spilt,
> In such a *Martyrdom*; to vex their eyes,
> Do crowne thy murdered Poem.

The alternative that the pastoral tragi-comedy offers to the ribald 'whitsun ales' which Fletcher's original audience lacked will lie in the area of notably fragile virtue. Innocence, chastity, vulnerability, wise-passiveness and (as Jonson notes) martyrdom are all matters of serious concern in the tragi-comic. And if this already suggests a move away, in regard to moral scheme, from the tragedy of blood, then it also suggests that new technical means might have been required to do justice to these new delicacies of moral vision.

An immediate indication of such links between vision and dramatic technique lies in the interest which Guarini took in developing a quasi-religious form of ritual theatre. Sannazaro had shown how the pastoral might encourage such an interest;[13] and Fletcher, if not Marston, seems in *The Faithful Shepherdess* to have shared it.

This is not, of course, to claim that any of the writers of pastoral tragi-comedy was a serious Christian thinker. Indeed, while Guarini overtly pursues some of the central themes of Counter-Reformation spirituality, his work – like that of some of the novella writers – could well be seen as one which seeks to evade any strict engagement with religious realities and with the censorship that had come to surround them. One may, however, suggest that, following Guarini, the two English writers set themselves to induce, in theatrical terms, a certain rhythm of attention in which our perception of the human figure – surrounded by ritual spaces – might be coloured by such otherwise religious emotions as wonder, awe or reverence. Such attention is likely to be all the more necessary since the moral perceptions which an audience is required to exercise will now fall not upon figures of heroic proportions but upon the modest and often tremulous humanity of shepherds and their nymphs. Often these figures will be called to express themselves in theatrical modes approaching that of balletic body language, scarcely articulate and at times relying as much upon the

13. See above, p. 148.

eloquence of a blush as upon the force of a mighty line. But as Charles Darwin reminds one, blushing is the most peculiar and the most human of all expressions.[14] It is also true that such a reaction is difficult to act. Tamburlaine does not blush easily; and a theatre in which the hero is required to blush – and where the audience is asked not to be embarrassed at the sight – might well claim to have advanced in dramaturgical no less than in moral sophistication.

THE THEORY AND PRACTICE OF MIXED FORMS IN CINTHIO AND GUARINI

To substantiate the claims of the pastoral tragi-comic form, one needs to look more closely at both the theory and the practice of Guarini's work.[15] For it is through a confusion or dislocation of genre expectations that there first arises the ethical freedom to view the stage character, or its actor, in a new light. Thus Fletcher himself, makes his own connection between the tragi-comic genre and the ethical issues which arise when we consider whether the figure on stage should die or not. Thus tragi-comedy, in Fletcher's phrase, 'wants deaths'; and in such a form the author will not actually mix mirth and killing, but rather seek, through a conjunction of moral and technical finesse, to avoid the representation of both. In practice, as the next chapter will show, the subtlest examples of such an evasion will be found in *Measure for Measure* and in *Cymbeline*. However, in theoretical terms, it is to Italy that Fletcher directs attention, and to the controversies which eventually produced *Il Pastor Fido*.

In discussing both epic and erudite comedy, one has seen something of the liveliness of Italian critical theory in the sixteenth century.[16] The study of Aristotle raised questions both of unified structure and of genre, but the work of Ariosto and Tasso greatly complicated the classical picture. Ariosto in the *Orlando Furioso* could already be said to have 'mixed' his genres, including comic, tragic and pastoral elements within an epic framework. Meanwhile, Tasso, though writing always with an eye on

14. See Christopher Ricks' discussion of this in *Keats and Embarrassment* (Oxford, 1974), pp. 50–68.
15. For an account of the controversy stirred up in Italy by Cinthio's account of tragi-comic writing and by *Il Pastor Fido* see Gilbert, op.cit., pp. 252–73 and pp. 504–33; also Weinberg op.cit., Vol. II, 1074–105.
16. See above, pp. 195–201.

regular practice, could escape in his own *Aminta* into a world where he boldly entertained the thought that 'whatever is pleasurable is legitimate'.[17] Moreover, the earliest theories of mixed genres are part of Cinthio's defence of Ariosto, the 'chamaleon' whose unity derives not from external prescription but from the internal harmonies of a personality which expresses itself throughout the 'body' of his work.[18]

Against this background, Cinthio goes on to develop, in both theory and in practice, a fully fledged conception of the tragi-comic. In fact, Cinthio himself speaks not of tragi-comedy but of tragedies with a happy outcome, *da lieto fine*.[19] By this he means tragedies in which the good receive their just deserts and the bad their due come-uppance. Moreover, on this understanding the tragi-comic play would be one in which, although there is always the danger of crime, no crime is actually committed, and where, consequently, repentance – in regard to unacted intentions – can all the more readily be secured. Such theories will show their merit in the study of *Measure for Measure* and *Cymbeline*.[20] But already it will be obvious that they reflect a considerable subtlety of ethical thought and require some sophistication of theatrical practice. Behind the theory of poetic justice lies the Counter-Reformation concern with the actions of Providence which range far beyond the understanding of human beings. As for the author, he – as the literary surrogate of providence – will be required to devise a plot in which death and disaster are always a plausible reality while simultaneously providing for an equally plausible deliverance from danger.

It is Guarini who proceeds to insist that, when successfully accomplished, a tragi-comedy will prove artistically superior not only to comedy but to tragedy itself. Thus, in the passage to which Fletcher may allude in his preface, Guarini writes:

> Pastoral tragicomedy involves the mingling of tragic and comic pleasure, and will not allow the hearers to fall into excessive tragic melancholy or into comic relaxation. From this there results a poem of most excellent form and composition, not merely corresponding to the mixture of the human body, which consists entirely in the tempering of the four humours, but also proving itself much more noble than a simple tragedy or simple comedy: it does not inflict upon us atrocious events and horrible and inhumane sights, such

---

17. See above, p. 187.
18. See above, p. 158
19. See especially *Intorno al comporre de i Romanzi, delle Commedie, e delle Tragedie* (Venice, 1542), selections translated Gilbert, op.cit., pp. 252–62, see especially pp. 255–6.
20. See below, pp. 284–7.

as blood and deaths; nor, on the other hand, does it cause us to be so relaxed in laughter that we sin against the modesty and decorum of the well-bred man. Truly if, today, men fully understood how to compose tragi-comedy (for it is not an easy thing to do) no other drama would appear upon the stage.

(Compendio, p. 13)

For Guarini, it follows that tragi-comedy is unambiguously the most advanced form of theatrical art. It represents, needless to say, a refinement upon simple comedy. As Guarini argues, comedy, particularly, the *commedia dell'arte*, has become nothing but 'a wandering public harlot', lawless and lascivious (ibid., p. 523). But tragedy, too, may well be thought to have degenerated into mere violence if one recalls that for Guarini the prevailing style of tragedy would have been Senecan tragedy – of the kind indeed which Cinthio was himself inclined to produce.[21] Against this Guarini makes a claim concerning the value of emotion and the subtlety of theatrical form which is far from negligible.

So, offering his own a version of the now-familiar question as to whether Christian tragedy is possible, Guarini assserts that tragedy is in fact wholly inappropriate in a Christian era:

And to come to our age, what need have we today to purge terror and pity with tragic sights, since we have the precepts of our most holy religion which teaches us with the word of the gospel. Hence these horrible and savage spectacles are superfluous. Nor does it seem to me that, today, we should introduce a tragic action for any other reason than to get delight from it.

(ibid., p. 523)

Here, as in Cinthio, there is an appeal to those certitudes of Providence and of Scripture which only the modern Christian can enjoy. But also, in the emphasis on the delightful contemplation which art should offer, there is an evident concern with the position of emotion in the response of such a Christian to the problems raised in tragedy; justice is less a matter of formal belief than a state of the sentiments:

Tragi-comedy can contemplate these tragic events; but it does so without dealing with the horrific, and thus restores the sense of internal justice.

(ibid., pp. 517–8)

It is at this point that the blush, implicitly at least, begins to make its presence felt. For the internal justice which Guarini seeks may certainly imply moderation but by no means repression: the emotions will be

---

21. See above, p. 229.

required to achieve their own balance through contemplation of an artistic well-formed object. Thus, says Guarini, 'to lose compassion is to lose humanity' (ibid., p. 516); and here, he declares that the ideal tragedy

> should not purge the affections in the stoic fashion by removing them totally from our hearts, but by moderating and reducing them to that proper consistency which can contribute to virtuous habit.
>
> (ibid., p. 516)

In tragi-comedy, then, there can be no crudely laxative effect of catharsis. If emotions are to be moderated, then they must first be brought into vigorous life; and the effect of an arousal in the mixed genre – proceeding from its comic as well as its tragic characteristics – will be to stimulate and healthily enliven our otherwise sluggish temperament. So:

> Tragi-comedy offers that restoration of which human life is so much in need; it refreshes the spirit. As a breeze is wont to drive away the thickened air, comedy shakes off that gloomy and foggy humour generated in us by too much thought, which often renders us slow in our activities.
>
> (ibid., p. 514)

One saw earlier how the excellence of the tragi-comic form was thought to reside in its correspondence to the well-balanced humours. Now, in regard to its effect, tragi-comedy is seen to surprise its audience into a comparable good temper; to that degree, the aesthetic disposition is also, it appears, an ethical disposition.

But how, technically – in terms of dramaturgy and stagecraft – is the 'breeze' which animates this disposition to be achieved?

In the first place, the choice of Arcadia as a subject must itself count for a good deal. In the Golden Age, law was thought to reside, not in precept or public pronouncement but inwardly, written in the heart itself and in the natural balance of the affections. In Arcadia, as Guarini chooses to picture it, this balance has been disturbed through the wrath of the Gods, and his concern is to picture the complications which arise in achieving the ultimate restoration of original order.

At the outset, as Guarini is quick to point out, his own Arcady is more of a Sophoclean Thebes than a Golden World: as penance for offences done to a long dead swain, the Arcadians must offer to Diana a yearly sacrifice of their fairest and best. This harsh imposition, however, will be lifted – so the oracles say – if two descendants of the God Hercules can be brought to marry.[22] The *Pastor Fido* proceeds to trace,

---

22. Cf. below, p. 272.

at extreme length, the way in which this solution is reached. As the play begins, there is an apparently insuperable obstacle, in that the only male Arcadian descended from Hercules – Silvio by name – prefers hunting to love and will have nothing whatsoever to do with the one remaining female of the appropriate bloodline, the shepherdess Amaryllis. Of course, a foreign shepherd, Mirtillo, who is much taken with Amaryllis, proves to be the long-lost, and hence Herculean, brother of Silvio. However, this only comes to light in the last act of the play. Here, as the Arcadian priests, who are also the fathers of the three Herculean offspring, are preparing themselves for the ritual execution of Amaryllis and Mirtillo, who by this time of course have become embroiled in *apparently* illicit passions. Enter, then, Tiresias, or rather (in Guarini's version) Tirenio, who reveals the truths that hitherto have lain without trace in the dark backward and abysm of time. A marriage is arranged, thus deftly avoiding the merely tragic or Sophoclean horrors of incest and self-mutilation. The importance of this marriage – as a truly modern expression of the Arcadian spirit – is further emphasised by the *intermezzi* which Guarini arranged when the play was performed in Mantua at the celebration of a dynastic wedding. Between each act a masque of the elements is performed representing – in each case through a mythological, and also softly pornographic, ballet – the Music of Earth, Air, Water and Fire: harmony will reign in the cosmos as in the sentiments.

The knottings of marriage, however, also have their counterpart in the formal 'knottings' of plot and resolution which in Guarini's view, must characterise the tragic–comic genre. Thus, in dramaturgical terms, Guarini in his notes to *Il Pastor Fido* emphasises that, in the first place, there must be a subtlety – a 'breeze' – in the text, wedding comic to tragic effect. Secondly, he points to the extreme skilfulness of his own plot construction, as – while preparing always for subsequent revelations and recognitions – he binds together the problems arising from character, situation and theme. Comedy in such a context is anything but a matter of comic relief. Rather, it lies in a perception of unexpected correspondences, which in turn gives birth to a delightful contemplation of *entrelacement*. Double or multiple plotting is a characteristic of the pastoral.[23] In Guarinian tragi–comedy, however, this device will be further strengthened by an urgent, if aesthetic, interest in the creation and resolution of narrative tension. Thus in his annotations to Act I of the play,

---

23. See William Empson, *Some Versions of the Pastoral* (London, 1986).

Guarini ostentatiously compares his own skill in narrative construction with the achievements simultaneously of Sophocles in *Oedipus* and to Terence in *The Eunuch*. In the same place he speaks, with some justice, of how, in Act I. i, his representation of the unwilling Silvio displays not simply an Oedipal *gravitas* but also, as is appropriate in tragi-comedy, a comic lightness – and delightfulness – of ornamentation. Guarini may be right; such compound effects are not very easy to achieve.

From a summary of *Il Pastor Fido*, and from Guarini's own chorus of self-justifying annotations, the impression could arise of an author obsessed with his own authorial omnipotence. Yet it needs to be emphasised how far any such effect would be from the effect which Guarini himself wished to create. In terms of Guarini's own culture, the breeze he attempts to create might well be seen as an aspect of *sprezzatura*, where, through long practice, a grace and seemingly artless poise can be achieved in the performance even of difficult exercises. Guarini himself stresses that the breeze of tragi-comedy should relieve an audience of 'too much thought'. It is a nonchalance of this sort which may have recommended Guarini to the connoisseurs among his English following – who would, after all, have recently seen in *Hamlet* what 'thinking too precisely on an event' might lead to. Yet the same capacity for courtly performance may also be seen, sympathetically, to have an ethical implication, in which harmony and moderation reveal themselves, not as principles of restraint, but rather as a lively and communicable expression of inward order. And certainly within the *Pastor Fido* itself these issues are carried through with a high degree of skill and energy. Wise passiveness is constellated with apprehensions of human frailty or of physical tenderness, and is at all times in counterpoint with an understanding of how merely comic, in the end, brute self-assertion must always be. We may have to wait for *The Tempest* for an author who can make self-abandonment a part of his own authorial practice. Yet the themes and the theatrical devices to express this abandonment are already present in *Il Pastor Fido*.

Thus in the first scene, the initial complication of the plot resides in the single-mindedness and self-assertions of the hunter Silvio, who is at one and the same time an Adonis and an *All's Well* Bertram.[24] So, Silvio insists upon defending his right to act according to his own name and nature – 'But as I am I'll do like Silvio' – and this already prepares for an ironic reversal when, in the denouement, it proves that Silvio's elder

24. See below, pp. 284–7.

and long-lost brother – the eponymous faithful shepherd, Mirtillo – had himself been known at birth as 'Silvio'. Their father, losing a first son, had given that name to his second. But nature, as well as name, is here at issue. For the apparently heroic integrity which Silvio so vigorously defends is itself recognised to be a barbaric wood in which he hunts while his unresponsiveness to love is the monstrous beast which he hunts there:

> La selva se' tu, Silvio,
> e la fera crudel, che vi s'annida,
> è la tua feritate.

(You Silvio are the wood; and the cruel beast which lurks there is your own cruelty.)

Only when, Oedipus-fashion, Silvio belatedly recognises what power he has to hurt, will he then do none; and thus by virtue of his own emotional wounding, rejoin the human race.

Yet his brother Mirtillo has known all this from the moment when he enters in Act I. ii, proclaiming himself, in immediate contrast, a martyr in the flames of his love for Amaryllis. Likewise in Act II. ii, it is Mirtillo – palpitating as ever – who narrates how, cross-dressed in Amazonian fashion, he has encountered Amaryllis in a kissing competition. Here, the words on the page stand merely, so to speak, as the score – which a sophisticated actor might indeed relish – for a blushful performance of psychosomatic responses. The breeze rises as Amaryllis 'dyes her cheeks in modest blushes':

> To show through her transparent skin
> That she is no less fair within
> Than she's without.

> (Di modesto rossor tutta si tinse,
> e mostrò ben che non men bella è dentro
> di quel che sia di fuori.)

This is a life of sensations but, even without thought, it has its own internal order. For precisely as Mirtillo's soul sensuously shrinks into a narrow volume ('chiusa in così breve spazio'), he realises the chaste restriction of shame in the face of Amaryllis's majesty – whom after all he has tricked into the kiss. So, sensuous as the scene undoubtedly is, it is still nothing like as strikingly piquant as the scene on which it is based from Tasso's *Rinaldo* of 1562, where the Amaryllis-figure easily recognises the gender of the kiss she has received. Here, as throughout,

Guarini distinguishes himself from the moral positions which Tasso had pursued in his own pastoral *Aminta*. In Tasso's work, there is that cult of luscious feeling which caused psychic as well as well artistic trouble in the *Gerusalemme Liberata*.[25] Where, however, Tasso declares in a moment of liberation that whatever is pleasurable is lawful, Guarini will constantly seek pleasure in conformity to the inner rule, asserting – with the authority of the choruses which end each act – that there is a law written in the heart of every creature:

> whose amiable violence
> And pleasing rapture of the sense
> Doth bias all things to that good
> Which we desire not understood.

The same point, along with a further investigation of virtue and vulnerability, is expressed even in the most obviously comic scenes of the play. These scenes revolve around a satyr and a confessedly lecherous nymph, Corisca, who has set her eye upon Mirtillo. But the voracious appetites of Corisca and the satyr are clearly held in judgemental parallel to the appetitiveness of the hunter Silvio. Thus Corisca's selfhood is made to depend entirely upon the violent sexual possession of Mirtillo's selfhood. This criticism translates into purely farcical terms when, at the height of a quarrel with the satyr, Corisca invites the satyr to pull off her head, which he does, falling to the ground with the violence of his exertions, only to discover, as – in mock vulnerability – he nurses his bruises, that the head in his hands was merely the wig of his cosmetically inclined antagonist. Selfhood, it seems, is not as graspable as might have been thought; and notably all purely physical, as opposed to psychosomatic, response is likely to be associated with the muscular comedy of the satyr, in whose make-up delicacy and wise passiveness have no part to play.

Even farce, then, can be an expression of moral theme. But the theme of vulnerability is also communicated – with subtler stagecraft – in, for instance, the comedy of Silvio's eventual conversion and in the religious theatricality which brings the play to its conclusion.

So Providence is eventually able to bring the reluctant Silvio to a realisation of how deeply he is loved by yet another nymph, Dorinda. But Silvio's heart is prepared for this reversal by a delicate echo scene, in the course of which the hunter's ferociously defended integrity is prised apart by a double voice: even the great 'I am' – 'sono' – becomes no more than an echo of the word for 'sound', 'suono'. The breeze blows

25. See above, pp. 174–5.

even through Silvio now; and, softened, he is ready for redemption. Thus, he discovers that the love-lorn Dorinda has followed him on his hunt; going to far greater extremes than Helena in *A Midsummer Night's Dream* – she has not only become his psychological 'spaniel' but has actually dressed herself as a hunted wolf, being wounded in that guise by an unintentional arrow from Silvio's bow. Only in inflicting this physical wound does Silvio realise the true extent of his erstwhile cruelty; and – tremulous now as hitherto only Mirtillo has been – he begs to receive a wound in his turn which might drive away the monster of his guilt.

Then, finally, we have the blind seer, Tiresias – or, in Guarini's text, Tirenio. Significantly, this figure arrives at a much later stage of the play than his Sophoclean counterpart; and where Tiresias offers an enigma to be answered by the protagonist himself in awful self-knowledge, Tirenio affirms to recommend, as the height of truth, the ignorance which all human beings are bound to acknowledge in the face of Providence:

> Vain men, how can you boast of knowledge so?
> That part of us by which we see and know
> Is not our vertue but drived from Heaven.

What value is there anyway in knowledge when Providence is secure? All we need to do, in Guarini's picture, is to approach the shadow of the altar: blushingly, we marry in the heartfelt realisation that each is the echo of each, and that neither God, nor any other advanced audience, will deride our blushes. How much better to contemplate this than the horrors of ancient Thebes.

It may well be thought that Guarini's work anticipates doctrines of art for art's sake; and certainly Guarini himself, when his main opponent, Jason De Nores, insists that poetry must be considered as a part of moral and civil philosophy, replies: 'Poetry has nothing to do with politics but is a member of sophistic and rhetoric'.[26] Yet, as is suggested by the appeal which his work was to hold for Romantic thinkers, there is more to Guarini than that. In particular, his cultivation of the aesthetic involves an attention to the otherwise invisible claims that might be made, in moral terms, for the claims of physical nature.[27] Certainly, Guarini is capable of indulging an appetite for scenes with a titillating

---

26. See Weinberg, op.cit., pp. 1085–6.
27. There is a marked correspondence between the claims implied for the aesthetic in Guarini's theatre and those elegantly stated by Terry Eagleton in *The Ideology of the Aesthetic* (Oxford, 1991), p. 13. In phrases which bear directly on the conception of the pastoral, Eagleton points to how Rousseau can speak of the original state of nature 'which no longer exists, which may never have existed, and probably never

frisson to them – as, for instance, in the semi-nudity which he prescribes in the *intermezzi*, where nymphs appear from behind trees 'entirely naked, except for a bright green, covering the unseemly parts'. But the claims for the moral temper which is eloquently expressed by the 'blush' also have their part to play in restoring balance. And turning now to Guarini's English followers, one discovers that, among the various uses to which they put Guarini's model, some involve an affirmation (on a political as well as an ethical front) of the values expressed in the sensitivities and vulnerability of the human body.[28] For the sixteenth century had seen not only the erection of orthodox edifices of power in the Counter-Reformation and in the growth of nation-states, but also the invention of the concept of power in the writings of Machiavelli. To some degree, however faltering, Guarini's pastoral might be seen as an attempt not merely to accommodate actual power but also to assert his interest in a power we possess to abdicate from power, either through self-sacrifice or else through an equivalent, in the cultivation of aesthetic form. And it is this interest which is shared and consciously developed by the two English writers to whom we now must turn.

PASTORAL TRAGI-COMEDY IN MARSTON AND FLETCHER

In both Marston and Fletcher, the definition of power in relation to freedom is a central issues – expressed, at least in Marston's case, in a well-developed critique of Machiavellian thinking. Also, both Marston and Fletcher were plainly interested in the connections to be drawn between power and sexuality and, more importantly, in the representation of these connections on the stage. In turning to Italy they discovered not only Machiavelli (or the perverse sexuality of Bandello's courts) but also, in Guarini's writing, a formal answer to the problems that these two issues raised.

Now the position to which the English pastoral moves is clearly expressed in the first scene of Fletcher's *Faithful Shepherdess*, when Clorin, amazed at her own power to subdue the Satyr, muses

---

will exist'. Even so, we must retain 'an adequate idea of this state in order to judge correctly our present position' (*Discours sur l'inegalite*); for 'feeling', says Rousseau, 'precedes knowledge; and the law of conscience is what I feel to be right'. The value of the pastoral is, in this perspective, also the value of the aesthetic which serves to remind the sophisticated mind of how (as Eagleton puts it) 'the world strikes the body, of that which takes root in the gaze and the gut'.

28. Empson, op.cit., stresses the invariably political nature of the pastoral writing.

What greatness or what private hidden power
Is there in me to drawe submision
From this rude man and beast.

As with the Faithful Shepherd so with the Faithful Shepherdess,
chastity, it seems, is the way to internal justice; and Fletcher's Clorin
maintains this position, dominating the play from the grave-side of her
lover. Already, however, certain differences begin to appear between
Guarini's emphasis and Fletcher's. For one thing, so far from dealing
here with descendants of Hercules, Fletcher presents a figure who stresses her own mortality and remains, by virtue of her devotion to a dead
amour, immune to any imposition of marriage. There is a security of
moral emphasis in Fletcher's play, and an admiration for human perse-
verance, which replaces Guarini's vaguer religious gesturing. And this
humane emphasis will be all the more apparent if one places Fletcher's
understanding against the the turbulent English background – as represented in Marston – from which it most immediately arose.

There can be no doubt about Marston's qualifications as a reader of
the *Pastor Fido*.[29] He had the advantage of Italian grandparents and makes
liberal use of the Italian language in *Antonio and Mellida* (as for example in
Act II. i. 234). At the same time, he is both a theatrical experimentalist
and a moralist of some penetration, in his plays as well as in his satires.
Moreover, he has an evident interest in the theme of Arcadia. Indeed, his
Histriomastix of 1610 reveals a theme which is directly relevant to the
present argument. Marston in this play shows, through an interestingly
dislocated structure of masque, meta-theatre and social realism, how
Arcadian peace generates idleness and dissolves into strife, want and
famine. In that respect, the theme is profoundly Machiavellian: human
beings are inherently corrupt, and this corruption reveals itself most
clearly when the power or *virtù* which is bred out of conflict lies dormant.[30] Yet it is not, in the end, to a Machiavellian *virtù* that Marston
here looks. The desperate cycle of peace, sloth and violence is finally
stayed by the emergence of a Virgin Queen, under whose golden reign,
the pastoral virtue of chastity ensures that peace can thrive.

The broad implications of the *Histriomastix* are carried further into

29. For Marston see George L. Geckle, *John Marston's Drama* (Cranbury, 1980); Philip J.
Finkelpearl, *John Marston of the Middle Temple* (Cambridge, Mass., 1969). References
to *Il Pastor Fido* can be found throughout the notes by Macdonald P. Jackson and
Michael Neill to their edition *The Selected Plays of John Marston* (Cambridge, 1986),
which is the edition quoted here. For Fletcher, see Leech, op.cit.
30. Compare Francis Bacon's Machiavellianism, above note to p. 100.

what T.S. Eliot thought was the best of Marston's play: *The Wonder of Women, or Sophonisba* (1606). This is not a pastoral or indeed a tragi-comedy. Nevertheless, the play takes great interest in the theme of power; and the solutions it foreshadows will be consistent with those which do emerge from pastoral tragi-comedy. Here three aspects of this play need to be examined. First, in both his Prologue and his Epilogue, Marston, like Fletcher, appeals for an audience of connoisseurs, endowed with particular moral sensibilities, who are ready for scenes 'exempt from ribaldry or rage' (*Epilogue*, line 11). Already in the prologue Marston has proposed an alternative to such scenes, offering – against the 'popular frown' (*Prologue*, line 27) – a spectacle in which wonder and admiration at human constancy are the guiding motives. From this point on, the word 'wonder' – along with words such as 'spectacle' and 'rarity' – will be as important as the words 'breeze' and 'blushing' have hitherto been in defining the effects at which this experimental theatre is aiming. For these terms, too, define an ethical perspective – which theatrical form may be expected to encourage – where fragile virtues can once again be appreciated, in opposition particularly to the manifestations of brute power.

Thus in Act II. i of *Sofonisba* Marston penetrates to the heart of the Machiavellian debate picturing, on the one hand, the politician Carthalon, who insists that even treachery must be used, at need, in 'soldering up' state purposes (line 60). Yet this position is immediately characterised by Gelosso – who expresses the claims of moral conscience – as 'a stage-like passion and weak heat' (line 74). He himself speaks out strongly on heroic moral grounds declaring: 'I am bound to lose/My life, but not my honour, for my country.' In its immediate context, this line is not wholly without a suggestion of moral self-indulgence, revealed when Gelloso declares: 'If treachery in state be serviceable/Let hangmen do it.' Yet Gelosso's position is expressed in a less suspect, less articulate way, when the heroine Sophonisba heroically drinks poison to avoid the prospect of capture at the hands of invaders. By this action, she becomes a silent monument, a 'long-lived story', 'a wonder of women'. The spectacle is one in which aesthetic perception is enlisted to identify values which lie beyond the reach of violent power – and in that respect, if no other, Sofonisba has much in common with Cleopatra. Here, as in Shakespeare's play, a display of apparent vulnerability proves – to the admiring eye – to be the assertion of a uniqueness or rarity which eludes the grip of any political machinery.

Similar considerations can be discerned in *Antonio and Mellida*. Here,

Marston, adopting a decidedly experimental stance, seems to envisage alternative endings to the play and – following an understanding of the relationship between genre and season – goes on to a tragic sequel for times when 'the rawish dank of clumsy winter ramps/The fluent summers vein'. But *Antonio and Mellida* is unmistakably a tragi-comedy. Here the potentially tragic theme of usurpation is displaced by romance themes when lovers, cross-dressed, overcome the enmity that exists between their families. Thus there is a direct parallel to be drawn between the Kissing-Competition of the *Pastor Fido* and the scene in which Antonio, dressed as an Amazon, woos the unknowing Mellida. This episode prepares for the swoon which Antonio suffers some scenes later, immediately establishing his credentials as a tremulous kinsman of Guarini's Mirtillo; and throughout the play it is evident that Antonio, until his love for Mellida is chastely realised, is indeed subject, in his bodily complexion, to an absence of internal justice: 'O how impatience cramps my cracked viens veins and curdles thick my blood with boiling rage' (II. i. 230). Against this, however, in Act I. i. 157, there is the breeze which comes from his admiration at the amazing rarity of the lady: 'Smile heaven and softest southern wind/Kiss her cheek gently with perfumed breath.' What follows, of course, is a speech in high heroic vein describing tempest and shipwreck. Yet, for the audience, the account of this horrid spectacle is clearly tempered, in directly tragicomic fashion, by the ironies arising from the visual imagery of this transvestite scene in which Antonio is already dressed in teasing ambiguity as an Amazon. There may be less of the pent-up sensuality here than one finds in Guarini, but there is a comparable value placed upon the subtly shifting reactions of the audience to a tantalising scene.

A comparable use of stage imagery precipitates a major resolution in the fourth act of the play and then again, in the final act, secures its conciliatory ending. At the end of Act IV. i, the audience is asked, by the choric voice of a page, to witness the high degree of confusion which the scene has generated – culminating in some eighteen lines of unrelievedly pastoral Italian. Mellida, now herself cross-dressed, meets the once-Amazonian Antonio; and the audience is required, in a benign spirit, to show some private respect which may 'rebate the edge of keener censure' (ll.218–9). But the scene had begun in quite a different way. Here the political theme of usurpation is voiced; and in contrast with that, there is an attempt on the part of the usurped King Andrugio to assert the familiarly stoic notion of a moral sovereignty over self: 'He's a king, a true right king, that dares do aught save wrong' (ll. 53–55). Yet, heroic as this position is, it is no more allowed to stand unqualified than it was in Gelosso's speech in *Sofonisba*. For just as Guarini's tragi-comedy denies that emotion should be repressed in the stoic fashion, so Marston here proceeds to dislocate Andrugio's heroic position, until the point is reached at which the page can point the audience to the 'Babel' that has been generated in the scene (line 209). But the Babel does not prove to be malignant. Thus, as the exiled father meets his exiled son, Antonio, something akin to Guarini's echo scene begins at line 91:

> Antonio. Ay echo I mean Antonio? Who means Antonio.

Heroic identity dissolves beneath the poetic breeze; and when it comes back to itself, it does so with a denial of self-knowledge – 'he's a fool that thinks he knows himself' (line 99) – a sentiment which would have sat well in the final act of the *Pastor Fido*.

Similar constantly shifting effects are observable in the concluding scene of the play. Here again it is a very self-conscious *coup de théâtre* that brings about the moral resolution. Andrugio enters, disguised, bearing the proclamation which places a price upon his usurped head, and demands payment. When his offer is accepted, he discloses himself and offers his head, still on his shoulders, to the mercy of the usurper. In a reaction which, by now, will surprise no one, the usurper is amazed by this imaginative affrontery. He blushes at the spectacle, and therapeutic emotion begins its political work.

A full study of Marston's position would lead at this point to the more complicated case of *The Malcontent* which includes direct quotation from *Il Pastor Fido* [31] and also pursues – as does Marston's *The Fawn* – an interest in the theme of Herculean descendants derived, conceivably, from Guarini.[32] At the same time, the work modifies Guarini's original model to the point of a parody in a way which will also be found in *Measure for Measure*. There are no religious spaces in this play, nor for that matter a great deal of authorial *entrelacement*. Rather, these are replaced by the psychological complexities, and strangely vulnerable omniscience, of the Malcontent himself: 'the elements struggle within him; his own soul is at variance within herself' (I. ii). Pitted directly

---

31. Largely in passages of anti-court satire identified by Marston's most recent editors, Jackson and Neill, op.cit.

32. The Hercules theme throughout the Renaissance had been associated with the heroic battle between Man and Fortune. Now the emphasis falls as much upon Hercules' vulnerability and subjection to others.

against the Malcontent is his Machiavellian shadow, Mendoza, who declares 'that Fortune smiles on those that cannot blush'. But it is the subtle music of the dance which here restores good order. Here, Marston envisages – far more seriously than in *Antonio and Mellida* or, of course, *Histriomastix* – a translation of the themes of the *Pastor Fido* on to a level where power, political observation and satire are evenly matched against the ethic of vulnerability and the final aesthetic evasion of death. Yet, as will be seen in *Measure for Measure*, these apparently realistic conclusions are themselves played out against a background in which Guarini is likely to have occupied an important position.

Returning, finally, to Fletcher's *Faithful Shepherdess*, the connection here with Guarini is direct and openly acknowledged. In circumstances which directly parallel Guarini's Arcady, there is in Fletcher's play a moral seriousness which draws its gravity, not from a Christian sentimentalism, but rather from a willingness to wonder at the rarity of human behaviour. This is a claim that could also be made for the best of Fletcher's (and Beaumont's) more accredited plays. In particular, *The Maid's Tragedy* – drawing directly on Sidney's pastoral *Arcadia* – creates its pathos through the image of a maid who dies in the ill-fitting armour of a knight.[33] In *Philaster*, too, there are similar effects where a derangedly Hamletian and very vulnerable hero retains his humanity through a readiness, shared by all tragi-comic protagonists, to wound rather than to kill. But effects such as these are traceable directly to *The Faithful Shepherdess*.

Thus, to begin with, there is an unmistakable breeze of emotional and imaginative ambiguity in this play, in both its verse and its structure. The story itself – while owing, no doubt, a good deal to *A Midsummer Night's Dream* and also to *The Faerie Queene* – is a sustained piece of *entrelacement*, where groups of lovers, in various states of desire, seek wholeness of heart in a sacred wood. Here Fletcher pictures the search for chastity itself as a magical impulsion. Indeed, even Pan, whose priests act as chorus throughout the play, is here transmuted into a demiurge of modesty. The conceit is apparent, and becomes the more obvious when the play is put, as Fletcher must have meant it to be, against Shakespeare's *A Midsummer Night's Dream*, where desire, in old and young and high and low, is unambiguously erotic in character. But Guarini is the ultimate source of such wishful thinking. Here, as in the *Pastor Fido*, wholeness of being depends upon the rediscovery of the law that lies not only in the heart but also in the well-springs or hollows of

33. See above, p. 182.

the wood and in the herbs that grow there. Thus Clorin, the Faithful Shepherdesss, rules the play not only as a grave-side oracle but also as a herbalist, able to distinguish the baneful from the healing weed. And, in time, all the lovers gravitate to this solitary, mourning presence, to receive, in appropriate degree, a remedy for their inner distempers. *Entrelacement* is all.

But in a similar way, on the level of verse, there is here a lightness which can be illustrated by Act I. ii. So, as two of the lovers set out for the grove, an understandable misapprehension occurs between them. 'A staine yet sticks', on Amoret's view, in the liver of young Perigot. At this point, as throughout, sensuality is linked — no less than in Guarini's thought — with physical disorder. But Perigot reacts, as most of his fellows would, with horror at the opaque corporeality of his girlfriend's thought, and rapidly translates the suggestion into a language in which selfhood becomes a part of the flow and interchange of elements:

> For to that holy wood is consecrate,
> A vertuous Well, about whose flowery bancks.
> The nimble footed Fairies daunce their rounds,
> By the pale moonshine, dipping often times
> Their stolen children . . .
>
> (I. iii. 100–5)

The comedy of this scene — given an abdication of normal comic expectations — seems entirely actable, not least because it is one in which a Guarinian flicker of sensuality contends throughout with the blush of refined perception.

In a similar vein, one must also refer to the interplay here of comic and tragic scenes which is, on the whole, far subtler than anything in *Il Pastor Fido*. For instance, the equivalent of Guarini's Corsica — she who loses her wig — is Chloe. Throughout, Chloe is the example of a rank, or by now perhaps refreshing, desire, unwilling to accept any chaste impediment. It is she, for instance, who declares: 'Thou cannot rape me I am so willing.' Yet, offensive as that protestation might now appear, Chloe is by no means presented as a baggage. Here, too, there is a lightness of touch, as lover after lover comes into her presence, only to shy away under the pretext of chastity. But Chloe is herself allowed to observe the approach of these timid males; and the audience, too, observes them, momentarily, through her choric comments before they can bring themselves to speak. So in Act I. iii. 97–99, she declares: 'I would sooner choose a man made out of snow and freer use an eunuch for my endes', and then outrageously changes her tune when the prey is in ear-shot.

Balanced against Chloe stands Clorin. But not as an inert presence. She too is capable of policy, though for remedial purposes; and so at Act IV. iv. 45–8, she is wholly prepared to assume, for a moment, the appetites of a Chloe, her aim here being to shock into sense a lover who is too much interested – as Angelo will be with Isabella – in her chastity. Thus when Thenot urges her to 'think but how blest/A constant woman is above the rest', her false-knowing rejoinder is: 'And offer up myself upon this ground to be disposed by thee.'

So *The Faithful Shepherdess* has its breeze which, given a chance, might wean its audience away from the crude expectation – whether generic or seasonal – of Whitsun ales, opening up a realm in which the intelligent analysis of parallels has it place and where there is also an enjoyment – both sentimental, sensuous and imaginative – of the un-settledness or relativity of the human figure. But if this is true on the formal level, then it is also true on the moral level. And here Guarini is outdone by Fletcher. For where Guarini is concerned with the dark spaces of the religious and providential scheme, Fletcher's concern is, much more consistently, with rituals that capture the trace and inter-trace of purely human actions. This is true even of the parodic rituals which are exemplified in Act III. i. Here a representative of male lust, the Sullen Shepherd, is pursuing a *Much Ado*-like stratagem to beguile the honest Perigot with a false image of his Amoret – dipping his accomplice in a well so as to transform her into the shape of her faithful counterpart. Before the illusion is complete, however, the ritual itself allows the sheer sensuality of touch to play with something approaching reverence, upon the physical form of the accomplice:

> I do thy sleepy body bind
> I turne thy head unto the East,
> And thy feet unto the West,
> Thy left arm to the south put forth
> And thy righte unto the Northe.
>
> (*FS*, III. 8–12)

Here a relationship which is momentarily established between touch and the simplest co-ordinates of the world we live in, North, South East and West;[34] and in that perspective mere voyeurism is dissolved. In this larger relationship, violent restraint – whether ascetic or sexual – becomes, as it were, a clarity of design. And it is this same clarity which Clorin, while marking the grave of her lover, consistently offers, in her

---

34. Compare the the funeral rites of Cloten and Imogen in *Cymbeline* below, p. 294.

healing rituals to those around her. Thus Perigot in Act V. iv enters with bloody hands. He is guilty, under the spell of illusion, of wounding his lover Amoret, and now seeks a rite of purification as urgently, if not as famously, as Orestes: 'O to what sacred flood shall I resort.' Clorin now performs the rite; and she does not do so merely by thought or by injunctions to future chastity. Her rituals show a tenderness towards 'the itching flame' and 'leprosie' which affect the body as well as the soul. She herself goes on to envisage an Arcady in which chaste spouses will use good husbandry to ensure that all can share the land which they possess and care for.

But at the last what Clorin and the tragi-comedy in which she appears both seem to aspire to is an Arcadian mode of perception which observes the uniqueness and fragile value of persons free from the confusions of mere power. So in Fletcher's play, in Act II. i. 10–11, one possible, and deleterious, mode of seeing is identified in the Sullen Shepherd, whose sexy loucheness is expressed through a crude appetitiveness of vision:

> all to me in sight
> Are equall . . . I can crowne
> My appetite with any.

But there is in the play an alternative to such possessiveness of vision. And it comes from the Satyr – by now long since converted to the value of modesty – in Act V. v. This is the concluding sequence of the work; and here the wonder which the Satyr has felt for Clorin from the first is translated into a form of seeing which is itself wholly unembarrassed and unembarrassing. Superlatives and pure light are here, but no inertia or sullen obsessiveness, rather, a rapidity of action in which Caliban seems to combine with Ariel. The eye is at work on behalf of the other senses, and translates the surrounding world, through microscopic attention, into a tactile and aesthetic expression of devotion to the human figure:

> shall
> I catch thee wantown fawnes, or flyes
> Whose woven winges the Summer dyes for many coloures.

In a word – the last word of the play – the Satyr is free. And, momentarily, the word 'free' is purged of all its lubricious ambiguities. It is this same freedom which the play itself offers as an alternative to Whitsun ales.

Chapter 8

Shakespeare and Italy

INTRODUCTION

It cannot be said with any confidence that Shakespeare was able to read Italian. Critics have traditionally assumed that he could not, and have been quick to seek French or English intermediaries even in cases such as *All's Well That Ends Well*, *Othello*, or *Cymbeline* where original sources exist in Italian. Such an approach strangely discredits Shakespeare's linguistic competence and curiosity. Shakespeare himself may not have travelled to Italy as Sidney did. But, as we have seen, English authors had never found it difficult to acquire a reading knowledge of Italian. In Shakespeare's own time, teachers of Italian such as John Florio were active in the circles which Shakespeare himself frequented, and Italian-language texts such as Machiavelli's *Discorsi* were even being printed and published in London by John Woolfe.[1] There is no reason to doubt that Shakespeare did indeed use the many French or English intermediaries that were available, either as a sole source or as a crib. It seems plausible nevertheless that in composing plays such as *Othello* and *Coriolanus* he should have been able to consult Italian texts.[2]

Positive testimony either for Shakespeare's knowledge of Italian or for his ignorance of the language is unlikely ever to be established. The fact

---

1. For Florio and Woolf, see above, p. 23. Also on Florio see Frances A. Yates, *John Florio* (London, 1934).
2. See Ann Barton in her essay 'Livy, Machiavelli and Shakespeare's *Coriolanus*', *Shakespeare Survey* 38 (Cambridge, 1985), pp. 115–29, speaks of Italian as 'a language which, on the evidence of his use of Cinthio for *Othello*, Shakespeare could read'. Noting that Machiavelli's *Discorsi* would have been available and read in England before their publication in this country, she concludes: 'I think myself it would be more surprising if it could be proved that Shakespeare had managed to avoid reading Machiavelli than if concrete evidence were to turn up that he had' (ibid., p. 122).

remains that Shakespeare makes reference to Italy in at least fourteen of his plays, choosing Italian settings, or employing story-lines from ultimately Italian sources. The range of reference would be much increased if one admitted the evidence of echoes, allusions and analogy. Plainly, Shakespeare shared with his contemporaries and immediate forebears a fascination with Italy. It is a natural conclusion to preceding chapters that one should compare the results of his fascination with the results of theirs.

There are three closely related areas of inquiry. The first – as in dealing with Renaissance comedy – is that of source and of influence, whether direct or through intermediaries. Here in the detail with which he reformulates his sources, as for example in *The Taming of the Shrew,* Shakespeare's literary craftsmanship will at once be apparent. So, too, will his appetite for experiment, and his particular readiness to respond, in plays like *Measure for Measure*, to the theoretical considerations which derived from Guarini's work.[3]

Secondly, there is the question of how the myth of Italy was used in Shakespeare's work. With the novella in mind, Shakespeare may be expected to have looked upon Italy as, by turns, an exotic and sophisticated otherworld or as a target for patriotic satire. More subtly, however, his use of the myth will display an ability to represent and analyse not only character types but also types of social and political organisation. Shakespeare did not share, perhaps, Machiavelli's political animus. But he does share a profound interest in the way that human beings operate in groups, and is alert to the possibility of institutional and cultural difference: in *Cymbeline,* the culture of the Italian Renaissance is compared – very unfavourably – with the cultures of ancient Britain and of ancient Rome.

Then, finally, as in discussing Spenser or Sidney, it is important to consider how Shakespeare dealt with the great inheritance of philosophical themes and literary aspirations which had developed in Italy since the time of Dante. There is no need here to argue that Shakespeare made any particularly deliberate contribution to the debate. But questions concerning, for example, the heroic individual, social order, rhetoric, education and love had been raised in very specific form by Shakespeare's predecessors, both English and Italian. One would do less than justice to the intellectual weight of Shakespeare's work and to the vigour of the tradition which he inherited if in the end one did not

3. See Madeleine Doran's contention that if there is a theoretical foundation for Shakespeare's work then it is to be found in Guarini's theory of mixed genres in *Endeavours of Art* (Madison, Wis., 1954), pp. 3–12.

measure him against the greatest of his forebears. Shakespeare had almost certainly not read Dante. Yet there is reason when considering the themes of love and justice in *Othello* to place this work – which, in regard to source and myth, displays an evidently Italian aspect – in a more speculative relation with works by Dante where the great issues of love and justice are also at voiced.[4]

THE ITALY OF SHAKESPEARE'S COMEDY: *THE TAMING OF THE SHREW* AND *THE MERCHANT OF VENICE*

Consider, first, two early comedies, *The Taming of the Shrew* and *The Merchant of Venice*, where Shakespeare, as well as experimenting with the formal features of the comic tradition, already displays considerable understanding of the culture and social order in Italy.

In *The Taming of the Shrew*, Shakespeare characteristically departs from the *commedia erudita* of his source – Gascoigne's *Supposes* – by inserting this source, as a sub-plot, into a scheme which relies heavily upon cross-reference, elements of metatheatre and even suggestions of dream-play.[5] The importance of such features in Shakespeare's dramaturgy will be confirmed by *A Midsummer Night's Dream* in which the Italian concern with the confusions and resolutions of city life are replaced by those which occur within the green world of rustic actors, phantasms and seasonal festivity. Yet Shakespeare, of course, does not abandon the city, as is clear from *The Merchant of Venice* and *Measure for Measure*. In *The Taming of the Shrew* itself, the play acted for Christopher Sly is largely, though not entirely, a city comedy; and the sub-plot is the point of departure for the contrasts and parallels on which the play as a whole depends.

Through the sub-plot Shakespeare introduces two traditional motifs of erudite comedy, that of the impeded marriage of Bianca and that of learning in the figure of the love-lorn scholar Lucentio and his associated pedants. But these motifs are quickly developed in Shakespeare's play. Contrasts are systematically drawn between Bianca's marriage – subject as it is to romantic impediment – and Kate's enforcedly unromantic nuptials. Similarly, contrasts are developed between the witty re-application of scholarly pursuits and the bitter psychological learning which Kate acquires through the crazed experience of 'taming'.

4. See Francis Fergusson's study of the two authors in *Trope to Allegory: Themes Common to Shakespeare and Dante* (Athens, Georgia, 1977).
5. See above, p. 184.

In expanding upon these themes, Shakespeare finds his way, critically, into the bourgeois – and essentially Boccaccian – world which had initially produced these motifs. Like Boccaccio, Shakespeare envisages in the Bianca plot a culture motivated wholly by principles of exchange, in which merchants 'of great traffic through the world' (*TS*, I. i. 12) travel from city to city (only briefly, it seems, regarding the countryside around them), learning itself bestows physical and mental mobility, and marriage here is a commercial transaction.[6]

Up to a point, Petruccio is an embodiment of the spirit of commercial mobility, being drive by

> Such a wind as scatters young men through the world
> To seek their fortunes farther than at home,
> Where small experience grows.
> (*TS*, I. 2. 49–51)[7]

These are the authentic tones of the piratical merchant venturer whose astuteness, in Boccacio's stories, combines with raw energy to promote the process of exchange.[8] Yet unlike Boccaccio, Shakespeare does not allow this energy – or the bourgeois ethos into which it might settle – to stand unqualified. Even before Petruccio's arrival, the frame has revealed a range of social positionings quite other than the bourgeois, which run from aristocratic revellers down to the socially challenged Sly who, significantly, claims for himself a lineage more authentic than that of his *parvenu* tormentors. Sly, after all, is descended from 'Richard the Conqueror' (Induction, I. 4). The revellers are Italianate in their brutal manipulation of the courtly apparatus of art and *haute cuisine*,[9] while Sly insists vigorously upon his connection to the Warwickshire countryside peopled with English names such as 'Marian' and 'Cicely Hacket' (Induction, 2. 21, 89). Sly's name will at one point be registered as the Italian 'Christophero' (Induction, 2. 5) as he allows himself to be drawn into the world of artifice. But even in the deepest trammels of art and

---

6. Similar themes occur in a similar Italianate setting in two early *Two Gentlemen of Verona* and in *Love's Labour's Lost* – where a Boccaccian oppositon of Nature and book-learning is combined with a sustained satire upon the most sophisticated forms of Renaissance educational theory and hermeticism. See above, pp. 000.

7. The edition used here and throughout is the *Oxford Shakespeare* general editors Stanley Wells and Gary Taylor (Oxford, 1988). The Oxford spelling of names is retained except (below) in the case of *Cymbeline*.

8. See above, pp. 36–81.

9. On Italian conceptions of the fine arts in Shakespeare see Leo Salingar, *Dramatic Form in Shakespeare and the Jacobeans* (Cambridge, 1986).

illusion, the verse is sensuous enough to remind one that there are the physical realities of 'sweet woods' and 'warm distilled waters' behind the *tromp l'oeil* furnishings which surround the victim (Induction, 1. 46–7). In a similar way, Kate displays energies of her own which oppose the bourgeois spirit of exchange: she has a name, and (resisting any anglicisation) she defends that name as fiercely as she defends her own selfhood from any exchange to which she does not consent.

This tightly woven nexus of parallels and contrasts has more in common with the Ariostan *entrelacement* of the *Orlando Furioso* than with the catalogue of errors generated in the *Supposes*. But in Shakespeare's play, rather than the ironies of Ariosto's voice or the moral positions of a Spenser, there are ambiguities which ultimately resist resolution. On the one hand, it could be argued that a residual sense of selfhood prevails in both Sly and Katharina, as Sly – like Bottom in his enjoyment of ear-tickling and provender – turns the illusory world of his transformation into a moment of sensual richness.[10] Kate, likewise, at least on one familiar reading, may be said to have discovered in Petruccio a match for her true self on a level of sexual mystery deeper than any merely social consideration. To touch her at all, Petruccio has to leave the city and expose Kate – in the muddy interstices of civilised life – to lunacies of the kind which in *King Lear* will be painfully educative. Yet it could also be said that the same scenes imply, in Sly's case, the victory of aristocratic luxury and wealth which buys and sells and disposes, while the bourgeois Petruccio goes deeper still and claims an ultimate power of transmutation in naming the sun and moon at will (IV. vi. 1–23). Then again, if that is one conclusion, what of Kate's final speech of submission to male 'sovereignty'? Bianca's astuteness had produced a very Boccaccian solution through wit and pragmatism. But Kate insists on absolutes and a hierarchy of established values, speaking in political terms which from the time at least of the Wilton Dyptich have been English rather than Italian. Her insistence upon order in 'matrimonye' – which would not be out of keeping with Sir Thomas Elyot's pronouncements –[11] provides a far more explicit closure than could be

---

10. One notes here a running disagreement with Terry Eagleton in *William Shakespeare* (Oxford, 1986), p. 98, where the body in Shakespeare's conception is seen as Shakespeare's conception of the body as 'a kind of symbol of the traditional feudal order'. Having associated Eagleton's views on the subversive power of the aesthetic with views expressed in Guarini, *Pastor Fido*, (see above, pp. 267–8.), I wish to attribute a similarly subversive power to the theatrical representation of the body in much of Shakespeare's work.

11. See p. 114.

found in the conventional terms of any erudite comedy. Yet, finally, the ambiguities and contradictions which the modern reader feels in this speech, as Kate counsels submissiveness to higher authority, cannot be unintentional. For the play ends not with Kate but with Sly. He, silent and scarcely visible, is left as a victim of autocratic power huddled over reactions which he cannot voice but which nevertheless re-open the question. This same resistence must be held in parallel to Kate's responses. The play within the play might exert a cruel closure; Shakespeare's own play retains a subversiveness through its ambiguity which would not be permissible even in Boccaccio's *Decameron*.

It has been said that if Shakespeare had seen Venice he would have been astonished at the extent to which that city was the product of human construction. Where, in an English town, one would usually be able to look out from the streets and see the fields which produced the means of basic existence, in Venice one would see nothing save the evidence of human ingenuity, expressed in buildings erected on watery foundations and in money which 'itself barren, had here proved strangely fruitful and multiplied itself hourly in the market place'.[12] Having explored such contrasting perceptions in *The Taming of the Shrew*, Shakespeare returns to them with increasing intensity in *The Merchant of Venice* as he will also in *Othello* and *Cymbeline*.

Although in writing *The Merchant of Venice* there are in a number of Italian *novelle* which Shakespeare might well have drawn upon,[13] the main interest of the play lies in its powerful recreation of a mythic Venice and the use it makes of this myth to investigate, as Boccaccio himself had done in the *Decameron*, the operation of the laws, bonds and relationships which underlie the life of the city. Jonson in *Volpone* was to make similar use of Venice, where he pictures a world constructed out of a welter of objects animated, it seems, 'less by souls or natural affections than by a strange lust for material possessions'.[14] *The Merchant of Venice*, however, is not a satire as *Volpone* is, nor – in spite of being a 'comical history' and in spite of its final act – does the play provide the festive conclusions which are always available in Boccaccio's *Decameron*.

12. A.D. Nuttall, *A New Mimesis: Shakespeare and the Representation of Reality* (London and New York, 1983), pp. 120–1.
13. Notably *Il Pecorone* (1558) by Ser Giovanni Fiorentino, which contains both an equivalent of the Belmont (though the suitor there must contrive to sleep with the Lady against the effects of wine) and also a bond theme.
14. Anne Barton, *Ben Jonson: Dramatist* (Cambridge, 1984), pp. 110–1.

It is famously a problematical play, impelled by an inquiring imagination which not only pictures accurately the workings of civic law and economic contract in an urban culture but also extends its investigations into questions of racial and religious law and parental imposition. Boccaccio, examining similar themes, would have considered the possibility that the grip of law might be released by the ludic effect of wit or the claims of nature. Thus the remote ancestress of Portia would seem to be Madonna Filippa (*Decameron*, Day Six story seven) who, accused of adultery in a city where adultery in women is a capital crime, boldly admits the offence and by the sharpness of her responses so entertains the court that it not only acquits her but also proceeds to repeal its ancient but unnatural edict. So, in outline at least, Portia circumvents the iron necessity of the Venetian law by the deviousness or 'wit' of her legalistic assault on Shylock's bond. Portia and Madonna Filippa speak from the margins of the social order in defence of values which the laws of that order seem not to have perceived. Yet underlying Boccaccio's position is the carnivalesque realisation that ancient laws of Florence have already been challenged by the disorder of the Plague. In Shakespeare's case, the possibilities of carnival seem plainly inadequate to the problems which the play confronts.

The complications extend even to Portia herself. Her first appearance in Belmont had shown her chafing at the paternal law which has attempted to dictate her choice of husband. Yet she herself in the last act has reassumed a position of authority; and even her Belmont holds the threat of a continuing rigidity which bears particularly upon the figure of the newly displaced figure of Jessica, who is 'never merry when she hears sweet music' (V. i. 69). It is true that the final phase of the action attempts to erase the memory of Shylock's continuing existence. Thus the metaphors employed by Lorenzo transfer attention through metaphor to a supernal order where the music of the spheres raises the mind above the 'muddy vesture' of disruptive physicality and where gold – ceasing to be the medium of exchange – is sanctioned now as a decoration in the celestial scheme (V. i. 58–65). But law cannot be wished out of existence in this play. Nor does wit prove to be a wholly reliable antidote to law. Graziano who is gratingly witty throughout the play – and who looks initially like an analogue to Boccaccio's anarchic Dioneo – is also responsible for much of the anti-semitic innuendo which the play voices; and in the final act he turns innuendo against the sexual rather than the racial body in an extemporisation on the theme of transfigured bodies, 'aughts' and rings (V. i. 144–183).

But if law and wit both prove menacing here, it is because both offend against a deeper principle, which is the integrity of the body itself. The body in this play has been threatened with living butchery as a result of an alliance between law and wit. It has been spat upon in a spirit of brutal carnival, despite the fact that a Jew has eyes, hands and organs. And nothing in this play has been able to articulate the full extent of such offences. Nor could Boccaccio – despite his interest in stories generated by sexual impulse – have provided a language in which to speak of bodily nature itself as it suffers, grows and moves from place to place. For that, a language of pity will be needed, to identify what cannot ultimately be exchanged, legalised or mocked. Such a language will not be available until the tragedies when, in *Othello,* Shakespeare returns to the same Venetian setting which, in *The Merchant of Venice,* first served to reveal the problem.

EXPERIMENT IN MIXED GENRES: *ALL'S WELL THAT ENDS WELL, TROILUS AND CRESSIDA* AND *MEASURE FOR MEASURE*

The three so-called problem plays deserve particular attention in an Italian perspective, not least because Shakespeare here seems to have entered a phase in which theatrical experimentation was combined with a close reading of Italian sources and an analytical attention to issues of central importance in the culture of the Renaissance. In *Measure for Measure* Shakespeare draws – through Whetstone's *Promos and Cassandra* – on a work by Cinthio which appears in both novel and dramatic form. In *All's Well That Ends Well* Shakespeare goes to the *Decameron,* via Painter for a main plot rather than a sub-plot. As for *Troilus and Cressida,* this work radically re-interprets the story which Chaucer first took from Boccaccio and in doing so engages not only with a medieval Italian source but also with the questions of heroism and of literary aspiration which throughout the Renaissance had been expressed in vernacular treatments of the epic story of Troy.[15]

In no work does Shakespeare follow Boccaccio more closely than in

---

15. On *All's Well That Ends Well* see G.K. Hunter's introduction to the Arden edition (1959) and Barbara Everett's introduction to the Penguin edition (1970); On *Troilus and Cressida* see Piero Boitani (ed.), *The European Myth of Troilus* (Oxford, 1989) and I.A. Richards in his *Beyond* (London, 1974). For *Measure for Measure* see J.W. Lever's introduction to the Arden edition (1965).

All's Well That Ends Well, and in few do craftsman-like changes to a source text have wider implications. Boccaccio's original appears in the Third Day of the *Decameron* in which all ten stories are intended to show how the protagonists achieve their desires or recover their losses through '*industria*', which is to say through hard work and enterprise. Here Boccaccian *virtù* expresses itself in the pursuit of goals which are almost always sexual, and the Helena figure illustrates this exactly: she is the daughter of a physician, socially inferior to the man she loves but endowed with her father's talents; and as in Shakespeare so, originally, in Boccaccio, she uses these inherited talents and her own ingenuity to win Bertram in marriage. She is thus a model of the Boccaccian woman, energetic in pursuit of her own interest. And there can be no doubt that Shakespeare has been impressed by this model. The pattern is there in Portia. Rosalind and Celia, too, in *As You Like It* can extemporise upon the Boccaccian triad of themes, speaking of how 'Nature hath given us wit to flout at Fortune' (I. ii. 38–54); and Rosalind, in pursuit of her own natural ends, achieves her goals through the Boccaccian ingenuity and courage which takes her to Arden.

When Helena, in Act I. i. 212, declares that 'our remedies oft in ourselves do lie', her position is exactly similar to Rosalind's. But Shakespeare proceeds to weaken this by omitting from his version of Boccaccio's story a section in which the Helena-figure is shown through her skill and industry to govern the country in the absence of her reluctant husband. Furthermore, Shakespeare introduces in the earliest scenes with Helena an interlocutor who, from the first, brings into disrepute the faculty of verbal ingenuity, the aptly named Paroles who has no counterpart in Boccaccio.

The initial effect is to distract attention from language towards the purely sexual urgency which motivates Helena. She has wit enough to deal with Paroles, but this in itself seems superficial compared with the sexual depths which are driving her forward and which enter even into the rhythms of her declaration of Boccaccian self-sufficiency: 'what power is it which mounts my love so high?/That makes me see and cannot feed mine eye?' (ibid., 216–8). As the play proceeds, so too parallels emerge between the affections which both Paroles and Helena entertain for Bertram, and these again point to the interest which Shakespeare takes here in the secret impulses of sexual attachment. Boccaccio's heroine displays her *virtù* clearly and decisively on a public stage: in Helena, Shakespeare seems deliberately to have entered a sphere of private and less articulate motivations.

Shakespeare's other additions to the original confirm this intention. Boccacio's king is a man almost entirely concerned with the proper management of the class system over which he holds sway. He is prepared to bend the rules of that system when Helena saves his life but would be loath to do so were it not that he had made a promise. Shakespeare's King, once restored to health, vigorously argues for virtues which lie deeper than social distinction (II. iii. 123–45). Significantly, the King in *All's Well That End's Well* has, from the first, been surrounded by an aura of mythic suggestion. In Shakespeare's treatment, but not in Boccaccio's, he is in part a figure from folklore – the king on whom the health of his country depends. The secrecy of a magical power combines here with the secrecy of sexual impulse to complicate the clear-cut oppositions of enterprise and rank with which Boccaccio had concerned himself.

This, finally, is true of Shakespeare's subtlest innovation, the introduction of Bertram's mother, the Countess. In one respect, the figure of the Countess does introduce into the play a dimension of social manner and rank. But again the motivations represented here are subtly private. There is a scarcely definable tact and delicacy in the behaviour of the Countess which allows her to overthrow the brutally conservative position of her own son and act simply out of a love for Helena which cannot be expressed in any social equation: 'there is more owing her than shall be paid, and more shall be paid than she'll demand' (I. iii. 100–4). At the same time, the presence of the Countess alerts one to affiliations between the members of an older generations – between herself, Lafeu and the King – who are all able to act generously in support of the obscure desires which the younger generation (and Bertram in particular) translate into rigid principle. Industry may have overcome such rigidities in Boccaccio, but in Shakespeare the agencies are sex, magic and discreet charm.

In creating this combination Shakespeare produces a Guarinian 'breeze' of tragi-comic effects.[16] The play is directly parallel to the *Pastor Fido* in its portrayal of a hero who is violently opposed to the claims of love; and in its own way the play is constructed as Guarini's was with an eye to the remote perspectives of time. But these perspectives are here translated from the realm of the gods to the realm of human generations. And when the miraculous 'unknotting' of the tangled situation

16. See above, p. 262; also see J. Whitfield, *Il Pastor Fido* (Edinburgh, 1976), pp. 33–5, for comparisons between Guarini's *Il Pastor Fido* and both *All's Well That Ends Well* and *Cymbeline*.

occurs, attention falls less upon the virtuosity of the author than upon the sexual and psychological tensions which had knotted the situation in the first place.

In its negotiations within the Guarinian tradition, *All's Well That Ends Well* deserves to be regarded as an experimental rather than a problematic piece. And if confirmation were needed of Shakespeare's propensity to experiment at this point in his career, one may turn to *Troilus and Cressida* where the tonalities are no doubt too brutal to be described as a 'breeze' but nevertheless oscillate violently between the tragic and the comic.

The experimentalism of *Troilus and Cressida* derives from the high degree of literary and theatrical self-consciousness which is displayed most obviously in the Prologue and Epilogue of the work. An 'armed' Prologue enters the literary arena not to challenge or to imitate, in High Renaissance fashion, the epic originals of the story but to speak with diffident self-consciousness of what 'may be digested in a play'. In terms of diction, too, the speech of the Prologue begins with a great rhetorical sweep – evoking the action of princes 'orgulous'. But it quickly descends to the scurrilous plane on which the subsequent action will be cast, where 'tickling skittish spirits' (Prologue, 20) rather than heroes are the protagonists. As always in the long history of the *Troilus* story, one is concerned with the margins of heroic action and with a fretful pause in the pursuit of epic purpose. It is as if epic ambition had here coalesced with the spirit of Bandello's *microstoria*.[17] And this suggestion is further confirmed by the dying moments of the play in which Pandarus (at least in the Quarto) concludes on a deeply unheroic note, asking the members of his audience to weep for a pandar and a bawd, and sending them away with a legacy of venereal disease.

On a full analysis, it would quickly appear that in *Troilus and Cressida*, Shakespeare, while not drawing directly on Italian sources, has substituted a theatre of gossip and embarrassment for the great literary themes of the high Renaissance. So Fame, which in Petrarch's understanding was the primary stimulus in literary work, here becomes a form of exposure to ironic opinion, most notably in Act III. ii. 168–205 when Troilus, Cressida and Pandarus step forward and confront the future half anticipating the dreadful fame which ensures that their names will indeed live but only as expressions of foolishness, prurience and perfidy. So, too, in Ulysses' speech (I. iii. 82–137), order, degree and honourable

---

17. See above, p. 233.

reputation become the instruments of Machiavellian policy which seeks nothing short of the destruction of Troy.

In *Troilus* Shakespeare explores the short-comings of the rhetoric which the Renaissance had drawn from the classical world and transformed to its own purposes. But in *Measure for Measure*, where Shakespeare's sources are ultimately Italian, he brings a similarly analytical eye to bear upon the codes and vocabulary of contemporary Christian culture. In doing so he engages – more consciously perhaps than in *All's Well That Ends Well* – with the issues which in the late sixteenth century had dominated the development of the mixed genre. His ultimate source here is Cinthio's *Hecatomitthi*, which he may have consulted directly since it seems likely he did so in reading the same work for the *Othello* story. In Cinthio's work, he would have encountered the themes of Providence and marriage which, as we have seen, were of central importance in Counter-Reformation forms such as the novella and the pastoral tragi-comedy. He would also have discovered here the author who, along with Guarini, was chiefly responsible for the theory of 'tragedy with a happy ending' – '*tragedia da lieto fine*'.[18]

It is of the essence in the *tragedia da lieto fine* that the situation it represents should contain serious possibilities of violence and danger while also envisaging an ultimate escape from death itself. In Cinthio's novella there is indeed considerable violence: 'Juliet' – or at least her legal status – is said in fact to have been 'violated' by 'Claudio'; and 'Isabella', to save her brother, does in fact sleep with 'Angelo'. Indeed, far from representing consistently the avoidance of death, Cinthio's novella shows 'Angelo' brutally reneging on his promise: at the moment in which 'Isabella' rises from his side, he presents her with the dead body and severed head of 'Claudio' who has, regardless, been executed at his command. Significantly, however, when Cinthio rewrites the novella as a play, he allows 'Claudio' to survive; and it is plain even in the novella that his purpose was not to dwell upon violence but to consider the remedies which might be found for the confusions and self-destructiveness of human beings. So 'Isabella' is shown to plead her case to the highest authority, who, in all versions except Shakespeare's, is the Holy Roman Emperor (which explains why the story is set in Vienna). This representative of God upon Earth is able to act as an agent of Divine Providence, and metes out justice, insisting first that Isabella – to preserve her legal integrity – should be married to Angelo, who will then at once be executed. At this point death is properly avoided, as Isabella –

18. See J.W. Lever, *The Elizabethan Love Sonnet* (London, 1956), pp. lv–lxiii, and above, p. 260.

now a dutiful wife – pleads forgiveness for her new husband.

Whetstone taking up this story preserves all its principle features, including the death of Claudio. Yet so far from being a slavish imitation, *Promos and Cassandra* (which is a two-part drama of contrasted tones) reflects the critical interest in the rectification of comic style which Whetstone expresses when, in his dedication of the play, he laments the indecorousness of English comic writing.[19] Whetstone shows considerable interest in the refinements of tragi-comic form. It is he who introduces fully developed low-life scenes, which Shakespeare retains. These serve partly as comic relief but also establish a strong interest in the theme of civic government. Whetstone displays a greater concern than Cinthio over the ways in which a city might control the corruption that arises within its walls. But like Cinthio he is also concerned to appeal finally to an authority far higher than any local magistrate. Indeed, the authority of the Emperor is underlined in Whetstone's play by the fact that he only appears in the second part when, *ex machina*, he majestically enters to ensure a happily married end for Isabella and Angelo.

In one respect, Shakespeare's intention seems to have been to write a play in which violence was more completely avoided than in the original and in which the happy ending was made happier still: neither Isabella nor Juliet is raped; there is no death here save the natural demise of a notorious pirate; and marriage seems to be conceived as a good deal more than legal convenience. Moreover, in terms of theatrical skill Shakespeare might here be aiming at that subtle interplay of comic and tragic tonalities which Guarini considered the highest form of drama. Thus the low-life scenes in this play do not provide merely comic relief; they are an integral contribution to the plot, and Lucio in particular moves like a witty (if maladorous) breeze from one level of the action to another.

Guarini's example may also be important in a less obvious way. Nothing, at first sight, is less like the pastoral world of nymphs and shepherds than this claustrophobically urban play. Here, Shakespeare seems to have regressed beyond the green world of his own comedies to an urban setting which would resemble that of erudite comedy were it not so realistically violent. But the enclosed spaces of palaces, prisons, nunneries, brothels and graves which haunt this play are so emphatically imprisoning as to cry out for the relief of pastoral world. Marston in *The Malcontent* – which stands in many ways as a parallel to the *Measure for Measure* – is acknowledged to have drawn on Guarini[20] in recognising, satirically, that the pastoral offered an alternative to the corruptions of an

19. *Elizabethan Critical Essays*, ed. Gregory Smith, (Oxford, 1904), Vol. II, pp. 58–60.
20. See Jackson and Neill, *The Selected Plays of John Marston*, op.cit.

'Italian lascivious palace' (*Malcontent*, III. ii. 36). And when in the romances Shakespeare does eventually create his own green world, there can be little doubt that the Italian pastoral was to the forefront of his mind.[21] If that influence has already begun to be felt in *Measure for Measure*, then it shows itself in Shakespeare's treatment of Marianna: she alone emerges, in however shadowy a fashion, from beyond the walls of the city and from a shadowy past to provide an unknotting of problems which the intensely critical present cannot encompass. In her extended 'romance time' she suggests an alternative to the highly compressed timetable which operates in the rest of the play.

Yet supposing that such parallels are plausible, they increase rather than diminish the problematical aspect of Shakespeare's play. This is particularly evident in Shakespeare's treatment of the Duke. This figure in Guarini would be the vatic and priestly presence which – at least in outline – Prospero is in *The Tempest*. In Shakespeare's immediate sources, he actually is a figure of unassailable and God-given authority. Yet while the Duke, as part of the character which Shakespeare has devised, may like to think of himself as a supreme authority, Shakespeare's treatment of his sources ensures that his position is surrounded by unprecedented ambiguities. Not only does he abdicate power, but Shakespeare's treatment ensures that, so far from being a *deus ex machina*, he is also involved throughout in the action of the play and is at least on one view demeaned or contaminated by contact with prison, brothel, and backstairs intrigue. Moreover, the conclusions which he produces in the marriages which end the play are certainly felt by many readers to be highly suspect.

None of this should lead one to abandon too quickly interpretations which emphasise the profoundly Christian aspects of this play.[22] There is certainly no more serious expression of Christian thought in Shakespeare's plays than Isabella's 'why, all the souls that were were forfeit once' (II. ii. 75). And while the Duke does not speak an unequivocally Christian language, nevertheless one might argue that in refusing the role of a spectacular *deus ex machina,* he becomes the searcher of intimate consciences.

Yet this view does not altogether square with the evidence. If the Duke were any sort of providential figure, then he would – as in

21. Footnote references to *King Lear*, Act IV, as being modelled on romance tonalties and themes.
22. Especially G. Wilson Knight, 'Measure for Measure and the Gospels' contained in *The Wheel of Fire* (London, 1930).

Guarini or in Shakespeare's Romances – surely be surrounded by an appropriate theatrical apparatus of ritual or masque-like effects. Shakespeare has plainly rejected these theatrical possibilities, even though Fletcher in *The Faithful Shepherdess* was soon to adopt them with enthusiasm. Nor does he return convincingly to a comic solution in which marriage would stand as a convenient emblem of social order. It is Shakespeare who decides that Isabella should marry the Duke rather than, legalistically, Angelo. Yet this marriage goes so strongly against the grain of Isabella's zealous commitment to chastity that it destroys, for most readers, any pretensions which the Duke may have to being an accurate judge of character. Indeed, so similar are Isabella and Angelo in their zealotry that Cinthio's solution of marriage between them might well have been preferred on the grounds not of convenience but of temperament.

The heart of the problem here is that the Duke sustains the principles of tragi-comedy while all the other major protagonists have the intensity of figures in a tragedy. So while the Duke may seem to pursue a concern ultimately with forgiveness, and indeed attempt to 'avoid deaths', Isabella and Angelo are both motivated by a violent appetite for high-minded principle, which leads them positively to embrace death and abnegation as instruments of moral design. When pushed to the limit, Isabella emphatically does not wish to avoid the death of her brother. Rather, she sees his death as the proper sacrifice to a principle which is the core of her own personality. But the same is true of Angelo. It is plainly insufficient to regard Angelo merely as a lustful hypocrite. That, certainly, is the way in which he appears in Shakespeare's sources, where he is seen as a younger and more hot-blooded individual than Shakespeare has chosen to make him. But Shakespeare here depicts a character who would not, as Angelo himself says, have been moved by Isabella had she not been virtuous. His own zealous commitment to justice is ironically thrown out of true by a woman whose own devotion to principle translates itself into a sexual attraction. But in the end it is Angelo who voices the intensity which he shares with Isabella by desiring – in full knowledge of his own unjust behaviour – to die as a victim of the law which he himself has both lived by and offended. The Duke, in insisting that he honour his marriage contract to Marianna, trivialises not only Angelo's self-knowledge but also the inherent realities of Isabella's personality which reveal that principle is as much an animating spirit in a personality as sexuality, or for that matter, legal domesticity.

To avoid death in this case is to prevent individuals from governing the span of their own lives and from controlling its beginnings and ends. Neither Cinthio nor Guarini, with their belief in a mysterious Providence (and authorial control) would have any difficulty with that position. Yet Shakespeare does. And in this regard he is both extremely distant from and extremely close to the writers of 'tragedies with happy endings'. Guarini in the *Pastor Fido* sees the human heart as a dark wood in which there lurks a beast of selfhood which can only be cured when selfhood comes to recognise its own vulnerability and smallness in the perspective of Providence.[23] In one respect, Shakespeare in *Measure for Measure* intensifies this understanding. Vienna is, after all, an irremediable stew of corruption; and, as the play ends, there is no sense that any solution has been found to the long-standing licentiousness of the city. On the contrary, Angelo's firm insistence on justice has been discredited and Isabella's chastity brushed aside. Moreover, corruption has by now been seen to extend beyond the relatively simple sphere of sexual misdemeanour. Here, the highest principles of chastity and justice are shown to produce cruelty and perversion. Claudio is the test case, a feeble, fearful and vulnerable representative of degenerate human nature. Neither Isabella nor Angelo can do more than use him as a pawn in their high moral designs. And the great irony of the play is that the Duke, in pursuing his own high principles of forgiveness and mercy, is no less guilty of manipulation than Isabella and Angelo. He constantly trivialises death, and is never further from the language of Christian redemption than when he taunts the terrified Claudio with Stoic injunctions to be 'absolute for death', knowing of course that death will not occur and that in any case it would lead, on a Christian understanding, to an after-life quite different from that which Claudio envisages: 'to lie in cold obstruction and to rot' (III. i. 118). Forgiveness – at least when enacted as a principle rather than as a response to the innner nature of the individual – is seen in *Measure for Measure* to be no less selfishly corrupt than the vanities of justice, chastity and sexual indulgence. In the tragedies, Shakespeare will move beyond this *impasse*; for lives there are lived to the last, and the deaths to which they lead allow a stark moral perspective to be established. An Othello seeking to establish a just assessment both of himself and of Desdemona through his own self-execution paradoxically exhibits a life which has arrived at a point of clear understanding. But in the experimental phase of the problem plays, Shakespeare works within the codes, whether Christian or classi-

---

23. See above, p. 267.

cal, which had been used in his own culture to articulate principles of the highest and most generous kind. He shows a remarkable understanding of the operation of these codes, whether Christian or classical. But he also demonstrates the emptiness of any view in which the realities of persons from birth to death are not actively explored. Providence, marriage and the Duke's formulae of 'measure for measure' are analytically seen to be distractions from, rather than defenders of, that ethical concentration on particular persons and particular situations which tragedy in Shakespeare's hands – unlike Guarini's exalted tragi-comedy – will properly explore. Meanwhile, it is Barnadine who best expresses the inebriated torpor which arises in that avoidance of death which, to the Duke, appears so noble a principle: 'away you rogue, away. I am sleepy' (IV. iii. 27).

CYMBELINE AND THE PASTORAL

Measure for Measure displays a desire both for the pastoral world and for the exhaustive examination of lives and persons which Shakespeare's tragedies will offer. The late romances largely reconcile these desires; and while Shakespeare displays characteristics in these plays which are distinctively his own, there is also clear evidence here of a continuing interest in Guarini's experimental theatre. *The Tempest*, with its priestly central figure and providential resolutions, answers to the pattern of Guarini's quasi-religious theatre, even though it greatly complicates the model by its concern, for example, with questions of usurpation, abdication and political power. It is, however, in *Cymbeline*, which seems to have been two or three years after Fletcher's *Faithful Shepherdess*, that such experimentation in pastoral and tragi-comic forms is most fully developed. But this play also draws upon a Boccaccian source and upon the myth of Italy, to develop an explicit and sustained comparison of English and Italian cultural positions.

At the centre of *Cymbeline*, in Act IV. ii, Shakespeare pictures the funeral rites for the dead Imogen and achieves in its own way almost everything that Guarini demanded in his theory. There is here a pastoral setting and a theatre of ritual; there is a tight knotting of plot-lines, as long-lost brothers meet their long-lost sister. There is a death which is not a death and a tonal 'breeze' which blows from solemnity, to comic misapprehension, to elegy as the brothers mourn Fidele, a twice-illusory being, neither true man nor true corpse. At the same time – far more daringly than Guarini – Shakespeare actually does include a death here, the death of Cloten, and produces from this, as a further tonal variant, the unparalleled violence of the moment at which Imogen smears her cheeks with the blood of her apparently decapitated husband. It is also significant that at the heart of the scene, in place of Guarini's reverence for the mysterious resolutions of Providence, there is a reverence rather for human beings themselves: even Cloten – for reasons which are not clear to his murderers but are forcefully seen by Belarius – deserves a fitting burial; and after the dirge, 'Fear no more the heat o'th' sun' (IV. ii. 259-282), his corpse is strewn with the same flowers that the brothers cast upon Imogen.

The rituals of the play will continually repeat effects of a similar kind. But in doing so they act as punctuation for an action which is not merely 'knotted' in its pastoral complications but epic in its temporal, geographical and political sweep. In this as in other respects, *Cymbeline* resembles its close chronological neighbour *Antony and Cleopatra*. Simultaneously, the play evokes the cultures not only of ancient Rome and of ancient Britain but also of Renaissance Italy, and deliberately frames its references to contemporary Italian decadence with a moral determination (which Machiavelli might have envied) to replace the corrupt courtliness of the modern world with an understanding of the older virtues which Romans and Britons share in their military and diplomatic encounters. Here, as in *The Faerie Queene*, politics is seen in a visionary perspective.[24] And to generate that vision, Shakespeare, like Spenser, returns to a myth of the past. In *Pericles* he had already made the medieval Gower his narrator. Now he bases his sub-plot on Boccaccio's *Decameron*, Day Two story nine. But this is a story which exactly illustrates the moment of transition from a medieval to a Renaissance view of the world: a merchant–husband wagers on his wife's virtue as if she were an object of exchange, and, precisely in admitting the possibility of such an exchange, the story calls into question that faith in the inalienable integrity of human beings which Dante had sought to establish in his celebrations of Beatrice – and which Shakespeare, in his *Sonnets*, had momentarily reaffirmed through what he calls the 'miracle' of his art.

The moral centre of the *Cymbeline* is Imogen, who clearly descends – in a highly developed form – from the enterprising women of Boccaccio's *Decameron*. By ingenuity as well as steadfastness, Imogen will

---

24. See especially the visions of Act V. v, which may be thought to contain at line 234 encomiastic references to King James I.

defend not only her own intrinsic qualities but also those of her husband
Posthumus. Yet, ironically, her efforts are seen against a background not
only of mercantile exchange but also of a literary degeneration in which
the story of the Roman Lucretia's virtue becomes a piece of erotic gossip. Throughout the Renaissance the story of Lucrece – whether in
Machiavelli's hands, Bandello's or Castiglione's – had become a test case
for contemporary attitudes to women and power;[25] and in turn there
are certainly strong connnections to be pursued between *Cymbeline* and
Shakespeare's *Rape of Lucrece*. In dealing, however, with Boccaccio's
story, Shakespeare decisively represents the wager sequence as symptomatic of a corrupt modern order in which persons – even grammatically
– can be reduced to the 'she's of Italy' (I. iv. 29). Posthumus only begins
to recover his own nature, which had degenerated during his sojourn in
Rome, when on British soil he 'disrobes his Italian weeds' and, suiting
himself 'as does a a British peasant'(V. i. 23), rediscovers an ancient *virtù*.

Yet Renaissance Rome has also proved capable of exporting corruption in the form of a perverse courtliness. The court of Britain is initially
under the malign sway of the 'drug-damned' Queen with her talent for
turning natural flowers into Italianate poisons (I. v); and the plainest
indication of corruption at the court is its inability to see clearly and to
identify the value of its courtiers. Glances here are froward and 'evil
eyed' (I. i. 1, 73 and 91). From the first, the play concerns itself with
acts of seeing no less profoundly than *King Lear*; and a resolution is only
achieved during the final scenes when, in a re-establishment of true
courtliness, eyes become free again to appreciate the value, virtue and
excellence of other persons in a 'counterchange'(V. vi. 397) of recognitions. Until that time, the action of the play concerns the attempt, for
which Imogen is largely responsible, to maintain as an alternative to
gossip and vindictiveness a power of truly courtly seeing.[26] For her, the
fullest indication of corruptions at the British court is the inability of the
court to recognise in Posthumus the virtues which Imogen herself sees
conspicuously displayed. Even in the eyes of the audience, Posthumus,
to judge from his behaviour, may no more deserve such regard than
Cloten deserves reverence from Arviragus and Guiderius. But the play
throughout invokes and expresses a faith in the value of particular
human beings; and Imogen's part is to sustain that intuitive perception
against the temptations offered by the false valuations of both the courtly
and the mercantile outlook.

25. See above, p. 208.
26. On such 'courtliness in Spenser, see above, p. 184.

There is here a clear reversal of gender roles. Thus it is Imogen, not her male counterpart, who acts the courtly lover, celebrating from an enforced distance the virtue of the loved object. And nothing is more striking in its combination of sexual drive and optical intensity than the lines in which she expresses the power of *amor de lonh*, her love-from-a-distance: as she hears of Posthumus's departure by ship from the English shores she exclaims:

> I would have broke mine eye-strings, cracked them, but
> To look upon him, till the diminution
> Of space had pointed him sharp as my needle;
> Nay, followed him till he had melted from
> The smallness of a gnat to air.
>
> (I. iii. 17–21)

Here like Cleopatra, as she laments the dead Antony, Imogen seeks to sustain her own understanding of a passive and even unworthy object. The eye here is trained on qualities so intense and specific that they eventually disappear in air, but such regard for what is imperceptible in another person is itself the expression of a reverence which the corrupt court could never command.

The intensities of vision which Imogen here summons up have much in common with those which characterised the mystic insights of a Neo-Platonist such as Ficino who, as we have seen, preferred the state of ecstatic irrationality to the understanding of the 'sober mind'.[27] But, strikingly, the verticalities of vision which were typical of such ecstasies – as in Spenser's *Hymn of Heavenly Beauty*[28] – are translated in *Cymbeline* into a decisive horizontal. So, too, in the last scene the restoration of harmony is achieved when the beneficent Roman Eagle disappears from view again along the horizontal – 'from south to west soaring aloft/(she) lessened herself'(V. v. 472–2) – leaving the British court free now to govern its own affairs. Plainly the effect of this departure is to liberate an appreciation not of some transcendent being but rather of that excellence in human persons which must underlie the healthy workings of the human order.

Throughout the play, the appalling perversions of perception which stand in opposition to this visionary mode have been embodied in the supremely Italianate figure of Iachimo. In direct contrast to Imogen's

27. See above, pp. 95–8.
28. See above, p. 96.

straining sight, Iachimo gazes luxuriously at Imogen herself as she lies asleep in her chamber. His purpose is emphatically to practise an exchange upon her person: in pursuit of his wager, he notes down her physical characteristics, precisely so that he can carry them back to Rome in a spirit of malicious gossip. Such looking has nothing to do with the open sky or with natural movement to and from the horizon. Indeed, Iachimo – for all his apparent courtliness – is a creature of confinement. He is transported in a treasure-chest and he seeks to confine the physical qualities of Imogen in an account book, 'mine inventory' (II. ii. 30). These particulars – 'rubies unparagoned', the 'mole cinque spotted', the 'enclosed light of her eyes'– all momentarily invoke in him an intuition of value and are 'riveted, screwed' to his memory (ibid., 43–4). Yet he dare not yield to this intuition or allow himself, in any natural way, to touch, kiss or revere what he sees (ibid., 16). To do so would be to distract this commercial Tarquin, from his avowed purpose, which is to catalogue these 'natural notes' and store them away in the conveniently portable form of a written script. Even books and words – the essential instruments of Renaissance culture – are here becoming dangerous as instruments of illegitimate exchange.

To see, however, how deeply Shakespeare resists the Italianate corruptions of a Iachimo, one must turn now to the tragedies and in particular to the play which draws most closely, in both a positive and a negative sense on Italy, *Othello*.

OTHELLO AND DANTE'S *VITA NUOVA*

Excellence, and the perception of excellence, are themes as important in *Othello* as they are in *Cymbeline*. *Othello,* however, is concerned to a far greater degree than the later play with the difficulties that arise in attempting to sustain any clear view of the value which displays itself in particular persons. The tragedy here is that Othello misapprehends and must die to reaffirm an excellence in Desdemona which is unhesitatingly acknowledged by every other character in the play, including Iago. Moreover, in Desdemona's eyes, Othello himself is excellent. While in this case, it is the audience who may well find difficulties in persisting in the irrationality of that perception, Desdemona is prepared to defend it with her dying breath.

In praising excellence of whatever kind, we identify and declare publically an understanding of what we think is good in human life. To that degree, any question of excellence involves questions of ethical response. But ethical considerations are here connected very closely to questions of cultural stand-point. Plainly enough, one will be taught by the culture one inhabits to discover excellence in particular kinds of action or skill or talent. Conversely, any culture may itself be seen as an historical concatenation of judgements; and, in that light, shifts of moral emphasis are possible at precisely the moment when a new excellence is recognised: to praise Hamlet where, once, one praised Tamburlaine is to register a moral change if not necessarily an advance.

These large considerations are relevant in a number of interconnected ways both to *Othello* and to Shakespeare's view of Italy – as well as to the closing pages of the present book.

First, they are directly reflected in the plot of *Othello*: a Moor is initially accepted as a hero in the European culture of Venice; the preconceptions of that culture are subsequently put to the test; but even if one said that Othello was eventually destroyed by these preconceptions (which is a doubtful interpretation), it would still be true that the Venetian state once agreed with Desdemona in finding virtues in Othello which it could not find among its native inhabitants. (Iago is a Venetian; Othello, like the less conspicuous Cassio, is a foreigner.)

Judgement, cultural preconception and the recognition of excellence are, then, already at play in the plan of Shakespeare's story. But these considerations become more acute when one realises that Shakespeare has not only drawn upon the myth of Italy in depicting what is, to him, a foreign culture but has also radically modified, in terms of ethical and cultural code, the original text which he found in Cinthio's *Hecatomitthi*. As may be expected by now, Shakespeare's treatment of the original is critical, but insofar as he alters Cinthio's work – in regard to its ethical vocabulary – the play stands as a register of the moral as well as the artistic choices which Shakespeare himself has made.

Likewise, in viewing the results of these choices, readers or audiences will also become involved in a cultural and ultimately ethical action. They themselves will bring to the play a range of expectations which, in some measure, will still be the remote product of the Italian Renaissance. However much may have happened since that time (and Shakespeare himself is one such happening), the views which a present audience takes about the excellence of individuals, or about heroism, or love or rationality, will be connected genetically to many of the notions considered in previous chapters. Indeed, so deep-rooted have many of these notions become that they can now seem like natural categories in human thought.

Othello, however, succeeds not only in calling some of the principles of Renaissance culture into question[29] but also in revealing the contradictions of thought which can arise particularly when we seek to attribute value to an individual person. He has done something similar in *Troilus and Cressida* and *Measure for Measure*, where ironically enough the Christian and humanist values which seemed to speak in broad terms of the heroism or redeemability of human nature are shown to be inadequate when applied to the complication of particular personalities. However, there is an evident difference between these two plays and *Othello*, not least because Iago comes to embody and channel many of the more cynical aspects which are voiced chorically in Thersites and Lucio. And Shakespeare's dramaturgy in *Othello* will be seen to encourage in its audience precisely those acts of evaluation, judgement and moral decision which are obstructed by the theatrical style of the 'problem' plays.

We are presented in *Othello* with the results of an analysis, of a kind which Spenser in his own way might have performed, on the ethical possibilities of the culture which Shakespeare himself inhabited. There are, of course, direct analogies between situations described in *The Faerie Queene* Book II, Canto IV and in *Othello*.[30] But on certain central questions of love and justice, Shakespeare heads back, as Spenser did, to the roots of his own tradition in the medieval world and, particularly, in the work of Dante. As has been suggested, Spenser, like Dante, found in courtesy a subtler alternative to the virtue of justice: at a certain point, law disappears and attention turns in courtesy to the values displayed in the lives and virtues of specific individuals.[31] This conception of courtesy has its place in *Othello*. But so, too, does the love of that excellence which may be perceptible to the 'courteous' eye. And in this regard, Shakespeare here comes to terms with conceptions which Dante began to define in his earliest complete work, the *Vita nuova*. Dante understands no less than Shakespeare how vulnerable and liable to distortion the love of excellence may be; and the *Inferno* is his picture of the conse-

---

29. M. Long, *The Unnatural Scene: A Study in Shakespearian Tragedy* (London, 1976), sees *Othello* as a portrayal of courtly culture in terminal decline. Much that follows here accepts the first moves in this analysis, while insisting that Shakespeare does not dismiss his Renaissance inheritance out of hand.

30. See Sister F. Potts, *Shakespeare and Spenser* (Ithaca, 1958). The episode in *The Faerie Queene* can be traced to Ariosto's *Orlando Furioso*, V. 5–74.

31. See above, p. 184.

quences and origins of such distortion. But in the *Vita nuova*, as finally in the *Paradiso*, Dante's characteristic theme is not condemnation but praise; and it is he who, in his praise of Beatrice, provides the simple and affirmative faith in human persons which lies to be rediscovered beneath the tragic agitations of Shakespeare's text.

Desdemona clearly descends from the line of Beatrice. From one point of view this is a dangerous admission. If both heroines are versions of the 'angelic' lady, then both may suffer the violent reversal which mysogynistically discovers the 'demon' at the centre of Dese*demon*a's name.[32] In Shakespeare's play, such a reversal does indeed momentarily occur, at least as part of Othello's psychopathology. The tragic fragility of any apparent idealisation of the lady is brutally revealed when Othello speaks of Desdemona as the 'cunning whore of Venice'(IV. ii. 93). Yet Othello is plainly at his nadir in this scene. The simple fact is that Desdemona is innocent. Readers, it seems, regularly overlook this truth. And perhaps with good reason. For it can be disconcerting, even shocking, to realise that individuals may indeed be good. A great deal is at stake in that realisation; and it is Dante in the *Vita nuova* who first explored what pressures the perception of goodness might exert upon the unprepared mind.

For in speaking of Beatrice, Dante's concern is not to develop an idea or a symbol but rather to tell of a particular person and of the goodness embodied in that person. Indeed, to arrive at an adequate mode of telling involves, on Dante's account, precisely an abdication of 'ideas' about love in favour of an intense moment of perception. The steps which he takes towards Beatrice in the *Vita nuova*, and which he repeats in the *Commedia*, involve, above all, an attempt to abandon all those conventions and linguistic categories which – necessary as they may be to communication between persons – ultimately fall short of the person as such. These attempts may seem logically doomed; and the logical strain of making them is dramatised in the Earthly Paradise (*Purg.*, XXX) when, in the moment of meeting Beatrice, Dante has to bid a painful farewell to the patriarchal Virgil who, hitherto, has provided him with the words, lessons and philosophical arguments which have allowed him to contain the disruptive experiences of Hell and Purgatory. The excellence of Beatrice lies beyond analysis, and is only

---

32. A point made strongly by Ann Barton in her Cambridge lectures on Shakespeare. For the classic expression of this position, see Sandra M. Gilbert and Susan Gruber quoted in Toni Moi, *Sexual/Textual Politics* (London, 1985), pp.57–8. See also the interpretation of Beatrice offered above, pp. 29–30.

to be realised in an act of contemplative love. So already in the *Vita nuova* Dante strives to find a language which does not project upon Beatrice the preconceptions which he had received from his poetic fore-bears. Formula after formula is cast aside – including of course the formulae of sexual infatuation which, as experience suggests, is one of the most highly conventionalised of all states of mind. Dante's aim is to speak not of sex but of an inherent goodness which if displayed initially in Beatrice may nevertheless be discovered, regardless of gender, in all human beings. It is this realisation which Dante embodies in his discov-ery of the praise-style in Chapter XIX of the *Vita nuova:* for in this style Dante actively refuses to seek possession through language of the reality of Beatrice, admitting that this reality must always lie beyond the scope of his verses. He cannot expect that his words will 'exhaust' her praises (*Vita nuova*, XIX, 'Donne ch'avete . . . ', 3). In the same vein, when Dante returns to Beatrice in the *Purgatorio* the only language he can adopt is one of sighs, tears and psychosomatic reactions more primitive than a spoken language could ever be (*Purg.*, XXXI. 13–21). The 'diffi-culty' of praise is that it requires us to abandon the conceptions and categories of thought through which hitherto we had articulated our own public selves. Law must be abandoned in an act of profound cour-tesy to the face of the individual person.

In *Othello* the equivalent of Dante's benign Virgil – possessed of words and skilled in the management of social language – is the malig-nant Iago. And though it is easy enough to see how vulnerable is Othello's apprehension of Desdemona's goodness, Dante again provides the simplest account of what it might be which moves Iago to assail Desdemona's integrity. On a Dantean analysis, the core of Iago's per-sonality is the sin of envy. For it is envy which Dante sees, particularly in *Purgatorio*, Canto XIV, as the vice that destroys the perceptions of true courtliness.[33] Envy, in the simple sense of Iago's response to Cassio's promotion, is clearly a motive as important in Shakespeare's play as sexual jealousy.

But envy can also appear, in the view expressed in *Purgatorio* (XVIII. 118–20), as a dark fear lest one should be unable to rise to excellence oneself or else be overshadowed by the excellence of others. The envi-ous, in this view, will seek to destroy the very light which they themselves desire to enjoy. And so it is with Iago, who plainly desires for

---

33. For a fuller account of this see R. Kirkpatrick, 'Courtesy and Imagination in *Purgatorio* Canto XIV', *Review of Modern Language Studies*, XXV (1982), pp. 15–30.

himself the same repute which, irrationally perhaps, has been bestowed upon Cassio. He is not satisfied with his own ironically demeaning reputation for honesty, but wishes himself to be seen, with the eye of love, as in some way excellent. In that sense he, like Dante's Satan, is a parasitical and even self-contradictory figure, seeking confusedly for himself the same good which he attempts to destroy in others. Indeed, like the Satan of *Inferno*, Canto XXXIV, Iago – for all his apparent frenzy of activity – is at last profoundly passive in his conduct of the plot: the energies on which he depends for his success are the energies which Othello displays first in his sexual rage and finally in his appetite for justice. And it is significant that Iago should not die at the end of the play but rather be left to waste away, wholly deprived of the regard he has sought for his own singularity.[34]

When Iago declares that Cassio 'hath a daily beauty in his life that makes me ugly' (V. i. 19), he reveals that unaccountable terror in the face of goodness which Dante knew as envy. Yet the same line may also indicate how the issue is dramatised in regard to the warring perceptions of the audience itself. Cassio may, on the evidence of the play, be as guiltless as Desdemona. Yet it is not immediately apparent that this Florentine – an arithmetician and a weak-headed whoremonger – possesses anything like a 'daily beauty' in his life. Nor is it clear, on pragmatic grounds, why he should be preferred for promotion over Iago. When, moreover, he reveals that, in his view, 'reputation' is his immortal part, one may well begin to suspect that a culture, such as the courtly culture of the Renaissance, which places a trust in public face is, to say the least, perilously flawed. Iago, with his public reputation for honesty, fuels these suspicions of 'face', while offering in his soliloquies the possibility of an inward if destructive sincerity to which the audience has privileged access. Yet Othello, Desdemona and even the Venetian state adopt a view which reveals, beneath the public face, the face of a private and wholly indefinable excellence, a face which expresses not qualifications or accountable virtues but rather a right to be loved. And if, at this point, one turns to Cinthio's *Hecatomitthi*, there will be found, among the many changes that Shakespeare makes to the original, some which abandon the clear-cut ethical positions that Cinthio had sought to promote. Greater weight is given in

---

34. Here, as throughout the play, Iago is described in terms of erosion and gnawing – 'more fell than anguish, hunger or the sea' (V. ii. 372). So too Time in the Sonnets – e.g. 66 – is seen as a force which erodes the monuments erected to particular persons by love and art.

Shakespeare's play to the possibilities of tragic confusion, but greater weight also to a mode of intuitive, even irrational, confidence in human beings which owes more to the High Renaissance – and ultimately to Dante – than to the orthodox sensibility of the Counter-Reformation story-teller.

There are many features of Cinthio's story which, had Shakespeare so decided, might have provided him with material for the bloody farce, domestic tragedy or celebration of demonic energy which sometimes his play is taken to be. 'Iago' here is at the outset in love with Desdemona; and his hatred stems from seeing how hopeless his love for her must be. For Cinthio, 'Iago' is an unambiguously active figure so that, even after the death of Desdemona, he pursues his passion for destruction in a long catalogue of crimes which Shakespeare, of course, wholly omits. Most importantly, he is shown actually to be present when 'Othello' murders Desdemona: to avoid leaving evidence of battery, the two assailants beat Desdemona around the head with a sock full of wet sand and then pull down the beams of the bed-chamber around her to provide a plausible cause of death. Subsequently, 'Cassio' loses a leg in a midnight scuffle and, believing, by 'Iago''s account, that it was 'Othello' who attacked him, precipitates the denouement by denouncing the Moor to the authorities for this crime. 'Othello' – after being arrested, tortured and exiled – is murdered by Desdemona's family, while Iago, returning to his homeland, continues in his evil ways. Some time later, under torture for an unconnected crime, he dies from a rupture of the intestines.

It would do no justice either to Cinthio or to Shakespeare to deride the original story. Beneath its contorted surface, Cinthio's novella still aims to emphasise the virtues of marriage, as a bulwark against social confusion, and to demonstrate that Providence will ensure poetic justice even where human beings have conspired to enact an undetectable crime. And these thematic considerations also prove consistent with the narrative form and language which Cinthio adopts.

Bandello-fashion, Cinthio authenticates his tale by asserting that it was passed down by an eye-witness, the surprisingly docile 'Emilia'.[35] Then, too, in picturing the married life of 'Othello' and Desdemona, he concerns himself precisely with those long periods of domestic acquaintance – including earnest conversations about career opportunities – from which, as some readers think, the Shakespearian characters themselves might have benefited. It is no 'down-right violence and storm of

35. See p. 234.

fortunes' which leads Cinthio's Desdemona to accompany the Moor to Cyprus but the considered affection of a companionate spouse. Once in Cyprus, jealousy takes a credible length of time to develop, and is fed as much by day-to day accidents or frictions – identified as the work of misfortune – as by flights of irrational passion. Even the handkerchief in Cinthio's story has none of the aura which Shakespeare casts around it: Desdemona enjoys visiting the Iago family and particularly delights in their baby daughter; Iago cunningly thrusts his child at the visitor and, while she coos over it, filches the handkerchief from her.

It is obvious, then, that Shakespeare, while allowing the domestic world to be one component in his play, also introduces an heroic and courtly strand which is simply absent from Cinthio's work, where Desdemona could never be spoken of as a 'fair warrior'. This is particularly evident in Shakespeare's decision to intensify the relatively realistic viewpoint of Cinthio's novella. In Cinthio's version, Venice is not actually at war with the Turks. Shakespeare, by choosing war as a background for his plot, indicates his interest in a situation which, so far from depicting the steady unrolling of a disaster, concentrates upon the critical moment of action, where perceptions, emotions and moral codes are tested by the extremity of circumstance. It is a further expression of such intensity that Shakespeare should have concerned himself very noticeably with the names of his characters. In Cinthio's novella, all the characters save Desdemona are eerily anonymous – the Moor, the Ensign, the Lieutenant. This is consistent with Cinthio's underlying interest in public roles and in the public confusions that follow when marriages go awry. Shakespeare, on the other hand, chooses names which are not only specific but also dense with suggestion and resonance: 'hell' lurks to be discovered in O*thell*o's name, an affirmation of selfhood in *I*-ago'. Far from leading to simplification or typicality, these names – in common with Shakespeare's accelerated time scheme – make the perception of inner characteristics all the more urgent yet all the more difficult to arrive at.

The most far-reaching changes which Shakespeare introduces stem from his refusal to adopt the machinery of Providence which had been central to Cinthio's moral purpose. For Cinthio, in a world where marriages fail and perfect crimes are possible, the final resort must be to a God who 'gazing into the human soul will not allow that wickedness should go undetected' (p. 442). But such pieties have no place in *Othello*. Instead, Shakespeare has chosen to set his play against the background of a coldly unresponsive 'marble heaven' (III. iv. 463). The characters – as in *Measure for Measure* – may speak a Christian vocabulary and it is a part of the characterisation of Othello himself that, as a stranger to Venice, he should overcompensate in his use of that vocabulary. But this language quickly reveals itself to be – as it was in *The Merchant of Venice* – the language of a particular cultural tribe, the Christian Venetians. *Othello* remains unique among the tragedies of Shakespeare's middle period in allowing no glimpse of a metaphysical world.

With Cinthio in mind, it is clear that Shakespeare has deliberately sought to construct in *Othello* a moral situation in which human beings are left, starkly, to their own devices. The tragic consequence is that the self-destructiveness of human beings stands plainly revealed. Yet this revelation does not lead back to the cynicism or desperation reflected in *Troilus and Cressida* and *Measure for Measure*. On the contrary, Shakespeare simultaneously sets himself to examine the capacities for Renaissance self-fashioning which Cinthio had seemed unable confidently to invoke and to picture the ways in which, through the utmost confusion and unsupported by Providence, justice and love might seek to build a scheme for human existence.

It is for this reason that the play gives such attention to the interlocking institutions of the public and private worlds. No other tragedy concerns itself with so wide a range of social situations,[36] from bed-chambers to diplomatic cocktail parties, from the midnight councils of the Venetian Republic to drunken mess parties in a colonial outpost. These are the institutional manifestations of self-fashioning. But it is both the strength and the weakness of these institutions that they should apparently be constructed, in both the public and private spheres, upon an intuition of human excellence. No human order could be or would be built at all if it were not animated by some sense of the value of its constituent persons. Desdemona and the Venetian State are, initially, of one mind in recognising those very virtues in Othello – who ought, if social preconception ruled, to be a rank outsider – on which both the public and the private spheres can be reliably founded.

The apparent irrationality of such choices prove to be their weak point. Yet throughout the play these same choices seem to be the only real safeguard against confusion. Desdemona pleads for Cassio on grounds of her intuition, and here, too, the State eventually concurs, in

---

36. Compare Michael Neil, 'Changing Places', *Shakespeare Survey* (Cambridge, 1984), pp. 115–31.

making Cassio the Military Governor of Cyprus. But the most ironic manifestation of this theme is in Othello's murder of Desdemona. Here, he proclaims a desire to do justice. Justice is, after all, the central principle of public life, and Othello himself has received something like justice from the Venetian state, at least in its support of his marriage. It now seems that even justice can become the plaything of jealousy and confused motivations.

Yet, on the account which Shakespeare offers, there is beyond justice a more truthful and essential principle: if Othello had yielded to his intuitive sense of Desdemona's presence, when her 'breath almost persuades justice to break her sword' (V. ii. 17), then there would have been no tragedy, and justice would in fact have been done.

As in *Cymbeline*, so in *Othello* there is behind a position such as this that affirmation of the superiority of blind love over rational attention which Ficino developed in his Neo-Platonic philosophy.[37] Shakespeare himself writes 'Love looks not with the eyes but with the mind/and therefore is winged Cupid painted blind' in *A Midsummer Night's Dream* (I. i. 234–5).[38] Likewise, in the sub-plot of *Much Ado about Nothing*, which is a comic analogue to *Othello*, Claudio's ill-founded trust in the rational evidence of his eyes can only be repaired when, with physical absence of Hero, the 'idea of her life shall sweetly creep into his study of imagination' (IV. i. 226–7). Yet when Iago is pitted against this mode of thought it is perhaps understandable that many readers should have experienced a surreptitious admiration for his low-minded reasonings. Iago's very existence make it difficult to sustain any trust in the inherent excellence of human beings. But so, too, does his way of thinking. And the irony here is that the modes of thought and discourse which he adopts are remarkably similar to modes which are frequently identified as the foundation of human dignity. Iago's mentality is self-assertively rational: he is concerned with evidence, and bases his thinking upon general observations and pragmatic procedures, all of which foreshadow, in the eyes of John Bayley, eighteenth-century styles of discursive thought and utterance.[39] The arguments with which he deludes Othello are based largely upon comparisons and reasonable estimate, and he makes great use of that apparently most Shakespearian of categories, the category of character. So Iago argues constantly – and quite subtly – from the 'nature' of people: Moors are lustful but in Othello's case are

37. See above pp. 95–8.
38. See Wind, Pagan Mysteries in the Renaissance (London, 1958), p. 58.
39. *The Characters of Love* (London, 1960), pp. 130–1.

also free, constant and loving in temperament (e.g. II. i. 292). And this mental technique is one which he uses to infect Othello's mind: so, if Desdemona has betrayed her father, she may very well betray her husband; in any case, Venetian women are all whores, so better kill Desdemona 'lest she betray more men'.

Now even within the play and within the sphere of Shakespeare's own culture, it is plain that such attitudes have a profound appeal. If they did not, then Othello would not himself have been ready to adopt them; and it is notable in Cinthio's story that Desdemona herself speaks categorically of her fate as a warning against the unnaturalness of mixed marriages. But Shakespeare has transferred this line of thought from Desdemona to Iago; and in doing so he suggests the resistance that needs to be made to these possessively rational claims. In his own *Sonnets*, Shakespeare had realised that 'false compare' is invidious, missing the essential particularity of the loved person.[40] And in Spenser, too, the apparently rational observations that might be made about courtly behaviour are seen as the essential enemy of courtly excellence: the Blatant Beast of *The Faerie Queene*, Book VI – who so accurately anticipates Iago – is rationality seen for what it can often become, an inclination to presumptuous gossip. In Iachimo, too, 'accounting', 'noting', description and title-tattle are evidently closely akin.

With this in mind, however, the question is how an audience at Shakespeare's play should view the action and the characters within it. On the one hand, the audience is certainly called to make a rational estimate of motives and actions. Othello in his dying speech asks that one should judge his case objectively and without malice; and one is bound, at some point, to ask forensically whether it is mere jealousy which moves Othello or whether a confused – and otherwise laudable – appetite for justice might not have impelled him to the murder of Desdemona. On the other hand, this diagnostic view could well lead back in the direction of Cinthio – and indeed of Iago – where one's conclusion might be, so to say, that 'mixed marriages were generally a mistake and that spouses should always take time to talk'.[41] The alternative is to look for excellence. Desdemona hears in Othello's account of 'anthropaghi' and 'antres vast' (I. ii. 143 and 138) not the character of the man but the indefinable *haecceitas* of his being. Significantly, Iago

---

40. See *Sonnet* 130: 'My mistress' eyes are nothing like the sun'.
41. As when Stanley Cavell in *Disowning Knowledge* (Cambridge, 1987), p. 136 suggests that Othello on his first night with Desdemona has suffered some obscure sexual shock.

cannot tolerate – in Roderigo's phrase – the 'wheeling' strangeness of this creature of here and everywhere (I. i. 138). The question for the audience is whether it is possible to praise that same strangeness which Iago abominates. As Desdemona is to Othello, so is Othello to the audience, a singularity to whom, in the midst of mental confusions, justice can hardly be done.

From first to last, the play is designed to exacerbate this debate.[42] It is, for instance, by no means inconceivable in the opening scene that Iago's views on Othello should sound plausible: an audience attuned to the Aaron of *Titus Andronicus*, or even to the Prince of Morocco, might be disposed in that direction; and even a modern audience could be misled if Iago presented to them the same convincing 'honesty' with which his fellow characters unanimously credit him. Yet any such opinion is clearly meant to be reversed by the sheer poise and self-possession which Othello displays at his first entrance, when he displays qualities which have led some to speak of an inherent goodness which approaches saintliness.[43] The audience here will be thrown off balance, not, as in *Troilus and Cressida*, by the undermining of value but rather by its unaccountable presence. From this point on, the play demands that we should track this excellence as it disappears under Iago's cloud, beginning, painfully, to re-emerge only as Othello frees himself from the presence of Iago and enters the bed-chamber to murder Desdemona.

At every point, the degree of Othello's subjection to Iago is registered in his language; and he is never further from himself than when his diction and logical pretensions inflate, to produce 'exsufflicate and blown surmises matching' Iago's 'inference'(III. iii. 186). Yet in the course of the final scene, a profound linguistic recovery takes place: Othello cries out, first, for care and modesty in judgement – 'soft you a word or two before you go'(V. ii. 347) – the speech then builds swiftly towards the gesture of his final exotic flourish, concluding with silence and the stroke of his own blade on the line 'took by the throat the turbanned Turk and smote him thus'. Here, in an intense form, are the paradoxical qualities which had allowed Othello – with his restrained yet flamboyant 'put up your bright swords' – to break through the net of gossipy judgements that Iago flung around him in the opening scene. And this paradox itself demands an imaginative rather than an analytical response.

42. See Giorgio Melchiori on the part played by paradox in this play, *Shakespeare Survey*, (1976)
43. Reuben Brouwer, *The Hero and the Saint: Shakespeare and the Graeco-Roman Heroic Tradition* (Oxford, 1971).

Yet, as a final paradox, Othello invites a forensic view of his own actions. Here the man who, as an outsider, fought on behalf of Venice simultaneously affirms both his alienation from and his consistent adherence to his adopted homeland. Using the language of justice which had so appallingly failed when he applied it to Desdemona, Othello here executes himself for what he truly is, an enemy of the Venetian state. Yet in doing so, he remains loyal to the principle that inspired his military career. There can be no doubt that, as a conclusion to the moral theme, the paradoxes which arise here deserve close attention; and certainly it is part of Shakespeare's advance upon Cinthio that he is prepared to envisage a final scene in which the human individual – unsupported by Providence and even at the expense of self-annihilation – should fashion justice for himself, rather than passively become the subject to justice. Here too a sentence – prohibited by the Duke in *Measure for Measure* – is coherently written to its bloody conclusion.

But the question remains as to whether Othello can be understood only in terms of the justice which he himself invokes. And by now the answer is surely clear. The paradoxes of his situation both defeat analysis and stimulate attention to the singularity of Othello's position; we are faced here with a self which can no more be defined or conceptually possessed than Beatrice in the Dante *Vita nuova*. The blackness of Othello, while important in stimulating many social and psychological considerations, has also been the principal focus for our response to his particularity. It is this physical attribute – always surely present, as nothing ever is sure is in the ever-masking Iago – which calls the audience to concentrate upon a being which, through the blur of racial taunts and preconceived sympathies, can only be identified by an act of praise. And praise will made the more acute by an awareness how fragile its object is.

This is where Dante has preceded Shakespeare. His own experience of the irreplaceable Beatrice – fragile enough to die before her time – evokes from him a realisation that only in the 'spaciousness' of praise can there be any adequate response to her singularity.[44] Othello knew that of Desdemona once. Now, Othello invokes the absolute language of judgemental distinction: where Desdemona is in Heaven, he sees himself bound for Hell, an exile accepting exile: 'Whip me ye devils from the possession of this heavenly sight' (V. ii. 284–5). Here at last

---

44. See John Bayley, who in the *Characters of Love,* op.cit., p. 162, compares Proust's picture of possessive jealousy with Shakespeare's demand for 'spaciousness': 'lovers do not place each other, and their incomprehension is paradoxically a form of spaciousness'.

Othello abdicates 'possession' and re-ascribes to Desemona the spacious-ness which Iago – and his own Iagan tendencies – have led him to infringe. But the audience, for its part, is called upon in the same instant to allow a similar 'spaciousness' to him. And the pattern for such a response could expressed in lines from the lyric poetry of both Shakespeare and Dante. In *The Phoenix and Turtle*, at line 46, love is said to have reason, 'reason none'; and it is an act of praise, expressed in the eloquent inarticulacy of a 'sigh' (line 67) – which is shown at last to identify the uniqueness, the 'Beauty, Truth and Rarity' of the dead lovers. So too in Dante's poem 'Tanto gentile . . . ' (*Vita nuova*, XXVI), addressed to Beatrice immediately before her death, the only appropriate attitude for the poet to adopt is one of praise, where, again, judgement is humbled before the deeper knowledge expressed in a sigh: 'che va dicendo all'anima: sospira'.[45]

45. I am happy to record, as a last note, a great debt of gratitude on points such as this to Martha Nussbaum, *The Fragility of Goodness* (Cambridge, 1986), who finds in Aristotle a recognition of the cognitive value of the emotions.

Select Bibliograpy

EDITIONS AND TRANSLATIONS

Aretino L., *Tutte le Opere* a cura di Giorgio Petrocchi (Milan, Mondadori, 1962).

Aretino L., *Selected Letters*, trans. George Bull (London, Penguin, 1976).

Ariosto L., *Le Commedie a cura di Michele Catalano*, 2 vols (Bologna, Zanichelli, 1940).

Ariosto L., *Orlando Furioso* a cura di Cesare Segre (Milan, Mondadori, 1964).

Ariosto L., *The Comedies of Ariosto*, trans. and ed. Edmond M. Beame and Leonard G. Sbrocchi (Chicago and London, University of Chicago Press, 1975).

Ariosto L., *Orlando Furioso*, 2 vols, trans. B. Reynolds (London, Penguin, 1975).

Bandello M., *Tutte Le Opere di Matteo Bandello* a cura di Francesco Flora, 4 vols (Milan, Mondadori, 1934).

Bibbiena B. Dovizio da, *La Calandria* in *'Commedie del Cinquecento'* a cura di Aldo Borlenghi (Milan, Rizzoli, 1959), vol I. (For trans., see Bentley below.)

Boccaccio G., *Tutte le opere* cura di Vittore Branca (Milan, Mondadori, 1967).

Boccaccio G., *The Decameron*, trans. G. McWilliam (London, Penguin, 1972).

Bruno Giordano, *Il Candelaio* introduzione e note Isa Guerrini Angrisani (Rizzoli, Milan, 1976). (For trans., see Bentley below.)

Castelvetro L., *On the Art of Poetry*, an abridged trans. of *Poetica d'Aristotele* by Andrew Bongiorno (Medieval and Renaissance Texts and Studies 29, Binghampton, New York, 1984).

Castiglione B., *Il libro del Cortegiano* a cura di Ettore Bonora (Milan, Mursia, 1972).

Chaucer G., *Troilus and Criseyde*: *'The Book of Troilus'* by *Geoffrey Chaucer*, ed. (with the text of Boccaccio's *Il Filostrato*) and intro. by Barry Windeatt (London and New York, Longman, 1984).

Chaucer G., *The Riverside Chaucer*, 3rd edn, ed. Larry D. Benson (New York, Houghton Mifflin, 1987).

Dante, *La Commedia secondo l'antica vulgata*, 4 vols, ed. G. Petrocchi (Mondadori, Milan, 1966–7).

Elyot Sir Thomas, *The Book Named the Governor*, ed. John M. Major (New York, Teachers College Press, 1969).

Elyot Sir Thomas, *The Boke Named the Gouvernor*, 2 vols, 1531 edition, ed. Henry Herbert Stephen Croft (London, Kegan Paul, 1880).

Fairfax Sir Edward, *Godfrey of Bulloigne*: *A Critical Edition of Edward Fairfax's Translation Together with Fairfax's Original Poems*, ed. K.M. Lea and T.M. Gang (Oxford, Clarendon Press, 1981).

Fenton Geoffrey, *Certain Tragical Discourses of Bandello*, 2 vols, trans. into English by Geffraie Fenton, *anno* 1567, with intro. by R.L. Douglas (London, David Nutt, 1898).

Ficino M., *The Letters*, ed. P.O. Kristeller (London, Shepheard–Walwyn, 1975).

Fletcher John., *The Faithful Shepherdess*, ed. Cyrus Hoy, vol. III in *The Dramatic Works in the Beaumont and Fletcher Canon*, general ed. Fredson Bowers (Cambridge, Cambridge University Press, 1976).

Gascoigne George, *The Complete Work*, 2 vols, ed. J.W. Cunliffe, (Cambridge, Cambridge University Press, 1907–10).

Guarini G., *Il Pastor Fido*, ed. J.H. Whitfield with translation by Sir John Fanshawe (Edinburgh Bilingual Library 11, Edinburgh, 1976).

Guarini G., *Il Pastor Fido* a cura di Ettore Bonora (Milan, Mursia, 1977).

Harington John, *'Orlando Furioso' in English Heroicall Verse 1591*, ed. Graham Hough (London, Centaur Press, 1961).

Hoby Sir Thomas, *Castiglione's Book of the Courtier as translated by Sir Thomas Hoby*, ed. Virginia Cox (London, Everyman, 1994).

Machiavelli N., *Tutte le Opere*, 2 vols, ed. F. Flora (Milan, Mondadori, 1949).

Machiavelli N., *The Prince and Other Writings*, ed. S. Milner (London, Everyman, 1995).

Marston John, *The Selected Plays*, ed. Macdonald P. Jackson and Michael Neill (Cambridge, Cambridge University Press, 1986).

Painter William, *The Palace of Pleasure*, 3 vols, ed Joseph Jacobs (New York 1890; reprinted New York and London, Dover Books, 1966).

Petrarch F., *Canzoniere* testo critico e introduzione di G. Contini (Turin, Einaudi, 1964).

Petrarch F., *Petrarch's Lyric Poems*, trans. R. Durling (Cambridge, Harvard University Press, Mass., 1976).

Sannazaro J., *Opere*, ed. E. Carrara (Turin, UTET, 1952).

Sannazaro J., *Arcadia and Piscatorial Eclogues*, trans. Ralph Nash (Detroit, Wayne State University Press, 1966).

Shakespeare W., *The Complete Oxford Shakespeare*, ed. Stanley Wells and Gary Taylor (Oxford, Clarendon Press, 1986).

Sidney Sir Philip, *Poems*, ed. W.A. Ringler (Oxford, Clarendon Press, 1962).

Sidney Sir Philip, *The Countess of Pembroke's Arcadia*, ed. Maurice Evans (London, Penguin, 1977).

Spenser Edmund, *The Faerie Queene*, ed. A.C. Hamilton (London and New York, Longman, 1977).

Surrey Earl of, *Poems,* ed. Emrys Jones (Oxford, Clarendon Press, 1964).

Tasso Torquato, *Poesie* a cura di F. Flora (Milan and Naples, Riccardo Ricciardi, 1952).

Tasso Torquato, *Prose* a cura di Ettore Mazzoli (Milan and Naples Riccardo Ricciardi, 1959).

Tasso Torquato, *Discourses on the Heroic Poem*, trans. with notes, Mariella Cavalchini and Irene Samuel (Oxford, Clarendon Press 1973).

Tasso Torquato, *Jersualem Delivered: Torquato Tasso*, trans. and ed. Ralph Nash (Detroit, Wayne State University Press, 1987).

Webster John, *The Complete Works*, ed. F.L Lucas (London, 1927).

Wyatt Sir Thomas, *The Collected Poems*, ed. Kenneth Muir and P. Thompson (Liverpool, Liverpool University Press, 1969) (also R.A. Rebholz, ed., New Haven, Yale University Press, 1981).

SECONDARY

This is a select bibliography of works largely of general and historical interest intended mainly for the use of English readers. Critical works concerned with specific issues are identified in the notes at relevant points in each chapter.

Abulafia D., *Frederick II: A Medieval Emperor* (London, Pimlico, 1990).

Andrews R., *Scripts and Scenarios: The Performance of Comedy in Renaissance Italy* (Cambridge, Cambridge University Press, 1993).

Ascoli Albert R., *Ariosto's Bitter Harmony* (Princeton, Princeton University Press, 1987).

Auerbach E., *Dante, Poet of the Secular World,* trans. R. Mannheim

(Chicago and London, University of Chicago Press, 1962). Originally *Dante als dichter der irdischen Welt*, Gruyer Berlin and Leipzig, 1929).

Baron Hans, *The Crisis of the Early Italian Renaissance,* Princeton, Princeton University Press, 1966*)*.

Baron Hans, *From Petrarch to Leonardo Bruni* (Chicago, University of Chicago Press, 1968).

Barton Ann, *Ben Jonson: Dramatist* (Cambridge, Cambridge University Press, 1984).

Barton Ann, 'Livy, Machiavelli and Shakespeare's *Coriolanus*', *Shakespeare Survey 38* (Cambridge, Cambridge University Press, 1985).

Becker Marvin B., *Florence in Transition*, 2 vols, (Johns Hopkins University Press, Baltimore, 1968).

Bentley Eric, *The Genius of the Italian Theater* (New York, Mentor Books, 1964).

Bergin T., *Petrarch* (New York, 1970).

Bishop M., *Petrarch and His World* (Port Washington, NY, 1973).

Boitani P., *English Medieval Narrative in the 13th and 14th Centuries* (Cambridge, Cambridge University Press, 1982).

Boitani P., (ed.), *Chaucer and the Italian Trecento* (Cambridge, Cambridge University Press, 1983).

Boitani P., *The Tragic and the Sublime in Medieval Literature* (Cambridge, Cambridge University Press, 1989).

Boitani P., (ed.), *The European Myth of Troilus* (Oxford, Clarendon Press, 1989).

Boklund Gunnar, *The Sources of the White Devil* (Uppsala, A-B Lundequistska Bokhandeln, 1957).

Boklund Gunnar, *The Duchess of Malfi: Sources, Themes Characters* (Camb. Mass, Harvard University Press, 1962).

Bondanella P and J.C., *Macmillan's Dictionary of Italian Literature* (London, Macmillan, 1979).

Boyde P., *Dante Philomythes and Philosopher* (Cambridge, Cambridge University Press, 1981).

Boyde P., *Perception and Passion in Dante's Comedy* (Cambridge, Cambridge University Press, 1993).

Boyd W., (with E. King) *The History of Western Education* (London, 10th edn., A. and C. Black, 1969).

Branca V., *Boccaccio medievale,* 3rd edn. (Florence, 1970) (a version is published in English as *Boccaccio: The Man and his Works*).

Brand C.P., *Tasso: A Study of the Poet and his Contribution to English*

Literature (Cambridge, Cambridge University Press, 1965).

Brand C.P., *Ludovico Ariosto: Preface to the Orlando Furioso* (Writers of Italy Series 1, Edinburgh, Edinburgh University Press, 1974).

Brucker G.A., *Florentine Politics and Society 1343–1378* (Princeton, Princeton University Press, 1962).

Burchkhardt J., *The Civilization of the Renaissance in Italy*, trans. S.G.C. Middlemore (London, Phaidon Press, 1965) (originally publ.1868).

Burke Peter, *Culture and Society in Renaissance Italy 1420–1540* (London, Batsford, 1972).

Burke Severs J., *The Literary Relationships of Chaucer's Clerkes Tale* (Yale Studies in English, XCVI, Yale University Press, New Haven, 1942).

Burrow Colin, *Epic Romance* (Oxford, Clarendon Press, 1993).

Burrow J.A., *Riccardian Poetry* (London, Routledge and Kegan Paul, 1971).

Buxton John, *Sir Philip Sidney and the English Renaissance* (London, Macmillian, 1954).

Campbell Lily B., *Divine Poetry and Drama in 16th century England* (Cambridge, Cambridge University Press, 1959).

Cassirer E., *The Platonic Renaissance in England* (Edinburgh, Nelson, 1953).

Cassirer E., *The Individual and the Cosmos in Renaissance Philosophy*, trans. Mario Domandi (New York, Harper Torch, 1963) (originally published as Vol. X in *Studien der Bibliothek Warburg* Leipzig and Berlin, Teubner 1927).

Chambers D.S., *The Imperial Age of Venice 1380–1580* (London, Thames and Hudson, 1970).

Cleugh James, *The Divine Aretino* (London, Blond, 1965).

Clubb Louise G., *Italian Drama in Shakespeare's Time* (New Haven, Yale University Press, 1989).

Cochrane Eric, *Italy 1530–1630*, ed. Julius Kirshner (London, Longman, 1988).

Cooper Helen, *Pastoral* (Ipswich, Brewer, 1977).

Cooper Helen, *The Canterbury Tales* (Oxford, Clarendon Press, 1991), p. 188.

Cox V., *The Renaissance Dialogue* (Cambridge, Cambridge University Press, 1992).

Crane W.G., *Wit and Rhetoric in the Renaissance (The Formal Basis of Elizabethan Prose Style)* (New York, Morningside Heights, 1937).

Cummings H.M., *The Indebtedness of Chaucer's Works to the Italian Works of Boccaccio* (Cincinnati, Haskell House, 1916 repr. New York, 1965).

Delany S., *Chaucer's House of Fame: The Poetics of Sceptical Fideism* (Chicago and London, University of Chicago Press, 1972).

Dodds E.R., Introduction, in S. McKenna (trans.), *Plotinus: The Enneads* (London, Faber, 1962).

Doran Madeleine, *Endeavours of Art: A Study of Form in Elizabethan Drama* (Madison, Wis., University of Wisconsin Press, 1954).

Durling R., *The Figure of the Poet in the Renaissance* (Cambridge, Mass., Harvard University Press 1965).

Durling R., 'The Epic Ideal', in D. Daiches and A. Thorlby (eds.) *Literature and Western Civilization*, 6 vols, (London, Aldus Books 1972–6), Vol. II, pp. 105–46.

Einstein L., *The Italian Renaissance in England* (New York, Burt Franklin, 1902).

Eliot T.S., 'Four Elizabethan Dramatists', in *Selected Essays* (London, Faber, 1951).

Eliot T.S., *Dante* (London, Faber, 1929 and 1993).

Emerton E., *Humanism and Tyranny: Studies in the Italian Trecento* (Cambridge, Mass., Harvard University Press, 1925).

Empson William, *Some Versions of the Pastoral* (London, Hogarth, 1986).

Falvo Joseph D., *The Economy of Human Relations: Castiglione's 'Libro del Cortegiano'* (New York, Peter Lang, 1992).

Finkelpearl P.J., *John Marston of the Middle Temple* (Cambridge, Mass., Harvard University Press, 1969).

Forster Leonard, *The Icy Fire: Five Studies in European Petrarchism* (Cambridge, Cambridge University, 1969).

Foster K., 'The Mind in Love', in John Freccero (ed.) *Dante: A Collection of Critical Essays* (Englewood Cliffs. NJ, Prentice-Hall, 1965).

Foster K., *Petrarch: Poet and Humanist* (Edinburgh, Edinburgh University Press, 1986).

Fowler Alistair, *Triumphal Forms: Structural Patterns in Elizabethan Poetry* (Cambridge, Cambridge University Press, 1970).

Freccero J., 'The Fig–Tree and the Laurel', *Diacritics,* 5 (1975), pp. 34–46.

Geckle George L., *John Marston's Drama: Themes, Images, Sources*, (Cranbury, NJ, Associated University Presses, 1980).

Gilbert Allen H., *Literary Criticism: Plato to Dryden* (Detroit, Wayne State University, 1970).

Gilbert F., *Machiavelli and Guicciardini: Politics and History in Sixteenth Century Florence* (Princeton, Princeton University Press, 1965).

Gleason John B., *John Colet* (Berkeley, University of California Press, 1989).

Goodman Anthony, with Angus Mackay, *The Impact of Humanism on Western Europe* (London and New York, Longman, 1990).

Grafton Anthony and Blair Ann (eds.), *The Transmission of Culture in Early Modern Europe* (Philadelphia, University of Pennsylvania Press, 1990).

Grafton Anthony and Jardine Lisa, *From Humanism to the Humanities: Education and the Liberal Arts in Fifteenth- and Sixteenth-Century Europe* (London, Duckworth, 1986).

Greenblatt S., *Renaissance Self–Fashioning from More to Shakespeare* (Chicago, University of Chicago Press, 1980).

Greene Thomas M., *The Light in Troy: Imitation and Discovery in Renaissance Poetry* (New Haven and London, Yale University Press, 1982).

Gregory Smith D. (ed.), *Elizabethan Critical Essays*, 2 vols (Oxford, Oxford University Press, 1904).

Grendler Paul S., *Schooling in Renaissance Italy: literacy and learning 1300–1600* (Baltimore, Johns Hopkins University Press, 1989).

Griffith Gwynfor, *Bandello's Fiction* (Oxford, Clarendon Press, 1955).

Gundersheimer W.L., *Ferrara: The Style of a Renaissance Despotism* (Princeton, Princeton University Press, 1973).

Guss Donald, *John Donne, Petrarchist* (Detroit, Wayne State University Press, 1966).

Hainsworth Peter, *Petrarch the Poet: an introduction to the Rerum vulgarium fragmenta* (London, Routledge and Kegan Paul, 1988).

Hale J.R., *Machiavelli and Renaissance Italy*, revised edn. (London, Harmondsworth, 1972).

Hale J.R., (ed.), *Renaissance Venice* (London, Faber, 1973).

Hale J.R., *Florence and the Medici. The Pattern of Control* (London, Thames and Hudson, 1977).

Hamilton A.C., (general ed.) *Spenser Encyclopedia* (Toronto and London, Toronto University Press and Routledge and Kegan Paul, 1990).

Hanning R. with David Rosand ed. in *Castiglione:the ideal and the real in Renaissance Culture,* (New Haven and London, Yale University Press, 1983).

Hathaway Baxter, *The Age of Criticism: The Late Renaissance in Italy* (Ithaca, NY, Cornell University Press, 1962).

Havely N., *Chaucer's Boccaccio: Sources for Troilus and the Knight's and Franklin's Tales* (Woodbridge Boydell and Brewer, 1992).

Hay Denys, *Polydore Virgil* (Oxford, Clarendon, 1952).

Herrick M.T., *Tragicomedy* (Urbana, University of Illinois Press, 1955).

Herrick M.T., *Italian Comedy in the Renaissance* (Urbana, University of Illinois Press, 1966).

Hogrefe P., *Life and Times of Sir Thomas Elyot, Englishman* (Iowa, Iowa State University Press, 1967).

Hough Graham, *A Preface to The Faerie Queene* (London, Duckworth, 1962).

Hunter G.K., 'English Folly and Italian Vice', in J.R. Brown and B. Harris (eds.) *Jacobean Theatre* (London, Stratford upon Avon Studies, Edward Arnold, 1960).

Hunter G.K., 'Italian Tragicomedy and the English Stage', *Renaissance Drama*, n.s., VI, (1973), pp. 123–48.

Hunter G.K., *Dramatic Identities and Cultural Tradition* (Liverpool, Liverpool University Press, 1978).

Hunter G.K., 'The Beginnings of Elizabethan Drama: Revolution and Continuity', *Renaissance Drama*, XVI, (1986), pp. 29–52.

Hunter G.K. and S.K., *John Webster* (London, Penguin, 1970).

Hyde J.K., *Society and Politics in Medieval Italy: the evolution of the civil life 1000–1350* (London, Macmillan, 1973).

Izard Thomas C., *George Whetstone: Mid-Elizabethan Gentleman of Letters* (New York, Columbia University Press, 1942).

Jardine L., *Francis Bacon: Discovery and the Art of Discourse* (Cambridge, Cambridge University Press, 1974).

Jayne S., *John and Marsilio Ficino* (Oxford, Clarendon Press, 1962).

Kalstone David, *Sidney's Poetry* (Cambridge, Mass., Harvard University Press, 1965).

Kay Denis (ed.), *Sir Philip Sidney: An Anthology of Modern Criticism* (Oxford, Clarendon Press, 1987).

Keen Maurice, *England in the Later Middle Ages* (London, Routledge and Kegan Paul, 1988).

Kent D.V., *The Rise of the Medici Faction in Florence* (Oxford, Clarendon Press, 1977).

Kirkpatrick R., *Dante's Paradiso and the Limitations of Modern Criticism* (Cambridge, Cambridge University Press, 1978).

Kristeller P.O., *Eight Philosophers of the Renaissance* (Stanford, Stanford University Press, 1964).

Larner J., *Culture and Society in Italy, 1290–1420* (London, Batsford Books, 1971).

Larner J., *Italy in the Age of Dante and Petrarch* (London, Longman, 1980).

Leech Clifford, *The John Fletcher Plays* (London, Chatto and Windus, 1966).

Lever J.W., *The Elizabethan Love Sonnet* (London, Methuen, 1956).

Levin Harry, *The Myth of the Golden World in the Renaissance* (London, Faber, 1969).

Lewis C.S., 'What Chaucer really did to *Il Filostrato*', *Essays and Studies*, 17, (1932), pp. 56–75.

Lewis C.S., *English Literature in the Sixteenth Century* (Oxford, Clarendon Press, 1954).

Lewis C.S., *Studies in Medieval and Renaissance Literature* (Cambridge, Cambridge University Press, 1966).

Lievsay J.L., *Stefano Guazzo and the English Renaissance* (Chapel Hill, University of Carolina Press, 1961).

Lovejoy A.O., *The Great Chain of Being* (Cambridge, Mass., Harvard University Press, 1936).

MacArthur Janet H., *Critical Contexts of Astrophil and Stella and the Amoretti* (Victoria, BC, University of Vienna Press, 1989).

Major M. John, *Sir Thomas Elyot and Renaissance Humanism* (Lincoln, Nebr., University of Nebraska Press, 1964).

Mann N., *Petrarch* (Oxford, Oxford University Press, 1984).

Martines L., *Power and Imagination: City States in Renaissance Italy* (London, Allen Lane, 1980).

Martines L., *The Social World of the Florentine Humanists* (London, Penguin, 1983).

Mason H.A., *Humanism and Poetry in the Early Tudor Period* (London, Routledge and Kegan Paul, 1959).

McFarlane K.B., *Lancastrian Kings and Lollard Knights* (Oxford, Clarendon Press, 1972).

McFarlane K.B., *England in the Fifteenth Century: Collected Essays* (London, Hambledon, 1981).

Miles Leland, *John Colet and the Platonic Tradition* (London, Allen and Unwin, 1962).

Minta Stephen, *Petrarch and Petrarchism* (Manchester and New York, Manchester University Press and Barnes and Noble, 1980).

Mitchell R.J., *John Tiptoft: 1427–70* (Longmans, Green, London, 1938).

Mortimer Anthony, *Petrarch Canzoniere in the English Renaissance* (Bergamo, Minerva Italica, 1975).

Norbrook David, *Poetry and Politics in the English Renaissance* (London, Routledge and Kegan Paul, 1984).

Nugent E.M., *The Thought and Culture of the English Renaissance* (Cambridge, Cambridge University Press, 1956).

Osgood Charles B., *Boccaccio on Poetry* (New York, The Liberal Arts Press, 1956).

Panofosky E., *Renaissance and Renascences in Western Art* (London, Paladin, 1970).

Pearsall D., *The Life of Geoffrey Chaucer: A Critical Biography* (Oxford, Blackwell, 1992).

Pearson J., *Tragedy and Tragicomedy in the Plays of John Webster* (Manchester, Manchester University Press, 1980).

Praz Mario, *The Flaming Heart* (New York, 1958).

Prince F.T., *The Italian Element in Milton's Verse* (Oxford, Clarendon Press, 1954).

Procacci G., *The History of the Italian People*, trans. Anthony Paul (London, Weidenfeld and Nicolson, 1970).

Prouty C.T., *George Gascoigne: Elizabethan Courtier Soldier and Poet* (New York, Benjamin Blom, 1942).

Pruvost René, *Matteo Bandello and Elizabethan Fiction* (Paris, H. Champion, 1937).

Pullan Brian, *A History of Early Renaissance Italy* (London, Allen Lane, 1973).

Raab F., *The English Face of Machiavelli* (London, Routledge and Kegan Paul, 1964).

Rabil A. (ed.), *Renaissance Humanism: Foundations, Forms and Legacy*, 3 vols, (Philadelphia, University of Pennysylvania Press, 1988).

Radcliffe-Umstead D., *The Birth of Modern Comedy in Renaissance Italy* (Chicago and London, University of Chicago Press, 1969).

Rebhorne Wayne, *Courtly Performances: Masking and Festivity in Castiglione's Book of the Courtier* (Detroit, 1978).

Rees D.G., 'Italian and Italianate Poetry', in J.R. Brown and B. Harris (eds.), *Elizabethan Poetry* (London, Stratford–upon–Avon Studies 2, Edward Arnold, 1960).

Reynolds B., 'The Pleasure Craft' in William Radice and Barbara Reynolds (eds.), *The Translator's Art: Essays in Honour of Betty Radice* (Harmondsworth, London, 1987).

Roche jnr. Thomas P., *Petrarch and the English Sonnet Sequence* (New York, AMS Press, 1989).

Rodax Yvonne, *The Real and the Ideal in the Novella* (Chapel Hill, 1968).

Rotonda D.P., *Motif Index of the Italian Novella in Prose* (Bloomington, Indiana University Press Publications, 1942).

Salingar L., *Shakespeare and the Traditions of Comedy* (Cambridge, Cambridge University Press, 1974).

Schless Howard M., *Chaucer and Dante* (Norman, Okla., Pilgrim Books, 1984).

Schmitt Charles B., with Quentin Skinner, *Cambridge History of Renaissance Philosophy* (Cambridge, Cambridge University Press, 1988).

Shapiro Marianne, *The Poetics of Ariosto* (Detroit, Wayne State University Press, 1988).

Simpson James, 'Dante's *Astripeta Aquila* and the Theme of Poetic Discretion in *The House of Fame*', Essays and Studies, 1–17 (1986).

Singer D.W., *Giordano Bruno: His Life and Thought* (New York, Greenwood, 1950).

Skinner Quentin, *Machiavelli* (Oxford, Oxford Past Masters Series, Oxford University Press, 1981).

Skinner Quentin, 'Ambrogio Lorenzetti: The Artist as Political Philosopher', *Proceedings of British Academy* 72 (1987).

Smarr Janet, *Renaissance Story-Teller* (Cambridge, Mass., Harvard University Press, 1973).

Smarr Janet, *Italian Renaissance Tales* (Rochester Mich., Solaris Press, 1983).

Sowerby R., *The Classical Legacy in Renaissance Poetry* (London, Longman, forthcoming).

Spearing A.C., *Medieval to Renaissance in English Poetry* (Cambridge, Cambridge University Press, 1985).

Stevens John, *Medieval Romance* (London, Hutchinson, 1973).

Stevens John, *Music and Poetry in the Early Tudor Court* (Cambridge, Cambridge University Press, 1979).

Tasso Torquato, *Lettere a cura di C. Guasti* (Florence, 1852–55), Vols I–IV.

Tasso Torquato, *Discourses on the Heroic Poem*, trans. Mariella Cavalchini and Irene Samuel (Oxford, Clarendon Press, 1972).

Taylor Charles, *The Sources of the Self: The Making of Modern Identity* (Cambridge, Cambridge University Press, 1989).

Taylor Karla, *Chaucer reads the Divine Comedy* (Stanford, Stanford University Press, 1989).

Thompson John A.F., *The Transformation of Medieval England: 1370–1529* (London, Longman, 1983).

Thomson Patricia, *Sir Thomas Wyatt and his Background* (Standford, Stanford University Press, 1964).

Tottel, *Miscellany*, revised edn. by Hyder Edward Rollins, 2 vols (Cambridge, Mass., Harvard University Press, 1965).

Trexler R.C., *Public Life in Renaissance Florence* (New York, Academic Press, 1980).

Trinkaus Charles, *In Our Image and Likeness: Humanity and Divinity in Italian Humanist Thought*, 2 vols, (London, 1970).

Trinkaus Charles, *The Poet as Philosopher: Petrarch and the formation of the Renaissance consciousness* (New Haven Yale University Press, 1979).

Ullman B.L., 'The Origins of Italian Humanism', in *Studies in the Italian Renaissance* (Rome, Edizioni di Storia e letteratura, 1955), p. 29.

Ullman B.L., *The Humanism of Coluccio Salutati, Medioevo e Umanesimo*, Vol. 3 (Padua, Editrice Antenore, 1963).

Van Cleeve Thomas Curtis, *The Emperor Frederick II of Hohenstaufen* (Oxford, Clarendon Press, 1972).

Wallace D., *Chaucer and the Early Writings of Boccaccio* (Woodbridge and Dover, New Hampshire, D.S. Brewer, 1985).

Wallace D., 'Chaucer's Continental Inheritance: The Early Poems and *Troilus and Criseyde*', in J. Mann and P. Boitani (eds.) *The Cambridge Chaucer Companion* (Cambridge, 1986), pp. 19–37.

Wallace D., ed., *Texas Studies in Literature and Language*, 32, 1, (1990).

Wallace D., *The Decameron* (Landmarks of World Literature, Cambridge, Cambridge University Press, 1991).

Waller Gary F. and Michael D. Moore (eds.), *Sir Philip Sidney and the Interpretation of Renaissance Culture* (London, Croom Helm, 1984).

Warren Leslie C., *Humanist Doctrines of the Prince from Petrarch to Elyot* (Chicago, University of Chicago Press, 1939).

Warwick Bond R., *Early Plays from the Italian* (New York, Benjamin Blom, 1911).

Watson G., *The English Petrarchans: A Critical Bibliography of the Canzoniere* (London, Warburgh Institute Surveys III, 1967).

Weinberg B., *A History of Literary Criticism in the Italian Renaissance*, 2 vols, (Chicago, University of Chicago Press, 1961).

Weiss R., *Humanism in England during the Fifteenth Century* (Oxford, Clarendon Press, 1948).

Wetherbee Winthrop, *Chaucer and the Poets* (Ithaca, Cornell University Press, 1984).

Whigam F., *Ambition and Privilege: The Social Tropes* (Berkeley, University of California Press, 1984).

Whitney Charles, *Machiavelli and Modernity* (New Haven, Yale University Press, 1986), p. 197.

Wickham Chris, *Early Medieval Italy Culture Power and Local Society* (London, Macmillan, 1981).

Wiggins Peter de Sa, *Figures in Ariosto's Tapestry: Character and Design in the Orlando Furioso* (Baltimore and London, Johns Hopkins University Press, 1986).

Wind Edgar, *Pagan Mysteries in the Renaissance* (London, Faber, 1958; Penguin, 1967).

Witt Ronald G., *Hercules at the Crossroads: The Life, Works and Thought of Coluccio Salutati* (Durham, NC, Duke University Press, 1983).

Woodhouse J.R., *Baldassare Castiglione: A Reassessment of The Courtier* (Edinburgh, Edinburgh University Press, 1978).

Yates Frances A., *John Florio* (Cambridge, Cambridge University Press, 1934).

Yates Frances A., *A Study of Love's Labour's Lost* (Cambridge, 1936).

Yates Frances A., *Giordano Bruno and the Hermetic Tradition* (London, Routledge and Kegan Paul, 1964).

Yates Frances A., *The Art of Memory* (London, Routledge and Kegan Paul, 1966).

Index